Praise for Beth Macy's

TRUEVINE

Selected as one of the Best Books of the Year

New York Times Book Review, San Francisco Chronicle, Tampa Bay Times, Houston Chronicle, St. Louis Post-Dispatch, Kirkus Reviews, BookPage, Amazon

"Expert.... You can feel Macy's admiration wafting off the page."
—Janet Maslin, *New York Times*

"'It's the best story in town,' a colleague told Beth Macy decades ago, 'but no one has been able to get it.' She now has, with tenacity and sensitivity. She gives a singular sideshow its due, offering these 'Ambassadors from Mars' a remarkable, deeply affecting afterlife." —Stacy Schiff, author of *The Witches*

"Extraordinary.... *Truevine* is at once poignant and rigorous, a compassionate dual biography and a forthright examination of codified racism. Macy is a resourceful reporter and a strong but never showy writer.... This book, her second after *Factory Man,* is the work of a journalist whose persistence, empathy, and commitment to accuracy can't be doubted.... *Truevine* may focus on events that began a century ago, but its guiding spirit couldn't be more urgent."
—Kevin Canfield, *San Francisco Chronicle*

"Beth Macy is a gifted storyteller and a dogged researcher, and readers will be riveted by her account of Harriett Muse's struggle to find her sons."

—Edward E. Baptist, *New York Times Book Review*

"An impeccably reported tale." —*Entertainment Weekly*

"Deep in circus history, beneath racist lies and family secrets, Macy found a gripping tale of the cravenness of human nature—and the power of family." —*People*

"Beth Macy's conscientious reporting (affirming the story's accuracy) and her vigorous storytelling make the saga of George and Willie Muse even more enthralling than fiction.... Macy is as tender and solicitous in telling their stories as she is in recovering, in print, the dignity of a family broken apart by avarice and injustice." —Gene Seymour, *USA Today*

"Macy earns a seat at the table of today's most accomplished nonfiction storytellers.... The tale of Willie and George Muse makes for a spellbinding read." —Jeff DeBell, *Roanoke Times*

"Expert.... Beth Macy has done Willie Muse's life justice in a riveting story that zigzags in unexpected directions.... Her enthusiasm never lags.... Even in the worst circumstances, Macy makes clear, the Muse brothers maintained their humanity."

—Jeff Baker, *Wall Street Journal*

"A vivid and moving history that uncovers much more than exploitation and racism."

—Randy Dotinga, *Christian Science Monitor*

"Deeply reported and told with the kind of nuance and grace that define Macy's storytelling. I have been a fan for a long time....It's also just a remarkable story...of a proud legacy, one that should be told, and thankfully, by a gifted writer."

— Maria Carrillo, *Houston Chronicle*

"Macy's digging, and how she chronicles her effort to find the truth...make *Truevine* a true mystery that provides insight into a long-gone world that still has echoes today."

— Dale Singer, *St. Louis Post-Dispatch*

"An entertaining, provocative, often moving search for the truth about the brothers....Like *Factory Man*, *Truevine* is rigorously researched and skillfully written....Macy provides rich detail about their lives....With empathetic storytelling, Macy raises questions about the brothers and their world, questions that persist. As we inch toward a forthright discussion of race in America brought on by police violence, Black Lives Matter, immigration, and a mixed-race president, *Truevine* elicits self-examination."

— Rob Walker, *Richmond Times-Dispatch*

"If over a hundred years ago there had been Black Lives Matter, the mother of George and Willie Muse would have joined and marched for the safe return of her sons. Back then, almost a century ago, she could only keep learning and finding folk who agreed she had a right to her family...a right to the love and protection of her sons. Beth Macy in *Truevine* has given us a stirring story of the persistence of faith...the strength of love...in this tale of a mother's journey to reclaim not only her sons but her right to them."

— Nikki Giovanni, poet and
one of Oprah Winfrey's twenty-five "Living Legends"

"*Truevine* not only puts the real faces and lives of George and Willie to the legend, but also speaks to the ongoing struggle for racial justice in the United States."

—Allison McNearney, *Time*

"*Truevine* is dominated by delight and triumph. Macy is a fine Blue Ridge wit....She paints vivid portraits of wily, creative minds....In a timely way, *Truevine* explodes the presumption that moderns are less gullible than in an earlier era."

—Jeff Calder, *Atlanta Journal-Constitution*

"You may find yourself wanting the tale of the Muse brothers to emerge as a simple tale of inhumanity and injustice. There's a certain satisfaction in that. But the story is too thorny and complicated for that approach, and Macy, whose last book was the *New York Times* bestseller *Factory Man*, does us the favor of respecting that complexity."

—Chris Vognar, *Dallas Morning News*

"A fascinating history....Macy puts their story into its larger historical context, giving the reader an understanding of the virulent, often violent racism of the Jim Crow era, which affected the Muse family deeply."

—Colette Bancroft, *Tampa Bay Times*

"Intriguing, enlightening, and multilayered....In so diligently and thoughtfully researching and writing this book, Macy has paid tribute to George, Willie, and Harriett and ensured that their life stories have finally been accurately and fairly told."

—Sharon Chisvin, *Winnipeg Free Press*

"*Truevine* is a moving attempt to reconstruct this David and Goliath story....If even 'Eko and Iko' can be given back their stories, there might be hope for us all."

—Julian Lucas, *New Republic*

"While it was clearly no picnic, Macy portrays life in a circus sideshow as a community experience that could provide emotional support, protection—and a living—to those who might otherwise have been ostracized or locked away."

—Susan Linnee, *Minneapolis Star Tribune*

"An inarguable page-turner, *Truevine* is a fascinating and shocking account of Jim Crow's legacy and America's strange (and often brutal) past."

—Dianca London, *Lenny Letter*

"Laying out her decades of journalistic persistence, Macy covers the uncomfortable aftermath that followed the boys' heroic rescue by their mother."

—Boris Kachka, *Vulture*

"Macy's exploration of the long-hidden fate of two young African Americans and how that fate illuminates the atrocities of the Jim Crow South is as compelling as Rebecca Skloot's *The Immortal Life of Henrietta Lacks*...both are absolutely stunning examples of narrative nonfiction at its best....Certain to be among the most memorable books of the year."

—Connie Fletcher, *Booklist*

"A deeply moving and endlessly compelling book."

—Alice Cary, *BookPage*

"Beth Macy has a way of getting under the skin of American life, burrowing into the seemingly ordinary to find the weird and wonderful taproots of our society. This true tale from rural Virginia will enrage you, inspire you, make you shake your head and rear your fist. And as the pages keep turning, you'll feel yourself slipping into a gothic world of freaks and geeks, and surreal racial thinking that seems both deeply strange and yet, sadly, all too familiar."

—Hampton Sides, author of *In the Kingdom of Ice*, *Americana*, and *Blood and Thunder*

"A sturdy, passionate, and penetrating narrative. This first-rate journey into human trafficking, slavery, and familial bonding is an engrossing example of spirited, determined reportage."

—*Kirkus Reviews*

"This compelling account of one family's tragic exploitation provides an important lens through which America's tortured racial history and the cruel legacy of Jim Crow can be seen anew."

—Bryan Stevenson, author of *Just Mercy* and founder and director of the Equal Justice Initiative

"Taking us into the dark corners of American history that are discussed only in whispers, Beth Macy shines a bright light on the racial profiteering of circus freak shows and the Jim Crow South. In the remarkable *Truevine*, Macy manages to do what all the exploitative showmen wouldn't dare; she humanizes the Muse brothers, and in doing so she has written an unforgettable story of both heartbreak and enduring love."

—Gilbert King, author of *Devil in the Grove*

TRUEVINE

TWO BROTHERS, A KIDNAPPING, AND
A MOTHER'S QUEST: A TRUE STORY OF
THE JIM CROW SOUTH

——————— ⌘ ———————

Beth Macy

BACK BAY BOOKS
Little, Brown and Company
New York   Boston   London

ALSO BY BETH MACY

Factory Man

Back Bay Books / Little, Brown and Company
Hachette Book Group
1290 Avenue of the Americas, New York, NY 10104
littlebrown.com

Originally published in hardcover by Little, Brown and Company, October 2016
First Back Bay paperback edition, October 2017

Back Bay Books is an imprint of Little, Brown and Company, a division of Hachette Book Group, Inc. The Back Bay Books name and logo are trademarks of Hachette Book Group, Inc.

The publisher is not responsible for websites (or their content) that are not owned by the publisher.

The Hachette Speakers Bureau provides a wide range of authors for speaking events. To find out more, go to hachettespeakersbureau.com or call (866) 376-6591.

ISBN 978-0-316-33754-0 (hc) / 978-0-316-33752-6 (pb)
LCCN 2015959853

10 9 8 7 6 5 4 3 2 1

LSC-C

Printed in the United States of America

To Tom,
for his big heart and humor,
and for keeping my eyes fresh

And in memory of George and Willie Muse

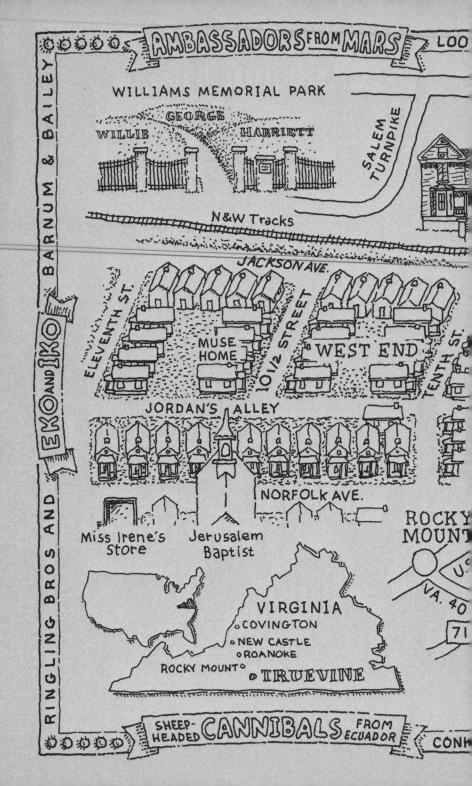

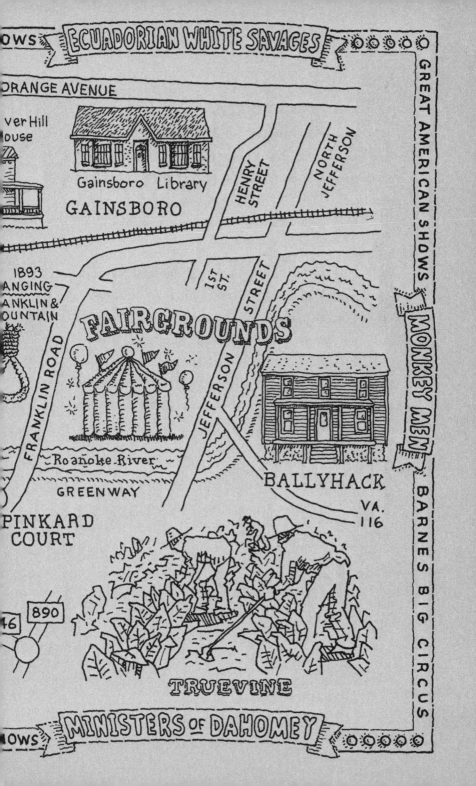

I am the true vine, and My father is the vinedresser. Every branch in Me that does not bear fruit He takes away; every branch that bears fruit He prunes, that it may bear more fruit.

—John 15:1–2

For the first time he sought to analyze the burden he bore upon his back, that dead-weight of social degradation partially masked behind a half-named Negro problem. He felt his poverty; without a cent, without a home, without land, tools, or savings, he had entered into competition with rich, landed, skilled neighbors. To be a poor man is hard, but to be a poor race in a land of dollars is the very bottom of hardships.

—W. E. B. Du Bois, *The Souls of Black Folk*

Contents

PART FIVE

TRUEVINE

Prologue
I Am the True Vine

Their world was so blindingly white that the brothers had to squint to keep from crying. On a clear day, it hurt just to open their eyes. They blinked constantly, trying to make out the hazy objects in front of them, their brows furrowed and their eyes darting from side to side, unable to settle on a focal point. Their eyes were tinged with pink, their irises a watery pale blue.

Their skin was so delicate that it was possible, looking only at the backs of their hands, to mistake the young African-American brothers for the kind of white landed gentry who didn't have to eke out a living hoeing crabgrass from stony rows of tobacco or suckering the leaves from the stems.

That was as true when they were old men as when they were little boys, back when a white man appeared in Truevine, Virginia, as their neighbors and relatives remembered it—that very bad man, they called him.

Back when everything they knew disappeared behind them in a cloud of red-clay dust.

The year was 1899, as the old people told the story, then and now; the place a sweltering tobacco farm in the Jim Crow South, a remote spot in the foothills of the Blue Ridge Mountains where everyone they knew was either a former slave, or a child or grandchild of slaves. George and Willie Muse were just nine and six years old, but they worked a shift known by sharecroppers as "can see to can't see" — daylight to dark. "Can to can't," for short.

Twenty miles away and twenty-seven years earlier, a man born into slavery named Booker T. Washington had walked four hundred miles from the mountains to the swampy plains, to get himself educated at Hampton Institute. "It was a whole race trying to go to school," he would write.

Forty miles in the other direction, another former slave, named Lucy Addison, had gotten herself educated at a Quaker college in Philadelphia. In 1886, Addison landed in the railroad boomtown of Roanoke, Virginia, where she set up the city's first school for blacks in a two-story frame building with long benches and crude desks, using hand-me-down books from the city's white schools. She became such an icon of education that some elderly African Americans still have her faded portrait hanging on their walls, right next to the Reverend Martin Luther King Jr. and President Obama. Addison inspired Ed Dudley, a dentist's son who would become President Truman's ambassador to Liberia. She taught future lawyer Oliver Hill, who would grow up to help overturn the separate-but-equal laws of the day in the landmark decision *Brown v. Board of Education.*

But such leaps were unheard of for black families in Truevine, where it would take decades before most learned to read and write. While Washington was on his way to fame and the founding of Tuskegee Institute, black children in Truevine were kept out of school when the harvest came in.

They had too much work to do.

*   *   *

Still, in this remote and tiny crossroads, where everyone knew everyone for generations back, George and Willie Muse were different. They were genetic anomalies: albinos born to black parents. Reared at a time when a black man could be jailed or even killed just for looking at a white woman—reckless eye-balling, the charge was officially called—the Muse brothers were doubly cursed.

Their white skin burned at the first blush of sun, and their eyes watered constantly. They squinted so much that they began to develop premature creases in their foreheads. So they looked down as they worked—they always looked down—heeding their mother's advice to never look toward the sun.

Harriett Muse was fiercely protective. She cloaked her boys in rags to keep their skin from blistering, and for the same reason she made them wear long sleeves when it was 100 degrees. When a vicious dog happened onto the tenant farm where they worked and lunged at little Willie, she chased it away with an iron skillet. She made the boys' favorite food, ash cakes, a simple corn bread baked over an open fire.

When it snowed she cobbled together a dessert called snow cream out of sugar, vanilla, eggs, and snow. When a rainbow appeared above the mountain ridges, she told them to take solace in it. "That's God's promise after the storm," she said.

She spoiled them as much as a poor sharecropper could, but George and Willie were expected to work, walking the rows of tobacco looking for bugs and picking budworms off the leaves when they found them, squashing them between their fingers as they went.

The boys were squinting, as they usually were, when the bad man appeared. What a surprise the well-heeled stranger was in this hodgepodge of dirt roads, tobacco barns, and shacks where tenants stuffed newspapers into holes in the walls to keep critters out, and the only dependable structure for miles was a white-frame meeting hall that doubled as a one-room school — a school the black community built by hand because the county provided a teacher but not a building for him to teach in.

The white man had arrived in the Virginia backwoods by horse and carriage. He cast a long shadow over the rows where the boys were crouched, working. He went by the nickname Candy, Willie Muse would later tell his family members, and he came from the Hollywood of that era: the circus.

At the turn of the twentieth century, the height of circus popularity, bounty hunters scoured the nooks and crannies of America's backwoods — and the world — looking for people they could transform into sideshow attractions: acts like Chang and Eng, the world's most famous conjoined twins, "discovered" by a British merchant in Siam (now Thailand) in 1829, or the Wild Men of Borneo, as P. T. Barnum pitched a pair of dwarf brothers to audiences in 1882 — though they actually hailed from a farm in Ohio.

Somehow the man had heard about the boys — maybe from a shopkeeper in nearby Rocky Mount, the county seat. Maybe a neighbor had seen the ads that circus showmen took out in newspapers and trade publications for freak hunters, as they were called.

"WANTED — To hear from the man that grows three feet in front of your eyes. . . . Call DAN RICE, Sioux City, Iowa."

Maybe even a member of their own family had given the boys up.

The white man found them working, alone and unsupervised, two snow-white field hands, no more than seventy pounds and four feet tall, dressed in flour-sack clothes and turbans jerry-rigged out of rags and string. As he approached, stepping over the tobacco rows, the boys stood and nodded respectfully, as they'd been taught to do with white men.

When they removed their head coverings at his request, the man gasped. Their hair was kinky, and it was golden.

It was money in his pocket.

Harriett Muse had warned her sons about copperheads amid the tobacco rows, about wolves in the outlying fields. They knew about the perils of what scholars call peonage, the quasi-slavery in which a man could be stripped to his waist, tied to a tree, and lashed with a buggy whip—for the bold act of quitting one farmer's land to work for better wages down the road. They'd heard the adults talk about the lynch mob in Rocky Mount in 1890, the year George was born, formed to rain vigilante justice down on five blacks accused of setting a fire that had destroyed much of the uptown. Two of the five were hung in the basement of the county jail before evidence surfaced, on appeal, that arson could not be proved.

"Before God I am as innocent of that charge as an angel," Bird Woods declared as a deputy slipped the noose around his neck. He spoke his truth even as his voice began to quake:

"I bear no malice in my heart towards any one, and my soul is going straight to heaven."

In 1893, the year of Willie's birth, a riot in nearby Roanoke erupted after a white produce vendor claimed that a black furnace worker, Thomas Smith, had assaulted her near the city market. Before the next sunrise, two dozen people were wounded and nine men were dead—including Smith, who was hung from a hickory tree, then shot, then dragged through the streets. As if that wasn't enough finality to the young furnace worker's life, the next morning rioters burned his body on the banks of the Roanoke River while a crowd of four thousand looked on, some clinging to pieces of the hanging rope they'd grabbed as mementos. The only evidence linking Smith to the crime was the victim's vague description of her perpetrator: he was "tolerably black," she said, and wearing a slouch hat, a tilted wide-brimmed hat popular at the time.

A Roanoke photo studio sold pictures of Smith hanging from the rope as a souvenir. It was the eighth known lynching in southwest Virginia that year.

The region had always been a dangerous place to be black. But it had never occurred to Harriett that some far-off circus promoter would steal her boys, turn them into sideshow freaks, and, for decades, earn untold riches by enslaving them to his cause.

But by the end of that swelteringly hot day, Harriett later told people, she had felt it in her marrow—something had happened, and something was wrong. A white man in a carriage had been spotted roaming the area, she heard, and now George and Willie were gone.

In a dusty corner of Virginia's Piedmont, in a place named Truevine—where the only thing that gave Jim Crow–era blacks any semblance of hope at all was the biblical promise of a better life in the hereafter—Harriett Muse knew it for a fact. She'd already been robbed of dignified work, of monetary pay, of basic human rights, all because of the color of her skin.

Now someone had come along and taken the only thing she had left: her children.

For more than a century, that was the story Willie Muse and

his relatives told. Their descendants had heard it, all of them, since the age of comprehension, then handed it down themselves, the way families do, stamping the memory with a kind of shared notarization. The story was practically seared into the Muse family DNA.

And, although it wasn't entirely accurate, not to the letter, the spirit of it certainly was.

The truth was actually far more surprising and, as it usually is, far more tangled.

PART ONE

1

Sit Down and Shut Up

The story seemed so crazy, many didn't believe it at first, black or white.

But for a century, it was whispered and handed down in the segregated black communities of Roanoke, the regional city hub about thirty miles from Truevine. Worried parents would tell their children to stick together when they left home to see a circus, festival, or fair.

A retired African-American school principal recalls, at age twelve, begging his mother to let him pick up odd jobs when a traveling circus visited town.

"They were hiring people to set up, but my mom said no. She was really serious about it," he said.

The myth of the Muse kidnapping was so embedded in the local folklore that, long before he became a social science professor, Roanoke-born Reginald Shareef remembers thinking it was bunk when his mother said to him: "Be careful, or someone will snatch you up," just as the Muse brothers had been.

But eventually an adult took him aside and told him that a circus promoter really had forced the brothers to become world-famous sideshow freaks, subjugating them for many years. And not only that, they had found their way back.

They were here. Now. Retired and hidden away in an attic of

one of the houses on a segregated Roanoke city block, one of them living into the early aughts.

While adults relayed the story as a cautionary tale, kids teased each other about it. Nobody seemed to know for sure whether the Muses really lived in an attic—and the handed-down stories had key points of divergence—but the truth didn't stand in the way of a good story: the brothers were the equivalent of Boo Radley. "The story had a mystery to it and a witchery in some people's minds," another retired educator told me. And some kids weren't sure whether it was the circus they should be afraid of—or the Muses.

In the 1960s, Shareef grew up in the same segregated neighborhood as the Muses; his grandmother lived two blocks away. He ran around with the great-nephews of the Muse brothers. "They were a nice family, but the men were always getting into something," he recalled. "It's a wonder the women in that family didn't go crazy."

In 1996, Shareef published a pictorial history of Roanoke's black community and included a long-hidden photograph of the Muse brothers he'd found in the dusty archives of Roanoke's Harrison Museum of African American Culture. The caption he wrote contained errors—they weren't twins, and they weren't exactly toddlers when they were kidnapped—but the gist was correct: "Albino twins [George and Willie Muse] were stolen at age three and featured as 'freaks' for many years in the Ringling Brothers Circus."

A Muse relative saw the photo in the book and called Shareef on the phone, asking, "Where'd you get that picture?"

The family didn't like to talk about what had happened to their uncles; they'd all been taunted about it as kids.

"Your uncles eat raw meat!" classmates shouted at them on

the playground. Or worse, curiosity seekers, blacks and whites, would show up on their front porch at all hours of the day and night, demanding to see George and Willie. Another albino relative, a niece, described that double curse of differentness rearing back on her. For years, she had a hard time leaving her house to go to the store.

Not long after Shareef's book came out, the Muse brothers' great-niece Nancy Saunders went to the owner of that image, Frank Ewald, who ran Roanoke's premier photo-finishing shop and gallery. A photo collector, Ewald had purchased the negatives of celebrated Roanoke street photographer George Davis, who'd taken the 1927 portrait of the brothers featured in Shareef's book. Ewald was in the process of launching a Davis photo exhibit when Nancy visited the gallery and politely said: take George and Willie out.

"She wasn't combative or threatening," Ewald recalled. "She just asked us not to exhibit them."

He didn't dare.

The first time painter and folk-art collector Brian Sieveking heard the story, he was an eight-year-old budding artist fascinated by circus sideshows. He'd seen the Muses' picture at the Circus World Museum, in Baraboo, Wisconsin, the original home of the Ringling Brothers Circus, and began drawing them in his sketchbooks next to other acts that struck his fancy, including Johnny Eck, the Amazing Half-Boy, and Chang and Eng, the original Siamese twins. "I got curious about the Muse brothers because you could easily understand the fat lady and the tall guy, but what exactly did these guys do?" recalled Sieveking, who is white and now a forty-nine-year-old art professor.

The summer he was twelve, his family moved from Cincinnati to a high-end subdivision outside Roanoke and enrolled him in a private school. He was lonely and bored, and took solace in a stack of decommissioned books for sale in a back room of the downtown library. There he stumbled upon a book called *You and Heredity*, a quasi-scientific tome on genetics published in 1939. Proponents of the eugenics movement often used sideshows as propaganda about the dangers of miscegenation and of allowing the lower classes, especially those with genetic "flaws"—and most especially African Americans with such characteristics—to breed.

In a chapter titled "Structural Defects," Sieveking was stunned to find a photograph of an unnamed George and Willie Muse with a caption describing Roanoke as their hometown. His new town!

The hobby turned into obsession. A few summers later, he was working as a grocery-store checkout clerk when the subject of the brothers came up in the break room. His coworkers were among the very few black people the teenaged Sieveking knew in Roanoke, which was, then and now, among the most housing-segregated cities in the South. They told him the Muse family lived "over in Rugby," a black neighborhood, where Willie Muse was approaching one hundred and still very much alive.

Sieveking sent word that he'd like to interview Willie, as he had done, once, with Johnny Eck. He wanted to know more about the brothers' careers, and he'd become particularly interested in the 1944 Hartford circus fire, one of the most devastating in American history (it killed 168 people). He would go on to paint a beautiful, haunting portrait of the fire—with the Muse brothers front and center. But he didn't get that interview.

"I wanted to ask Willie Muse about the fire," Sieveking recalled. "But I was told in no uncertain terms not to mess with Nancy," his primary caregiver.

As a young journalist who'd arrived in Roanoke in 1989 to write feature stories for the *Roanoke Times,* I took two years to muster the nerve to mess with Nancy. A newspaper photographer had told me the bones of the kidnapping story, based on rumors he'd heard growing up in Roanoke. "It's the best story in town, but no one has been able to get it," he said.

By the time I poked my head into her tiny soul-food restaurant, with the idea of writing a story about her famous great-uncles, it was very clear that all personal details were going to be closely held, trickling out in dribs and drabs—and very much on Nancy Saunders's timeline. The first time I asked if I could interview Willie Muse, she pointed to a homemade sign on the Goody Shop wall. A customer had stenciled the words in black block letters on a white painted board and given it to her as a gift.

The sign said SIT DOWN AND SHUT UP.

Willie was not now—nor would he ever be—available for comment. So, hoping to generate some goodwill for a future story on her uncles, I wrote a feature about her restaurant, a place where the menu never changes and isn't even written down. You're just supposed to know.

Legions of black Roanokers could already recite the daily specials I would eventually commit to memory: Tuesday is spaghetti or lasagna, except every other Tuesday, which is pork chops. Wednesday is fish, and Thursday country-fried steak. Friday is ribs, but you'd better come early because the ribs always sell out quickly. The line out front starts forming at noon, though lunch doesn't officially begin until 12:15 and not a minute before—and later if Nancy has to run home to check on Uncle Willie and finds him in the midst of a bad day. (His favorite special? Spaghetti Tuesday.)

For most of December, the place is closed so the Saunders women—Nancy and her mother, Dot; cousin Louise; and aunt Martha—can work on the hundreds of yeast rolls, cakes, and pies they make by advance special order for Christmas.

Among the other unwritten rules in the Goody Shop code: "Don't criticize, especially the fruitcake," I wrote. "When a novice Goody Shopper grimaced at the very mention of the jellied fruitstuff, Saunders snapped, 'I beg your pardon! You're getting ready to step on the wrong foot!'" She pointed, again, to her sign.

She also kept a painted rock on top of her cash register, a gift from her preschooler nephew, whom she helped raise. She was not above picking it up—presumably in semi-jest—should a customer offend her.

When I returned for lunch, two days after my story ran—Rib Fridays were my favorite—Nancy shook her finger at me, and it was clear I was not getting anything close to a pat on the back. Dot sat nearby peeling potatoes, watching *The Young and the Restless* and cringing at what she knew her daughter was about to say.

Nancy had been ready to send me packing the first time I walked in the restaurant and blithely inquired about her uncles, but softhearted Dot persuaded her to let me stay and do the restaurant feature. A *Y&R* fan in my youth, I'd bonded quickly with Dot over the characters and was helping peel potatoes in her kitchen before the episode was over, much to Nancy's chagrin. (Victor Newman was a scoundrel, we agreed.)

"You know what your story did?" Nancy barked. "It brought out a bunch of crazy white people, that's all!"

Paying customers, I might have added, but she was in no mood for backtalk. She walked past me without further comment. She was leaving now to feed Willie and turn him in his bed, as she often did throughout the day, leaving the Goody Shop as many as five or six times a shift.

If Nancy Saunders had her way, her great-uncles' story would have stayed buried where she thought it belonged. The first time she heard it, she was just a child, and she found the whole tale embarrassing, and painfully raw. The year was 1961, and black and white people alike wanted to know: Were the light-skinned brothers black or white? Had they really been trapped in a cage and forced to eat raw meat?

These men deserved respect, Nancy knew. They did not deserve the gawkers who came by their house at all hours, banging on the front door.

By the time I came on the scene, no one talked about savages or circus freaks in front of Nancy, a sturdy woman with a no-frills Afro, graying at the temples, whose skin was nearly as white as the chef's coat she wore to work. She baked bread every bit as good as her great-grandmother Harriett's ash cakes — and she was every bit as fierce. Even Reg Shareef, who knew the family well, had never contemplated bringing the subject up with her.

"That is one exceptionally guarded family," he told me, advising baby steps. "You have to think of them as a tribe. They fall out with each other sometimes. But if you fall out with one of them, they will come roaring back at you like an army."

It was ten more years before Nancy warmed up enough to let

me cowrite a newspaper series about her uncles, and only after Willie Muse's death, in 2001. She didn't reveal much, though. She invited my fellow reporter Jen McCaffery, photographer Josh Meltzer, and me inside the Muse brothers' house exactly once.

She made reference to a family Bible that we were not permitted to view, and for years after the series ran, whenever I visited the restaurant she hinted that there was so much more to the story than we had found.

Our newspaper was the same one that had mocked her family's version of the kidnapping story decades before. It had looked the other way when city officials decimated two historic black neighborhoods in the name of midcentury progress, via urban renewal, or, as the black community called it, Negro removal. The newspaper cheered when the city knocked down hundreds of community homes and buildings, including the Muse family's Holiness church. It refused to print wedding announcements for black brides until the mid-1970s because, the wealthy white publisher reasoned, Roanoke had no black middle class.

I myself had used a pair of pregnant black teens to illustrate a story about Roanoke's super-high teen-pregnancy rate in 1993, a story that went viral before that Internet term existed and made the girls the object of ridicule; even Rush Limbaugh joined in with a rant. When the girls dropped out of school shortly after my story ran, it was devastating, including to me.

Words linger and words matter, I learned, and it's not possible to predict the fallout they can have on a subject's life.

It would take me twenty-five years, finally, to earn something *nearing* Nancy's trust; to convince her I wasn't one more candy peddler intent on exploiting her relatives for the color of their skin—or purely for my own financial benefit. As the literary critic Leslie Fiedler has put it, "Nobody can write about Freaks without somehow exploiting them for his own ends."

George and Willie Muse had come into her care in the 1960s, a situation Nancy considered her privilege as well as her duty, and her loyalty to them extended to everything from coordinating their retirement activities and doctor visits—restoring the love, respect, and dignity that had been stolen from them as children—to holding their story close.

By 2008, she had begun, in her inimitably gruff (and usually funny and occasionally even sweet) way, to warm toward me. When I set out to write a ten-part series on caregiving for the elderly, Nancy was the first person I called for input.

"You gotta keep it real," she said, sharing names and numbers of people who would eventually become primary sources for that project. She periodically counseled me about other career and family stresses, advising me, "You can handle this. Listen, girl, if you can get back into Dot's kitchen, you can do anything."

When I hit a snag updating the story of the pregnant teens more than twenty years after my explosive first story, it seemed fate that Shannon Huff, now a thirty-seven-year-old mother of four, lived just around the corner from Nancy's northwest Roanoke ranch house. After some angry relatives tried to bully me into not running the story—physically threatening me and demanding a meeting with my newspaper bosses—Nancy reassured me, "You don't need their permission to do the story, just like you don't really need mine to write your book. Not *really*, you don't."

And yet, months earlier, Nancy's permission is exactly what I sought. On the eve of publishing my first book, about a third-generation factory owner who had battled Chinese imports to save his company, I had given her an advance reading copy of *Factory Man*, dog-earing a chapter on race relations I'd found particularly hard to write. It detailed decades of mistreatment of black furniture-factory workers and the sexual harassment of black domestic workers, who often resorted to wearing two girdles at the same time as a defense against their bosses' groping hands and outright rape.

"It's been that way down through history," Nancy said. "A friend of my mom's, she'd be vacuuming down the steps [on a housekeeping job], and the husband would be feeling her up from behind. My mom had to fill in for her one day. And so she told the man first thing, 'Don't make me open up your chest!'"

By which Dot Brown meant: with the tip of my knife.

Nancy and I had come a long way from the days of sit-down-and-shut-up.

Still, it was by no means a gimme when I called her in November 2013, asking for her blessing to pursue her uncles' story as a book. She was in her midsixties and recently retired, after closing the Goody Shop. I wanted her help delving into the family story as well as connecting with distant Muse relatives, including one albino Muse still living in Truevine.

"I'll think about it," Nancy said, and the message was clear: I was not to call back. She would call me.

More than six weeks later—oh, she enjoyed making me wait—she finally called. "I waited so I could give it to you as a present," she said.

It was Christmas morning, and Nancy had decided to let me write her uncles' story with her help and blessing. But on one condition: "No matter what you find out or what your research turns up, you have to remember: in the end, they came out on top."

I knew the story's ending, I assured her. I'd already interviewed several people—nurses and doctors, neighbors and lawyers—all of whom described the late-life care she'd given her uncles as impeccable and extraordinary.

I was less certain about who had forced them into servitude in the first place, about their struggle to have their humanity acknowledged and their work compensated. How exactly, during the harsh years of Jim Crow, had they managed to escape?

2

White Peoples Is Hateful

Driving into Truevine today, you still see hints of the hopelessness that hung over the tiny enclave a century before. Chestnut Mountain stands sentinel to the west, and farm plots give way to sagging trailers and tidy brick ranch houses. Joe-pye and pokeweeds wave along the roadside, and rickety tobacco-curing barns — most of the logs hand-chinked by Franklin County slaves and their descendants — are not Cracker Barrel postcard throwbacks: they're a decaying nod to the cash crop that has long driven the economy of the region, most of it farmed on the backs of minority labor.

But year after year, the past grows fainter. Another barn crumbles. A CLOSED sign hangs askew on the door of an antiques shop that was once a thriving country store. There, sharecroppers who plowed for their supper and pulled tobacco for their shelter used to buy hundred-pound sacks of pinto beans to last their families the winter long. The largest structure for miles in Truevine was a brick school built for black children in the 1940s. Closed shortly after integration, it was reopened by a small textile factory that operated for a few decades before it, too, shut down, in the wake of the North American Free Trade Agreement.

From slavery to segregation, from integration to globalization—the economic history of the American South intersects in this isolated, unincorporated crossroads. Truevine is a speck of land where slaves and their descendants became sharecroppers, then sewing-machine operators, then unemployed workers before, finally—those who could afford to, anyway—they fled.

Truevine and neighboring Sontag, Penhook, and Snow Creek: these close-knit Franklin County enclaves are memories now more than working communities, places where farmers once grew millions of pounds of the highest-grade cigarette tobacco in Virginia's so-called Old Belt. A few large tobacco operations are still in business, though tractors and giant metal curing barns have replaced the log structures and mules.

"We've always grown the kind of tobacco that is the worst for you," says Penhook farmer Johnny Angell, who cultivates eighty-five acres of flue-cured tobacco with the help of a dozen or so Mexican guest workers who spend ten months every year doing the work the black sharecroppers used to do. Angell credits his tobacco's richer taste to rolling topography and weather, especially cool Franklin County mornings drenched in big, foggy dews. With wide, leathery golden leaves, the region's "bright leaf" tobacco is distinguished by its thick tar content, such that a worker pulling leaves off stalks will find his hands black and sticky by the end of the day.

This isolated cluster of tobacco communities has always stood apart from its larger counterparts a few counties to the south—not just for its tar-laden tobacco, but also for the character of the people who grow it. For their moonshine and music, for their nineteenth-century dialect quirks that still linger on the tongue.

Truevine is a place where children are still called chaps, and the word *only* is pronounced "onliest," as in *Till the factories came, 'cropping was the onliest way we had to make money for our chaps.*

When one neighbor offers another a good deed—a driveway plowed, a bag of homegrown tomatoes dropped off on a porch—thanks is still offered in the language of Isaiah and Moses: *God bless you a double portion.*

To understand the world the Muse brothers came from, I talked to African Americans who have stayed in and around Truevine, some out of commitment to the home they love and others because they have no viable alternative. All had the Muse name tucked somewhere in their family tree, though those trees are marked by holes and missing limbs. In a culture where census takers didn't bother recording the names of slaves, the first black Muses to enter the public record are noted only as property, documented by gender, age, and dollar value.

Most of the people you talk to in Truevine have no idea where their slave ancestors actually toiled, though it was likely nearby. Slavery in the American South, as Harvard sociologist Orlando Patterson has written, decimated the black family unit of the 1800s, and it still plays a lingering role in black poverty and the relatively large numbers of families headed by single mothers today.

As retired Franklin County library genealogist Diane Hayes, who is African American, explained it, "Slavery was so painful that black families, like Holocaust victims, didn't talk about what happened for a long time. Lots of times the families would be split up so badly, sold off when their owners died or given away as gifts when someone in the [white] family got married, that people don't know" the names of their ancestors.

Before the publication of Alex Haley's *Roots,* in 1976, slavery remained such a taboo subject among blacks that when mid-century museum workers at Colonial Williamsburg tried to introduce a recording about slavery into an early interpretive program, the tape was repeatedly sabotaged—by the black maintenance staff.

Even then it was still too raw, still too soon.

The stories flow more easily now, about brutal work conditions that didn't vary much from the time of emancipation to the American civil rights movement. Without fail, from the wealthiest black entrepreneur to the retiree getting by on food stamps, the opportunity afforded Franklin County blacks throughout the first half of the twentieth century echoed Booker T. Washington's sentiment from 1865: "To get into a schoolhouse and study this way would be about the same as getting into paradise."

Most children of sharecroppers didn't go to school during harvest, a period extending from August to December; they were too busy wiring tobacco leaves onto sticks, hanging them from rafters to dry. When their stomachs began to rumble, they were told to chew a leaf or two—as an appetite suppressant.

"In the fall, you only went to school when it rained or snowed," said Janet Johnson, seventy-one, who'd been among the last generation in her family to work tobacco. She recalled dropping out of Truevine School in the sixth grade when she got tired of watching the white farmer's children go to school while she and her siblings stayed home and worked the crop.

Her mother, ninety-eight-year-old Mabel Pullen, hadn't gone to school at all. Mabel didn't learn to read until she was in her seventies, when she took a few night classes run by the county's adult education program. Her husband, Charles, never did.

The Pullens live in Sontag, not far from Truevine, in a tar-papered bungalow, heated by wood and supplemented by a pungent kerosene space heater. Mabel was ninety-seven when we first met in 2013, hard of hearing but still sharp. I had met her daughter quite by chance while working on a newspaper article about proposed cuts to the federal food-stamp program. Janet, who retired when the furniture factory where she worked into her early sixties closed, was picking up a box of food from a nearby food pantry to share with her parents.

Charles and Mabel qualified for food stamps but refused to apply because, as Janet put it, "You talk about pride!"

To supplement their Social Security benefits, the extended family raised chickens, canned apples and tomatoes, and shared a plot of mustard greens — their salad patch, they call it — in the yard between their cluster of modest trailers and homes.

By the time I returned to ask about sharecropping in Franklin County, it was almost a year later. Janet agreed to introduce me to people from Truevine, including some Muses who still lived in the area. She was descended from people, I later pieced together, who crossed paths with Harriett Muse's husband, Cabell Muse.

As a child, she'd heard that the circus had kidnapped the brothers right from under their mother's nose, but details were scant. She'd thought about them often over the years, with pity for their trauma but with a touch of longing, too.

Only in a place like Truevine, she thought, could the notion of being kidnapped seem almost like an opportunity.

*   *   *

"It's hard talking to you about this," Janet said, abruptly, during a follow-up interview.

Our earlier talks had been fluid and friendly. A year before, Janet had asked me to help her and a sister track the family's genealogy back to slavery, looking up forebears on my Ancestry.com account. When I hit a dead end, I introduced her to a researcher friend, who also couldn't overcome the record-keeping gaps.

But during this interview, our fourth, Janet was hesitant to open up. It wasn't just the difference in our skin tones. It seemed to be my education and my presumed life of ease. It was every white kid who'd ever spit on her from a school-bus window while she trudged the four miles by foot to the one-room school. It was the still-vivid memory of a slave in Truevine, passed down through the generations at Truevine School: he was standing naked atop a tree stump with pork grease slathered on his muscles—so he'd show better, so he'd bring a better price—and his family never saw him again.

"White peoples is hateful," Janet said, finally. "And I like you, I do. But it's hard for people to understand, my grandkids even...to know how hard it was when me and Mama was coming up. That white peoples treated us like dirt."

It was Mabel's ninety-eighth birthday. She stared out the window, and she didn't seem to be following our conversation, until suddenly she jumped in:

"They would feed you outdoors," she said, her voice reedy and resonant.

She was speaking about the farmers she 'cropped for from the 1920s through the '60s, and her parents before that. "They had a little table under the tree by the big house, and when it was lunchtime they'd raise up the kitchen window and hand you out the food—like you a dog or something. Then you'd eat at that table."

"They said they didn't like 'niggers in the house,'" Janet explained. "That was the rule."

That was the kind of world George and Willie Muse were born into in the 1890s, when the only hope the son or a grandson of slaves had—somehow, some way—was to buy a piece of land. Cabell and Harriett Muse had been reared during Reconstruction, a time when former slave owners had adopted sharecropping as a system for retaining control over almost four million ex-slaves, most of whom had no means of sustaining their families—or of leaving the land where they'd once been bound. With a cash-poor farm economy dominating the South, cotton and tobacco crops became the main sources of credit, and black families rented small plots of land in return for a portion of the crop.

But whites determined how blacks should be paid, how much they should work, and how many members of their family would do the work. The 'croppers weren't compensated until the tobacco was sold, at which point they generally got one-quarter to one-half of the money the farmer received. Half-shares, people called it.

But that was *if* the farmer was honest about how much the crop brought. And *if* the 'cropper hadn't taken out too many liens against his wages from the farmer or the store. Interest rates on loans and cash advances typically ranged from 21 to 53 percent, and often the 'cropper earned nothing at all on "settling-day" once he paid back his debt, ensuring he'd have no choice but to return to that farm another season—and sink even deeper into debt.

Like the Muses, the Pullens lived in shoddy tenant cabins along the perimeter of the farmer's land. "There were holes in the walls and the roof, too," Janet said. "That farmer was such a mean man. He'd carry that tobacco and sell it in Danville, but we never did get to go," she recalled of the warehouse where the crop was auctioned every fall. "He'd [show] you what it brought, but Daddy never could read any of it."

So it went across the South, where only a fool would question the landlord's math. "If you raised the slightest question, you ran the risk of being forced off the land," explained Berea College historian Andrew Baskin, who has researched slavery and its aftermath in Franklin County. "Everything was in the hands of the whites who owned the land."

Most rural blacks didn't challenge the system. Alabama sharecropper Ned Cobb explained why in Theodore Rosengarten's landmark 1974 exposé, *All God's Dangers*. When Cobb's neighbor Henry Kirkland questioned his landlord's accounting, he "flew in a passion—he toted his pistol all the time—...over that book business and throwed that pistol on old Uncle Henry and deadened him right there." He shot the man's son, too.

Nelson Whitten, the Freedmen's Bureau Records official sent to Franklin County in 1867 to "provide for more efficient government of the Rebel States," wrote to his boss in Washington, D.C.: "I find an inclination on the part of the whites, though not universal, to override and take advantage of the freedmen whether they are working for a share of the crops, or for wages."

The entwinement of former slaves with land and white landowners continued after the Civil War. And, in the remotest parts of the rural South, so it persisted for another century and beyond.

*　　*　　*

Up the road from the Pullens' and past a small field of bright-leaf tobacco, Thelma Muse Lee remembered feeling entrapped. "We 'cropped for eighteen years, till after our kids left home," she said. "It was the onliest way we had to make money. But you could never make enough to buy any land. Because you had to give half to the farmer, then he'd take out what we owed him for fertilizer. Then in the spring we had to borrow money from him again for seed," she said.

It was an Indian-summer day, with temps in the upper 80s. The year was 2014, but looking at the landscape behind Thelma's house, it could have been a century before. Thelma was boiling thirty-seven and a half pounds of green beans she'd canned over the weekend, she told me proudly. She had grown the beans herself—at the age of ninety-three, managing every aspect of the garden, except the tilling, which fell to her son—and now she was sealing the jars atop an outdoor wood fire the son had started at five that morning, before he left for work.

When I asked if she was trying to keep her kitchen cool by boiling the jars outside, she and Janet shot each other a bemused look. *White people.*

"No, honey," Thelma said, shaking her head. "I'm saving on electric."

Thelma remembered hearing about the Muse kidnapping as a child. It was the same cautionary tale the blacks in Roanoke had been taught, but with a different setting. "They got stoled from a fair they used to have up here in Rocky Mount," she said.

Thelma thought they were related to her—her maiden name was Muse, and she had albinos in her family, including a daughter who lived a few houses up Sontag Road—but she wasn't sure exactly where George and Willie fell on her extended-family tree.

A few miles away, under the shadow of Chestnut Mountain, the Muse lineage was similarly vague. A. J. Reeves didn't get much further in school than Janet Pullen or Thelma Lee. But he chopped the wood for the potbellied Truevine School stove, same as they did, and he, too, had Muse family blood. He figures that his grandmother Queen Victoria Muse probably descended from the same Truevine-area family as Cabell Muse.

One hundred years old at the time of our interview, Reeves was sporting a pair of new replacement knees that carried him to his backyard workshop every morning. The centenarian spends most days building and repairing clocks—mantel clocks, grandfather clocks, clocks of the sort you set on your desk. A farmer-turned-sawmiller-turned-contractor-turned-plumber, Reeves performed his last plumbing job in 2007 on a Habitat for Humanity house at the age of ninety-three. He still lends out his tools and advice to the many neighbors who stop by regularly to chat. A hand-lettered sign in his workshop that hangs from the ceiling says IN GOD WE TRUST. ALL OTHERS PAY CASH.

Asked to describe living conditions in Truevine during the era when the Muse brothers disappeared, Reeves cracked a sly half-smile, leaning back to unleash a cacophony of squeaks from his rusted office chair.

"You want the truth?" the clock maker asked, tilting his head. "Are you *sure* you want the truth?"

He was as serious as a copperhead in a wood stack.

His grandparents were Franklin County slaves, freed at the end of the Civil War, he told me. His grandfather Armistead Reeves even participated in it, one of 534 Franklin County slaves requisitioned by the Virginia governor to join the Confederate war effort. Armistead was sent to Richmond to cook for the troops and tend their horses in 1862.

Details of Armistead's war experience were not recorded, but I found parallels in the records of a contemporary, Samuel Walker, born into slavery in nearby Snow Creek and married to yet another Muse. Walker described his first memory at the age of five in 1847: watching the sale of his mother to a Georgia plantation owner. He ran after the wagon that took her away, calling her name, but she never looked back.

Walker married Naomi Muse, who belonged to prominent Truevine landowner Elizabeth Muse, along with thirty other slaves—including, probably, Cabell Muse's parents. Elizabeth Muse had threatened to sell Naomi during the war, prompting her to fret over who would care for her "chaps," as Naomi later recalled. But the family stayed together until 1862, when Samuel was conscripted to serve as a teamster and fortification builder; he was eventually sent to the front lines shortly before Lee surrendered to Grant. The first time their names appear together in an official record is in 1870. But because they were illiterate, the census taker misspelled Naomi's name as Onelly.

"Perhaps one of the greatest tragedies of institutional slavery in North America was that it robbed millions of African Americans—and countless Virginians—of their heritage," wrote journalist Bill Archer, who chronicled Walker's painstaking efforts to receive a small Civil War pension. It wasn't approved until six decades after the war ended, in 1925. For the remaining eight years of his life, Walker's quarterly war pension amounted to $6.25.

Walker saved the money to buy his first piece of property not by farming but by sending two of his sons off for jobs with the Roanoke-based Norfolk and Western Railway, which was expanding into the West Virginia coalfields in the 1880s to link Appalachian-mined coal to the port of Norfolk and, eventually, the Great Lakes. Using the funds they sent home, he built his first house in Franklin County, his granddaughter, Grace Roten, proudly remembered, complete with weatherboarding and "store-bought windows."

That same quest for upward mobility prompted Cabell Muse to leave Franklin County not long after the births of George and Willie. The first time his name appears in an official record is 1900, a time when thousands of African-American men, tired of trying to earn a living off the land, wandered the countryside seeking jobs in work camps and mines scattered throughout the South. They were building levees in Arkansas, gathering turpentine in Georgia, and mining coal in West Virginia and Tennessee—making far less than their white counterparts and sometimes, if their company-store debts were large, earning nothing at all.

Cabell and scores of other young men from Truevine ventured to Rock, West Virginia, looking to earn the first cash money of their lives. They were, in the words of a prominent union organizer, "seeking a man's chance in the world . . . looking for true American citizenship." Most were tasked with hard labor, digging out coal, hammering metal into spikes, and building track to carry the coal using pickaxes, shovels, tie tongs, and mallets.

In a posed photo from the Norfolk and Western archives, fourteen black men (and one white laborer) clutch shovels while four white bosses loom large in the foreground, one with his hand on hip and another leaning authoritatively on his leg, his foot perched atop a handcar. Rocks litter the sifted dirt, which gives way to scrubby grass, crooked electricity poles, and mountains rising from both sides of the tracks in a wide V.

It was rough work performed largely by rough people, black and white. In 1904 in nearby Williamson, West Virginia, two drunken vagabonds who were caught wandering the work camp at night shot and killed a policeman and a railway telegraph operator. The officer was shot for refusing to drink the tramps' whiskey, and the night operator was shot when he tried to intervene.

Blacks lived in segregated communal housing, and as with the Mexican immigrants who would one day replace their kin in the tobacco fields, their families relied on them to send money home. Only the luckiest black workers like A. J. Reeves's father managed to learn blacksmithing, a physically easier skilled trade that brought better pay.

Masterless men, they were called, as the presence of tens of thousands of black men in work camps across the South instilled fear in whites, who saw them as job competition and free agents, no longer attached to the land or beholden to landlords.

As sociologist W. E. B. Du Bois framed the situation, emancipation had transmogrified into a "race feud" in the southern states. "Not a single Southern legislature stood ready to admit a Negro under any conditions, to the polls; not a single Southern legislature believed free Negro labor was possible without a system of restrictions that took all its freedoms away; there was scarcely a white man in the South who did not honestly regard Emancipation as a crime, and its practical nullification as a duty."

Back in Franklin County, more than a dozen tobacco factories fashioned cigarettes and plug tobacco, but blacks typically weren't permitted to apply for factory jobs. Imprinted in the minds of most white southerners was the notion that black people lacked the necessary intelligence to operate machinery. They dismissed their dialects, mannerisms, and supposedly narrow skills, viewing them as inferior in every way.

But A. J. Reeves's father returned from his West Virginia blacksmithing stint with an entrepreneurial work-around of that mind-set: "My daddy came back and bought a hundred and fifty acres of this land before I was born, for five hundred dollars," Reeves recalled, gesturing to the property that abuts his church and the original wood-frame Truevine School (now the site of a church picnic shelter). "He was a farmer, but he also had his own blacksmithing shop right down the road. He never worked for anybody but himself, and he taught me that. Because you saw the way the 'croppers were treated. Even if they treat ya good—and most didn't—they're still taking part of your labor because you're working one day for yourself and one day for them. I want to work every day for myself."

It was simple math, as commonsense as the minute hands and moon dials marking time along the perimeter of his workshop walls.

Cabell Muse wanted to work for himself, too. He traded blisters from the tobacco hoe for blisters from shoveling rocks and dirt. But, unlike Robert Reeves, he did not come home to Truevine with a pocketful of cash.

By the time he came back to Virginia, George and Willie had not returned home, and their mother was panic-stricken. The police hadn't lifted a finger to help her find them, and a children's-rights agency in Virginia had mounted only a brief, halfhearted search.

She probably imagined the worst. Just an hour east of Roanoke, in Lynchburg, Virginia, news was reverberating of Ota Benga, whose story would become the low point of scholars' search to find the "missing link" bridging human and ape. Hailed as a "pygmy" who'd been "liberated" from the Congo by an American missionary, Benga was first displayed at the 1904 World's Fair in St. Louis alongside Eskimos, Filipinos, and Native Americans. In an exhibit that was two parts Barnum and one part pseudo-science, they'd been forced to wear loincloths in the cold winter wind.

In 1906, Benga—his real name was Toa Benga—came to live in a guest cottage at the Bronx Zoo, where he was caged with an orangutan. The zoo director had the idea to display the pair together, with a sign on their cage that read: THE AFRICAN PIGMY, OTA BENGA. AGE, 23 YEARS. HEIGHT, 4 FEET 11 INCHES. WEIGHT, 103 POUNDS.... EXHIBITED EACH AFTERNOON DURING SEPTEMBER.

The exhibit drew forty thousand visitors on a single Sunday. But a scandal flared up almost immediately, led by indignant black clergymen who prevailed on zookeepers to release Benga to an orphanage. "Our race, we think, is depressed enough, without exhibiting one of us with the apes," the Reverend James H. Gordon said. "We think we are worthy of being considered human beings, with souls."

But a *New York Times* writer opined otherwise, in an editorial that perfectly captured the white-supremacy zeitgeist of the day: "As for Benga himself, he is probably enjoying himself as well as he could anywhere in his country, and it is absurd to make moan over the imagined humiliation and degradation he is suffering."

Eventually he did land at a black-run Baptist seminary in Lynchburg. Though he was happier there than anywhere else he'd been in America—he'd come under the tutelage of Harlem Renaissance poet and Lynchburg resident Anne Spencer, and through Spencer he met both Du Bois and Booker T. Washington—Ota Benga was taunted every time he went out in public. As he walked through Cottontown, a white working-class section of Lynchburg, boys cursed him and threw rocks.

"Why they do that?" he wanted to know.

In 1916, he shot himself in the heart next to a campfire he'd built for himself in the woods. "I guess he decided these are Christians and, with Christianity, you have a soul. And he thought he'd shoot himself, and his soul would go back to Africa," said Spencer's son, Chauncey, in a 1993 interview.

A distraught Harriett tried to make up for the loss of George and Willie by birthing three more children in three short years—Tom and Annie Belle, and Harrison, who had the same white-blond hair, milky skin, and watery eyes as the older brothers.

Relatives recalled that she took her brood to church every time the doors opened. She asked neighbors and fellow parishioners to alert her when they heard of a traveling carnival or circus playing in the Rocky Mount or, more likely, in the closest cities of Roanoke or Martinsville.

But Roanoke was almost forty miles to the north, and Martinsville was almost that far to the south. As Booker T. Washington had put it, Franklin County was extremely isolated, "about as near to nowhere as any locality gets to be."

Harriett kept her other children close, especially Harrison. The boy was a blessing and a constant reminder to his mother, who swore that she would find George and Willie one day—or risk her life trying.

3

And Still the Cry Against Us Continues

When Harriett landed in Roanoke, by about 1917, she was following a well-worn migration pattern. She was looking for information on her sons, of course. But she was also looking for opportunity, just like the more than four thousand other African-American migrants who'd flocked to the so-called Magic City in its earliest years, making the nascent boomtown the fastest-growing city in the post–Civil War South.

In 1882, a group of ambitious tobacco merchants and entrepreneurs had persuaded the Philadelphia-based Norfolk and Western Railway to launch a terminus, machine shop, and corporate hub in a Virginia outpost named Big Lick. To sweeten the deal, they offered the Philly industrialists rights-of-way, cash bonuses, and tax exclusions. The N&W provided cheap access to iron and coal lodged in the mountains, which in turn spawned industrialization of the region as investors raced to set up mines, furnaces, and mills along the winding tracks.

As an additional incentive, the town fathers even offered to change the name of the town from Big Lick, with its hillbilly salt-lick implications, to Kimball, in honor of the railroad president. When Kimball demurred, they switched it instead to

Roanoke, a Native American word that translated loosely—
and fittingly—to *money*.

Nearly a third of the city's early residents were black, former
sharecroppers and sons of former slaves who made their way to
Roanoke by wagon and by train to work as Pullman porters,
janitors, and manual-labor assistants to the machinists and railroad brakemen.

Some of the men sold illegal liquor on the side, and their
wives cleaned white people's houses, and, all in all, it was still
a hell of a hard time to be black because the white establishment told African Americans where to eat and where to live
and where to sit in public spaces.

But it beat sharecropping.

"Had an old Virginian fallen asleep in 'Big Lick' last year to
wake up to Roanoke today, he would have been as much bewil-
dered as Rip Van Winkle was when he awoke in the Kaatskills,"
gushed a writer in *The Industrial South*, a weekly newspaper. A
New York Times reporter enthused that Roanoke's fledgling
businesses were now poised to exploit the state's coal deposits
with the goal of returning Virginia "to something like its old
position in the Union."

There were growing pains galore, including a relentless spate
of typhoid that people called Big Lick fever. A bawdy, thriving
saloon and brothel scene clashed with the boosters' view of
Roanoke as a shiny symbol of the so-called New South.

In a town dominated by single working-class men, there
were more saloons than any other kind of business in Roanoke's downtown, not counting all the illegal speakeasies,
called nip joints. At night, "with the red-light beacons of the
bar rooms all ablaze over the plank sidewalks, and the music of
the violin and banjo coming through the open doors and win-

dows, the town suggests a mining camp or a mushroom city of Colorado," a *Baltimore Sun* reporter wrote.

Built atop a bog, Roanoke grew faster than its public sanitation system could handle, with a death rate in its early years that was higher than New York City's. Early residents threw down stepping-stones in front of themselves to avoid losing their shoes in the mud.

There were no public gardens, parks, or libraries, no public squares or tree-lined avenues. By 1907, Roanoke had transformed from a village of five hundred people to a city of thirty-five thousand without much concern for aesthetics or the greater civic good.

As renowned urban planner John Nolen quipped, the place had simply gone "from Big Lick to Bigger Lick."

The city was as divided as the railroad tracks that separated black from white. Most new arrivals were farmers from the countryside who let their cows and chickens roam free into their neighbors' lots, and they were looked down on by the city's burgeoning business class. When a couple from rural Franklin County rode downtown in their beat-up wagon, they startled at the sight of a passing bicyclist, then jumped again at the sound of a fire alarm being tested, one reporter noted. Bystanders burst into laughter at their "hayseed" ways until finally the couple fled, embarrassed and confused.

Blacks were even bigger targets for ridicule, turning out in such numbers at a fair "as to threaten a watermelon famine" and singled out for press coverage only when accused of crimes. Whites even blamed the periodic smallpox waves on "the Negroes" and once torched the homes of infected blacks.

If Franklin County had been a tough place to be black, at

least the tensions there had been spread out over a half-million acres of hills and hollows. Here, blacks and whites competed for jobs. While they lived and worked in very different social strata, they also brushed against one another with regularity on streetcars, in stores, and, for those employed as domestic workers or chauffeurs, in the homes of the wealthy.

"Roanoke was incredibly hostile to African Americans," said Rand Dotson, an author and historian who chronicled Roanoke's earliest years in a 2007 book. "There was a level of hostility that most people today can barely comprehend," from segregated public accommodations and segregated housing ordinances to outright violence on many occasions.

"Whites were scared of blacks and despised them. They thought they weren't really people. And yet they hired them to work in their homes, cook their food, and do their laundry, which was just bizarre."

The relationship was as oddly intimate as it was degrading.

For the rest of their working lives, that is exactly how the Muses paid their rent and fed their children: Harriett working as an in-home maid and picking up laundry jobs on the side, and Cabell driving white men and women around — first in a wagon, later in a car. (In what must have been a disappointing entrée into Roanoke work life, before becoming a chauffeur, Cabell spent part of 1917 doing the same kind of manual labor he'd done on the railroad — digging trenches, fixing leaks, and laying water pipelines for the Roanoke Water Company.)

Harriett and Cabell weren't allowed to vote because they couldn't read, nor could they afford to pay poll taxes, requirements written into the 1902 Virginia Constitution, which replaced the old Reconstruction-era Underwood Constitution forced on it in the aftermath of the Civil War.

"Discrimination! Why, that is *exactly* what we propose," boasted constitution delegate and future senator Carter Glass when asked whether the new voting restrictions were discriminatory.

The goal, Glass explained, had been the "the elimination of every Negro who can be gotten rid of, legally, without materially impairing the strength of the white electorate."

To celebrate the new constitution and the complementary Jim Crow laws that banned the mixing of races in public places, restrooms, trains, and water fountains, municipalities across Virginia planted oak saplings in courthouse squares.

It didn't matter who you were, if you were black; just strolling into the wrong Roanoke block could land you in jail—or worse, depending on what was going on at the time. In 1904, a white shop worker named George Shields went home for lunch and found his wife and three-year-old daughter lying in pools of blood, victims of a robbery and assault. His wife, Alice, survived the attack—barely—to describe her perpetrator as a black man.

A manhunt sprang up, and no black male in the city was spared suspicion. The entire race was blamed as hundreds of whites took to the streets and demanded vigilante justice. Newspaper writers used the crime to justify holding down African Americans, blaming the crime on "the black menace" and "the beast in the Negro."

Four days after the attack, rumors circulated that a black civic leader and minister, the Reverend R. R. Jones, had given a Sunday sermon suggesting that George Shields himself had committed the assault. A mob of a thousand whites went look-ing for Jones, storming through black neighborhoods and shoot-ing up Jones's home, tearing down fence pickets, and blasting pistol shots into the sky. Jones denied making the remarks, but whites still papered the city with placards, vowing he'd be lynched if he failed to leave town by nightfall.

Born into slavery, Jones, a Roanoke preacher for thirty years, walked seven miles through the woods to secretly catch a train heading north—never to return. The black-owned *Richmond Planet* advised him that he should only dare to do so once he'd made his own funeral arrangements, bought a shotgun, and killed a few of the "white hoodlums" who were sure to show up at his house.

When a "Negro roustabout" in nearby Salem was accused of making a "dastardly statement" about the case, a mob hauled him away and stripped him, tying him to a telephone pole and whipping him with electric wires. When he screamed, they stuffed handkerchiefs in his mouth.

Several other black men were run out of town, and some were fired from much-coveted railroad jobs. A black woman was spared only when she went into "spasms" after a mob threatened to flog her, too.

Two weeks later, a black drifter named Henry Williams was captured in the West Virginia coalfields by the Baldwin-Felts Detective Agency, the railroad's crime-busting arm, and con-fessed. Following a short trial that historians would later deem a sham, a judge ordered him hung until he was "dead, dead, dead."

No apologies were issued to the scores of black citizens who'd been wrongfully accused of harboring the offender or challenging the narrative of the blood-hungry mob. The Shields case cemented racist sentiments in the region, paving the way for segregation ordinances, more violence, and lingering tensions in a city demographers still consider among the most segregated in the South.

The courthouse oaks grew taller and leafier. And across Virginia, blacks lived under a canopy of subjugation. In 1915, Roanoke officials passed a city ordinance forbidding blacks and whites from living on the same block and carved out five segregation districts, saying the presence of a black person living on the same block as whites "offends the general sense of community," increases tensions, and decreases property values.

Most blacks in Roanoke were too afraid to speak up, but the editor of the *Richmond Planet* cataloged the indignities: "We have been denied the right to vote, the right to hold office, the right to live on the same block with the white man, the right to ride in the same railway car, the right to occupy a seat in a street car beside a white man, the right to worship in the same church, the right to drink at the same bar, the right to be buried in the same cemetery—and still the cry against us continues."

In response, the *Roanoke Times*—the newspaper that had once opined, "Lynching has its place"—devoted most of a page to an open letter titled "The Negro Question." It claimed black crime was endangering "the future of our beautiful southern land." The solution, the editorial writer proposed, would be the formation of a white man's league that would exert a repressive influence on the "lawless negroes."

By the mid-1920s, Ku Klux Klan membership had surged to five million members, with chapters from California to Maine, including a thriving Klan in Roanoke, named after Robert E. Lee. With the government's permission, a national parade of

Klansmen marched down Pennsylvania Avenue in the nation's capital in 1925 and past the White House, then occupied by Calvin Coolidge, to express superiority over not just blacks but also Jews, immigrants, Catholics, and radicals.

The entire country was obsessed with the notion of separating people into greater and lesser breeds.

But city life, as racially charged as it was, still held the potential of progress as Cabell and Harriett Muse moved to Roanoke, drawn by the same desires that motivated most other blacks from the countryside: with the prayer that Cabell would land a coveted job on the N&W. As a popular blues lyric went, *When you marry, marry a railroad man / Every Sunday, dollar in your hand.*

"Everybody was leaving the country, coming to town, like they thought they were gonna be picking up money off the streets," recalled A. L. Holland, ninety-eight, a onetime railroad janitor and civil rights leader who broke barriers in the 1960s when he finally got to use his college degree in an office job. In 1898, his father, Gus Holland, had migrated from a tobacco farm in Chatham, near Truevine, to work as a railroad blacksmith, a relatively plum job he landed only because of his experience shoeing horses on the farm.

"He never bought an automobile, but we never did live in a rented house," his son proudly recalled. "He knew owning property was more important, so he walked to work every day."

By the time Cabell and Harriett Muse first show up together in Roanoke records, in the 1910s, Cabell was finished "doggin' the rails," as the backbreaking work of building railroad track was called. In West Virginia, he had resented the way the company required African Americans to purchase platefuls of corn bread and beans while white workers and supervisors received balanced meals. In West Virginia, black workers on assignment had to bring their own spoons, a typical Jim Crow humiliation, and racial tension in the camps was high. A black track worker on assignment in the coalfields recalled whites posting a sign: BLACKS READ AND RUN. IF YOU CANNOT READ, RUN ANY DAMNED WAY.

So no one blamed Cabell when he landed easier, slightly more dignified work as a chauffeur, a job with more independence and a higher status, while Harriett labored as a domestic worker and laundress. They lived in a black enclave near the N&W rail yard, a cluster of shacks and shotgun shanties near the city's West End that old-timers still refer to as Jordan's (or Jerden's) Alley.

They were just a few blocks away from the Victorian mansions owned by the likes of the *Roanoke Times* publisher and those Philadelphia-bred railway executives, close enough so Harriett and her neighbors could walk to their back doors, pick up the laundry, and carry it back home to scrub by hand.

The Muse home at 19 Ten-and-a-Half Street was set on an alleyway, more or less, a red-dirt road with an alley on one end and a sooty rail yard on the other. Engines were maintained at the yard's roundhouse, so a near-constant cacophony of steaming locomotives, blowing whistles, and train-car clatter hovered over the neighborhood. Cinders belched from the engines, enough to make a resident's eyes water at times. With six houses crammed together on the Muses' side, and four across the street, the entire road was just a half-block long.

Most born in the neighborhood lived quiet lives, more modest than the blacks who lived closer to downtown in Gainsboro, home to a thriving Henry Street business district. An aspirational middle class was forming there around a growing number of doctors' and lawyers' offices, several black-owned businesses, and a hotel/nightclub scene that brought in such rising stars as Louis Armstrong, Ella Fitzgerald, and Cab Calloway. The musicians played epic, late-night sessions in the black-owned Dumas Hotel after performing for crowds at the whites-only Hotel Roanoke owned by the railroad.

But having status in Gainsboro didn't much matter when Dr. I. D. Burrell, a black physician and druggist, became deathly ill in 1914. He'd been working toward starting a black hospital. But when white Roanoke hospitals refused to treat him, he was left to attempt a trip to a Washington, D.C., facility instead.

Dr. Burrell died en route. When Roanoke's first hospital for blacks finally opened on Henry Street in 1915, it was named for him.

Gainsboro was also home to a young Oliver Hill, whose work on the landmark 1954 *Brown v. Board of Education* Supreme Court case overturned the "separate but equal" laws of the day.

I interviewed Hill in 2006 about segregation in Roanoke. He was one hundred at the time, but he remembered clearly the injustice of Jim Crow dawning on him in 1918, when he had to awaken at 5:00 a.m. for basketball practice in the combination auditorium-gymnasium at Harrison School. "You had to clean up and put the chairs away before you could play. And you knew they had a gymnasium and showers and everything in the white schools," Hill recalled.

In his autobiography, Hill described trying to sell discarded whiskey bottles he'd collected as a child to a Roanoke distillery to earn some extra change. "When I got up on the second floor, someone yelled out, 'Grab the little nigger and cut his balls out,'" which sent Hill scrambling for his life.

*   *   *

If Gainsboro was a place that occasionally produced Supreme Court litigators and foreign ambassadors—the Talented Tenth, as Du Bois called the black leaders of his day—then Jordan's Alley was home to the lower 90 percent. Its businesses were comparably much smaller, many of them run by recent Syrian immigrants who lived over their shops. Willie Mae Ingram, known to the community today as Mother Ingram—an honorific given to the wives of pastors—was raised by her grandparents around the corner from Ten-and-a-Half Street, near the same stretch of railroad tracks. Her grandfather kept hogs in a communal pen up the street, and a creek ran through the area where she picked creasy greens. Few houses had furnaces, and it got so cold in winter that her grandmother used to take an old flatiron, heat it on the back of the coal-fired stove, and tuck it into the foot of her bed, wrapped in blankets, to keep her warm.

Willie Mae was eighty-four years old when I spoke to her in 2014, and she is one of a handful of people still living in the community with firsthand knowledge of the Muse brothers. She remembers Harriett Muse because she was strikingly tall and old-fashioned-looking, "with a black dress and an apron, like someone you'd see on a wagon train."

Everyone knew everyone else in a community where life was lived in the public eye, on the sidewalks, front porches, and alleyways. "You walked everywhere," said Regina "Sweet Sue" Peeks, eighty-four, including to Harrison School, a mile away in Gainsboro and across the bridge. She was raised near the rail yard by an aunt and uncle, Cora and John Holmes, whom she still refers to as Mama and Daddy. Her biological mother, Genova, lived with them off and on, and worked domestic jobs on Maiden Lane, a white neighborhood across a bridge and a couple of miles away, for a family who refused to pay her extra for Sunday work and made her use the "servants' bathroom" in their dank, unfinished basement. "They had a pony, and once they even let the 'poor little colored girl' come ride it," she said.

I winced when Sweet Sue told me the family's name, which I recognized immediately from the deed on my house. I've lived on Maiden Lane for fifteen years, and I winter my geraniums in the sink of that very same dank basement (after a heavy rain, it still leaks). When I asked how Genova got to the house, she told me she took the streetcar to Grandin Village, a quaint commercial area filled with restaurants, shops, and a movie theater, then and now.

"And then from there, I suppose she walked," about eight blocks.

Sweet Sue's daddy—meaning her uncle, whose nickname was Big John—"hustled for a living." By which she meant he hopped the passing N&W trains when the Baldwin-Felts policemen who provided private security for the railroad were sleeping on the job and rode in a boxcar to West Virginia, where he picked up corn liquor in ten-gallon cans. Big John sold that liquor for ten cents a shot glass out of an unmarked nip joint he ran from a rented house on Tenth Street, where Cabell Muse must have been familiar, judging from the proclivities that would later dominate family stories and news accounts. Once automobiles became popular, the men in the neighborhood stopped hopping the trains and simply drove to Franklin County, the unabashed moonshine capital of the world.

Another nip joint, across the street from the church, served food and liquor—and rented rooms by the hour. "You could get anything you wanted to in there, and you could dance and, if the wives didn't catch them there, the men could have all their money spent before they ever made it home," Sweet Sue said. "You'd be surprised at the people who'd buy whiskey when they wouldn't have nothing to eat."

Only whites lived on nearby Salem Avenue in those days, she told me. On her way home from school, she passed the home of an elderly white lady who kept trained parrots on her screened-in front porch.

When she was little and first started walking to school, she dreaded having to pass that Victorian house. But, seeking comfort in numbers, she talked some neighborhood kids into walking with her. Almost eight decades later, Sue still thinks about those parrots every time she passes the spot, though it's now just a grassy lot.

She still remembers, word for ungrammatical word, the taunt of those parrots when they spotted her and her friends.

"See them little niggers coming," they squawked.

Sweet Sue and Mother Ingram both grew up as regulars at the spiritual center of the neighborhood, Jerusalem Baptist Church, now 116 years old and still a neighborhood beacon. A few bungalows from the early 1900s still exist, many in states of disrepair, and Sweet Sue pointed them out to me as I drove her around the streets on a crisp autumn day in 2014, along with the long-gone churches and nip joints, and the home of the racist parrots.

Jordan's Alley, now part of the West End, is still the poorest section of the city, still overwhelmingly black; the rate of neighborhood-school students qualifying for free and reduced lunch is by far the highest in the city, at 98.17 percent. But as Sweet Sue and Mother Ingram described the community the way it was when the Muse family migrated there, I realized I had to look beyond the peeling paint and the sagging porches. I sensed there were plenty of rich histories waiting to be unearthed on the tongues of octogenarians, in old scrapbooks, and in remote courthouse files. I just had to dig.

Mother Ingram had a memory of her own to share, along with a clue about the early lives of George and Willie Muse. She had seen them only once in her life.

She remembers it because they were *just so different-looking*. That woolly blond hair, for one thing. And their watery blue eyes. In her neat living room, decorated with Asian-inspired wall hangings and a plastic-covered couch, she demonstrated the way their eyelids fluttered constantly, like butterflies on a milkweed stalk. "I was only nine years old, but I remember it like it was yesterday."

Their skin was milky white, and they reminded her of Burl Ives. "They were both real fat," she said.

She understood that, years since they'd last seen their family, the circus had reluctantly sent them back to visit their mother, with a guard to keep watch over them. A white man stood next to them as they sat on their mother's porch. "He hovered over 'em, like a person who was in charge," she explained. "So they wouldn't run off. The circus *owned 'em,* you see."

But that was in the late 1930s, years after Harriett Muse first risked her life to bring her boys home, years after she begged the Lord to send her a sign about her firstborn sons.

Though she couldn't read, Harriett looked everywhere for clues when she first landed in Roanoke—in the pictures of the newspapers she saw in the homes of the city's well-to-do, on billboard signs, in the faces of people getting on and off the trains.

While Cabell blew too many paychecks in the neighborhood nip joints, Harriett kept her pennies close, sewing clothes by hand out of feed sacks for herself and the children, using patterns she made from the cast-off newspapers she took from her employers' homes.

She worried about Willie, the younger boy, especially, and the more tender one of the two. Whenever she spotted a rainbow hovering over the mountain-ringed valley, she thought of God's promise, and she prayed that his big brother, George, was looking out for him, wherever they were.

PART TWO

4

Your Momma Is Dead

Picture a life about as far away from rural Virginia as you can get. A life lived constantly on the move, spanning locales as disparate as Park Avenue and Paris, Texas.

Picture a life far removed from the Franklin County tobacco fields, one where people actually rode, ate, and slept in the railroad cars that passed by Jordan's Alley at all hours of the day and night. Sweat-stained and stinky, traveling-show performers and roustabouts traversed the country by train, boasting a pride of calling that bordered on arrogance. They developed their own rhythms, their own hierarchy, and even their own language: people they worked with and who understood what they did were "with it." Everyone else was a "mark."

Now picture a single car, usually somewhere near the front of the train, full of human misfits—a bearded lady, a skeleton man, a conjoined twin complaining that she hadn't slept because her sister was tossing and turning all night. The freaks, people called them, in politically incorrect language that fit right in with other offensive circus lingo. Which was fine by most of the freaks because, well, they had their own pride of calling, too. As the art photographer Diane Arbus once said of sideshow performers: "Most people go through life dreading they'll have a traumatic experience. Freaks were born with their trauma. They've passed their test in life. They're aristocrats."

They would capture the imaginations not only of marks across America but also of America's finest artists, starring in the short stories of Eudora Welty and Carson McCullers, the films of Alfred Hitchcock and David Lynch, and the journalistic dispatches of E. B. White.

Modern sensibilities and medical advances would ultimately change, if not erase, the spectacle of the circus sideshow. Plain old decency would ultimately relegate the phenomenon to kitschy camp, mythology, and a curious set of resurgences evident in today's cable-TV shows, Broadway-musical revivals, and reality television.

But a century ago, when the Muse brothers were young, they and other people who didn't match physical norms were exhibited for profit and titillation in ways that today would be considered demeaning at best. They were gathered and displayed as a consortium of dwarves, giants, microcephalics, and fat ladies who (compared with today's heavier body norms) don't look all that fat.

Some freaks weren't so different-looking physically, but they could perform special tricks — swallow swords or stuff dozens of balls into their mouth, or blow smoke out of their eyeballs. Women draped themselves in pythons and became knife-throwing targets, and men contorted their tattooed bodies into pretzel shapes.

All were exhibited onstage, arranged in a kind of off-kilter school-yearbook assembly. The dwarf usually stood next to the giant (who splayed his arms out like wings), the fat lady adjacent to the thin man.

The Congress of Freaks, they were called. Or the World's Strangest People.

Money-hungry managers pitched them in ways that alternately humiliated them and enhanced their prestige and, above all, made money for the predominant form of American entertainment between 1840 and 1940: the circus.

The sideshow was so named because it was placed to the side of the main circus show or big top, under a separate tent and with a separate admission fee. More commonly known as the freak show, it was also called the pit show, odditorium, kid show, and ten-in-one—for the number of typical acts you could see with a single ticket.

Presented on a platform, under a tent and behind a thick canvas wall (to keep the nonpaying out), the sideshow was meant to instill fear and wonder in its audience. Capitalizing on the scientific naïveté of the day, it was also supposed to inspire educational curiosity. Once customers were inside the tent, a "lecturer" (oftentimes a magician who also performed tricks) would lead them on a walking tour from one attraction's section of the stage to the next, describing each act. Then, one at a time, the freak demonstrated his or her special skill.

Limbless people, for instance, would roll a cigarette or write with a pen between their toes. Johnny Eck, aka the Only Living Half-Boy and the World's Greatest Mistake, did acrobatics, sang show tunes, and told jokes. He was happy not to have legs, Eck told the audience, because he didn't have to press his pants.

At seven feet seven and a half inches, the Texas giant Jack Earle was pretty much just tall. Circus publicity photographs featured him playing cards with his buddy Harry Earles, the dwarf who would become the lead character of Tod Browning's cult classic film, *Freaks*.

As outlined by Lew Graham, Ringling's longtime announcer and freak-show impresario, a freak act in the 1910s had to adhere to three basic rules: "The abnormality must be remarkable, if possible unique; it must be exploitable by an accompanying talent or dexterity; and it must be inoffensive to public taste."

For example, he offered: "The fat lady may not be a repulsive mass of blubber; she must be delightfully curvaceous." The midget had to be perfectly symmetrical and, above all, fabulously cute.

Before movies, radio, and TV, people saved their pennies for the one time of year when the circus came to town. The upper-middle classes and those aspiring to be like them wore their best clothes to the circus, then brought home photographs and other souvenirs to show off later to visitors. Giants sold oversized "giant rings," so a person could have the tactile experience of seeing how small their own fingers were compared with the giant's. Dwarves sold miniature Bibles.

"Siamese twins were at the top of the pecking order because there were so few of them. Below that were the one-of-a-kinds, someone like Johnny Eck," said sideshow researcher and collector Warren Raymond. "Giants were fairly common, and the good ones among them brought good money."

Harriett Muse might have had no idea where her sons were. But they were actually becoming famous from Butte, Montana, to Binghamton, New York, where their pictures could be seen on cartoonish banners designed to mock their milky-white skin and African features — and draw more quarters and dimes.

As albinos, they were among the rarer finds, somewhere between a giant and a limbless man in the freak-show pecking order. Inside the tent, lecturers introduced George and Willie to ticket holders — or rubes, as the showmen referred, dismissively, to customers behind their backs — via a hyperbolic spiel, or lecture, which began like this:

The brothers were descended from monkeys in the dark continent....With Neanderthal heads, caveman bodies, and tremendous shocks of hair that stand out on their heads like the wigs on Raggedy Ann dolls....

Two Ecuador white savages...they are pure Albinos, with skins as white as cream, and with all of the facial characters of South African bushmen....

All for the insignificant sum of one dime, two nickels, ten coppers, one-tenth of a dollar — the price of a shave or a hair ribbon — [you can witness] the greatest, most outstanding aggregation of marvels and monstrosities gathered together in one edifice. Looted from the ends of the earth....

Sparing no expense, every town, every village, every hamlet, every nook and cranny of the globe has been searched with a fine-tooth comb to provide this feast for the eye and mind....Step right up, ladies and gentlemen, and avoid the rush!

They were cast, in other words, as anything but what they actually were: a pair of black boys from Virginia with callused hands and alabaster skin. Boys who cried themselves to sleep at night.

They cried especially hard during their early days on the road, when their captors shushed them repeatedly. "Be quiet. Your momma is dead. There's no use even asking about her," Willie later recalled being told.

Tell that to a child long enough, and the repetition turns into story turns into truth. Tell that to a pair of boys dependent on you for food and shelter, for clothing and comfort, and as weeks turn into months and months into years, they'll believe anything you say.

Especially if you hide them away from anyone who might tell them otherwise.

"Be quiet," the men told them. "Your momma is dead."

While their parents tried to carve out a life in the newly industrializing South, the Muse brothers traveled the country—and, eventually, the globe—by rail, by boat, and, later, even by airplane. I worked out a rough chronology of their early careers by scouring century-old issues of *Billboard* and *Variety* magazines, and newspapers ranging from the *New York Times* to the *Big Spring (Texas) Daily Herald* to the *Baltimore Afro-American*—archives that were not readily searchable online (or in some cases via microfilm) when a colleague and I wrote our initial newspaper series about Willie and George in 2001.

There were more surprises tucked away behind paywalls in esoteric databases and faraway circus-museum archives, especially regarding their earliest years as performers. A former circus owner and Canadian author tipped me off to rare, out-of-print books and more people to talk to ("Call Philadelphia Eddie's Tattoo and ask for a sideshow collector named

Furry, and be sure to tell him I sent you"). I was also helped by a collector in Silver Spring, Maryland, a specialist in souvenir giant rings whose wife is on the hunt for anything pertaining to Siamese twins. The couple own more than sixty thousand pieces of memorabilia, including a souvenir cup purchased by the Muse brothers for their own use and engraved with their show names at the Iowa State Fair.

A Roanoke sandwich-shop operator gave me a dusty duffel bag full of circus memorabilia collected decades before by a relative who'd worked as a handbill poster for the John Robinson Circus and said, "Keep it—just bring back what you don't use."

A Baltimore archivist directed me to other people to call, advising me to pay special attention to "visual clues"— photographs and pictures of sideshow banners—since I couldn't assume I knew all their stage names. The one thing I could be sure of: nowhere among the copious press clippings would they ever be referred to as George and Willie Muse.

A sideshow collector in Chapel Hill, North Carolina, who was writing a book on the sword swallower and Muse brothers' sideshow colleague Mimi Garneau put together an especially helpful binder of clippings and photographs. Bob Blackmar invited me to tour the basement he calls his Nauseum, with sideshow memorabilia from floor to ceiling that feature old posters, random beer lights, and a photograph of tattooed man Jack "Dracula" Baker, photographed by Diane Arbus for a 1961 issue of *Harper's Bazaar*. "Jack is tattooed simply because he wants to be," Arbus told the magazine. In Blackmar's basement, a fuzzy copy of Arbus's picture sat framed and propped against a black marble box containing Jack's ashes. "I was his last living friend," he said.

By the time I wrapped up my research, I was tapped into a trove of freak authorities, from retired sideshow operators in

Gibsonton, Florida (aka Gibtown, once home to Percilla the Monkey Girl and Grady the Lobster Boy), to act-specific memorabilia collectors ("My specialty is souvenir rings sold by Irish giants"), as well as to circus-interested sociology and theater professors across the country, one of whom spent hours analyzing my photographs, enthusing, "I find this very exciting!" And: "Historical menswear is my passion!"

The professor was speaking of a photograph of George and Willie labeled "1905" that had been unearthed from the massive archives of Howard Tibbals, a wealthy Florida benefactor and circus junkie who'd given $10.5 million to the Ringling Museum in Sarasota to preserve his collection of circus memorabilia. For decades, Tibbals had collected materials for his lifelong pursuit of building model circuses, which became the basis of the museum's eleven-thousand-square-foot Howard Tibbals Learning Center.

"I hate sideshows," Tibbals said when I reached him at his home in Longboat Key. Seeing people with disabilities displayed for profit made him uncomfortable, lending a dull and lowly cast, he thought, to his middlebrow hobby.

As the writer James Baldwin put it in his 1985 essay collection, "Freaks are called freaks and are treated as they are treated— in the main, abominably—because they are human beings who cause to echo, deep within us, our most profound terrors and desires." The true grotesque, in Baldwin's view, isn't the monster or the freak but rather members of mainstream society who, clinging to safety, abhor differentness.

As they did Tibbals, sideshows made me uneasy. My tattooed twenty-one-year-old son raved about *American Horror Story: Freak Show,* insisting I watch it as research for this book.

But forty minutes into the first episode, I had to turn it off. I couldn't take any more of the murderous clown or the murderous Siamese twins (actually, only one of the twins was murderous). And the freak orgy, rendered as a kind of silent-film sex tape, was just way too dark. ("But Mom, freaks need love, too!" my son said.)

Watching Tod Browning's *Freaks*, I bounced along a gaping spectrum of curiosity, pity, and guilt (for having pitied), as I conceded to my friend and former film professor Richard Dillard when he screened the movie for me in his theater classroom at Roanoke's Hollins University.

"Yes, but in this film, the freaks are the good people!" Dillard said. The bad guys are the able-bodied circus workers who conspire to murder the sideshow-starring dwarf, so they can steal his fortune—until the freaks see to the bad guys' comeuppance. "The freaks are leading their regular lives, and they're functioning, but they're never frightening or upsetting."

Dillard went to his first sideshow in Florida, where his father was stationed during part of World War II. More fascinated than repulsed, he stands firmly in the camp of sideshow enthusiasts, who argue that most freaks were willing subjects, grateful for the work, and happily in on the sham.

"Most sideshow freaks took pride in being a burden to nobody," author Al Stencell wrote in *Seeing Is Believing*. "The sideshow allowed them to escape being institutionalized or stuck inside a home . . . and gave them independence, self-worth, friends, and a support system to help them achieve as normal a life as possible."

As the sideshow star Zip, born William Henry Johnson, was said to have told his sister on his 1926 deathbed: "Well, we fooled 'em for a long time, didn't we?"

No one knows whether Johnson, who was arguably the world's most famous freak, actually uttered that line. It could have been like 99 percent of all sideshow accounts: written by a reporter with a knowing wink-wink to the press agent who choreographed all the stunts, backstories, and jokey quotes. With brown skin, a diminutive stature, and a balding tapered head that P. T. Barnum accentuated with a tuft of hair at the crown, Johnson was said to be a pinhead, or someone with "microcephalous idiocy," as the disability-rights expert and sociologist Robert Bogdan has put it.

Here's how showman Barnum juiced up Johnson's narrative after a freak hunter "discovered" him in New Jersey in 1860 at the age of four: gorilla explorers had found him naked and walking on all fours along the river Gambia. Zip-the-What-Is-It? (as he was originally named, reportedly by Charles Dickens) ate only raw meat and spoke gibberish, and was therefore "a most singular animal," as Barnum said, "something between man and monkey, without a language."

When Barnum handed Zip a cigar, he ate it, as instructed. "He has been examined by some of the most scientific men we have, and pronounced by them to be a connecting link between the wild native African and the brute creation."

From an early age, Zip was smart enough to participate in the ruse, a relative later told reporters. After all, Barnum had paid him a dollar a day *not* to talk.

But which freaks were in on the joke, and what of those whose abilities didn't rise to the level of informed consent?

And which category fit children like George and Willie Muse?

Tibbals doubted he had anything on the Muse brothers in his archives, but he did send me to a friendly Ringling Museum archivist who was midway through sorting the collection Tibbals had donated, including piles of yellowed scrapbooks compiled by other circus buffs. A few days later, she e-mailed a photo of the young Muse brothers that Tibbals had acquired decades earlier (and had either never seen or forgotten).

It was my first physical evidence of the Muse brothers as child performers.

Dated 1905 (probably in error, I would later learn), the portrait had been printed as a souvenir postcard sold by circus performers as a way to enhance their managers' earnings. In post–Civil War America, visitors entering the parlor of a well-appointed home would often be shown lavish photo-album collections — posed family portraits capitalizing on the brand-new photography craze but also pictures of famous people, from Abraham Lincoln to General Ulysses Grant to, even, "human oddities, who were not only fascinating but quite acceptable as Victorian houseguests — as long as they stayed in their albums," as Bogdan wrote in his 1988 book, *Freak Show.*

If the date on the card was correct, the brothers would have been twelve and fifteen years old. In the picture, they stand stick straight, their arms pressed against each other from their shoulders to their hands. An inch or two taller than Willie, George is devoid of expression. Like a junior-high choirboy following instructions to stand stiffly, he gives nothing away. His arms are perfectly taut at his side, his fingers outstretched and dainty-looking, the calluses presumably gone.

Willie leans forward slightly, his posture more tentative. His bow tie is crooked, and his expression befuddled, possibly afraid. His fingers are clasped and his mouth agape, as if awaiting inspection — or maybe a whack on the head.

Maybe they're just uncomfortable, stuffed as they are into

woolen suits that look two sizes too small. The suits are respectable garments designed in the trendy-for-the-time Edwardian style, commonly manufactured by Brooks Brothers and similar brands. But there's more to see in the too-short sleeves and wrinkly stress lines running from the back of their necks to their armpits: "They've already been wearing those suits for a couple of years," pointed out Joshua Bond, a costume historian at the College of Charleston.

With knickerbockers for pants and hair pulled into short, white-blond dreads, the look evokes a pair of innocent young kids. And yet it doesn't.

"To me, it looks manipulative, like they're trying to say two things at once," Bond said.

Between the tight suits and the off-center bow ties, "they were dressed with some care for the ruse but not really that much attention to detail."

As if a showman, for instance, had kept them from their family and had no intention of truly caring for them himself— or taking them home.

The showman gave the boys stage names right off the bat. For the next half-century, the monikers would morph, with added appositives, occasionally disappearing for a year or two at a time but always returning to the singsong names that forever bound them together: Eko and Iko (pronounced "EE-ko" and "AYE-ko").

Spellings changed occasionally, such as when they appeared in *The New Yorker* magazine as Ecko and Iko. Their ethnic origins shifted in the media narrative, too, from one circus season to the next.

The boys had been discovered floating on a barge in the Gulf of Mexico. Along the Amazon. In the wilds of Ecuador. Off the coast of Madagascar.

Their albinism was the main draw, of course, the only thing that really set George and Willie Muse apart from ordinary African-American children — before the circus got hold of them.

Black albinos were considered important finds for a sideshow operator, something the average person didn't run across — a blurred boundary between black and white. One in 36,000 Europeans is born albino; for people of African descent that figure is higher, one in 10,000, with particularly high incidences among the Zulu and the Ibo of Nigeria. Usually caused by a deletion in the P gene, the most common mutation disables one of the enzymes (around day twenty-eight after conception) used in the making of skin pigment. The absence of pigment makes albinos sensitive to light; the red in their eyes' whites are actually the retina's blood vessels showing through.

Many are legally blind at birth, from a condition that cannot be corrected with glasses and has sometimes historically resulted in them being stereotyped as cognitively impaired when in fact they're not; they suffer from horizontal nystagmus, which makes their eyes rotate back and forth. "The eyes are trying to focus, but they can't," said Bonnie LeRoy, a genetic counselor at the University of Minnesota. And when they walk into the bright sun, "they squint because it hurts. They can't block out the sun with the iris because they have no color in their iris. Even indoors, many wear sunglasses because the light still hurts." (The Dutch dismissively called albinos *kakerlaks*, or cockroaches — things that scurried around in the night.) During the rise of Nazism in Germany, people with albinism were despised as being "effeminate."

The biblical Noah was thought by some scholars to be the first albino, evidenced by text in the Dead Sea Scrolls that described him as having "the flesh of which was white as snow, and red as a rose; the hair of whose head was white like wool, and long; and whose eyes were beautiful. When he opened them, he illuminated all the house, like the sun."

Many modern-day pop-culture depictions of the condition are sensational and dark, portraying albinos as villains and henchmen. In films like *The Da Vinci Code* and *The Matrix Reloaded,* albino villains drive around cities at night, shooting people—which would be impossible, of course, given that often they are legally blind.

International advocacy and research groups to support people with albinism have surged in recent years, particularly in response to disturbing news accounts in Malawi and Tanzania, where modern-day witch doctors have murdered and kidnapped albinos, claiming that potions made from their harvested body parts have magical powers. With his antibullying platform Positive Exposure, fashion photographer Rick Guidotti has launched a campaign to show the beauty of people with albinism and to include positive messages about children with all kinds of genetic differences, including cleft palates and mobility issues.

"As an artist, it's our responsibility to steady that gaze a little bit longer.... To start seeing beauty in difference," he said in a popular TED Talk.

But it was centuries before the stigma surrounding albinism would lift enough to create a space for Guidotti's stunning albino supermodels. (Sunglasses weren't even mass-produced until 1929.) The negative stereotypes were embedded in the mind-set of America's most heralded founding father, the author of the Declaration of Independence.

A little more than a century before Willie Muse's birth and a hundred miles north of Truevine, a future president named Thomas Jefferson had become fascinated with black albinos. And perplexed. In 1783, he surveyed his fellow plantation owners in Virginia, asking them about the presence of slaves with unusually white skin. Henry Skipwith wrote back to tell him about three sisters whose skin is "a disagreeable chalky white" while their parents are "the ordinary color of blacks (not jet)."

Darwin's *On the Origin of Species* was still decades away (1859). The word *scientist* hadn't been coined (1833). And the mysterious gorilla of Africa was not yet known to the scientific world (1847).

Jefferson compiled his findings into a catalog of the state's flora, fauna, and mineral deposits, placing albinos squarely between his accounts of fish and insect varieties in his taxonomic tome, *Notes on the State of Virginia*. A major book, it also put forth Jefferson's suggestion that Africans had sex with apes.

Governor of Virginia at the time, Jefferson was grappling with the genetic quirk of black albinism, nervous that it might dissolve the boundaries between the races. The skin of the albino was "a pallid cadaverous white, untinged with red," he wrote.

With life around him in chaos—his daughter had recently died, the Revolutionary War had just come to Virginia, and the approaching British troops had forced his government out of Richmond—Jefferson was desperate to bring order to the natural and social world, according to the literary critic Charles D. Martin, who explored the topic in his 2002 book, *The White African American Body*. For slave owners like Jefferson and his neighbors, black albinos raised an ominous specter. "The image of the African American deprived of blackness—slaves transforming, degenerating, possibly regenerating—fired the political imagination and insinuated its way into the debate on race," Martin wrote.

In 1791, the Philadelphia painter and museum entrepreneur Charles Willson Peale stumbled upon a mulatto slave named James whose skin had begun turning white over the course of many years, a rare condition called vitiligo. (It's the same pigmentation disease that pop star Michael Jackson would struggle with near the end of his life.)

Peale painted his enigmatic portrait, titled it *James the White Negro,* and hung it in his Philadelphia museum, later known as Peale's American Museum, part of the nascent nation's efforts to sanction gathering spots that weren't taverns but salonlike places where citizens could meet and mingle to discuss taxonomical displays and other educational and cultural pursuits. Peale also exhibited people with missing limbs and albinism and other "human curiosities," as he called them, but he thought such attractions got too much frivolous attention, insisting that it was more scientific to study regularly occurring specimens, not the unusual. But the paying public disagreed.

Such museums were designed to have a civilizing impact on nineteenth-century Americans, who were fascinated by physical abnormalities—and to underscore notions about white superiority. An influential physician of the time speculated that black skin was the result of leprosy, arguing that lightening skin or vitiligo spots were actually a kind of early-stage cure for blackness.

One well-known case was that of Henry Moss, a black Virginian whose skin began to lighten radically in his midthirties. While Moss began exhibiting himself for money in Philadelphia taverns in the late 1790s with great success, museums soon became the dominant place to learn about oddities, especially in New York City's Bowery District.

Though Peale had been the first to exhibit albinos, it was Phineas Taylor Barnum who added the bling. He brought together dramatic and musical acts with freaks (he preferred the term "oddities") in his American Museum, located at the intersection of Broadway and Ann Street, in the heart of bustling New York. He transformed the stuffy, scientifically focused museums into amusement centers where families brought picnic lunches and spent the entire day.

The so-called father of modern-day advertising—Barnum was, after all, credited with the phrase "There's a sucker born every minute" (a slogan he believed, though never actually said)—he was the first businessman to advertise aggressively, hanging banners on the exterior of his museum and luring in passersby with lively storefront bands. He spun wild yarns about his human exhibits: albinos, fat people, bearded ladies, giants, dwarves, and gypsies. Barnum's so-called dime museum, which hosted some forty-one million patrons, spawned a major new form of entertainment that endured from the 1870s to the turn of the century.

Barnum initially displayed William Henry Johnson as Zip the Man-Monkey to capitalize on Americans' fascination with all things Darwin, whose theory of natural selection argued that humans descended from an apelike ancestor.

So Barnum dressed Johnson in a fur jumpsuit and had him carry a stick, then hired Civil War photographer Mathew Brady to take his publicity shots, art-directing Johnson to pose in positions mirroring early drawings found in natural-history taxonomies of apes.

Off and on throughout his early career, Johnson was displayed inside a cage, with a "keeper" nearby who made up stories about him walking on all fours before his "discovery," eating raw meat, and being a cross between a native African and an orangutan. He was an immediate favorite of Barnum's—and a favorite target of press mockery.

As the Bowery grew sleazier, city dwellers moved on to newer amusements like popular song-and-dance acts. But the freak show still prevailed in cities and towns across America's heartland, in circuses, carnivals, and street fairs. By 1900, there were one hundred traveling circuses in America, and the sideshow was a highlight.

Piggybacking on the craze for Darwin, a full-time occupation had been birthed: freak hunting. As one circus publication described it, "Scouts are sent abroad to outlandish places searching for that human being upon whom nature has played a trick. It is a hard job, and freaks are frequently found in places where you least expected to find them."

In New Jersey, for instance (Zip).

Or in Mount Vernon, Ohio (the Wild Men of Borneo).

If an act actually did hail from a foreign country, the details were exaggerated to portray the performers as cannibals, polygamists, or dog eaters. Facts changed with the season: a New Zealand albino named Unzie was said to have been found by a benevolent explorer who saved him from being sacrificed by his own tribe. A more realistic account went that Unzie was taken, by permission of his parents (and with remuneration to them), by an English colonist and first exhibited in Melbourne, Australia, before being brought west.

Among the most celebrated albinos in the sideshow, Unzie was said to see in total darkness—a member of the Night People, as albino blacks were sometimes called. He fixed his hair in curling papers when he went to bed at night, then brushed it out and into a six-foot-wide mushroom in the morning.

"I never tip my hat to the ladies," he used to say from his freak-show platform, wearing an elegant high hat and dress suit. "If I should, they'd think a bombshell exploded." After which he promptly removed his hat, causing his enormous white hair to bounce out as if his head were submerged within a cloud.

As dime museums gave way to circuses and movie theaters entered the public domain, many predicted the freak show as entertainment would spiral to a close. A *Washington Post* reporter wrote a premature obituary in 1911, using a morose midget named Mike as his expert source.

Mike described sneaking into a movie theater to watch a silent film—"If people could see us passing along [out in public] they wouldn't pay over their dime at the door"—only to have the popularity of moviegoing then threaten to put his kind out of work. "We didn't imagine that we were going to our own funeral," Mike said.

The reporter bade a premature good riddance to the pastime of profiting off the misfortune of others (though he did sympathize with sad, unemployed Mike). "No good ever came of staring at the frog-boy, nor of questioning the ossified man," who'd lived out his final years as a hermit, six feet tall and just eighty pounds. He'd been found dead in a hut on the outskirts of Providence, Rhode Island, a few months earlier.

"Is it not a healthier sign of the public mind that it is no longer interested in the sad misfortunes of others?"

And yet, as dime museums faded, circuses and carnivals did nothing of the sort. Factory jobs made entertainment affordable for ordinary people, many of whom now had a modicum of leisure time, with half-days off on Saturdays and modest vacations. The country's booming railroad system carried traveling entertainments deeper into America's heartland and kept the freak hunter busy, judging from frequent ads in *Billboard*, the weekly trade magazine:

WANTED—FREAKS...NOVELTIES...STRANGE PEOPLE.... Any act suitable for a real, live Pit Show. Send photo. State salary with full particulars.
WANTED—Fat Man, Midget, Glass Blower, Magician, anything suitable for high-class Pit Show.

In a special column called "Freaks to Order," *Billboard* ran a weekly compendium of abnormal births, leaving no species unturned: twin lambs born on a Bluffton, Indiana, farm, one black and one white.

A cat in Cynthiana, Kentucky, birthed a kitten with the head of a fox terrier. A child was born in Kankakee, Illinois, with two heads.

A man in Binghamton, New York, couldn't stop walking owing to a nervous disease. He paused only to take brief naps, standing up.

So you can see how a pair of albino brothers from rural Virginia might have made it into a show of this sort. But though modern-day relatives had always believed George and Willie were kidnapped around 1899 from Truevine, some of the facts I uncovered were casting doubts on the timeline that had been handed down through generations.

The brothers had definitely been exploited, made to work without pay, then traded between various showmen like chattel. They were without question sequestered from their family for many years, just as Mother Ingram had observed: *The circus owned 'em, you see.*

But an alternative narrative was taking shape around the genesis of their circus lives, a story stream that would parallel, and sometimes conflict with, the family's long-standing, sacrosanct account.

And the water in that alternative stream wasn't just murky; from the family's point of view, it was fraught.

What is certain, though, is that sometime during the drought-ridden summer of 1914, the brothers from Truevine gave their first documented sideshow performance.

A few months earlier, the Great American Shows had been launched by Morris Miller and Ben Klein, veteran carnival operators who had assembled twelve train cars full of attractions, a carousel, concessions featuring everything from candy to handicrafts, a merry-go-round, and a Ferris wheel. Klein had gone south in search of "show property," according to *Billboard*, and Miller to Buffalo, New York, to buy up tents and railcars from two carnivals that had gone belly up. The operation carried its own lighting plant and a cookhouse, the tent where all staffers were fed.

As usual, the carnival was an exciting draw for the lot lice — the nickname carnies and showmen gave townies who gathered to watch them unload and lingered on show grounds. Lot

lice were an integral part of the show world's free advertising;
even those who couldn't afford admission to the big show would
often hang around and spend their scant dimes on sideshow
admission, concessions, or souvenirs—then spread the word to
their friends.

Moose Lodge No. 159 of Flint, Michigan, gave the show its
banner week of the season, according to a *Billboard* write-up
submitted by Klein late that summer. The lineup featured trick
horse riding and high-diving dogs; Alex Thomas, a weight jug-
gler and strong man; Colonel Fred, the horse with the human
brain and musical education; a midget show; and Professor
John Zenga's Excelsior Concert Band.

It also featured two albinos performing under the name
Eastman's Monkey Men, part of the show's seven-in-one freak
show: aka Willie and George, exhibited probably as they were
in their woolen suits in the Tibbals picture, as normal—and
scared—teenaged boys. (The scrapbook photo dated 1905
was, thus, most likely taken around 1914 or 1915.)

All urban sideshow obits aside, there was no need—yet—to
dress the Muse brothers up in costume: being black with white
skin was still different enough. Especially in Fort Wayne, Indiana, where the newspaper described them, simply, as "monkey-face
men." As another freak-show historian described the spiel:

Let me tell you about these other two strange creatures
you see before you! Very strange indeed! Not only are
they…from the heart of deepest Africa…. They are
"albinos"—weird creatures in whom normal pigmentation
does not exist! In fact this is why we are able to bring
them to you today. They were rejected by their fellow
tribesmen because of this strange condition!

That summer the carnival traveled from Flint to Elkhart, Indiana. The only day it rested was Sunday, when blue laws forced businesses to close. That explained the long-standing tradition of the "Sunday boil-up," when troupers bathed in makeshift bathhouses to delouse and boiled their clothes in buckets, creating a smoky haze visible for blocks around their campsite.

So they moved from Chicago Heights to DeKalb, Illinois, from Ligonier, Indiana, and on through Kentucky before ending the show in November with a weeklong engagement in Hot Springs, Arkansas, where they wintered and those with cash on hand took advantage of the nearby casinos, healing baths, and, if they could afford them, ladies of the night.

One of the show's top draws was the Motordrome—or Wall of Death—a daredevil act in which motorcycles raced around a cylindrical track pitched at an angle of eighty-four degrees, daringly performing "feats that seem impossible." The riders were German immigrants, and one of them would leave abruptly the next fall, called away by the German army to enlist as a lieutenant in the motor squad.

The Ford Motor Company had just announced its revolutionary eight-hour workday. Charlie Chaplin featured the incompetent Keystone Cops in his second silent-film release. England merged two African territories to form Nigeria. And the archduke Franz Ferdinand of Austria was assassinated, triggering the start of World War I.

How much George and Willie knew about any of that is unclear. During their earliest carnival seasons, their ears were probably more attuned to what was happening in the insular world behind the canvas: in Ottumwa, Iowa, an eighteen-year-old carnival barker named Clarence McCormick murdered the boss of his twenty-year-old snake-charmer girlfriend, Ruth McCullough, on account of the boss "getting too friendly" with her.

With their mother foremost in their thoughts, George and Willie might have noticed that black sharecroppers in the Deep South began turning out in greater numbers at their shows. In the fall of 1916, profits at southern carnivals boomed; for the first time in years, attendance was not marred by the dreaded boll weevil, and earnings were up.

"The Southern darky is in clover this fall," noted a *Billboard* writer in racist language that was ubiquitous in most white-run newspapers of the day. "For years he has been in debt to the cotton merchant and storekeepers, who have held him up from year to year, but this fall cotton is king, with a capital K. The colored man is out of debt...and the colored girls are decked out in gaudy raiment and flashy boots and money is being literally thrown away.

"The showman was quick to take advantage of the changed conditions, and some sections of the South are fairly overrun" with one-night carnival stands, the magazine noted.

It was while researching George's and Willie's early days in the circus that I came across the thread of evidence that first made me doubt the Muse family's long-held beliefs about how the boys came to be in the circus and led me to ask: Had they really been taken from a tobacco field without warning in 1899? Or was it possible that Harriett actually *did*, at least initially, know where they were?

The first written reference I found to Eko and Iko, from a 1914 *Billboard* story, did not dovetail with the stolen-from-Truevine narrative that Nancy and her relatives had long championed.

The account would call into question several basic facts: where exactly the Muse brothers had lived, when they were born, their real surnames, their paternity, and — most critically — the birth of their circus careers.

"Those sideshow people had complicated lives," said author Al Stencell, a Canadian sideshow expert who left his hometown as a teenager to run the candy-wagon trailer for a traveling carnival and never looked back. ("My mom didn't want me to go. My dad said, 'Oh, he'll be home in a few days; he'll get tired of it.'" He was on the road full-time with a Toronto-based circus by the next year, 1963.)

"So much of [the narratives] are made up," Stencell said. "But you can't just say, 'I found this three-armed kid sitting on his porch so I scooped him out to save him.' *Somebody* had left him on that porch alone!"

Dozens of sideshow operators he has interviewed over the years have told him about attractions ambling up to the ticket box and begging: *take me in.* Some were dropped off by relatives hoping to unburden their families — in exchange for cash.

Few freaks, Stencell maintains, were kidnapped outright.

Another historian, a former Circus World Museum curator, cautioned me not to be like most industry outsiders, writers who condemn sideshow employment without garnering a broader historical understanding. "A question that needs to be answered: What would the guys have done had they not been on tour, especially in the 1910s?" he wrote.

Where were the brothers, and what were they doing? Harriett Muse must have been wondering that in the fall of 1914, when somehow it came to her attention that George and Willie had gone missing from the Great American Shows carnival.

"How are the wonders 'Eko' and 'Iko' doing?" mused an anonymous reader of the *New York Clipper,* a trade publication, a few months later.

The day after Christmas, a friend apparently helped Harriett write to the Readers' Column of *Billboard,* explaining that she was "anxious to learn the whereabouts of her two sons, known as Eko and Iko." True to the marketing hype, the resulting notice in the magazine described them as being of Ethiopian blood, but with perfectly white skin and curly white hair: "They were exhibited by Charles Eastman and Robert Stokes with Morris Miller's Great American Shows. Eastman separated from Stokes, leaving the boys in his charge, and it is thought that Stokes is exhibiting them in store shows" or dime museums.

Tips about their whereabouts, including "information direct from Stokes," should be sent to Eastman's address, on West Thirty-eighth Street in midtown Manhattan—today the site of a cellphone store.

Harriett wanted them back immediately, the story implied, though it's possible that Eastman was the author of the notice. They were supposed to have been returned to her at the end of the season, in plenty of time for Christmas.

Lacking any mention of a kidnapping, the reader is left to assume that they had left her care temporarily not some fifteen years before but that summer, with the showmen and possibly *with her permission*—until one of the men decided the brothers belonged instead to him, and took off with them.

I'd heard of James Herman "Candy" Shelton, the brothers' longtime manager. He'd put truth to the idea they'd been abducted, even if not initially. Until his dying day, Willie Muse would curse Shelton and call him a "dirty rotten scumbag," saying it was Shelton who had "stolen" him and his brother as children, kept them from their mother, and exploited them for decades for his own personal gain.

But Stokes and Eastman were brand-new names to me.

And in a way so was Harriett, since in her introduction to *Billboard* readers she went by a different name entirely: Hattie Cooke.

Census records showed her living under that name (though this time spelled Cook) in 1910, with her five children, whose last names, including George's and Willie's, were also given as Cook. Though she was recorded as married, there was no father listed as living in the home.

A renamed and reconfigured family had turned up in a different locale entirely, and a very unlikely one at that. They were living in the secluded mountains of New Castle, Virginia—a resort town at the turn of the twentieth century better known today for its marked absence of black people, an active KKK chapter, and a tourism board that sponsors the Annual New Castle Open Carry Day, which actively promotes the wearing of handguns in public as an exercise of Second Amendment rights.

A branch in Truevine had sprouted a story tendril in a surprising place, and it was up to me to follow its fickle, creeping path.

5

Some Serious Secrets

I drove over Catawba Mountain, then higher into the Allegheny Mountains the following week, looking for signs of Harriett and her children in New Castle—a courthouse document, a marriage or birth record, anything. She had taken out the *Billboard* notice with the help of a friend named Anna Clark in Covington, Virginia, where records showed Harriett working as a maid for the Industrial School and Farm for Mountain Children and Homeless Boys, later renamed the Boys Home of Virginia. She and Anna had been neighbors in New Castle, a resort town the next county over, in the late aughts and early teens. And my hunch, guided by the 1910 census, was that Harriett (nicknamed Hattie) had followed the Clark family to Covington, a small city in the neighboring county, seeking a better job and a friendlier racial climate.

In 1910, around seven years before she moved to Roanoke and set up house in Jordan's Alley, Harriett was working as a washerwoman in the company town of Fenwick, which had sprouted up on the outskirts of New Castle, with some three hundred residents. It had mushroomed to serve the flourishing Fenwick Mines, whose iron-ore deposits drew hundreds of workers to the lush highlands. Anna Clark's husband, Porter, was a superintendent at the mines, and Harriett's other neighbors were night watchmen, iron-company machinists, and miners.

Scores of Franklin County blacks and Italian immigrants — nearly all of them single men, or married men who'd left their wives and children back home — migrated to mountainous Craig County between 1900 and 1910 for work, part of iron-mining and furnace operations that extended through the Appalachian Mountains from New York to Alabama and beyond. The Italians' goal, as one Craig County old-timer recalled it, was to save up a thousand dollars, then return to Italy, "where they would be considered rich."

A smaller version of the Roanoke boomtown story playing out some forty miles to the south, Fenwick was an offshoot of the same post–Civil War story: the rural South was transforming from a self-sufficient, agrarian society to a capitalistic cash economy managed by absentee northern capitalists who were feasting on cheap southern labor, much of it minority. Timber, coal, and iron were the new economic drivers of the Appalachians.

The courthouse turned up no Muse/Cook documents, but some friendly court clerks told me about New Castle native Jerry Jones, the only one from the region who knew anything about the brothers' connection to New Castle. A retired guidance counselor and an amateur historian, Jones had grown up at the knee of his great-aunt Leslie Craft (1896–1980). Jerry had spent many hours as a child listening to her and her sister discuss life during the resort town's prime, back when it was a summertime playground for the wealthy (President Cleveland was a fan).

"My great-aunts would smoke cigarettes, serve candy laced with alcohol, and talk for hours," Jones told me. They sometimes mused about the lives of George and Willie, having played with them as children and run into them once again, quite by chance, many years later—while visiting a circus. "Miss Leslie!" she remembered them exclaiming, in unison, as if they'd all been wading together in New Castle's Craigs Creek the day before, their mother scrubbing clothes on a nearby rock.

The story had captured Jones's imagination as a child, but that was as much as he knew.

"Who ever thought they would be the county's most famous citizens?" he marveled. "It's true: the last shall be first."

On a wintry afternoon, I drove around the deserted mines, now part of the George Washington and Jefferson National Forests, with retiree Don Charlton. A seventy-nine-year-old Craig County native, Charlton made a career of selling land and other property, including several KKK robes he'd auctioned off four years before. "One of 'em brought sixty dollars," he said, shaking his head.

In 1976, the *Roanoke Times* sent its first black reporter, twenty-five-year-old JoAnne Poindexter, up to the county to write a story headlined MINORITY OF 12 IN CRAIG; BLACKS LIVE THERE TOO. The county had just recently stopped paying to have the handful of black children bused across the state line to West Virginia schools. "There were times when the white people were lousy, and you wouldn't have thought they had hearts," one mother told Poindexter. "But I have no complaints…as long as my children aren't bothered in school."

Now, four decades since the integration of Craig County schools, Confederate flags still hang from homes surrounding the abandoned mines, tied to trees and displayed from sagging front-porch railings. Charlton said it would be OK if I took pictures of the scant shacks and the trailers that still lined the dirt road, never mind the NO TRESPASSING signs posted by unseen occupants. A broken tricycle was tipped over on the front yard of one unpainted wooden shack, and I could picture Harriett scrubbing the workers' clothes in the creek behind it, pinning them on clotheslines to dry.

There were few remnants of what had passed for Fenwick a century before: no signs of the commissary, a hospital, the separate black and white churches, the school, or mule stable, all of it infused with ethnic tensions as seventy Italians and thirty black workers lived on one side of the tracks and thirty-seven whites on the other, with some fifty children among them. To distinguish everybody, the homes of white families were painted gray, and the homes of blacks red. The non-English-speaking Italians lived in gray houses and were given the most dangerous jobs in the mines.

There was a school for children of white workers but none within walking distance for blacks — though blacks and whites were allowed to attend film screenings, in separate sections, at the playhouse. In January 1914, a five-year-old whose family lived near Harriett at Fenwick burned to death while playing "with fire which it had kindled in the yard when its clothing took fire."

In my newly discovered scenario, the teenaged George and Willie would have worked dirty, menial, and dangerous jobs, especially given their visual impairment.

Geographer Lori LeMay, who researched Fenwick history for the U.S. Forest Service in the early 1990s, said the few black children living at Fenwick were put to work servicing the tipple, culling piles of rock near the spot where ore cars were emptied. The miners, she said, dropped their clothes off for

Harriett to wash — outside, in an iron kettle over an open fire — next to her small company-owned house.

A local named Old Man Wilson sold dandelion beer, home-made pies, and other goods to the workers, who knew they were being ripped off by the high prices at the company com-missary. Fenwick was an isolating place for black families; the only other black woman there was married to the stable boss, the man who took care of the mules that carted the ore out of the mines. The mules were kept underground during the week but allowed to graze outside the stable on Sundays — to keep them from going blind.

They must have captured the attention of the young George and Willie, animal lovers with poor vision and extremely sensi-tive eyes. Harriett had listed them as being just nine and eleven in the 1910 census, though other official documents have their births listed several years earlier — which would put them at sixteen and nineteen during the Fenwick stint. Maybe she kept them officially young to keep them from working inside the mines?

And what of the mysterious Mr. Cook? Census records showed a Hattie and Moses Cook living together in Roanoke County in 1900 — he worked as a farm laborer, she stayed at home. But when I looked for proof of their marriage and/or subsequent divorce or his death record, it was as if he had van-ished from public record. (Only Tom, the third son, would offi-cially, albeit briefly, use the Cook name in adulthood, in his 1930 census entry. On his 1924 marriage license, he was living in Cabell Muse's rented house and went by the name Thomas Muse.)

Though I never established the Muse brothers' paternity with certainty, months later I discovered the name of their paternal grandmother, America Cook, in an errant 1920 census document that had the entire family misfiled under the name Mules. That information led me down more inconclusive paths, ancestry tracks that were muddied by generations of systematic servitude, illiteracy, and careless record keeping on the part of census takers.

America Cook was most likely a former slave, born in Virginia in 1827. After the Civil War's end, she worked as a housekeeper and remained living in the household of John Cook, a miller and white landowner who had probably been her slave master. In 1870, she was living with John Cook and her two mulatto children, twelve-year-old daughter Elizar and toddler Henry, who was one and a half.

Though the handwritten census documents are literally hard to read and even harder to project onto the Muse family tree, my best guess is that Henry Cook was George and Willie's father, and that landowner John Cook was the brothers' grandfather. That was a common, though rarely recorded, scenario in the Reconstruction-era rural South, especially in and around Truevine. And it's another reason why African-American ancestry is so hard to track.

Hanging on his bedroom wall, an incomplete family document still occupies the mind of ninety-four-year-old J. Harry Woody, a Truevine native who lives in a four-square home in Roanoke's West End. It's his grandparents' 1878 marriage license. Where the young couple's parents' names are listed, there's a single line where the groom's father's name is intentionally blank, as if he were immaculately conceived.

"My great-grandfather was a white man," Woody told me, recounting the story his father told him. "See, the landowner would have sex with his black maid, and then tell her that she should feel honored that a white man would want her!" he exclaimed from his living-room hospital bed.

"It was happening from slavery all the way down to when I was growing up" in the 1930s, he added. "They'd force all the maids, and they had kids of all different colors."

As proof, he points to the thin skin of his forearm, the color of coffee with full-fat cream. "And didn't none of them ever claim their children," he added, his eyes blazing, more than a century later, with the indignity of his own grandfather's father-lessness. "They were ashamed to claim their children, but they weren't ashamed to force sex on the maids."

I wondered aloud how the white children living nearby iden-tified him. Like Janet Johnson and A. J. Reeves, he remem-bered walking miles to Truevine School—"sixty kids and one teacher in a single room"—while the white children took county-furnished buses and taunted the black walkers along the way.

"They called me *nigger!*" he said, and scoffed.

Then he changed the subject, staring at a prepublication postcard I'd given him that featured the cover of this book.

Mr. Woody positively lit up, reading the tobacco field on the cover like he was divining tea leaves, and this is what he saw: "Looks just like tobacco from the thirties," he said, pointing to the yellow-tinged leaves. Immature plants, still months away from harvest. The yellowed leaves meant that the farmer who planted the crop was poor—and probably black. "Back when blacks wasn't able to buy fertilizer because they didn't have the money to pay for it. You can tell that 'cause the leaves are turn-ing yellow before they got to be full-sized."

He wanted to know when this book would be for sale. Publication was still more than six months away. He said younger people, black and white, needed to understand the harsh realities of their ancestors. "They think we're lying! They say, 'That was then, this is now.' They think everything was roses, but ain't nobody making any of it up."

I'd been sitting at this bedside for going on two hours. It was a crisp April morning. He'd ended the interview twice already, saying he was tired, then kept telling stories when I stood up to go.

Fenwick itself was a short-lived enterprise, closing in 1924, two decades after it opened, when ore discovered in Minnesota, Ohio, and Pennsylvania was found to be easier and cheaper to extract. The town bank, the railway spur, and several of the resorts followed suit. The buildings that housed them are long gone. Some were moved when the mines closed; others were buried when the area was turned into a wetlands and recreation area.

Don Charlton recalled his mother writing letters for an illiterate elderly black man who had worked at the mines and remembered the way he pulled three cents to pay for the stamp from his coin purse. Uncle Ed, as Charlton called him, wore a pungent asphidity bag around his neck as a talisman. Popular at the time, especially among African Americans, the bag contained rotted herbs that were believed to ward off polio and the flu.

Judging from the *New Castle Record*, the biggest news of the day, not counting the heated debates over Prohibition (the paper was pro) and women's suffrage (con), focused solely on the land-owning whites: Whose cousins were coming to visit to take the healing waters of Craig? And what on earth had happened to the prominent citizen convicted of murder who had broken out of jail, the last trace of him being a set of bloody footprints found on the top of Burks Mountain?

His trial had been such a spectacle that Anna Clark took the train from Covington to her old New Castle hometown to watch it unfold.

Charlton and I drove past the clear, rushing creeks that have drawn visitors to Craig County since Thomas Jefferson's time. He pointed out the old rail bed that once held the Chesapeake and Ohio Railway spur, which probably carried Harriett and her children to Covington, where so many blacks migrated for work in the thriving paper-mill factories—and to escape the burgeoning presence of the KKK.

Charlton beamed at the gorgeous Fenwick Mines Recreation Area, a U.S. Forest Service park shelter. With a boardwalk for the wetlands and its handicapped-accessible creek-side trail, the mining site has become a big draw for birders, especially those chasing red-shouldered hawks and pine warblers—proof, as a cultural geographer researching the area once noted, that "humanity's disruptive influences can be erased from the earth."

In 1998, KKK chapters from Maryland and Tennessee held a picnic at the area. It was not a rally, a park-service employee assured the media, just a "pitch-horseshoes-and-eat-hot-dogs sort of thing."

Nancy Saunders knew her great-grandmother Harriett had worked briefly at the Episcopal Diocese–run boys' home in Covington sometime before her move to Roanoke in the mid- to late teens. She'd wondered what it must have felt like for

Harriett to watch the homeless boys play on the spacious grounds, attend school in the charming brick cottages, and entertain visits from Santa and Boy Scout leaders—while her own sons weren't just homeless, they had vanished entirely, and to where? Not even their original carnival managers seemed to know.

But the scenario of Harriett mothering children by someone other than Cabell Muse, whom she wouldn't marry for seven more years, came as an unlikely detour on the family's long-accepted timeline. (Neither Willie nor George ever mentioned the surname Cook, according to family members, and when Harriett and Cabell married, they both listed themselves as single on the marriage license.) The implication that Harriett may have initially contracted with a traveling carnival to put her boys to work was another, even bigger surprise.

If that version was true, it would replace the narrative of two child sharecroppers being plucked from the fields.

I was more than a little nervous about broaching the new revelations with Nancy. "She still doesn't trust you all the way, but she's working on it," her best friend, Marsha, told me a few weeks before. (Halfway through the reporting of this book, Marsha attended a talk I gave at the Library of Virginia in Richmond, introducing herself only afterward—then reporting back to Nancy what I'd said publicly, during the Q&A, about this book. "She has me checking on you," Marsha said, winking.)

For months, I'd been e-mailing Nancy every new photo I found featuring her uncles—and never once gotten a reply. I'd mailed her reprints I'd had made of a portrait of the brothers for her cousin Louise. Nancy returned most of my phone calls, but only after several days, sometimes weeks, had passed.

But I knew the Hattie Cook surprise could be unwelcome news. To ease (and speed) the conversation along, I delivered a small Christmas gift in early December, one that represented our two common interests—plants and food. I left a ten-dollar pot of rosemary on her front porch, though the metaphor didn't hit me until later: rosemary is a symbol of remembrance, as in *Would it kill you to return my calls?*

The tug on her southern manners worked. When Nancy called a few hours later to thank me, we exchanged pleasantries. Then I told her about the *Billboard* article.

She was stunned, recalling the marriage license located a month earlier between Harriett Dickerson and Cabell Muse—from 1917, much later than the family had imagined. "After that, I was wondering if they were even Cabell's children," she said. "But I swear I never knew their mama was a Cook!"

This time she was curious, open, and not at all defensive. She seemed relieved by the possibility that she was not kin to Cabell Muse. Long ago she'd adopted her uncle Willie's position that Cabell was a philanderer and a drunk, and—as I would soon learn—a very tragic figure.

She had long wondered why many of her nonalbino relatives were extremely light-skinned and now wondered if George and Willie's father was perhaps white. Her grandmother Annie Belle, who helped raise her, was so pale that many mistook her for white. Nancy herself is very light-skinned. And though she is not technically albino, Erika Turner, Nancy's teenaged cousin—who has albinism on both sides of her family tree—often gets bombarded with rude questions from classmates about her auburn-blond hair and hazel eyes.

"To be albino in the African-American community, you don't fit in anywhere. You're not black, and you're not white; it's hard now, but back then, it would have been extremely hard," said Bonnie LeRoy, a University of Minnesota professor and genetics counselor.

George and Willie's father, whoever he was, was probably teased mercilessly because of his sons' condition. Even in modern times, some fathers at the clinic where LeRoy counsels families with albinism, skeptical of the child's paternity, have abandoned their families altogether, she said.

"Maybe Mr. Cook's the one who sold them," Nancy said, referring to Willie and George.

It was the first time she was willing to entertain the idea that maybe they hadn't been kidnapped from the start, despite what Willie himself had always maintained. But she firmly and resolutely believes that Harriett was not involved. "I don't dispute what you found, but I can't imagine all these years and all these people who knew the family, and nobody brought it up before," she said.

Besides, as she'd told me many times before, Uncle Willie himself insisted they'd been kidnapped. "And my uncle Willie was not a liar."

Nancy's mother, Dot, had made the same argument. So had her grandmother Annie Belle, who was just a toddler when the boys left home. Neither had ever mentioned the name Cook — even though Cook must have been Annie Bell's childhood name.

But what if Willie himself didn't actually recall? Maybe he was too young when it happened to remember, or too traumatized? Maybe he'd heard the story so many times that what he remembered wasn't the reality of having been kidnapped — *that piece of candy coming toward him, proffered by a stranger in a sweltering tobacco field* — but the memory of hearing that story told?

Or maybe Willie Muse remembered his early days in the circus the way a child, any child, recalls the first time a parent inflicts pain, even unintentionally. My own mother loved me to the moon and back, and yet my first recollection of her is a story I've never recounted before out loud or in print—because it makes her look bad. She accidentally burned me with a cigarette during a raucous game of euchre while I was seated on her lap at our kitchen table.

This is nothing like contracting with a carnival showman to put your two young teenagers on a train, granted, even if you thought he'd bring them back. But who is anyone to judge the pressures facing an illiterate washerwoman raising five children alone in rural Virginia during the harshest years of Jim Crow?

Nancy seemed excited that I'd found a new story thread, albeit one that raised more questions than it put to rest.

"Old people, you know they could keep some *serious* secrets," she said, finally.

She would see if she could nudge anything new out of her ninety-two-year-old aunt, Martha Turner—the only living member of her mother's generation.

But the Cook name was also a mystery to Martha, she reported back a few weeks later.

Serious secrets weren't unheard of between showmen and the parents of sideshow acts. Circus-goers had long clamored for exotic acts from the so-called Dark Continent, and several African Americans had been recruited to portray African natives. Black sideshow musicians, many hailing from New Orleans, took jobs playing such African "savages" on the side.

"There was a circus term for it, even," said Bernth Lindfors, a University of Texas literature and African-American studies professor who has written about black sideshow performers. "You'd pretend to be someone running around with a spear and a grass skirt, and that was your 'Zulu ticket,'" he explained.

That was certainly the case with William Henry "Zip" Johnson, whom Barnum claimed to have found in West Africa in a "PERFECTLY NUDE STATE, roving among the trees and branches, in the manner common to the Monkey and Orang Outang."

But Barnum hadn't been the first to display Johnson, the son of former slaves William and Mahalia Johnson. In 1860, he bought the rights to exhibit him from the much smaller Van Emburgh's Circus, located in Somerville, New Jersey, not far from Johnson's hometown. Many years later, a woman claiming to be his sister recounted that he'd been sold at the age of four "by his parents in need of funds." The details of that initial contract have been lost to history, but the Johnsons had six children to feed, and the money offered by that first circus must have felt like a fortune to the newly freed slaves—even if their teenaged son was forced to screech and rattle the bars of his cage, pretending to eat raw meat.

One obituary writer noted that for the first ten years of his career, Johnson "had almost to be forced to mount the platform," suggesting that he was coerced, at least initially, to perform.

Was the remuneration worth the early family loss? Or was Johnson better off playing the role of Zip?

How do you measure a life?

In dollars, by Barnum's accounting. And so, regardless of how much Barnum supposedly grew to love his favorite performer, he also fiercely controlled his every movement onstage and off, from profit margins to publicity stunts. Johnson's true backstory was suppressed in trumped-up press accounts and steeped in a racist, exploitative climate that underscored the ideological mainstream of the day: black people were subhuman.

Like Johnson's backstory, the genesis of George and Willie Muse's career is largely undocumented. If their mother did initially contract with the Great American Shows, it is clear from her beseeching notice in *Billboard* that she was "anxious to learn the whereabouts of her two sons" and to get them back. Being black, illiterate, and husbandless at the time, she certainly wouldn't have had the upper hand in contract negotiations. "She couldn't read her own name if you put it in front of her," Nancy said—and if she did sign a contract, it was only with an X.

Like her sharecropping relatives on settling-day, she was dependent on the honor of the white man to explain, and live up to, the written word.

Billboard updates written by the show's business manager, Ben H. Klein, made the touring company sound like the most cheerful and beneficent family-oriented affair. The wife of his partner, Morris Miller, ran the candy concession and held down the fort with Klein while Miller went on buying forays to Chicago, for instance, to shop for new train cars. (Miller's goal, he told *Billboard* in 1914, was to double the carnival's size, amassing a twenty-car train, by the next season.)

The carousel operator took a vacation to his home in New Kensington, Pennsylvania, to visit his wife. And Klein himself

vacationed on a two-week "pleasant sojourn" before returning
to find that carnival-goers in Ligonier, Indiana, "were wearing
a smile that won't come off."

In Fort Wayne, a newspaper referred to George and Willie
only as "strange creatures," highlights of a small sideshow affair
that also featured the "smallest woman in the world."

But George and Willie never made it to the carnival's Hot
Springs, Arkansas, winter quarters. By the late fall of 1914,
their co-manager Robert Stokes had broken off from the Great
American Shows and was exhibiting them as a solo act (or sin-
gle-O) in store shows and dime museums, according to Harriett's *Billboard* notice. George and Willie were now being
exhibited as the Ethiopian Monkey Men—very much in the
vein of Zip, only full-sized and albino, and not yet so famous.

Where Stokes took them next is unclear. In one showman's
account, George and Willie performed during that period in a
Boston dime museum called Austin and Stone's, a block away
from Faneuil Hall and Quincy Market. An offshoot of Barnum's American Museum, the venue exhibited carnival freaks
and curiosities, both real and phony, with a stage next door for
vaudeville acts. Presiding over the spectacle was a barker
named Professor William S. Hutchings, a former Barnum and
Bailey Circus lecturer whose spiels were so loquacious that
Harvard forensics professors liked to dispatch their students to
observe him and take notes.

"The Professor was loath to use one word if eight or nine
would do," one showman wrote of Hutchings, who ended every
story by mumbling "Marvelous, marvelous!"

Austin and Stone's was so cutting-edge in its day that it even had its own air-conditioning system: large blocks of ice were placed in a trough and covered by a grate running along the center aisle. As one advertisement ballyhooed, "Our Lecture Hall always maintains the leading curiosities of the day from all parts of the world, and lectures on the same are delivered hourly, by PROF. HUTCHINGS, the most eloquent descriptive orator in America or Europe."

The details about the Boston museum were all true. But George and Willie could not have performed there, I realized, after discovering the museum had been torn down in 1912, shortly after the professor's death. The demolition paved the way for the new vaudeville theater, Scollay's Olympia, where comedian Milton Berle would get his start, sometimes performing in blackface.

For the Muse brothers' earliest career, then, my timeline relies only on Harriett's anxious plea for more information and the Tibbals picture: George and Willie standing there in their too-small suits, looking not very marvelous.

The man who printed the picture, in fact, turned out to be so much better documented than his teenaged subjects: Albert R. Bawden lived in Davenport, Iowa, where he ran a novelty postcard-making service and print shop with his brothers in the 1910s and '20s, and also worked as treasurer of a local bank. His wife held society luncheons while Albert ran the local merchants' bowling league, his average a respectable 170.

The novelty-postcard business was thriving, judging from the hundreds of weekly *Billboard* classifieds. In fact, in every nook and cranny of the country, any number of enterprises seemed to be eager to sell goods to traveling showmen — or to join their tribe. From a sampling of one of the six-page classified spreads:

Porcupines perfect for "a good pit show attraction" could be purchased by writing to "FLINT" in North Waterford, Maine. One could find a fellow in Kansas who promised to display his own brand of "DARE-DEVIL DEED-DEFYING DANGER and death in an entirely new and unequaled motorcycle act."

With this molasses-slow version of eBay, a buyer could locate such hard-to-find items as shooting galleries, popcorn wagons, and a rebuilt Edison moving-picture machine.

And people, too, according to the messages and ads:

"The thinnest man alive"—or in Chattanooga, anyway—was keen to join a store show or carnival. An aging but still employable "good freak born with feet and no legs" could be leased by contacting Eli Bowen in Thayer, Indiana. (Bowen had supposedly been discovered by Barnum at an Ohio country fair and already had a long career as the Legless Acrobat—but, now seventy-four, he seemed to be hearing the call of the road.)

The father of Fred Pettit wanted to hear from his wanderlust-filled son, who'd presumably run away with the circus, "before too long."

An elderly couple sought a house-sitting job for traveling show people.

The so-called Kid Albino from Stamford, Connecticut, who doubled as a famous hypnotist, offered himself for hire to any "high-class vaudeville act."

And a multitalented family consisting of man, wife, and child posted a notice about its "BIG NOVELTY ACT," promising to deliver "real fancy shooting; we also use whips, violin, cornet, piano and sing."

Despite such a wide range of documented human spectacle, for two years the Ethiopian Monkey Men were curiously absent from both the media and the marketplace. If Stokes was exhibiting them in stores, as Harriett believed, he was being quiet about it.

Back home in Virginia in late 1914, it had just become illegal for any child to be employed in factories, shops, mines, mercantile establishments, laundries, bakeries, and brickyards. The groundbreaking labor activist Lewis Hine was in the process of photographing several small children from Roanoke, including twelve-year-old Mamie Witt, who was helping support "an able-bodied, dependent father," and a seven-year-old, Frank Robinson, who swept the floors of the Roanoke Cotton Mill in bare feet. Across the nation, Hine's muckraking photographs began to change the way Americans thought about children's rights. ("I counted seven apparently under fourteen and three under twelve years old," he wrote of one Roanoke factory.)

Teenagers working in the sideshow may well have thought, "These people are going to stare at me anyway, so why shouldn't I get something for it—and help my family out at the same time?" pointed out historian Jane Nicholas. That had been the case with the legless, teenaged Bowen when he hired himself out to a traveling showman, shortly after his father's death, to help support his mother and seven siblings.

Besides, it was easier than sorting rock at the Fenwick Mines.

"One of the hardest things for modern audiences to understand is, parents sometimes did this, and yet they still loved their children. It's that combination of love and financial need that can be so hard to tease out," Nicholas told me. "People will say, 'If they really loved their children, they wouldn't have done that,' but people do all sorts of things for their children."

During the time the Muse brothers began performing, Nicholas pointed out, adults could legally and literally *mail* children — by affixing stamps to their shirts and putting them on a train.

I wondered if the Muse brothers felt like the dislocated and orphaned Eskimo Minik, who had been brought to the United States in 1897 at the age of six or seven with his father and four other villagers from Greenland at the request of exhibit-hungry explorers and museum directors. They'd been displayed to paying customers aboard the ship *Hope,* then housed and exhibited at the American Museum of Natural History. They were ostensibly there to be interviewed, examined, and measured, but all except Minik and his father died soon afterward from diseases their immune systems were not equipped to handle.

From a patronizing *New York Times* account written in October 1897: "The unfortunate little savages have caught cold or warmth, they do not know which, but assuming it was the latter their sole endeavor yesterday was to keep cool. Their efforts in this direction are a source of amusement to several scores of visitors."

When Minik's father died the following February, the museum faked a funeral for him to deceive Minik about the body's whereabouts, wrapping a corpse-length log and covering it with fur. It was nine more years before Minik discovered that his father's body was actually inside a glass case at the museum. His impassioned quest to retrieve his father's remains and give him a proper Inuit burial — the subject of a remarkable 1986 book by Kenn Harper called *Give Me My Father's Body* — was not successful during his lifetime.

"You're a race of scientific animals," Minik said in 1909,

railing against the museum. "I know I'll never get my father's bones out of the American Museum of Natural History. I am glad enough to get away before they grab my brains and stuff them into a jar." (It wasn't until 1993, many decades after Minik's death, that his father's remains were repatriated for burial in the family's home village. Four years later, a commemorative plaque was installed at the Greenland gravesite, with a phrase that translated to *They have come home*.)

Uprooted and orphaned, Minik lived what Harper described as a "tortured and lonely life," unable to entirely adapt to either country. "It would have been better for me had I never been brought to civilization and educated," Minik told a reporter after he'd journeyed back to Greenland, only to find himself missing America and then returning to New York. "It leaves me between two extremes, where it would seem that I can get nowhere."

While Minik's narrative varies greatly from the Muse brothers'—especially the ending—the two arcs share parallel threads of cultural, familial, and geographical displacement. When the literate Minik eloquently describes what it was like to be dislocated, ripped from his family, and exhibited at the dawn of the twentieth century, I can picture Willie and George feeling exactly the same way:

"Aside from hopeless loneliness, do you know what it is to be sad—and to feel a terrible longing to go home, and to know that you are absolutely without hope?" Minik wrote about the period following his father's death. Even after being "adopted" by a kindly family, he still cried most of the time and fretted constantly about the possibility of being returned to the museum.

When he enrolled in college, Minik felt like a "freak to those about me," he wrote. Only after being taken in by a farm family in New Hampshire, where he labored in obscurity as a lumberjack, did he describe being content. But he died soon after, of the Spanish flu, in 1918. He was believed to be twenty-seven or twenty-eight.

Unlike in Minik's case, there was relatively little media discussion of the ethics of exhibiting black sideshow performers, most of whom were unschooled and unable to leave a written record of their own experiences. The *New York Times* noted in 1914 that Zip was the oldest freak still performing with the Barnum and Bailey Circus. The reporter gushed as he recollected Barnum's 1864 Cooper Union lecture, "How to Get Money," with Zip and the Wild Men of Borneo flanking him onstage. "Zip is almost entirely devoid of mentality, but a peculiar look comes over his face whenever there is shown to him a photograph of his first protector and for that matter, owner, the late Phineas T. Barnum," the reporter wrote.

The so-called Wild Men were forty-pound dwarves named Hiram and Barney Davis who lived on a farm outside Mount Vernon, Ohio, when their family was first approached by a showman in 1852. Their parents initially declined to part with them, but the mother reportedly changed her mind when the showman returned with an irresistible pile of cash.

When Barney Davis died at eighty-five, in 1912, his niece held his funeral at her home, pointing out that her uncle was a real person and not a freak. While Barnum had pitched them as being monkeylike and having paws, she pointed out Barney's perfectly formed hands and told mourners that the brothers conversed easily, though they'd been instructed to speak gibberish in their act.

"I wanted people to see that they were not freaks," she told an interviewer. "Wouldn't you have done that for them?"

The Davis brothers' specialty—which they displayed while decked out in short pants and leotards—was performing feats of strength, routinely lifting the heaviest volunteers in the audience as one of several featured stunts. Dressed elaborately in an effort to aggrandize their appearance and inflate their status, they were like the Muse brothers in that their looks deviated from that of the general population, but they were otherwise able-bodied and capable of demonstrating talents.

As with the Muse family, the Davises had lost track of the brothers by the time they had become regulars in the circus world. In 1880, they even instituted a lawsuit to have them declared legally dead—at the same time Hiram and Barney were about to be hired on with the Barnum and London Circus.

A century before the Internet, it was harder for an isolated family in rural America to keep tabs on far-flung relatives— even those who appeared on the front pages of the *New York Times.* It was not so hard, then, to whisk a person's loved ones away and never return them, leaving their families to lie awake at night, wondering if they were dead or alive.

The Muses' special skill? Nothing the showmen recognized right off the bat.

But it wasn't long before someone heard them singing a popular song, an Irish ballad recorded by tenor John McCormack in 1914 that soon became a World War I anthem, sung by soldiers on their way to the Western Front. The brothers began a lifelong obsession with "A Long Way to Tipperary," a ballad about longing for home:

It's a long, long way to Tipperary,
But my heart's right there.

Christmas 1914, their first of many away from their mother, people were talking about the unexpected Christmas Day truce along the Western Front. Snatches of "Stille Nacht, Heilige Nacht" had been heard drifting across a frigid Belgium battle-field, littered with fallen soldiers. *Silent night, holy night.* Men who'd been shooting to kill put their weapons down for the day, allowing corpses to be recovered and buried.

Back in Virginia, Harriett followed news of the war, and she sang along with the radio at work.

It's a long way to Tipperary,
It's a long way to go.

It was quiet in the tiny Boys Home quarters she shared with her three youngest children. Harriett waited for a response to her *Billboard* notice, but every day after the mailman had come and gone, Anna Clark sighed and shook her head.

In her mind's eye, George and Willie were frozen at chin height, their blond curls still short. She prayed George was reminding Willie to stay out of the sun.

She must have known it by now: she had been duped. The boys might have been kidnapped by the circus, or they might have been loaned to it. They might even have seen it, at first, as a kind of adventure. But they were most certainly trapped in it now, wherever they were.

She would never reveal to them — or any of her other relatives — how they came to join the circus.

She would take that serious secret to the grave.

But first, Harriett Muse would right the wrong done to her boys. Their mama was very definitely *not dead,* not yet, and she wanted them back. One day George and Willie would know that with certainty.

And so would the circus.

6

A Paying Proposition

The brothers' birthdays came and went, George's on Christmas Eve and Willie's in April, celebrated often around Easter—holidays now made all the more poignant for their mother.

D. W. Griffith's film homage to white supremacy, *The Birth of a Nation,* based on the novel *The Clansman,* premiered in 1915, and Franz Kafka published his landmark novella, *The Metamorphosis,* about the absurdity of existence and the cruelty of power the same year. In 1916, not long after Pancho Villa tried to reclaim New Mexico, President Wilson announced he was running for a second term literally by throwing his hat into the middle of the Ringling Brothers and Barnum and Bailey Circus center ring—and forever cementing a cliché. (A lifelong circus fan, Wilson had wanted to accept Charlie Ringling's invitation to ride an elephant, but his advisers nixed the idea of a Democrat riding on the symbol of Republicanism, and so did the Secret Service.)

As Americans shed their Puritanical prudishness, and factory work began to give people in rural areas and small towns money for amusements, the circus became the pinnacle of popular culture. Barnum, who died in 1891, may have been the Walt Disney of his day, but as the market for the circus grew, his successors were reaching more customers than the pioneer showman could have dreamed. In the American West, the Al G. Barnes Circus grabbed headlines with thirty train cars full of its wild-animal menagerie and circus-stunt acts, and had a near-monopoly in the western states. Farmers sold hay and grain so they could afford to take their families to the eye-popping shows.

At the turn of the twentieth century, ninety-eight circuses and menageries traveled across the country, the most in American history. The largest among them were traveling company towns, mammoth three-ring railroad circuses that rattled across the nation, toting more than a thousand employees and hundreds of animals.

In the Midwest and along the East Coast, Ringling Brothers and Barnum and Bailey—the two entities combined in 1919— moved its version of a small city on a near-nightly basis, shrewdly timing its course to bring in the most dollars. In the South, that meant fall, after the cotton crop was picked, and right after its tour through the midwestern states, timed to capture the wheat farmers when they were flush with harvest cash. Its "big top," or main performance tent, seated fifteen thousand people for its daily afternoon and evening performances, which were held at 2:00 and 8:00 p.m.

By contrast, the carnivals George and Willie Muse first traveled with were much smaller affairs. When they stopped in a town, they tended to stay for a week at a time.

But there were dozens of such shows back in the 1910s and '20s—enough to take up several pages of news in *Billboard*, which was sold weekly in local pool halls, newsstands, and tobacco shops across the nation. For people who already worked in the industry but dreamed of "hopscotching," or switching shows, *Billboard* was typically sold in front of the cookhouse entrance. It was also manna to bored teens who dreamed about ditching it all and joining the carny life. Circus people even had a nickname for *Billboard,* as they did for a lot of things. They called it the *Educator.*

Carnivals tended to be somewhat smaller affairs, with five or fewer rides, a Wild West show, maybe some clown and wild-animal acts, and a freak show with five or six exhibits. They were often sponsored by local Elks clubs as a way to attract new members, and Elks organizers would close the Main Street down for a week at a time to make way for the rides, acts, and food stands.

"Circus people thought they were more highbrow than a carnival, but the term wasn't really applicable to either of them," the collector and researcher Fred Pfening III said. "Watching a circus was a nonintellectual activity."

But to a nation straining against its Puritan rigidity—"We have yet to learn again the forgotten art of gayety," as Nathaniel Hawthorne put it—a traveling show was a break in the dreary monotony of farm and factory life. As Ringling pitchman Dexter Fellows noted, "People flocked to tent shows as though drawn by some overmastering spell," often wearing their Sunday finery.

Barnum had been the first to go against midwestern ministers' teachings that the circus was "Satan's own show," and he did it with clever subterfuge: he issued free passes to clergymen. Early in their careers, the Ringling brothers boosted their audience by taking advantage of the growing number of "drummers," or traveling salesmen, who canvassed the country. They issued them special credentials that came with free admission privileges to any Ringling show.

*   *   *

George and Willie hadn't yet caught the attention of such sprawling circuses. The regional carnivals they traveled among were fly-by-night affairs that changed names often to give the appearance of offering patrons something new, to entice return patronage. "Quite often the carnivals would change their name, as you would change your underwear," said the collector and author Warren Raymond.

Stokes and Eastman had named the Muses the Ethiopian Monkey Men sometime during the 1914 season. They also exhibited them as Stokes's Monkey Men and Eastman's Monkey Men.

But it was the brothers' next manager who would make the biggest impact on—and the most money from—George and Willie Muse. Sometime between 1914 and 1917, Candy Shelton anointed himself their caretaker and their captor, their supervisor and their sponge.

He changed their stage names regularly, and working with the tacit approval of subsequent show owners, he refused to pay them—or return them to their mother.

In a nod to the ghost of Barnum, for a time Shelton named them Barnum's Original Monkey Men. At other times they were pitched as Darwin's Missing Links, thought to represent something between ape and human—just as Barnum had done with William Henry "Zip" Johnson and the Bronx Zoo with Ota Benga—except when they were heralded as the Sheep-Headed Men, in which case the ruse evoked a ram.

Depending on the crowd, the brothers were said to have been discovered on a raft floating off Madagascar, or the Gulf of Mexico, or somewhere in the South African bush, cavorting with the springbok.

The truth was considerably less colorful. And more cruel. Heralded as "nature's greatest mistakes," George and Willie were modern-day slaves, hidden in plain sight, at a time when naïve and eager audiences didn't think to ask questions about contracts or working conditions, and civil rights didn't much exist for children, women, or blacks. Circus- and carnival-goers simply smiled and took the sideshow lecturer at his word.

For an itchy-footed farm boy from Powder Springs, Tennessee, trying to work his way up the carnival ranks—first in concessions and, now, as an act manager and lecturer/announcer—Candy Shelton waxed effusive in an ever-shifting spiel about the brothers' geographic origins.

His distinguishing feature, according to a nephew, was that he was missing four of the fingers on his left hand. He'd been grinding meat on his family farm as a teen when the stool he was sitting on slipped out from under him. When he instinctively reached to right himself, his hand went into the grinder.

"He still had his thumb," the nephew, Don Nicely, said.

When his family migrated to Detroit in the mid-1910s so his father could work the lines at Ford Motor Company, Shelton, the eldest child, was in his mid- to late teens. Rather than accompany the family, he joined a little-known traveling carnival passing through and headed south with it. Before long he had ditched the middle name his family members always referred to him by—Herman—and was christened Candy by fellow concessionaires.

According to Al Stencell, the sideshow expert and retired circus operator, the nickname stemmed from his first carnival job as a candy butcher. A pre–Civil War phrase that dates to the very first person to work selling candy in the carnival stands, it was initially used to describe the man who'd been the town's meat butcher, and the name stuck.

Back in Virginia, Prohibition was proving a boon to the Franklin County moonshiners, who'd formerly catered to just the local market. In Roanoke, a black pharmacist who lived near Jordan's Alley was tried for practicing medicine without a license and received a six-month jail sentence, though it's unclear if he actually served the time. Still, John Pinkard's mostly black patients continued flocking to the "yarb doc," or herb doctor.

Pinkard was taking advantage of Roanoke's segregation laws by developing a black subdivision on the Roanoke County outskirts called Pinkard's Court, not far from the Franklin County line, touted as "exclusively for colored people." With a flair for fashion and chauffeurs to drive his new cars, he erected a cast-iron arch at the entrance to the development and built his own fence out of ceramic jugs emptied of the alcohol he mixed with wild cherry bark, tobacco, and sassafras roots for his treatments.

Two generations removed from slavery, Pinkard's Court represented black Roanoke's aspirational suburban middle class, a neighborhood of matching two-story houses peopled by silk-mill and railroad workers. It would have made an impression on Harriett when she passed it en route to her shack on Ten-and-a-Half Street shortly after marrying Cabell Muse, in 1917.

Her hope was to marry a railroad man, someone who could take care of her and her youngest three children, who were now teens; maybe even buy a house.

The Great Migration was under way, the organic movement between World War I and the 1970s of six million African Americans from the rural South to urban centers in the northeastern, midwestern, and western states. Eager to escape the state-sanctioned violence encouraged by Jim Crow laws, former sharecroppers also migrated en masse to southern cities like Roanoke, an internal migration that was sometimes the first stop on their northward quest for freedom—for the vote, for the chance to make a living and acquire property, for the right to live without fear of being lynched.

As the historian Benjamin Quarles has written: "Whatever the Southerner had surrendered at Appomattox, he had not surrendered his belief that colored people were inferior to white."

In Florida, a black person could be given thirty-nine lashes for "intruding himself into any religious or other assembly of white persons." Mississippi blacks were allowed to vote only if they paid a poll tax, showed proof of residency, and read and interpreted a section of the state constitution.

In Virginia, too, poll taxes had been cemented by the addition of the so-called understanding clause, part of the new Virginia Constitution of 1902. The tax was $1.50 per head, to be paid six months in advance of any election, and voters could register only if they could read and explain any provision of the newly written state constitution.

The clause gave extraordinary powers to county and city registrars, who got to ask questions of prospective voters—and judge their replies. Answers from white Democrats were usually right; the replies of blacks and Republicans were often not.

Fearing Virginians would not vote to disenfranchise

themselves, delegates had opted not to submit their new constitution to a vote and simply proclaimed it law. After various court challenges, the Virginia Supreme Court of Appeals backed the politicians, ruling in favor of the new constitution. Voter participation dropped significantly, especially among blacks.

The segregationist-written constitution remained in effect until July 1, 1971.

It had been more than two years since she'd last been in contact with her sons. Harriett knew nothing of Candy Shelton or their whereabouts when *Billboard* boasted in March 1917 that Barnum's Original Monkey Men "will undoubtedly be among the big money getters of the season." George and Willie were now performing with the Fort Worth, Texas–based J. George Loos Shows carnival, where the banner attraction was Booger Red's Congress of Rough Riders. A droopy-eyed Texan who got his start in the business running a traveling burlesque show, Loos was known for mentoring a host of carnival operators during his forty-year career.

"Quality first seems to be the slogan of this company…the shows are all clean and meritorious," a newspaper in Corsicana, Texas, gushed after the carnival's first performance there, in 1916—though it changed its tune a few years later when Loos was convicted of running an illegal gambling operation.

While it's not clear how Shelton and Loos met—both listed Fort Worth as their home base in official documents over the next decade—they oddly shared a left-hand deformity: Loos's second and third fingers were webbed.

And they shared an affinity for African-American performers, judging from a 1916 classified ad taken out by Loos:

"FREAKS WANTED FOR TEN-IN-ONE. Colored pianist, also singers and dancers with good wardrobe and ability for [minstrel] show. Talkers and man to handle show."

With a novel freak act now in his possession, Shelton used his salesman's gift of gab to exploit their differences: he knew how to exaggerate their attributes to patrons inside the side-show tent.

As their manager, Shelton would have negotiated the brothers' contracts with the carnival or circus owner, outfitted them, and arranged for their photographs and banners. He made sure they got fed — but maybe not that well, judging from their skinny stature in the Tibbals photo.

The arrangement was probably not unlike the contract written for Johnson (aka Zip), made between his manager, Captain O. K. White, and Ringling Brothers, which outlined monthly $40 payments to White, with proceeds from the photo souvenirs split evenly between Ringling and White.

And like the Muse brothers, Johnson was paid only in food and board.

"Zip was treated like a trained dog," said Pfening.

A similar contract was written for George Bell, "the colored giant" and minstrel, who stood seven feet eleven inches tall (and wore a size 23 shoe). But that agreement was issued directly between Ringling and Bell, with the latter signing an X. Bell was paid only $12 a month but appeared to have more agency in his circus dealings. As Pfening put it, "I am sure Bell was of at least average intelligence and just got screwed being black in a lousy time to be such.... He had no need for a representative to handle his financial affairs, as Zip did."

Freak-show hierarchy, then, paralleled the order of the day: a white giant working during that same period for the Ringling-owned Forepaugh-Sells Brothers Big United Shows earned $25 a month, which was paid to him directly—more than double what Bell earned.

Traveling by rail in sixteen cars, the Loos carnival featured not only the Monkey Men but also a musical group called the Dixieland Minstrels, "an array of talent that will be hard to equal in the colored minstrel line." (Carnival workers dismissively called the minstrel shows plant shows, short for *plantation*.)

The Loos show also exhibited a fat girl named Jolly Vallera, "who has a neat frame-up... and is everything that the name of fat girl implies," and Booger Red's Wild West act, featuring twenty-five riders and ropers. Boasting that it was the only outdoor amusement enterprise that had been on tour more than four hundred consecutive weeks without closing, Loos took out ads in *Billboard* proclaiming, "You Can't Lose with Loos," and promising "SUCCESS" and "PROSPERITY" in an all-caps spiel.

Shelton displayed his ambitions early on, working his way to bigger jobs and better shows. "Most people in management start out with smaller jobs and work their way up," Al Stencell told me. Many workers who managed acts had secondary positions, their so-called cherry-pie jobs, and Shelton was frequently also listed as both a manager and ticket seller in circus programs.

Ticket sellers often engaged in shortchanging customers—a common practice that shortchange, or shortcake, artists took pride in. They developed elaborate dialogues and faux-counting routines designed to distract or confuse the circus-goer while they were busy palming a quarter (or more) from the person's change.

Shelton could stretch the truth to match the arm span of a circus giant. In 1920, he told census takers in Belton, Texas, where he and his new wife, Cora, were wintering, that he was the manager of a traveling sideshow when he was really just overseeing one of its acts. In 1923, he bragged to a newspaper reporter in Hamilton, Ohio, that he owned his own circus when, again, he was only managing one of several entertainers.

Shelton not only pocketed the Muse brothers' earnings; he also kept the money he made by selling their photos, proceeds of which were split between him and the lecturer, who spoke inside the tent as the acts were being exhibited.

Shelton is mentioned sparingly in press accounts and doesn't even merit his own file in the country's circus museums. But Harry Lewiston, a longtime contemporary of Shelton's who was also a ticket seller and sideshow manager at many of the same circuses, described the lifestyle unblinkingly, down to the shortchanger's code of honor: "That we would never short change a child, a woman, a cripple, a man with a child in his arms, an elderly person, or a man we didn't think could afford the loss." (Circus operators shortchanged more often than carnival operators because they were only in town for one night— and less likely to draw the ire of police.)

"Ringling and all the big shows would go on and on about being clean 'Sunday School shows,' which was pure B.S.," Stencell told me. "The only reason for anyone taking a job around a show as a ticket seller was to shortchange."

The circus was a grift-filled enterprise that attracted adventurers and others drawn to society's fringe, especially those eager to ditch sad histories and societal restrictions. Some circuses even hired professional pickpockets to circulate throughout the carefree crowds—as long as they split their take with management.

Shortchangers were aided and abetted by "fixers," or "patches"—circus employees who arrived at new venues and immediately headed out to grease the palms of public officials, policemen, and fire marshals, persuading them to bend the rules.

Lewiston, for instance, employed his show's patch every time he exhibited the naked hermaphrodite Mona Harris, against a town's decency laws, as his show's "blow-off," or special-admission attraction offered at the end of the regular sideshow.

A red-haired, buxom woman who had both a penis and a vagina, Mona also "had a split personality as far as sex was concerned," Lewiston wrote. "She seemed to be equally attracted to both men and women, and would carry on a romance with either sex if she got the chance." State sodomy laws criminalizing homosexual acts might have been the law of the day, but a culture of sexual openness permeated the live-and-let-live circus culture.

"There were a lot of gays in show business because back then it was about the only career open to them," Stencell said. "Those shows were full of interesting and ethnic people, and people running away, and criminals and everything else.

"But for gay people especially, the circus was a place you could escape to and make money, and not worry too much about being accepted." Though no one was much coddled.

One beloved gay colleague of Stencell's was a cook who would counter slurs from his straight coworkers by slipping the cellophane from individually wrapped slices of American cheese into their grilled cheese sandwiches.

*   *   *

The fact that, from the earliest years of Barnum and Bailey Circus, James Bailey had deemed wives to be "time-wasters," preferring to hire bachelors, may have also hastened the preponderance of gay men in the circus. (Single men were also easier to fit on train bunks than married couples, fitting in bunks stacked three high or two to a bunk in coaches.)

High jinks were permitted behind the scenes, as long as the big top could still be broken down in an hour or so, then packed onto waiting railcars. And paid cherry-pie job or not, every employee was expected to earn his or her keep. In towns where officials refused to be paid off by fixers, Mona Harris made herself useful by babysitting the show's microcephalics when they weren't onstage.

The sad backstories, of course, were never part of the ballyhoo. For "Darkest Africa," a sideshow Lewiston ran in the late 1930s, he freely admitted that he had "bought" four microcephalic teenagers from their parents, Beulah and Joe House, resurrecting an earlier act. Their heads were shaved, except for a bushy knot at the top, in the style of Zip. Cast as African pygmies, the House children had been taught years earlier to perform various "native" dances, "knowing full well that if they didn't they would be beaten" by an earlier manager, a Mississippi showman who'd "owned" them for a spell before returning them to their impoverished parents.

When Lewiston rediscovered the family living in a ramshackle Memphis shack, Joe House greeted him warmly with "We sho' missed you, Mistah Lewiston. And we sho' do miss that money," according to Lewiston's account.

So Lewiston engaged with their parents to buy the children

back at a rate of a hundred dollars a week, plus food and transportation, with the caveat being that African Americans were
not permitted to ride in the sleeper cars with the other performers; they had to sleep sitting up in the coach cars, and they had
to eat in a separate cook tent and dining car, Lewiston wrote.

The Houses eagerly accepted that deal, and the children
were happy on the road, Lewiston claimed, though "they were
still retarded as ever" and often refused to use the toilets provided for them, openly urinating in front of audiences and
"adding to the amusement of the crowd."

In such a lurid and unseemly environment, where children and
disabled people were bartered like horses, it is not known exactly
how or when George and Willie Muse crossed paths with Shelton, who in 1916 was working as a carnival announcer and usher
for Paul's United Shows, a competitor to the Loos shows.

"Candy Shelton, that's the man that took them, and that's
the man that told them their mama was dead," insisted their
niece, Dot Brown, Nancy's mother, in a 2001 interview. "And
when you keep telling a child for so long that 'your mother is
dead, and there's no need to go back,' the child believes it."

More recently, Nancy described the brothers' complicated
dependence on their manager as Stockholm syndrome. Though
the term wasn't coined until 1973, when hostages held in a
Swedish bank developed an attachment to their captors, it has
been used to describe scenarios ranging from Patricia Hearst's
helping her kidnappers rob a California bank in 1974 to, more
recently, the nine-month kidnapping of teenager Elizabeth
Smart, who was tortured and sexually abused.

Candy Shelton was the "onliest person Uncle Willie ever
said anything bad about," Nancy recalled. But when they were

young, Willie and George learned that he was also the key to their being fed, housed, and clothed.

The captor is your abuser, but he's also the only person who can keep you alive.

Despite the inconsistencies in the story of their early circus careers, documents show the parallel narrative streams converging into a single moving current from the time Shelton took charge. And often the ripples turned into rapids.

Shelton's reputation wasn't so stellar among his colleagues, judging from a 1920 *Billboard* ad taken out by managers of the Loos show, offering a twenty-five-dollar reward for information leading "to the whereabouts of J.H. (Candy) Shelton, Manager of Iko and Eko Monkey Men."

Shelton had absconded with George and Willie Muse, chasing a bigger show and more pay—and not for the last time.

In an as-told-to biography that is as self-servingly promotional as Lewiston's is blunt, showman Al G. Barnes recounts running into the unlikely trio in the mid- to late 1910s. A native Canadian, Barnes had started out as a wild-animal trainer, beginning with a pony and a "talking" dog: he spent months training his childhood pug, Rowser, to say the words *I won't, yes* (which the dog emitted in a sort of sneeze) and the name Barney, then worked out a monologue routine featuring those words as a kind of punch line. The animal acts were a common feature among earlier, smaller circuses in the late 1800s, and the inspiration for another cliché that breached the circus-tent walls to become part of the American vernacular: the "dog and pony show." Barnes owned one of the largest train shows in the West, based in Southern California. It had quickly grown into a thirty-car traveling spectacle of dancing horses topped by dancing girls, an "aerial" lion act (lions riding on the backs of horses), tiger and elephant attractions, and a sideshow run by Bobby Fountain.

As Barnes tells it, an early manager — Stokes, perhaps — had been traveling with the Muse brothers in a small midwestern town, exhibiting them under timeworn names that didn't adequately cash in on the public's fascination with all things exotic and savage, from the Monkey Men to the Ministers from Dahomey, an African kingdom (now Benin) that had been an important location in the Atlantic slave trade.

Cast as albinos from Africa, the Muses did nothing but stand there blankly while a lecturer made up wild stories about them, punctuated with a few kernels of geographic truth.

When spoken to, they replied in gibberish, as instructed.

Shelton "didn't know how to exploit them," Barnes declared. "In fact, he knew little or nothing of showmanship."

But with his decades of experience, the man known as Governor Barnes and the Prince of Showmen knew he would eventually figure out how to perfect their act.

"I quickly realized their possibilities," Barnes said in his memoir. "And when the manager asked me to permit him to join the show with the boys, I agreed, thinking I could buy them from him."

That season, the Muse brothers morphed from the Monkey Men to the Ministers from Dahomey to Darwin's Missing Links to, finally, the name they used for the duration of their stint with Barnes: Eko and Iko, the Ecuadorian Savages.

Showmanship, as Barnes viewed it, required a continental shift. And fiercer facial expressions.

The brothers were now featured exhibits of the Barnes Big Circus Sideshow, located stage left of Barnes's three-ringed big top. The sideshow had always taken a backseat to the big top, where Barnes's menagerie reigned supreme. In his book, he imbues the animals he describes with more humanity than he does the Muses, for instance.

The spectacle was a rich, two-hour stew of wild animal acts, dancing girls, music, and clowns — all billed as "The Show That's Different." The highlight was Mabel Stark (real name: Mary Haynie), pitched alternatively as the Greatest Woman Animal Trainer in the World and, later, when she worked for Ringling Brothers, the Intrepid Lady Trainer. Stark was hailed for her ability to tame lions, tigers, and even sea lions, though she was mauled several times throughout her fifty-seven-year career and carried lifelong scars. (She credited her cat-training prowess to strategically doling out meat rewards, as opposed to just beating the tigers into submission, as her predecessors had done.)

A brunette with Barnes (she turned blond for Ringling), Stark took her work seriously, clad in a militaristic white suit and trousers — especially when she had her bare hands (or head) in the mouth of a lion. At the height of her Barnes act, she would sit astride a lion on a platform that slowly ascended inside the tent. With the lights dimmed, a shower of fireworks would emanate from her head as she reached the top.

With the GIs returning from World War I in the spring of 1919, Barnes played on the patriotic fervor of the day and the increasing popularity of wild-animal shows by dedicating one of his lions to the returning 303rd Infantry. He introduced himself to each town he visited by leading a parade of circus acts from astride a six-ton elephant named Tusko as a prelude to each show.

A few years later, during a stop in a Washington logging town, Tusko escaped, upsetting cars and knocking over trees, fences, and telephone poles. Barnes eventually unloaded him on a carnival operator, but the elephant continued to unleash "a trunkload of trouble" before his death, at the age of forty-two. Criminal poisoning was suspected.

It was common practice for most of the larger rail circuses operating from Barnum's day through the late 1920s to kick off every stop with a free parade to drum up customers for their shows—until the ubiquity of the automobile finally made the practice unwieldy. Newfangled traffic lights messed up the processions, and it was hard to turn corners in a sixteen-horse wagon without bumping into parked cars.

In his sideshow, Barnes strived never to display anything that would "offend good taste." Always on the lookout for new finds, he had once enlisted a freak hunter who had adventured to Africa, where he captured a "hideous-looking Negro" with a foot-long tail. Arriving in San Francisco, the man had been quarantined at Alcatraz Island, where Barnes inspected him and deemed him "too repulsive" for display. Later, when the Smithsonian Institution made an "exceptionally large offer for the specimen," Barnes lamented—in the interest of science, of course—that he had already sent him back.

Barnes's favorite freak (and best moneymaker) had been a woman with two bodies, both perfectly formed from the shoulders down. "We found her in the backwoods of Texas where she was living on a ranch with her husband and three children," two born from one side, and one from the other, he wrote. "She traveled with the show for several years...and the women especially were very taken with her," asking to examine her after the show, which she permitted. Her husband became a ticket seller and didn't get too mad when his coworkers ragged him with Mormon bigamy jokes.

Despite his claim of being highbrow, Barnes had intuited what Stencell came to define as the three keys to sideshow success: "Displays of sex, horror, and strangeness consistently open the purses." The best showmen adapted to the fact that two heads trumped one, and three breasts trumped two.

Crowds strolled by as the lecturer Eddie Thorn ("The Innovator") took turns exaggerating the qualities of the various performers, beginning with snake enchantress May Blasser, who demonstrated her python-charming prowess. Snake handling was a popular sideshow act of that time, judging from the myriad *Billboard* classifieds to buy and sell snakes.

Next they watched the "peerless" Billy Pilgrim, born with no arms or legs, roll a cigarette with his mouth while Fountain's wife, the sideshow's "xylophone artist," played a song. Mabel Gardner presented a show with talking cockatoos, while Carmelita the Lady with the Marvelous Hair and Nettie the Texas Fat Girl simply sat or stood as Thorn hyperbolized away. Eko and Iko were on the billing, though accounts from that time don't mention exactly what more, if anything, they did beyond standing there and answering an occasional question or two.

At an Ohio stop in the fall of 1919 — Barnes's farthest trip east in a while — the *Cincinnati Times* called the entourage "by far the oddest and most entertaining show ever seen in Cincinnati. The modern and smooth-faced Noah, which is Barnes himself, has Jack Londonized the circus, kicked out vaudeville and set up only that which is of red-bloodedness and highly satisfactory with a preface which is all beauty and muscle."

A few years later, another newspaper gushed, "The whole

show proved to be as advertised, was fine from Eko and Iko in the sideshow, to the grand ensembles under the big tent. There was only one drawback. There was just too much for one pair of eyes to see."

In Scranton, Pennsylvania, Eko and Iko took top news billing out of a Barnes cast that included 1,080 circus performers and workers, with a picture of the brothers looking fiercely at each other, in profile and frowning, their hair jutting out every which way. BODIES OF ZANZIBAR YOUTHS ARE COVERED WITH FINE WOOL, the headline trumpeted.

Three days later, the same paper described the brothers' marching in the pre-show parade as "Eko and Iko, two wild and uncivilized men from the jungles of Equadore [sic], who are covered with wool from their heads to their feet." Marching next to them were Mr. and Mrs. Tiny Mite, the Smallest Married Couple in the World, and John Aasen, the Norwegian boy-giant, said to be not just the largest but also the tallest man alive. Tusko, the paper noted, was sitting this parade out due to his bulk, which varied by several tons depending on which press agent was spinning the numbers. "He only weighs ten tons," the Scranton reporter wrote, up four tons from an earlier account.

George and Willie's mother had been married to Cabell Muse since 1917, and around that time the couple relocated the family to Roanoke. But the brothers had no idea what was happening with their relatives back home—or even where that home was.

They later said they'd believed all along that their mother was still alive, but it seemed possible they might never see her again.

*   *   *

As Barnes recounted in his book, the circus returned later in fall 1919 to its winter quarters in Venice, California. That's around the time Eko and Iko's manager—who is unnamed in Barnes's account but presumably was Stokes, working with Shelton—asked to borrow some money so he could travel east.

Barnes boasted about the transaction in loan-shark terminology, underscoring that the "boys," now grown men, meant nothing more than chattel to him. "I lent him the desired amount, taking the boys as security," he wrote. "He stated that if he did not return, I might have the boys. He did not show up again, so we started out with the boys next season."

Around that time, Barnes anointed Shelton, then twenty years old, the Muses' sole manager and caretaker. By this time Shelton was already working as a ticket taker for the sideshow and may have been co-managing them earlier with Stokes or another intermediary manager (Barnes doesn't say, and I could find no other direct references to pre-Shelton managers in the trade publications between 1915 and 1918).

Shelton immediately "realized the boys' possibilities," asking if he could pay off the debt contracted by the former manager and thereafter work with Barnes on a percentage basis. "I agreed to do this, and we made the boys a paying proposition," Barnes wrote, candidly.

In a photo from 1922, Al G. Barnes stands in front of a sideshow tent with his arms draped casually over George's and Willie's shoulders. Willie squints and leans to the side, clenching his fists, while George looks more relaxed (or at least open to the pose), his hands steepled elegantly in front of him. On Barnes's left hand shines a gleaming wedding band, acquired from his second wife after an extended fifteen-year divorce battle, including five separate lawsuits filed to end his first marriage. The divorce was granted in 1921 on desertion charges; Barnes married a different woman the next day.

But that didn't go so well either. Barnes filed for divorce against his second wife in 1923, claiming she horsewhipped him, and six years of litigation followed.

"The legal battles he engaged in, most of them due to domestic difficulties of one sort or another, never seemed to lessen his zest for life," a reporter wrote in Barnes's 1931 obituary. "As he rushed from tent to tent he would shout his answers to the reporters drawn there by a new lawsuit."

With the shift in management, the Muse brothers' native lands changed, and a new anthropomorphic tale was honed: "There was a story to the effect that the boys were members of a colony of sheep-headed people inhabiting an island in the South Seas; that they had been captured after many hair-raising escapades, and that they were the only specimens in captivity," Barnes had written.

The captive-history narrative only added to the irony of their present lot.

They were already captives, of course — just not in their native lands.

But what Barnes claimed next would bedevil the brothers from Truevine for most of their lives: "The boys had a very low grade of intelligence, and the press-agent story fitted them well."

For the next several decades, that assertion would rear its head repeatedly, inspiring heated debate among their caretakers, lawyers, and relatives, and scholars, too. Were George and Willie born mentally incapacitated, or did the environment they were thrust into—kept away from their family and denied education—make them that way?

Or were they in on the ruse and pretending to be dull-witted, per Candy's orders, just as Zip followed the instructions of O. K. White?

It's also possible that, like their enslaved forebears, George and Willie feigned servitude to give the impression of being attached to their captors. A survival technique designed to make Shelton think they were more childlike than they were, the behavior could have become internalized, as the historian Stanley Elkins has described in his famous but controversial study of slavery's effects.

Maybe George and Willie hid their opinions and their wits because they were champion observers of life during Jim Crow. Maybe they instinctively understood that it was dangerous to know too much. As the poet Paul Laurence Dunbar wrote in his landmark 1896 poem, "We Wear the Mask," about black Americans forced to hide their frustration behind a façade of happiness:

> *We smile, but, O great Christ, our cries*
> *To thee from tortured souls arise.*
> *We sing, but oh the clay is vile*
> *Beneath our feet, and long the mile;*
> *But let the world dream otherwise,*
> *We wear the mask!*

One other plausible explanation, according to albinism expert Bonnie LeRoy: during the early twentieth century, the brothers' rapid eye fluttering was routinely misinterpreted as a symptom of mental impairment. "It's still not uncommon for people to misdiagnose albinism, or not to understand that the vision isn't correctable, or that the patient is cognitively fine.

"But back then, there would have been very minimal understanding" of horizontal nystagmus, she said, a condition also known as dancing eyes.

Housed among the freaks, the brothers were already trapped in the "rigid caste system of the circus," as Lewiston described it. Sideshow folks "didn't mingle with the big top performers except in dice and poker games." But big-top performers refused to acknowledge sideshow workers when they met them on the street.

Freaks, then, were the most isolated of all, tucked away from nonpaying eyes lest they exhibit their wares for free. They were often moody, and most of them were illiterate, one prominent manager wrote, adding that "they succumbed quickly to professional jealousy."

A keen audience observer, Barnes was astute enough to understand that simply being albino was no longer freaky enough at a time when the nascent movie and radio businesses were competing with the circus. As early as 1901, a *Billboard* writer had observed that albinos no longer brought in customers the way they once did. "They're too common," he wrote. If they could also sing and/or dance—or were married to women who did—the act was more valuable.

Novelty—something the public had never before seen—was always the goal.

To be a big draw in the 1920s, the brothers would have to up their game.

Barnes credited himself for what happened next: "We taught them to play a mandolin and guitar so that they could strum the instruments passably well." It's likely they had picked music up earlier, either from their neighbors in Truevine or from the minstrel shows that traveled with Loos.

But as Willie himself told the story, the first time Shelton gave them instruments, it was meant to be a joke. A photo prop, the instruments were placed in their hands for a pitch-card pose. Shelton assumed they had no marketable skills beyond their appearance. He had no idea they harbored the potential to hear a song one time—and re-create it on just about any instrument.

By all accounts, music came naturally to George and Willie, especially playing stringed instruments. Relatives recall Willie insisting he was the better player—and singer—of the two.

> *I'll wear my high silk hat and frock tail coat*
> *You wear your Paris gown and your new silk shawl*
> *There ain't no doubt about it, babe,*
> *We'll be the best dressed in the hall.*

"Eko and Iko could play anything," one of their coworkers told Stencell. "They could hear a tune just one time and play it perfectly."

Finally, the brothers had something they could take solace in, besides each other.

In an undated photograph from their Barnes stint, George and Willie look to be in their late teens or early twenties. Posted under tent frames, they sit in chairs draped with striped ribbons. Willie holds a banjo while George clutches a saxophone, a ukulele balanced against his knee.

Their costumes are bolder and sharper than before, and they're certainly better-fitting, with wide-lapel jackets, short pants, and above-the-knee socks. The first time I saw the photo—found during a late-night search online — I glimpsed a white horizontal stripe above their knees and instinctively thought I was seeing straps designed to tether them to their chairs.

The next day, I realized, I'd mistaken the narrow space between their socks and knickers for shackles, when in fact what I was seeing were stripes of bare, white skin. It was a powerful reminder to look beyond the story I *expected* to find as I set out to untangle a century of whispers from truth.

I've spent hours trying to suss out that photo, my favorite from the stack, seeking the opinions of historical-costume, circus, and music experts alike. George's chin is raised, almost defiantly, while Willie looks straight into the camera, this time with confidence. His right hand is held in the playing style known as clawhammer, thumb out from the body of the banjo and fingers tucked.

Popular among old-time mountain musicians, clawhammer is a style of playing first popularized in minstrel shows of the 1820s and '30s in which players thump their downstrokes on the strings. Plantation owners sometimes sent musically inclined slaves to New Orleans or New York to learn the violin for their cotillions. The earliest banjos, made of gourds, horsehair, and animal hides, were brought to the United States from Africa by slaves. But when slaves were alone in their quarters, African souls seeped into Irish fiddles, and a new style emerged.

Minstrelsy was originally performed by white banjo players who copied black music and performed in blackface applied using the singed bottom of a cork. As the scholar Eric Lott has argued, it grew out of the theatrical genre's encapsulation of both white desire for and fear and loathing of African Americans. The caricature was a warped meshing of cultures that was as strange and unsettling as the sideshow itself. In the 1830s Barnum even got in on the act, naturally, promoting jig-dancing contests between an African-American New York City dockworker and anyone who would challenge him.

By the 1860s and '70s, black musicians had reclaimed the co-opted music for their own use, and blacks and whites alike "blackened up" so they could get work. (The term "Jim Crow" came from a minstrel song of that period called "Jump Jim Crow" and was initially used pejoratively by whites to describe someone acting like a stage caricature of a black person.)

Minstrelsy began a slow decline with the advent of the twentieth century, but it held on for a few decades in the rural South. It was quite popular, in fact, among blacks and whites in the Piedmont area of Virginia, where George and Willie were born.

"Clawhammer-style playing is what you would have heard in rural, isolated places that didn't have access to traveling medicine shows or vaudeville shows or that kind of thing," said musicologist and historian Kinney Rorrer, who hosts a popular public-radio show called *Back to the Blue Ridge*.

"You look at that picture [of George and Willie] and those costumes, and you think of minstrel shows immediately," Rorrer said. The music was popularized by Al Jolson, the white singer who claimed that performing behind a blackface mask "gave him a sense of freedom and spontaneity he had never known." Comic entertainer Bert Williams, the last major black entertainer to perform in blackface, rose to play with the Ziegfeld Follies, where his humor was as critically acclaimed as it was complicated. Blackface minstrelsy reinforced horrific racial stereotypes, while it also elevated African-American music and made Williams one of the highest-paid black entertainers of his time. W. C. Fields called him "the funniest man I ever saw, and the saddest man I ever knew."

Rorrer described minstrelsy as "a patronizing mentality, an attempt to see black people, slaves, and their descendants as 'the happy darkie,' as the expression went. They were supposed to be so happy because being enslaved wasn't so bad if you were able to play the banjo and sing and dance."

Rorrer came away from studying that picture with a question: Did circus people really teach the Muse brothers to play, or had they already learned how in Truevine? Though he was a few years younger than the Muses, a Franklin County musician named Lewis "Rabbit" Muse would go on to become a heralded country blues player, sought out for ethnography recordings and radio and festival performances, popular among black and white audiences alike.

Loose-limbed, light-skinned, and long-jowled, Rabbit also played kazoo and danced a jig that blended tap with mountain flatfooting. He called it "the dance that don't have no name; I just get into all kinds of shapes."

Rabbit decided to take up the ukulele, his main instrument, after seeing a traveling minstrel show around 1920. When he left home to try show business for himself, his father intervened.

"My daddy had to come and get me off the train," he told the *Roanoke Times* in 1977. "He sent a policeman in." And though he would go on to record such tunes as "Darkness on the Delta," Rabbit did not stray far from home again. He started a family band with a cousin on the washboard, his mother on accordion, and his father singing and playing guitar. When he wasn't working as a sawmill laborer, Rabbit was often with his band, playing house parties and county fairs, jamming in tobacco warehouses and on the streets.

What difference did the gift of music create in the brothers' lives? They still couldn't move about freely, still signed their names with an X. They still were told that the person they loved most in the world—their mother—was dead. Their vision problems were growing by the year, providing future circus pressmen with an endless array of "night vision" jokes.

But from minstrelsy to American jazz, the mastery of music gave marginalized blacks a freedom and power that many white musicians of that era couldn't fathom. African Americans bent rhythms and upended traditional white tonal patterns. They threw in swoops, growls, slides, and glissandos, infusing the music with a passion and spirituality that made it uniquely their own. "It's why I'd much rather listen to old black jazz than old white jazz," Rorrer said. "It was music played by people who couldn't read or write their names, but they could play with more authority than anyone out there."

And, whether they were pretending to be from Ecuador or from Ethiopia when they played it, Willie and George now had something that connected them, even obliquely, to their roots.

It also gave them something to do behind the scenes of the sideshow, and in the cookhouse, dressing tents, and stables where the show folks hung out.

Music seemed to lessen the brothers' misery, and it made them special for something, finally, besides the strangeness of their skin.

It gave them a skill they would each carry with them, literally, to their graves.

*   *   *

For several seasons, Barnes recalled, the Ecuadorian Savages made for "a great feature in the sideshow, until the new owner [presumably Shelton] had a better offer from another circus and left my show," likely in 1922 or 1923.

The name of that casually mentioned circus is curiously omitted from Barnes's account. At the time, a dozen large railroad shows competed for the best fair dates in North America. But Barnes was talking about the circus that had boasted Jumbo, an elephant so huge and so famous that its name had long ago slipped into the American vernacular.

The circus that was the home, for decades now, of the zany and inimitable Zip.

It was the circus that employed Lillian Leitzel, the so-called Queen of the Air. So famous was the looping aerialist during the Roaring Twenties that she was known the world over by just her last name.

Not long after the two largest circus entities on the planet had merged their traveling tents into one mega-show, this circus played to as many as two and a half million people in some 125 cities and towns.

Pick your superlative. It was either the Big One or Big Bertha, or the Greatest Show on Earth.

It was the golden age of the Ringling Brothers and Barnum and Bailey Combined Shows.

And the Muse brothers were now among the most elite of freaks.

7

He Who Hustleth While He Waiteth

In a silent-film documentary from the early 1920s about Ringling's behind-the-scenes staging, Willie and George Muse appear briefly. They are impeccably dressed in matching tan sport coats, bow ties, and newsboy hats. In the most dandy-like touch of all, they carry matching wooden canes, which they use, carefully, to propel themselves into the back of a truck—and probably to feel their way among objects they can't quite make out.

EVEN EKO AND IKO GET UP EARLY, the title board announces in ornate art deco font.

Dawn breaks just as the steam engine delivers the Big One and all its accoutrements to Chicago. The show travels in a caravan the size of a small city, more than a hundred railcars filled with sixteen hundred people, nine hundred horses, and nearly as many tigers, sea lions, zebras, and clowns. Showers are...what showers? Workers are allotted two metal buckets of water daily—one for sponging off, the other for washing out their clothes.

In the primitive movie technology of the day, the brothers' movements come across as swift, jerky, and out of focus.

They step gingerly into the motorized open-air truck, or gilly, that carries them from the steam-driven railcar to the circus lot. They take a seat across from the sideshow fat lady, Ruth Smith—aka Ima Waddler and Baby Ruth. Unaccompanied by handlers or guards, George and Willie converse cheerfully with the others in the truck. They do not appear to be mentally encumbered, incapacitated, or slow.

Minutes later in the film, they are seen along the sideshow banner, a cartoonish painting of them clad in tuxedo pants and white shirts, to the right of the sideshow entrance. It's an astonishingly bad likeness, lacking any hint of their African-American heritage. With reed-thin noses and blondish hair that's wavy and long (with feathery bangs), they look like waiters in a fancy restaurant, or members of a 1980s heavy-metal band.

Their skin looks neither black nor albino but rather a garden-variety vanilla. "The thinking was, you wanted to ward off an unpleasant or unfavorable reaction from the potentially racist general public," said Rob Houston, who has written about black performers in the sideshow.

After all, at Coney Island, carnies of that time were still selling white patrons on "three balls for five" to "dunk the nigger."

Like the other Eko and Iko sideshow banners of the day, the racial skewing on this one reminded Houston of Sadie Anderson, a black woman with white spots (or vitiligo) whose career intersected with the Muse brothers'. Promoters had Anderson's sideshow banners painted with her skin tones reversed so that she looked like a white woman with brown spots instead.

The truth comes through, though, in the beautifully choreographed *Congress of Freaks* large-format photographs Ringling allowed the Manhattan banquet photographer Edward J. Kelty to take every year. One season he placed the brothers front and center, flanking Sadie and her sister, Rosie. While the Muses wore tuxedos with sashes, in stark contrast to their wild and dreadlocked hair, the Anderson sisters wore halter tops and short skirts to bring optimum exposure to their pearl-colored patches.

An independent contractor, Kelty gave half his proceeds to circus management in exchange for its cooperation in the elaborate group portraits. He made most of his money from selling prints to circus employees and fans, and via publications like *Billboard*.

Kelty's drinking binges were legend, prompted, people said, after he returned shell-shocked from World War I. When money grew tight, he was known to pawn his negatives to settle his bar bills at his favorite midtown saloon. This might have been bad business, but it ensured that there was, and continues to be, no shortage of his annual photographs in circulation.

Throughout the 1920s and '30s, Kelty would photograph the Muse brothers in costume—encircled by hundreds of animals and big-top performers in the center ring, surrounded by wild bushmen and fat ladies and the diminutive Doll family. He shot them in front of the dime-store museums where they sometimes worked in the winter off-season.

In one of my favorites, from 1938, the Muses stand directly in the center of a thousand people—the Big One in all its glorious humanity. To their right is an elephant. On the other side, Texas giant Jack Earle is holding up Harry Doll, just before he broke into Hollywood by landing the role of a Munchkin in *The Wizard of Oz*.

It was the height of Jim Crow, when blacks and whites in southern states couldn't attend the circus together or share a taxicab. In the wake of World War I, the huge migration of blacks to northern cities had increased tensions across the country, partly triggered by job competition. Returning black veterans who now expected common decency for their service were rebuffed at every turn, spurring race riots from Chicago to Longview, Texas. Klan membership soared, peaking at five million members in the mid-1920s.

And yet there are George and Willie in newsreels, easily chatting up the white circus workers on the gilly truck.

"Uncle Willie told us they were considered white when they traveled," Nancy Saunders remembered. "They did not have to use the 'colored' bathrooms."

That was hard to believe, initially, the concept of the Muse brothers actually "passing," as the practice is known, for whites. From today's lens, the Muse brothers' facial features would easily identify them as very pale-skinned African Americans.

But halfway through the research for this book, I found a 1924 ship's manifest with their names. They were sailing from Los Angeles to Hawaii aboard the SS *Calawaii*. The Ringling season had ended a few months earlier, and they were going to work a sideshow in Honolulu, with Candy Shelton and his wife, Cora, in tow.

Their names were listed as Eko Shelton and Iko Shelton, and they were traveling, presumably, as the couple's kids.

As whites.

In the Ringling film, sideshow manager Clyde Ingalls stands behind his ticket box, talking up the show and giving the audience a "bally," or free tease, of what's inside the tent. (The term comes from *ballyhoo*, the press-generated excitement that precedes the show.) Dapper in a wide-brimmed panama hat,

Ingalls leans over a lectern, presenting two performers as bait. First up is the bushman Clicko, though Franz Taibosh just stands there; he does not perform his trademark bushman dance from his homeland of South Africa, reserving that for inside the tent.

Shoeless and wearing a leopard-skin robe, Taibosh was said to be a favorite among Ringling executives — Frank Cook, a Ringling legal fixer, or adjuster, was his legal guardian. Cook and other managers plied him with beer, his favorite drink, and Cuban cigars, and bailed him out of trouble when he disappeared in search of "a nice mama."

The blond and beautiful Grace Earles is showcased next in the bally. A preteen and the youngest of the diminutive German performers known as the Doll family, she stands atop Ingalls's ticket box, nervously tugging at her sundress. The sister of Harry Earles/Doll, the star of Tod Browning's *Freaks,* she slept in a sleeper car with miniature furniture "that looked like something out of *Gulliver's Travels,*" recalled one observer, while the giant Jack Earle (different spelling, no relation) had to have two berths knocked into one, with a ten-foot-long mattress.

Ingalls, whose loud velvety voice made him a bally master, was never happier than when the big top was already sold out, because that gave him an overflow group of disappointed fans who might be content to attend the sideshow instead. Besides, they had money in their pockets they were itching to spend.

Even better, the more they spent, the more Ingalls himself took home, since he kept 10 percent of the door. Lewiston described the front-end life on the sideshow, sharing bally duties with both Candy Shelton and Ingalls: Ingalls allowed them to shortchange, as long as they gave him a cut of the proceeds, and he took pleasure in correcting Lewiston's errors when he referred to Clicko as a *pigamy* instead of a pygmy and pronounced the word *Italian* "EYE-talian."

Gesturing emphatically, Ingalls himself spoke with grand, alliterative flair:

"They're all real, they're all alive, and they're all anxious to meet you, ladies and gentlemen, girls and boys," he intoned. "You can talk to them, they will talk to you. The cost for entering our capacious, clean, and comfortable pavilion is a mere twenty-five cents for the gentlemen and gentle ladies, a thin dime for the young ones."

Once enough people gave over their quarters and dimes, the freaks paraded into the tent and took their spots on the sideshow platform, at which point each act had five minutes to perform or otherwise interact with the audience.

When Ingalls wanted a breather, he would shout "Bally, P.G.!" and sideshow bandleader P. G. Lowery, a renowned cornet player, would cue his all-black band to play a few bars of Dixieland jazz. Though his group was not permitted to play with Merle Evans's all-white band in Ringling's big top, Lowery was a pioneer in circus minstrelsy and the first African American to have his own concert band in the sideshow. Heralded for his association with Scott Joplin, who wrote songs for him, Lowery gave employment to hundreds of black musicians over the decades, from Harlem to New Orleans.

His formula, as he shared it with members of his band, was perseverance plus pragmatism equals, eventually, success. "Good things come to he who waiteth as long as he hustleth while he waiteth," he said.

Lowery's band had its own space at the end of the platform,

Tobacco was Virginia's dominant cash crop for more than two centuries. Farmed initially by slaves, it was planted, tended, and dried by sharecroppers in Virginia's Southern Piedmont for decades after slavery's end. (*Cook Collection, The Valentine*)

In 1893, rioting broke out in the fledgling boomtown of Roanoke, Virginia, after a furnace worker named Thomas Smith was accused—probably falsely—of assaulting a white female produce vendor. Smith was hanged from a hickory tree, then shot, then dragged through the streets, and, finally, burned. A Roanoke photo studio sold this picture of Smith hanging from a rope as a souvenir; it was the eighth known lynching in southwest Virginia that year. (*Anonymous archive*)

Census figures from 1900 indicate that Cabell Muse, along with scores of other Franklin County sharecroppers, migrated to Rock, West Virginia, to lay track for the booming Norfolk & Western Railway. The identities of the workers in this picture were not recorded, but it was taken around the same time just outside Rock, West Virginia. (*Courtesy of Norfolk Southern Archives, Norfolk Southern Corporation*)

Truevine native A. J. Reeves was the grandson of Franklin County slaves. While other men left the region to escape tobacco sharecropping and seek equally tough but better-paying railroad work, Reeves's father, Robert, returned from his West Virginia railroad blacksmithing stint with enough savings to buy 150 acres of land, enough to farm and to build this once-glorious Victorian-era family home on. Reeves, ninety-nine when this photo was taken, still lives on family land and has always followed his father's advice to never work for anyone but himself to avoid mistreatment. (*Photograph by Beth Macy*)

"White peoples is hateful," former Truevine-area sharecropper Janet Johnson (left) recalled of her family's treatment on a Franklin County tobacco farm. Shown here in 2013 with her mother, Mabel Pullen, and father, Charles (now deceased), Janet had painful memories of not being allowed to attend school when the tobacco harvest came in, and of a farmer-boss serving the family's lunches through the window. "They said they 'didn't like niggers in the house,'" she explained. *(Photograph by Stephanie Klein-Davis; copyright Roanoke Times, reprinted by permission)*

This photo, probably taken in the mid-1910s, is the earliest known photograph of George (left) and Willie Muse as child sideshow exhibits. Their woolen suits are too small, indicating they've already been wearing them a long while. "They were dressed with some care for the ruse but not really that much attention to detail," one historic costume expert said, as if a showman had kept them and had no intention of truly caring for them himself—or of returning them to their mom. *(Courtesy of the John and Mable Ringling Museum of Art, Tibbals Collection)*

William Henry "Zip" Johnson, who was arguably the world's most famous freak, was "discovered" by P. T. Barnum, who claimed he found him naked and walking on all fours along the river Gambia. Barnum was said to have paid him a dollar a day to pretend to be "something between a man and monkey"—and not talk. *(Photograph by Sverre O. Braathen, courtesy of the Milner Library Special Collections, Illinois State University)*

Sideshow manager Clyde Ingalls (left) was a colorful fixture with Ringling Brothers & Barnum-Bailey Circus. Trying to woo potential patrons into his tent, he often spotlighted top performers such as Johnson aka "Zip" (right) on the bally platform, in an attempt to "turn the tip," or gather enough quarters for another sideshow performance to begin. *(Courtesy of Circus World Museum)*

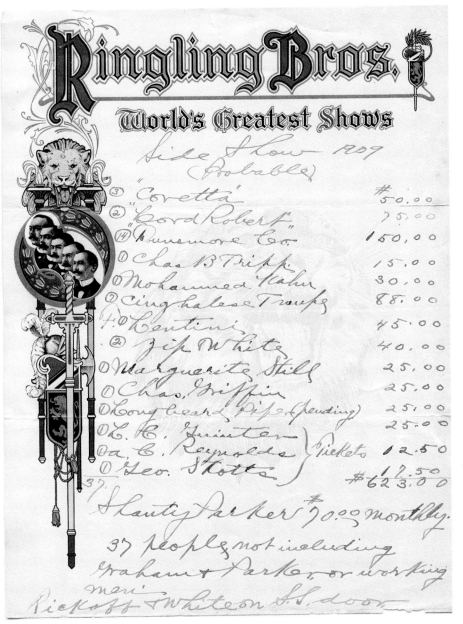

Ringling Bros.

World's Greatest Shows

Side Show 1909
(Probable)

③	"Covetta"	#50.00
②	"Cord Robert"	75.00
⑭	"Dunsmore Co."	150.00
①	Chas B Tripp	15.00
①	Mohammed Kahn	30.00
⑨	Cinghalese Troupe	88.00
④	Centini	45.00
②	Zip White	40.00
①	Marguerite Still	25.00
①	Chas Griffin	25.00
①	Long beard Piper (pending)	25.00
①	L. C. Twister	25.00
①	a. C. Reynolds ⎫ Tickets	12.50
①	Geo. Stotts ⎭	12.50

37.

#623.00

Shanty Parker #70.00 monthly.

37 people not including
Graham + Parker, or working
men
Rickoff + White on S.S. door.

Sideshow impresario Lew Graham would search the world "freak-hunting," then write regular letters back to John Ringling estimating the cost of the following season's exhibits—including, in this list, William Henry "Zip" Johnson, whose manager, O. K. White, was to be paid $40 for his services in 1909. (Note: Johnson's name is referenced as Zip White.) (*Courtesy of the Milner Library Special Collections, Illinois State University*)

This is the second-oldest known photo pitch card of Willie (left) and George Muse, shown here circa mid- to late 1910s, playing the banjo and saxophone. Though they were falsely regarded as being cognitively impaired (probably owing to their oscillating eye condition and lack of socialization and schooling), their managers and co-workers conceded that they were brilliant musicians. (*Collection of Warren Raymond*)

Taken sometime between 1918 and 1922, this is the only known photograph of the Muse brothers with one of their captors, showman Al G. Barnes, who bragged in his memoir about "buying the boys" and "making them a paying proposition." (*Collection of Josh Meltzer*)

The Al G. Barnes Circus was massive, as evidenced by how much lakeside real estate it took up in Cleveland, Ohio, in 1922. Across America at the turn of the last century, "Circus Day" was second only to Christmas Day in popularity. (*Courtesy of Circus World Museum*)

Kelty's annual "class photographs" of the sideshow exotics heralded the new Ringling Brothers & Barnum-Bailey Circus season and were taken at Madison Square Garden, this one in 1924. George Muse is third from the left, upper row, standing next to William Henry "Zip" Johnson. Willie Muse is third from the right, standing between the Doll family and Franz "Clicko" Taibosh. (*Courtesy of the John and Mable Ringling Museum of Art, Tibbals Collection*)

The all-black Ringling Brothers and Barnum & Bailey Circus sideshow band was led by P. G. Lowery. The Muse brothers are visible both in the Kelty "class photograph" that hangs from the sideshow entrance and in a cartoon-like banner, just to the right of the tent's entrance, which casts them as tuxedo-clad people with white features, including thin noses and blond hair. *(Courtesy of the John and Mable Ringling Museum of Art, Tibbals Collection)*

Circus archivist and collector Dick Flint found this mid-1920s-era photograph of George and Willie Muse being clutched by Ringling Brothers & Barnum-Bailey Circus minders in the circus backyard, likely owing to their poor eyesight. *(Courtesy of Richard Flint)*

ARE THEY
AMBASSADORS FROM MARS?

Sideshow banners, hung from the exterior of sideshow tents, often exaggerated the features of the acts inside the tent. George and Willie Muse were cast as whiter than they were, all traces of their African-American heritage erased. "The thinking was, you wanted to ward off an unpleasant or unfavorable reaction from the potentially racist general public," said Rob Houston, who researches black sideshow history. *(Photograph by Sverre O. Braathen, courtesy of the Milner Library Special Collections, Illinois State University)*

Longtime manager and captor Candy Shelton (far left) with George and Willie Muse in the water in Margate, Florida, on Christmas Day 1926. According to Candy's wife, who wrote a dismissive description of the photograph on the back, the Muse brothers were "taking their annual bath." *(Courtesy of The John and Mable Ringling Museum of Art, Circus Museum Collection)*

Edward J. Kelty took this picture of the brothers for Ringling Brothers & Barnum-Bailey Circus in 1926 with the handwritten caption "Are They Ambassadors from Mars." The brothers hadn't seen their mother in at least twelve years at that point. (*Courtesy of Circus World Museum*)

This 1929 sideshow photo is essentially the same makeup of the RB&BB sideshow the year The Greatest Show on Earth made its first—and most dramatic—stop in Roanoke, Virginia, in 1927. (*Edward J. Kelty photograph courtesy of the John and Mable Ringling Museum of Art, Tibbals Collection*)

Franz Taibosh—aka Clicko the Dancing African Bushman—shared the sideshow stage with the Muse brothers for much of his time touring with the Ringling Brothers & Barnum-Bailey Circus sideshow. "He was rather snooty" about the brothers, his biographer said, despite sharing the experience of having been long exploited by showmen. (*Photograph by Sverre O. Braathen, courtesy of the Milner Library Special Collections, Illinois State University*)

Harriett Muse's act of confronting circus lawyers and Roanoke police officers to reclaim her sons was particularly bold in light of the fact that the chief prosecutor in Roanoke in 1927 was Col. Kent Spiller, the founder of the local KKK. (*Courtesy of Donald Caldwell, Commonwealth's Attorney, city of Roanoke, 2015*)

The Roanoke chapter of the KKK, named for General Robert E. Lee, was the largest in the state under Spiller's direction. Shortly after Spiller's election, the KKK held a parade through the streets of downtown Roanoke, headed by a huge fiery cross and an oversized U.S. flag held up by fifty people. (*Photograph by George Davis courtesy of the Virginia Room, Roanoke Public Library*)

Virginia reporting legend Melville "Buster" Carico, shown here at age ninety-nine, recalled that when he first started working at the *Roanoke Times* in the 1930s, "If a black was in the news, you had to put 'comma, colored' after his name." His mother admired the local KKK for its protection of women, and Buster remembered an open-air Ford passing down his hilly blue-collar Roanoke street chock-full of Klansmen who had donned white robes and hoods. (*Photograph by Beth Macy*)

A Roanoke street photographer took this family portrait behind the family home at 19 Ten-and-a-Half Street shortly after Harriett Muse (far right) claimed her sons and brought them back to the tiny shotgun house she shared with her husband, Cabell (left), and other relatives. (*Photograph by George Davis, courtesy of Frank Ewald*)

Harriett Muse hired soon-to-be-famous Roanoke litigator Warren "Squeak" Messick (center) to file a lawsuit against the Greatest Show on Earth in October 1927, claiming the circus owed her $100,000 in damages and back pay. (*Courtesy of Harvey Lutins*)

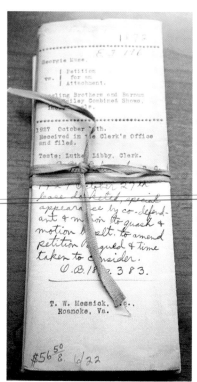

The original petition for damages and back pay filed for Harriett Muse by her attorney, Warren Messick, on file at the Library of Virginia. Such loose court papers, called "shucks" and tied together with red cord, gave birth to the bureaucratic form "red tape." (*Photograph by Beth Macy*)

Ringling lawyer J. M. Kelley fired back immediately in response to Messick's lawsuit. (*Photograph by Sverre O. Braathen, courtesy of the Milner Library Special Collections, Illinois State University*)

By the time the Muse brothers decided to rejoin the circus, they took their younger brother, Tom, along to work as a circus roustabout. This photograph, from 1926, shows a typical Ringling Brothers & Barnum-Bailey Circus tent-erecting scene, with the "lot lice" looking on in wonder. (*Courtesy of Circus World Museum*)

Eko AND Iko
sheepheaded CANNIBALs
from ECUADOR

Once the Muse brothers were being paid regularly for their work, their act took on comic undertones. "Black 'wildmen' were sometimes exhibited in cages as uncivilized brutes who subsisted on raw meat and bit the heads off chicken or snakes. But these two, in comparison, look like Boy Scouts," said the scholar Bernth Lindfors, referring to this 1928 picture. Perhaps that's because they were now performers who were being paid—for a while, anyway. (*Courtesy of Bernth Lindfors*)

The Muse brothers were widely considered "good examples of contented freaks," wrote *The New Yorker* magazine, which snidely reported that the brothers returned to the circus because "the fried chicken had soon given out at Roanoke." (*Collection of Robert Stauffer*)

where musicians played everything from opera to popular minstrel tunes to the latest jazz. They played during the pre-show bally and at the end of the freak show, performing two or three numbers as a minstrel show, some of the black musicians in faux blackface, their lips exaggerated and painted white.

The standing audience, having wandered in a semicircle from the first freak to the sideshow band, would exit the tent. Then Ingalls went to work trying to drum up people for the next showing.

Sideshow performers were on call all day long, with intermittent shows given whenever Ingalls lured enough people off the midway and into his tent for a new show—or, in circus lingo, when he had turned the tip.

Which is partly why even Eko and Iko got up early, as the silent film had put it. The freaks were always the first to eat breakfast at the cookhouse, so they could arrive at their appointed tent well before the big-top performers were on call. The tent-canvas crew, or roughnecks (aka rousties, for *roustabouts*), would sit on one side of the cookhouse, the managers and performers on the other. The freaks sat on the performers' side but at a table to themselves.

On a good day, Ingalls told a reporter, the sideshow could take in $1,200 or more.

Ingalls was so smooth-talking, so beguilingly good at what he did, that he managed to woo the diva Leitzel into marrying him in 1920—never mind that he was married to someone else when they had started cavorting a year earlier. Bandleader Evans had caught them rustling around in the predawn inside a pitch-black tent. "On the circus, everybody's crowded together like candy in a gumball machine," Evans said. "No secret can survive long."

By the time the Muse brothers joined Ringling, Ingalls had moved on to a British-born widow who managed Ringling's gorilla act. And Leitzel would eventually find love with Ringling's number-two draw: Alfredo Codona, the Mexican trapeze artist known for his movie-star good looks and his mastery of the triple flip.

For George and Willie, the work was dirty, and it was grueling. You had to stand there most of the day, playing and saying the same things over and over, all day long, just about every day. But it was almost never boring.

You could read that on the faces of the lot lice who came to watch the rousties putting up the tents and taking them down. The big top was so breathtakingly scary and so alive, while the sideshow had the lure of the forbidden and perverse.

Maybe I'll run off with the circus. You could see the moment the thought crossed their stunned, starstruck faces.

The mobile city moved at night. Back in the 1870s, James Anthony Bailey had designed his Cooper and Bailey Circus to travel that way, the only problem being that eventually the thing grew so much that it was too big to move easily. A protégé of P. T. Barnum's, Bailey had grown up an orphan in a Pontiac, Michigan, livery stable. At the age of thirteen, he bolted from his abusive caretakers and ran away with a circus. "I told the [showman] I was an orphan, with no friends, and would like to go with the show," he recalled in 1891. "He took me along, making me useful where he could. I have never done anything but circus work since, and I never want to."

Bailey blamed his frenetic, obsessive work habits on having been beaten severely as a child. The abuse fueled him with a desire that was as motivating as it was destined to earn him a mint.

A self-taught circus engineer, Bailey mastered speedy techniques for loading and unloading trains. He designed tent-lot layouts that became the industry standard. He also figured out transatlantic travel in the 1880s, determining how to lift freight cars full of lions, tigers, and elephants — by crane — into the holds of ships. He transformed his circus from a single-ring enterprise to two rings and, later, three.

Bailey was so adept at logistics that a quartermaster general with the German military would shadow him in the late nineteenth century to learn the best ways to move men, animals, and equipment by rail.

The key was his scrupulous attention to detail: Bailey not only knew how many horseshoes he carried with him on any given day, his underlings claimed, he could tell you in exactly which bin they were located.

When the stress of managing thousands of employees and animals overwhelmed him, he gnawed on rubber bands. He saved his important decisions for Fridays, which he considered the most auspicious day of the week.

If Barnum had been the Walt Disney of his era, Bailey was the back-end brains behind Barnum and Bailey's Greatest Show on Earth when the two joined forces in 1880. The polar opposite of Barnum, Bailey hated publicity. A tall but slender and wiry man — with energy emanating from his pores — Bailey had one-upped Barnum when they were competitors by refusing to sell him a baby elephant, the first born in captivity. Not only did he turn down Barnum's bid of $10,000 for the young pachyderm, named Columbia, Bailey out-Barnumed the master by turning the refusal into an advertising promotion. He placed posters and handbills with copies of Barnum's telegraphed offer under the caption WHAT BARNUM THINKS OF THE

BABY ELEPHANT. Had he been born a century later, he would have been a master of Twitter.

Bailey became "an ideal 'silent' partner for the noisy Barnum, but a canny one as well. By the time Barnum died, in 1891, Bailey owned a controlling interest in the corporation," wrote Fred Bradna, the Ringlings' longtime equestrian director and stage manager.

Meanwhile, in Baraboo, Wisconsin, five brothers—the sons of a German harness maker—were busy putting on their first show. Premiering in 1882 with an admission price of 25¢, it was called the Ringling Brothers' Carnival of Fun, and the brothers starred in and managed every aspect of it, from spinning plates and juggling (Al Ringling) to playing the cornet (Alf T.) to playing the violin and acting in skits (Charles) to portraying a Real Live Dude (John) and booking the shows (Otto). Al's wife, Lou, did double duty as equestrian and snake charmer in the gang's nascent wagon-show days. To give the impression the operation was larger than it was, Al had the idea to make the performers change costumes and reappear in another ring. Al himself had mastered a second trick of balancing a plow— on his nose.

Initially, they were "an awful exhibition of faltering nerve… and a demoralized lot," Charles Ringling would later write. The brothers first traveled by farm wagon, wintering in the off-season in Baraboo, where they stowed their equipment and played occasional concerts.

And plotted their ascendency. In two years they saved $1,000 from ticket sales and garnered the stamp of support from the circus veteran Yankee Robinson.

A bona fide circus operation was born. The Ringling Brothers

Circus went on the rails in 1890, giving it access to markets beyond the Midwest and, eventually and with support from Robinson, the ability to buy out some of its competitors. This naturally raised the ire of James Bailey, who worried some about the explosive growth of his young competitors. But, apparently, not enough: Bailey underestimated the Ringlings' ambitions when he took his Greatest Show on Earth to Europe in 1898 — and stayed five years. The Ringlings took full advantage of the openness of this newly competitive field and vastly expanded their routes south, west, and into Canada. By the time Bailey returned, "the Ringlings were by now so strongly entrenched in the favor of the American people as to be almost impregnable," their nephew wrote.

But Bailey fell ill in 1906 at the age of fifty-eight, following an insect bite that infected him with erysipelas. (Bitten on a Thursday, he died the following Wednesday.) He'd been supervising the preparations for opening day at Madison Square Garden, and true to character, he insisted he could return to work, which he did — until, literally, he collapsed and died.

The following year, the brothers from Baraboo bought Barnum and Bailey for $450,000 from Bailey's widow — an amount they earned back within a year. Operations for the two were kept separate until they merged into one colossal show in 1919.

John Ringling was the Bailey-like taskmaster of the combined operation, and he was considerably more flamboyant in his affairs than his brothers. He moved the headquarters to Sarasota, Florida, in 1927 and built a palace he anointed with a Venetian name: Ca' d' Zan, or House of John. He kept a long black cigar in his mouth and a pet monkey at his elbow, and he loved working late into the night, devouring two roast chickens and several pints of beer before going to bed at 4:00 a.m.

With his African-American chauffeur Taylor Gordon at the wheel, he rode in a Rolls-Royce and kept a firm hand on all aspects of the family dynasty, slinking around to covertly watch the RB&BB parade from a side street—to make sure no one was shirking.

"He dressed soberly, like a banker, but conducted his affairs like a Moorish potentate: ornately, glitteringly, incredibly," recalled Bradna. At six feet one, he was swarthy, with drooping eyelids and a low, deep voice.

"The brothers who owned the show—Al, Otto, Alf T., Charles and John—were sort of Hydra, with five rather than nine heads, which could look everywhere at once," Bradna wrote. "And the competitors who, like Hercules, tried to lop off these heads, soon discovered that when one was cut, two others immediately sprang up. By canny management, superlative showmanship, aggressiveness and doggedness, they succeeded ultimately in crushing virtually all their opposition. By 1929, they had ruined, absorbed, or bought every important rival in the land"—including the Al G. Barnes Circus.

And still John Ringling clutched the reins. When another elephant in the Barnes circus went amok, in 1929, crushing a woman to death, wrecking a car, and injuring two trainers, he personally wired: "Kill Diamond in some humane way." The elephant was led to a clearing in the woods and chained to a tree while five marksmen pumped more than fifty bullets into him from six yards away.

To hype ticket sales and massage the media, the Big One employed Dexter Fellows, a Boston-born media darling who'd already worked with circuses across North America and in Europe. Fellows could quote literature from Balzac to Dickens and knew hundreds of reporters. He had a soft spot for animals, naming his Irish terrier after a character in a Balzac story and keeping sugar cubes in his pocket for the Ringling elephants.

Reporters from Seattle to Sarasota called him the Dean, and in New York especially they looked forward to the RB&BB's annual spring opening stand at Madison Square Garden because they knew Fellows would spoon-feed them a new and crafty angle on the routine story.

As a *Times* reporter gushed of Fellows, "His keen sense of humor, his delightful ways and his broad culture gained him entrée into offices where more exalted personages had to wait in ante-rooms to be in turn ushered in."

Fellows could place just about anything he wanted in any newspaper, from the gossipy pages of *Billboard* to the front page of the *New York Times*. "He could improvise the type of story that would 'make the front page,' and he invariably had the material to back it up; there was generally plenty of it in the shape of strange beasts, human freaks, clowns, equestrians, and all the rest that make up a circus," a *Times* reporter marveled.

Fellows had a special place in his heart for freaks, marveling at audiences who paid to feel better about themselves, or sought to pity rather than to gloat.

"Sideshow people have a pride of calling," he argued. "They have the hauteur of Shakespearean actors of the old school and the temperament of grand opera stars.... And a good many of them are in a position to buy and sell the majority of citizen paupers who come in to shed a tear over them."

Most experts I interviewed agreed with Fellows's laudatory assessment of sideshow performers. Al Stencell said the circus was the rare place in America where misfits of all stripes were welcomed. Most were "towners who were fleeing bad homes or aching to sow their wild oats. Gays were just glad to find somewhere that welcomed them," he wrote, especially in the clown and sideshow departments.

Sociologist Robert Bogdan said he found show people in general to be more tolerant of human variation than the general population. "The other thing is, if you treat people badly, then they don't cooperate. So there was a certain built-in incentive to keep the sideshow exhibits happy," he told me.

A loyal camaraderie developed among the traveling performers, who cast the show-goers as provincial and naïve. A carny who played a show near his hometown was called, dismissively, a forty-miler.

The cool thing, the superior thing, was to be alive and on the road—unlike the people in the towns, who were thought to be sleeping through their lives. Those poor pitiful rubes.

Fellows had no trouble publicizing the fact that Ringling sideshow announcer Lew Graham had just made ONE OF FINDS OF HIS CAREER, or so blared *Billboard*'s main circus page in August 1922. While the Barnes circus had just been waylaid by a railroad strike along the East Coast that summer—and stuck in Zanesville, Ohio, of all boring places—the Ringling trains had moved on to Chicago and were now, thanks to Eko and Iko, "the center of a curious and interested audience."

By moving the Muse brothers from Barnes's show to Ringling's, Shelton had done what people along the sawdust trail call blowing the show, or switching circuses.

"Mr. Graham is exhibiting Iko and Eko, two Ecuador [*sic*] white savages," *Billboard* noted, as if writing about them for the first time. "They are pure Albinos, with skins as white as cream, and with all the facial characteristics of South African bushmen, aside from their color. The two strange creations are elaborately dressed in robes of royal purple, and their great masses of cream-white hair add to their striking appearance."

The brothers' hair grew so woolly and quickly, according to one newspaper, that it could make the equivalent of three new shirts a year. It was also said to grow from their scalps in knots, like some Jazz Age version of a chia pet.

In their earliest Ringling sideshow banners, Willie and George are portrayed as tall and elegant, with European-looking features. Their tuxedos are adorned with diagonal, vaguely militaristic sashes across their chests. And contrary to photographs, in which they appear extremely well fed by the mid-1920s, their early Ringling banners picture them as being almost as slender as Peter Robinson, the fifty-eight-pound Human Skeleton.

Fellows called a press conference to brief reporters on Ringling's latest find, saying the brothers were around forty years old—at least a decade older than they actually were—and describing them as quiet, eccentric, and "childish" men, "the center of a curious and interested audience." A paper in Syracuse, New York, said they spoke a language understood only by the two of them—their tribal dialect from Ecuador—but that they'd also absorbed "sufficient English to carry on a conversation."

Sideshow manager Ingalls was said to have found them floating on "some peculiar wreckage near the coast of California," Fellows stated in his typically alliterative prose.

Due to the strange language they spoke, the *New York Sun* reported, people at first thought they hailed from Hollywood.

Farce or not, the brothers from Truevine were now part of the top tier of the sideshow world. They worked hand in hand with Zip, now considered the dean of freaks; with the beloved Texas giant Jack Earle; and with Lionel the Mexican-born Dog-Faced Boy, who was then the highest-earning sideshow act, hauling down $250 a week, the equivalent of $3,400 today.

Candy Shelton had moved up to the big leagues with them, managing the brothers and working as a sideshow ticket taker. No longer would he have to "Chinese," a racist bit of circus lingo that had morphed into an action verb for doing unpaid heavy labor around the show grounds. "Chinese is what you did in exchange for your sleeping quarters and cookhouse accommodations," Stencell said of the slang, whose roots lie in the nineteenth-century Chinese immigrant laborers who built the transcontinental railroad. "The candy butchers, especially, they pulled a lot of Chinese."

In one of the few photos I found of Shelton from that era, he stands among the RB&BB circus staff with a host of other ticket takers and back-end workers. He's paunchy, a shock of dark bangs dangling from his receding hairline. His sleeves are rolled up, his vest left open, and his trouser fly is cinched with a safety pin. He drapes his arm jocularly around a man named Charles Hummell, the only named guest in the picture.

By 1924, Shelton was pocketing $400 weekly for George and Willie's work—a pretty penny, the equivalent of $5,400 today. And that didn't count what he made from their photo-postcard sales, judging from a newspaper story about how well paid circus freaks were at the time. But that story may have been just another Fellows fiction, another alliteration-filled riff designed to engender admiration for Ringling—and more quarters for the sideshow tent.

What's clear, according to *Billboard* briefs that chronicled his whereabouts, was that Shelton was very well connected among managers of all the largest circuses and carnivals. He hobnobbed with diva Leitzel. He was friendly with Al G. Barnes and the managers of famed conjoined twins Daisy and Violet Hilton. He spent Christmas 1924 with the prominent carnival sideshow entrepreneur Pete Kortes and dined occasionally with Charles and John Ringling and John's wife, Mable.

A *Billboard* writer even made up a Christmas poem featuring Shelton and the brothers one year—though he got one of their names wrong:

Candy Shelton, Harry Wilson
And Bob Crawford, too,
All line up in front
As the ticket-selling crew

Then there's Eko and Mike [sic]
The Ambassadors from Mars
But we doubt if they ever
Have "mingled with the stars"

The wool on their heads
Is like that of the sheep
And they sit there as peaceful
As if in a sleep

In the fall of 1924, *Billboard* covered the backstage Halloween shenanigans of the Greatest Show on Earth, an annual party held as a masquerade ball in the big top, this time in Anniston, Alabama. The main stages of the big top were used as dance floors, and bandleader Evans furnished the music. Leitzel—by now she had both a private railcar and her own dressing tent—dressed up as a Boy Scout.

It's not clear whether George and Willie were invited to the party—Alabama's Jim Crow laws prohibited biracial fraternizing—or whether their presence was merely echoed, sneeringly, at the ball. The wife of a Ringling horse trainer dressed up as one of the Muses, while Shelton's wife, Cora, played the role of the other brother in a mockery whose "impersonations were clever" and "had the show folk guessing."

But which of the "rope-haired wonders," as they called them backstage, was Eko? And which was Iko?

The Ringling brass hadn't bothered figuring it out. But what a wild celebration it was.

Billboard recounted the event in a brief that was spoon-fed to it by Fellows, who liked to twirl his graying mustache as he typed. He was proud of the nickname his reporter friends bestowed on him: the Minister Plenipotentiary of the Greatest Show on Earth.

It was getting to be so effortless; they reprinted his every word.

What the Minister Plenipotentiary never saw coming was the literal media circus into which he was about to be jammed.

If Harriett Muse had her way, the reporters could print all the racist poems and jokes they wanted. But George and Willie would have the last laugh.

8
Comma, Colored

If Dexter Fellows couldn't tell one brother from the other, he sure didn't know where their mother lived. In his autobiography, he says authoritatively that the Muse brothers hailed from "the Carolinas."

He certainly had no idea they had an entire family living in Roanoke. But he did understand just how harsh the racial climate in Virginia's booming rail town was.

Fellows's most recent trip to Roanoke had been three decades earlier, as an advance man for Pawnee Bill, a cowboy-oriented Wild West show whose acts included Annie Oakley and Buffalo Bill.

By his own vivid accounting, Fellows's brief time in Roanoke had been a haunting one. The drama unfolded the moment he happened into town in September 1893, when a hotel proprietor urged him to attend a public event taking place that night.

"Better come uptown with me," S. A. Vicks said. "They're going to lynch a nigger...Why, the whole town is turning out."

Indeed, Fellows had just stumbled into the most violent and chaotic scene ever witnessed in Roanoke, before or since: the Thomas Smith lynching of 1893. Thousands gathered around the city jail, threatening to storm it. Evidence was flimsy, historians would later agree, that Smith had actually attacked a woman earlier that day, as the media and police claimed at the time.

But the crowd "snarled and snapped like wolves encircling their prey and their ululating cry, as it could be heard blocks away, throbbed like the thundering bass of an organ," Fellows wrote in a four-page description that dovetails, paragraph by paragraph, with the confirmed historical account. (While his press releases were full of hyberbole and outright myth, Fellows hewed to the facts where the lynching was concerned.)

"Come on, let's get the bastard!" someone shouted.

Shots rang out, and though Vicks initially insisted otherwise, it became clear—there was blood everywhere—that the bullets were not blanks. Separated from Vicks in the chaos, Fellows took refuge under a porch while soldiers ushered Smith out of jail during a brief lull, transporting him outside the city limits.

When the shooting quieted down, Fellows wrote, he found the hotel proprietor lying dead in the street, one of nine people killed.

By nightfall, Smith's corpse dangled from a hickory limb, bullets riddling his body and signs hanging from him that read MAYOR TROUT'S FRIEND on his back and DO NOT CUT DOWN BY ORDER OF JUDGE LYNCH.

After scores of people carried away fragments of Smith's clothing, after they burned Smith's body on the banks of the Roanoke River, after hysterical women tore ribbons from their dresses to throw into the funeral pyre, Fellows walked back to the proprietorless hotel, as he described it. He closed the scene by reciting the lamentations of a poem by Paul Laurence Dunbar, the best-known black writer at the time:

I bent me down to hear his sigh;
  I shook with his gurgling moan.
And I trembled sore when they rode away,
  And left him here alone.

By the mid-1920s, Roanoke's racial climate hadn't changed much, though Smith's lynching was the city's last. What had evolved, though, was the cultural cachet of the Gainsboro neighborhood, along the northern edge of downtown. The black-owned Dumas Hotel on Henry Street, popularly known as the Yard, was beginning to attract the likes of Duke Ellington, Marian Anderson, and Louis Armstrong. It was home to scores of black-owned businesses, too — barbershops, law offices, smoke shops, nightclubs, and cafes. It had its own tiny branch library, initially housed in the flood-prone basement of the black YMCA in 1921.

The Yard also had people like the feisty young Virginia Y. Lee, a librarian who covertly put up black-history displays against the wishes of her white downtown-library bosses, who told her to "slow the pace." Because the city was pitching in only $20,000 toward a proper black library — just one-twelfth of what it was planning for its new main branch downtown for white residents — Lee found herself walking toward the grand, imposing Catholic church at the top of a steep hill near the Yard. She wanted the priest to donate land for the stand-alone building she had literally sketched out herself, a beautiful, sun-drenched brick Tudor building that would become the beacon for the neighborhood as it exists today — and, where, incidentally, I began my research for this book.

"On the way up that hill, I was saying a little prayer that God would be with me; that I would not have to tolerate non-interest in what I was going to ask," she recalled in a 1982 ceremony in her honor. The priest signed on to donate the land, after garnering written permission from Pope Pius XII.

A few blocks away, a young Illinois-born novelist-turned-filmmaker named Oscar Micheaux had set up an office on the Yard called the Micheaux Film Corporation, and he had grand plans for Roanoke's mini–Harlem Renaissance. From the gritty railroad city, Micheaux was on his way to becoming the most prolific filmmaker of the silent period, black or white. He used local actors—including a young Oliver Hill—in his *House Behind the Cedars,* a film that shocked viewers for its depiction of an interracial couple, one of Micheaux's favorite themes.

The oldest surviving feature film by a black director is his 1920 *Within Our Gates.* The sprawling story of racial injustice was created in partial response to D. W. Griffith's 1915 *The Birth of a Nation,* which had featured a cast of inflammatory caricatures: noble white people who liked nothing more than to lynch lazy, lecherous blacks.

Virginia-born President Wilson, a staunch supporter of segregation, made *The Birth of a Nation* the first film shown inside the White House, helping spark a resurgence of the KKK. Calling Griffith's racist saga "the finest motion picture of all time," the *Roanoke Times* noted that its local premiere featured a special orchestra and select seats that sold as high as $2, the equivalent of $46 today.

Micheaux's return salvo was released the same week the National Association for the Advancement of Colored People announced that nine African-American World War I veterans had been lynched. *Within Our Gates* featured especially bold and graphic scenes of two blacks being lynched and the near rape of a black woman by a white man—who stops only when he realizes that the victim is, in fact, his own mulatto daughter. The man had been stealing from the parents who raised her, his tenant farmers, for many years, and long before, he had also raped her mother, never realizing that he had sired a child.

Criticized for its graphic nature and banned in some cities, Micheaux's film was positively audacious at a time when whites were still cheering Griffith's work. Across the country, lynching had almost turned into a spectator sport, with special railroad excursions planned around established lynching sites — a practice W. E. B. Du Bois called the new "white amusement."

Unlike most of the black leaders Du Bois hailed as the Talented Tenth, Micheaux didn't just portray blacks as heroes. He was rare among black artists because he also explored the negative traits of his characters, airing such dirty laundry as gambling, drug use, conspiring with white men for selfish advancement, and crime. He even stepped on the toes of the black clergy, openly mocking what he perceived as their greedy and sanctimonious behavior.

"The black intelligentsia attacked him," said Bayer Mack, a documentary filmmaker who explored Micheaux's life in a 2014 film. "He was saying the church was dead asleep and for sale to the highest bidder."

With his liberal use of black dialect, "he was saying we are not properly educated. He was pointing out that urbanization gave blacks a different problem than they had in the South: competition for jobs," Mack added.

"If you're looking at civil rights and [the 2015] riots in Baltimore, Oscar was just light-years ahead of his time."

In Roanoke and elsewhere in the South, Jim Crow laws had reached their zenith in the late 1910s and '20s. Some progress had been made in Virginia since emancipation. Blacks now owned $53 million in property, a pittance compared with the $920 million of white-owned land. Still, it was "a big step forward from the days of slavery," a newspaper writer noted in 1924. And yet, more than fifty years after the abolition of slavery, three-quarters of African Americans living in the South were still working as day laborers or sharecroppers.

"Separate but equal" segregation, legitimized by the 1896 U.S. Supreme Court *Plessy v. Ferguson,* was now fully entrenched, with stringent Jim Crow laws in places like hospitals, jails, and businesses in southern states, not to mention the voting booth. Under the oligarchy of segregationist Virginia governor Harry F. Byrd and his so-called Byrd Machine, ordinances forbidding blacks and whites from living on the same block were enacted in many cities.

As a visiting Swedish writer observed: "Segregation is now becoming so complete that the white Southerner practically never sees a Negro except as his servant and in other standardized and formalized caste situations."

Black-white interactions could now be as bizarrely intimate as they were brutally snobbish. In Jordan's Alley, black maids were so close to their white employers that they washed their undergarments outside their own shanties but could not ride in the same railcars. In the executive car of the Norfolk and Western Railway, the black chef served elaborate meals for his white bosses garnished with the parsley he'd grown and snipped in the backyard of his home—located, of course, on a blacks-only block.

The *Roanoke Times* heralded the establishment of the region's KKK klavern, or chapter, named for Confederate general Robert

E. Lee, and attributed its creation to a "surge of patriotism." World War I had just ended, and in the next year more than seventy African Americans had been lynched, many of them still wearing their military uniforms.

Membership was no doubt helped along by having the right kind of haters in the right kind of places: local Klansmen were led by a prominent lawyer and Spanish War and World War I veteran, Colonel R. Kent Spiller, who would go on to serve as the city's commonwealth attorney, or chief prosecutor, in 1925. Shortly after Spiller's election to that post, the KKK held a parade through the streets of downtown Roanoke, headed by a huge fiery cross and an oversized U.S. flag held up by fifty people.

Under a hazy October sky, some fifteen hundred men, women, and boys joined the parade, and thousands more came along to watch, filling streetcars and causing one of the city's earliest traffic jams. The parade started at a downtown park and wended its way down the Jefferson Street main corridor and on to the city fairgrounds, near the edge of downtown.

Led by a robed horseman, the marchers encircled the grounds, and cheers rang out from the grandstand. More than two hundred converts took oaths of allegiance to the Invisible Empire. Hooded figures then gathered in the shadow of a burning cross. The newspaper recorded "the color and mystery of the organization with the fiery cross," and a local radio station broadcast the event so people who couldn't be there could listen from home on their brand-new Atwater Kent radio sets.

Spiller and company declared they "hated neither negroes, Catholics or the foreign born; that their organization was simply to keep the states under control of white native-born Protestants."

Spiller was a member of the prestigious St. John's Episcopal Church in downtown Roanoke and of the upper-crust Shenandoah Club—which wouldn't admit Jews, blacks, or women until the late 1980s. He was descended from an old Virginia family, prominent slave owners and land-grant recipients from the British sovereign during the colonial era. His father had served as a captain in the Confederate army and fought in the Battle of New Market, and Spiller saw himself as a law-and-order defender of racial integrity and white Protestant supremacy.

Roanoke's Robert E. Lee Klan No. 4 was a prestigious group to be a part of, something local business owners joined to help boost their reputations, akin to Rotary and Kiwanis clubs today. "They were just plain, everyday citizens," recalled one black Roanoker, in an oral-history interview he gave to the Harrison Museum of African American Culture in 1992. For years the man couldn't understand why his boss at the insurance agency where he did low-level work was so mean to him—until he saw him marching in a Klan parade.

At ninety-eight years old, retired but still a legend among Virginia newspapermen, Melville "Buster" Carico told me he remembered a weeklong singing and dancing extravaganza sponsored by the local Klan in 1926. A musical that toured across the South, *The Awakening* relied on local Klans to provide backup for its professional troupe. The city's best-known department stores sponsored the play, tracing the Klan version of Reconstruction: outrages perpetrated by "negro officers" and "low class" whites, followed by the "awakening" of the South, all thanks to the gallant and patriotic Klan.

Buster was ten years old at the time and didn't go to the show. But he read about the opening-night crowd of twelve hundred in the afternoon newspapers he delivered. He recalled an open-air Ford passing down the hilly blue-collar street where he lived with his divorced mother and spinster schoolteacher aunt. It was chock-full of Klansmen, wearing white robes and hoods.

"My mother admired the KKK, not for its racial stance but for how they protected women. If a man was known to be cheating on his wife, the Klan would go to him and persuade him to stop," recalled Buster, who said he knew not a single black person growing up. "A lot of the best people in Roanoke were in the Klan."

It did not surprise him to discover, after being promoted to *Roanoke Times* reporter at the age of nineteen, following stints as a paperboy, mailroom hand, and switchboard operator, that the print establishment treated blacks as subhumans, covering only their crimes or, on rare occasion, their church- or library-related events.

The paper ran a syndicated comic strip called *Hambone's Meditations,* featuring a character in blackface who said things like "I ain' stud'in' 'bout borryin' trouble — dey's 'nough uv it come to me FREE!"

"When I started on the paper, if a black was in the news, you had to put 'comma, colored' after his name," Buster said.

During Prohibition, Spiller was as adamantly opposed to bootleggers as he was to blacks, though he was careful not to look too hard for them, knowing full well that everyone from judges to church deacons made their own beer and wine. Advertisements for hip flasks were a routine sight in the *Roanoke Times.*

The nip joints in Jordan's Alley were in full swing, and in a spectacular moonshine-conspiracy trial that took place in the 1930s, a clearer picture of illegal '20s drinking would soon emerge: Franklin County alone had turned 17,000 *tons* of sugar into moonshine in one three-year period, and everyone seemed to be in on the action, from sheriff's deputies to a state Prohibition officer to a twelve-year-old boy who ran whiskey regularly from Franklin County to Roanoke.

"Few had scruples about violating the unpopular law," wrote the Roanoke historian Clare White. "A whole generation came to adulthood in an atmosphere of permissive law-breaking never before seen."

Spiller tended to focus his laser beam of justice elsewhere, waging a campaign to eliminate gambling devices of all kinds and in particular slot machines. Roanokers were "gambling away money needed for pork chops, bacon, and beans," he argued.

While the *Roanoke Times* ignored the things Spiller turned a blind eye to, it paid special attention to the crimes being committed by blacks, such as in these typical "Police Court Notes" items: "Eight colored men, charged with gambling, were dismissed. They said you couldn't get fifteen cents out of the crowd. Their defense, in addition to that: 'Jest in dah talkin' about de good games we used to have 'en how close times is now 'en how hard money is to git.'"

It was OK for judges and clergymen to have a little home brew going in their basement or moonshine in their hip flasks. But when Novelle Smith attempted to cross the county line from Franklin to Roanoke, a patrolman, shocked that a black woman could have the resources to own her own vehicle, pulled her over, searched her car, and found whiskey stashed in the trunk.

"She offered him $100 to let her go...but he refused, bringing her to headquarters," the court reporter wrote.

"I think I would have let her go," the judge quipped, and the courtroom erupted in laughter.

But it was only a joke, as he then abruptly pronounced "Fifty and thirty" for Novelle Smith, meaning a $50 fine and thirty days in jail.

The Muse family had been on the radar of city police since Cabell's arrest in 1920 for reckless driving, a charge he appealed but ultimately lost, incurring a $5 fine. In 1923, the same year a wire-service reporter described Willie and George as shedding all their hair on their heads every six months, their younger, albino brother, Harrison, was arrested for felonious malicious assault. His victim was a laborer named A. W. Wade, whom police said Harrison had "feloniously and maliciously cut, stabbed, stricken, beaten, held, wounded, bruised, and ill-treated" with the intent of disfiguring and killing him.

An all-white jury sentenced the twenty-one-year-old Harrison, who had recently married but was still living in his parents' two-room shanty, to five years in prison. Harrison appealed the ruling. He claimed he was at home—nowhere near the scene of the attack—and that, besides, it was too dark that night for Wade to have reliably identified him as the attacker. But the judge overruled his motion to appeal. (One wonders whether Harrison, legally blind from albinism, would have been able to see his purported victim.)

With one son in prison and two others missing, it must have been a relief for Harriett Muse to have her lone daughter, Annie Belle, living around the corner from her with her husband, Walter Herbert Saunders, who delivered coal and eventually worked his way into a coal-yard management job. Most of the extended family attended church at the tiny Mount Sinai Holiness, where Annie Belle sometimes preached as a lay minister. In the photo Nancy Saunders displays of them in her living room, her grandparents are dressed in Sunday finery. Herbert has his arm around Annie Belle, who wears a white dress with silver buttons down the front and a matching thick-brimmed hat.

No such family memento exists for Cabell Muse, who, early in the marriage, became known throughout the neighborhood as a philanderer, a gambler, and a bully—the kind of man Oscar Micheaux might have featured in one of his films.

When I asked Nancy and her cousin Louise whether Cabell abused Harriett's children, Nancy gave a resolute no. She would not have tolerated it.

Louise agreed and made a reference to the woman whose fiancé (now husband), an NFL star, was arrested for assaulting her in an elevator in 2014: "She would've beat the bricks off him. Harriett would've shown Ray Rice's wife what to do with him!"

"Don't you know this by now, Scoop?" Nancy said to me, her eyebrows arched into an angle, like shark fins. "The women in our family have always been strong, backboned people."

But what options did a black maid, even a strong, backboned person, in a racist southern city have for finding her missing sons beyond simply working and keeping her ear to the ground?

Harriett hustleth and she waiteth, and finally, in the fall of 1927, she heard some potentially promising news.

The circus was coming to town.

PART THREE

The Prodigal Sons

The idea, when it first came to her, was so bold it was practically suicidal. She could have been arrested. She could
have been killed.

Harriett Muse could not have read the advance press Dexter
Fellows had spoon-fed and finagled *Roanoke Times* reporters
into writing in October 1927. THE WORLD'S LARGEST CIRCUS IS
HERE, the newspaper trumpeted in a preview story about the
upcoming spectacle of four locomotives, one hundred railcars,
sixteen hundred people, five rings, six stages, and the circus's
most famous star of the moment, a special-guest albino elephant from Burma.

It was the first time the combined RB&BB shows had ever
played Roanoke, and Ringling's advance team had been busy
placing newspaper ads in the weeks leading up to the performance. The billing crew plastered handbills for the two shows
all over the city ahead of time, and the adjusters secured the
usual permits. The Big One had just recently grown from a
four-ring to a five-ring affair.

At the Roanoke Fairgrounds, there was no WHITES ONLY sign
posted. But this was the same venue where the KKK rallied,
and blacks across the South already knew they could not just
wander the show grounds at will. In Louisiana, for instance,

officials had gone to the trouble of mandating racially separate ticket booths and entrances and exits, down to the declaration that black and white accommodations had to be twenty-five feet apart.

While carnivals performing weeklong stays typically set aside a midweek day as Colored Day or Black Achievement Day, circuses that played just one day afforded no such access. Blacks arriving at a one-day event such as the 1927 Roanoke show would have had to view the big-top performance from a restricted area in the back of the tent—the back-end blues, as show people called it.

By the fall of 1927, the Ringling caravan was finishing up its late-season swing through the southern states, having already looped through Texas, Louisiana, Arkansas, and Tennessee. Taylor Gordon, John Ringling's longtime chauffeur, had described what it was like for black circus workers from the North to journey through the land of Jim Crow: the shock of seeing signs out his Pullman car window that read NIGGERS AND DOGS NOT ALLOWED and of learning to introduce himself to white southerners as "Mr. Ringling's niggah" to stave off criticism and attacks.

Gordon was wisely defensive. In 1920, a lynch mob had gathered outside a circus tent in Duluth, Minnesota, declaring that three black workers for the John Robinson Circus had raped a white girl. Though the young woman's doctors found no physical evidence of the rape, the mob hanged the men anyway in one of the most notorious events in American circus history.

And yet consider: even those heinous events had not been held in locales where the city's chief prosecutor was the founder of the largest Klan organization in the state.

Indeed, the biggest threat of danger on this day was not to any circus employee. And it had nothing to do with the usual unpredictability of Circus Day, that rare moment when country and city life converged; when preachers got to see the wonders of God's animal creations but also rubbed elbows with some of the drunkest, meanest people in town; when middle-class farmers and townsfolk were put within eyeshot of "educational" but naughty "hoochie coochie" strip shows — aka the cooch show.

No, the gravest danger that day was to Harriett Muse, who'd made her way from her clapboard shack on Ten-and-a-Half Street through the downtown and to the fairgrounds in suburban south Roanoke late that afternoon, probably by streetcar.

For decades, Roanokers would speculate about how she learned her long-lost sons were playing that day in that circus. Maybe a neighbor had seen them performing earlier in the day and sent word. Maybe one of the families Harriett did laundry for casually mentioned noticing one of the posters plastered all over town. Maybe one of her other children, now grown, heard it through the Jordan's Alley grapevine.

Her granddaughter Dorothy (Nancy's mother, Dot) had been born to Annie Belle and Herbert Saunders on October 4, just ten days before. That little girl would grow up hearing a lot about Harriett's brave actions that day. Discussed at every family reunion and every Sunday potluck, the story would become the Muses' single most vivid piece of lore, passed down like tales of a grandfather's war heroics, or a cousin's brief brush with notoriety, or the meeting of the immigrant great-grandparents when the man saves the pretty lady from stepping on a snake.

After all those years of searching and worrying, Harriett

woke up the morning of October 14 with an absolute certainty of where she should go.

Her husband would be of no help to her; that was nothing new. The last thing he thought they needed now was more mouths to feed.

Harriett was entirely alone.

But she was convinced. And she was unflinching.

"It came to her as she was sleeping," Dot told me in a 2001 interview.

"She saw it all in a dream: 'Go to the circus.'"

The New York Yankees had just won the World Series, slaughtering Pittsburgh in four straight games. Babe Ruth had just come off his record-setting season of sixty homers, and Lou Gehrig had led the charge. Aviator Charles Lindbergh was touring the nation in the *Spirit of St. Louis,* the single-seat monoplane he'd flown from New York to Paris a few months before. The first nonstop transatlantic flight, his feat was another in a long string of firsts for Americans in the 1920s. From modernized plumbing and electricity to movie theaters, cosmetics, bobbed haircuts, and radio—so much about the Roaring Twenties was brand-new. "You Need Never Change Your Oil If You Own a Buick," boasted an ad for the Watson Motor Company, a Roanoke dealership that offered coupes for $1,195.

The city had just celebrated the opening of its first bowling alley to welcome women bowlers—as long as they were white. The local police court was full of the usual drunk-in-public arrests and Prohibition still busts. In the past fourteen months alone, two policemen and two Prohibition agents had been shot and killed during liquor raids.

Ben-Hur, "the mightiest of all epic spectacular romances," was playing at the Jefferson Theatre downtown for fifty cents. Street photographer and Roanoke studio owner George Davis had been busy documenting the installation of new underground water lines and taking other snapshots of life in the growing city, stopping only to shoot breaking news for the newspaper—such as when a downtown furniture store caught fire, or the local Klan gathered.

A thin man with penetrating eyes, Davis had long had his antennae dialed in to local happenings. When news broke, he sped off toward it after hoisting his massive, 111-pound Eastman camera, with eight-by-ten-inch glass-plate negatives, in the rumble seat of a friend's borrowed car. He preferred photographing places to photographing people, though he wasn't opposed to marrying the two when something visually interesting occurred.

Among the images that particularly fascinated him were portraits of African Americans he'd either collected or shot himself: a domestic worker sitting atop her back-porch stoop, eyes sorrowful and hands wrinkled and worn; four men hanging lifeless by their necks from a tree somewhere in southwest Virginia, a group of white men sneering at them below—in the middle of the day.

Though I found no photos of the 1926 Klan parade, Davis did use large-format film to document the 1931 statewide KKK convention in Roanoke in similarly exquisite detail. CHARTER NO. 6 WOMEN OF KKK, ROANOKE, VA. read banners held by rows of young white women, clad in cheerful white uniform-style dresses, with white stockings and black Mary Janes. The one deemed prettiest got to stand at the front of the picture. SECURITY GUARDS ON HAND — BRING YOUR PASTOR AND THE

ENTIRE FAMILY one poster for the event read, and another said ABSOLUTELY NO PROFANE LANGUAGE OR DRINKING BY ANYONE ON OR OFF STAGE.

The KKK queen, with her pious half-smile, sports a black satin sash with a single word splashed across the front of her white tea-length dress: JUSTICE. Confidence-exuding smiles are on every face. "More than likely those are daughters of some of the most prominent families in Roanoke," Buster Carico had described it, remembering the Klan events.

Their body language conveys triumph and a wholesome righteousness that is hard to fathom some eighty years removed. But here it is, another glimpse of stop-time morality, preserved in crisp black-and-white.

When the circus came to town that bright fall day, George Davis had no idea that his 111-pound camera would soon turn its lens on Harriett Muse.

Roanokers had already been treated to the Dexter Fellows full-court press. The October 14 show would spotlight Ringling's "biggest, newest, and most amazing features of all time gathered from every country in the world," the newspaper boasted. Aside from Pawah, the Burmese elephant, the headliners were the soon-to-marry aerialist couple Lillian Leitzel and Alfredo Codona, dangling from wires, rings, and swinging trapezes. The sideshow wasn't mentioned in the ads, as was custom, but an advance story in the *Roanoke Times* did herald the collection of "all strange oddities combined in one sideshow, continuous from morning till night."

Among the lot lice, buzz had been building all week for the Friday shows. The paper advised readers to borrow alarm clocks so they could join the throngs at dawn, when the trains would steam into the rail yard. The night before, rousties had folded the tents up in Bristol, Tennessee. After Roanoke, the performers had just one more week of stops in Virginia and North Carolina; then the troupe would call it quits for the season, having traversed 13,618 miles of train track that year.

Thirteen years. That's how long it had been since Harriett had last laid eyes on her sons. As far as she knew, they were still being billed as the "missing link" between man and monkey, with references to African jungles and simian features in their names and banner drawings. Things had changed a lot, though, since George and Willie left home in 1914 and especially since they joined Ringling in 1922.

Their hair, for one thing. Their show names, for another. Not to mention their hometowns, home states, home countries — and even their planets.

A page-one publicity stunt trumped up by Fellows in 1925 had made them the stars of a hairdressers' convention. Seated in the front row of a Hotel Astor ballroom in New York, they were no longer from Ethiopia or Ecuador. This time, the story went, they were found floating off Madagascar by John Ringling himself!

They'd gone incognito to the hairdressers' convention, their dreadlocks tucked into roomy, newsboy-style caps. "As the convention president rapped his gavel to start the day's proceedings, Eko and Iko removed their hats and allowed their monstrous hair to be photographed against a background of groomed stylists," Ringling stage manager Fred Bradna recalled.

One hairdresser complained about the circus interrupting his convention with a practical joke, but he was soon placated when Fellows later pointed out that some fifty newspapers not only printed pictures from the event, they also named the hair-stylists' association.

The brothers fit announcer Lew Graham's qualifications for a successful freak act to a tee: They were unique. They were good musicians. And, dressed in finery with red sashes and tuxedos— the outfit topped off by that explosive, anachronistic hair—they were far more interesting than they were grotesque.

It's hard to imagine people today being shocked by the sight of dreads, so common today on Bob Marley T-shirts, hipster bohemians, and even the occasional middle-aged white lady.

But during a time when it was rebellious for women, black or white, to bob their hair, few people had adopted, or even wit-nessed, a hairstyle born in ancient Egypt and popular among pre-Columbian Aztec priests, Islamic Sufis, and Masai warriors.

In later years, Whoopi Goldberg would have no problem finding a New York salon to care for her do, but Clyde Ingalls and Candy Shelton surely had to scramble to find a dreads-savvy hairdresser. (While I spotted pictures of "colored barbershop" tents in the Ringling archives at the Circus World Museum, I found no record of anyone styling the Muse brothers' hair.) It's possible they picked up some tips from Clicko, whose manager soaked his much-shorter dreadlocks in flat stout ale.

The strangeness of the brothers' skin color was now sur-passed by the strangeness of their hair. And Shelton took full advantage. During a stop in Cleveland around that period, a *Plain Dealer* writer described them wearing "an enormous cap filled with the long wooly hair which makes them different from the rest of us, hence objects of curiosity."

A writer in Fairfield, Iowa, added: "The boys are as vain of it as a woman of her hair, and shampoo it every second day."

And: "They let you pull it to see that it won't come off."

Patrons could have their picture made with the brothers, but it would set them back the equivalent of almost thirty dollars in today's currency—payable to Shelton, of course.

Over the previous thirteen years, the press coverage of the brothers from Truevine featured a multitude of origin stories, but the planetary story was perhaps more fantastic than them all:

In 1923, they'd been spotted climbing out of a hole near the remains of their spaceship, wrecked in the Mojave Desert.

They were the first interplanetary freaks, now hailed as Eko and Iko, Ambassadors from Mars.

"Actually they were amiable lads, particularly Eko [usually George], who loved all animals, wanted to become an equestrian [like Bradna], and when he was not performing could be found behind a menagerie wagon gazing fondly at the lead stock," Bradna wrote.

The New Yorker magazine agreed, noting in a "Talk of the Town" column that George seemed to be "a shade brighter" than Willie, who looked to his brother for "conversational guidance": "If you said 'Hello,' the bright one would reply: 'How do,' and the other would immediately pipe up, 'How do.' If George said he was feeling fine, Willie would thereupon furnish the same report."

The writer claimed that scientists had pronounced them both "subnormal." But he also asserted that the brothers "shed their hair from time to time, as a chicken moults."

Could they carry on an intelligent conversation? One elderly Roanoker who met them as a child remembered that Willie had the habit of parroting whatever his older brother said.

When I asked Nancy that same question, she bristled. "Don't make my uncle Willie out like he was some kinda damn fool!"

As young men around the age of thirty in 1927, the brothers could have been hampered in terms of sentence construction—because they'd been denied education and cloistered in the sideshow, a distant relative explained. More likely, they were just playing a role.

It's clear the capacity for learning was there, as the brothers were later described as more vocal and more articulate. In late life, doctors said they conversed easily and possessed a quick wit.

Attorneys who interviewed an elderly Willie Muse told me he was "in no way incapacitated mentally or in any way incompetent in his thinking." One of the lawyers, John Molumphy, had happened to interview Willie in mid-December, "and I remember thinking, 'He's got a better handle on his Christmas shopping list than I do at this point.'"

As their humanity began to be recognized, in the circus back lot as well as in the press, their personalities began, slowly, to emerge.

For now, though, as far as their media representation, they were cartoon characters, and always the butt of the joke.

Fellows was so adept at corralling the media, feeding the *New York Times* such headlines as EKO AND IKO PLAY VIOLA AND GUITAR AND THE ANIMALS JUST CURL UP, that another *New Yorker* writer predicted it would be impossible, looking back, to know the truth of what really went on under the sideshow tent and in the circus backyard, the behind-the-scenes zone that was a walled-off city unto itself: "Mr. Fellows's stories are taken for granted and treated by the rewrite men with almost unfailing good humor, but what are historians a hundred years hence going to think of us when, along about the end of March in each year's carefully preserved files, these startling sidelights on metropolitan life in the early thirties begin to show up? We hope that Mr. Fellows is still alive at that time to explain proudly."

Amid all the trumped-up press accounts, all the racist faux dialect, and all the "comma, coloreds" that made up the media coverage of the Muse family saga, that observation is one of the very few thoughtful, and accurate, statements I've encountered.

Though Harriett had no idea where her boys were, most people in New York paying any attention to the comings and goings of the circus would have. Eko and Iko were often among the top tier of sideshow headline grabbers, especially during Ringling's annual four-to-six-week indoor opening-season engagement at Madison Square Garden, in which John Ringling was a major shareholder. As eighty-four-year-old Zip lay near death at Bellevue Hospital in the spring of 1926, reporters poured on the love, hyping the various ways in which his fellow freaks were grieving: Clicko allegedly stopped doing somersaults, for instance, and the Texas giant was mooning in a corner. "Even the Ambassadors from Mars, who don't say much as a rule but look at the monkeys and at Big Bill the rhinoceros, are standing in front of his seat in the basement of the new Madison Square Garden, scratching their yellow matted heads and mumbling in low tones."

One thing the elbow nudging between Fellows and the press undoubtedly demonstrated was just how famous the brothers from Truevine had become. Their strange, singsongy names had entered the mainstream vernacular everywhere Ringling

played—especially New York. As early as 1922, the REO
Speed Wagon that ferried Ringling sideshow performers
between their dressing rooms and performance tents was a
jalopy that resembled an old milk truck, with six letters painted
on the side: EKO & IKO.

Perhaps the best indicator of their fame came in an unre-
lated *New York Times* book review of a new work by Gertrude
Stein. The reviewer hated the book in particular, hated Stein's
repetitive modernist style in general, and, in a harsh bit of trash
talking, likened Stein fans to "people who have paid good
money, gold or boloney, to be amused by the gift of tongues,
whether exemplified by Miss Stein talking nonsense, Eko and
Iko muttering gibberish, or Habu, the man with the iron
tongue, lifting three-hundred-pound weights from the sideshow floor."

They were objects of ridicule, yes. But they were also bona
fide characters, as exaggerated and outsized as the banners fas-
tened to their sideshow tent. With their silk sashes and
faux-official medals, the Ambassadors from Mars had been
gawked at by millions of people from Hawaii to the Hudson
Valley of New York.

But not by their mother.

Not yet.

Seeing how they were held up as amiable lads in one account
and ridiculed as slow-witted mutterers in the next, I wondered
how much control Candy Shelton still exerted over their public
image and in their daily life in 1927. Divorced by 1926, he'd
spent that Christmas with the brothers, according to an eerie
photograph recently found by the curator of the Tibbals collection at the Ringling Museum of Art in Sarasota. (The picture

was attached to belongings associated with Candy's first wife, Cora, also known as Frankie. She's the one who mockingly dressed up as a Muse brother for the 1924 Halloween costume party.)

Wearing long one-piece bathing suits and standing thigh deep in a Florida lake, the Muse brothers lean on each other for support. They appear to be in a water amusement park— one that's strangely barren but for them and the two men flanking them, as if they'd all jumped the fence and snuck into the empty park for Christmas. One of the men sits on the high end of a teeter-totter while the other—the pudgy Candy—holds the seesaw firmly in place with his foot underwater.

"Eko and Iko on Xmas day, taking their annual bath," someone, presumably Frankie, scribbled on the back of the picture.

It was the thirteenth Christmas in which Harriett had not seen, or heard from, her sons.

The following spring, in its coverage of Ringling's 1927 opening day, the *New York Times* made note of a new performer in the sideshow, a bearded lady hired after her predecessor's beard had deliberately been singed by the fire-eater. Or so the story went.

The sabotage was sheer luck for Madame Adrienne, the new bearded lady, and a sign, the reporter wrote (apropos of nothing at all), that "Eko and Iko knew their home planet was in the ascendency."

The past year, in fact, had brought with it a lot of change to the circus, including three deaths that would portend the end of an era for the Ringling sideshow: Zip, the dean of freaks; Krao Farini, a Laotian-born bearded lady who was also much beloved (she'd asked to be cremated so no spectators could view her body after her death); and the December 1926 demise of Charles Ringling, the best-loved brother and known as Mr. Charlie by all, including the rousties. It was Charles who'd managed daily circus affairs while John began chasing riches in Oklahoma oil fields and Florida real estate.

But George and Willie were about to see how, when your home planet's in ascendency, as the astrological theory goes, you have greater power and influence over others.

The line was a throwaway gag for the reporter—and no doubt dictated by the Minister Plenipotentiary himself. But the joke would backfire on the Greatest Show on Earth.

George and Willie can't read the WELCOME TO ROANOKE sign as their train car rolls through the mountains east from Bristol, past the crimson fall foliage and into the booming city, where civic leaders had fretted that Roanoke wasn't big enough yet to host a spectacle of Ringling's size. They probably recognize the topography of their childhood, though, as the sun rises and the train chugs through the red-clay hills where the Alleghenies meet the Blue Ridge. Past Poor Mountain, past Twelve O'Clock Knob, then past Fort Lewis until, finally, the train cars come to a creaky halt in Roanoke, where Mill Mountain stands sentinel over the town.

The four-engine, five-ring behemoth arrives in Roanoke at 9:00 a.m. The tents and banners are hoisted, the animals disembark. Walking into the fairgrounds late that morning, George and Willie are as surprised as anybody to run into a familiar face.

It's Leslie Craft Crawford, their neighbor from New Castle. They haven't seen her since childhood, not since they played together in Craigs Creek. But they recognize her immediately, exclaiming "Miss Leslie!" together and waving their arms.

Surely it occurs to them how close they are to home: if Miss Leslie's here, then maybe their mother is also nearby—if she's alive.

The brothers take their place on the sideshow stage, and when it's time to introduce themselves and play the mandolin and guitar, they squint hard, their eyes scanning the standing, milling crowd. (As is typical with Ringling and other large circuses, there are no chairs inside the sideshow tent, making it the rare place in the circus where segregation codes often break down.)

Their vision has dimmed considerably in recent years, but if they squint just right, they can make out the faces near the front. They sing their favorite song as they strum:

It's a long way to Tipperary,
It's a long way to go.

Outside the tent, Harriett probably spies her sons' banner picture first, though it's doubtful she recognizes them from it. Their cartoon likeness is displayed near Clyde Ingalls's platform. The banner takes up prominent real estate, just to the right of the sideshow entrance—with a giant sign announcing continuous performances and topped by waving American flags.

ARE THEY AMBASSADORS FROM MARS? it says at the top, just to the left of the banner for Jolly Irene (real name: Amanda Siebert), who at 620 pounds likely suffers from an untreated thyroid disorder.

Harriett Muse is not your typical mark, or rube. She finds her place near the back of the crowd as the inside lecturer wanders from one performer to the next, giving his spiel.

As the crowd follows him, she nudges her way toward the front.

George and Willie are halfway through "Tipperary" when their mother's face comes hazily into focus.

There are worry lines on her forehead, a deep crease between her brown piercing eyes.

She's wearing a hand-sewn black dress, its collar cinched by a safety pin, a belt circled loosely around her waist. Her dress is so long that it almost touches the tops of her creased, laceless shoes.

Georgie spots her first and stops playing the moment he does. He elbows his brother, in a scene the family would recount often, with pride, over the years.

They tell the story so often that each member recites it consistently and verbatim, down to the stilted, old-fashioned vernacular the brothers often used.

"There's our dear old mother," Georgie says. "Look, Willie, she is *not dead*."

The crowd is puzzled when the brothers drop their personas, along with their instruments, and rush from the stage.

They greet their mother, folding themselves into her tall, sturdy frame.

Ingalls is so flabbergasted that he can only resort to his fallback cry for his bandleader, P. G. Lowery, "Bally, P.G.!"

He who hustleth while he waiteth, Lowery is no doubt thinking as he stifles a grin, then strikes up his band.

But all the Dixieland jazz on the planet will not cloud this astonishing reunion, this almost-surreal instant in time.

The memory of this moment will outlive everyone inside the

tent. It will surface and resurface. It will be repeated so often and for so long that one day people will just assume it's a myth.

Their mama went down there and got them…
It had come to her, you see, in a dream…
Don't wander off from me at the fair, now, or you'll be
*   kidnapped, too.*

Before the Dixieland is over, Candy Shelton appears. *Who is this woman, and why is she disrupting my show?*

Harriett stands firm, clutching her sons. It's dawning on her that he's the man in charge, the man responsible for the trafficking of her sons.

For the thirteen years of family holidays, birthdays, and weddings that have passed without word of their health or whereabouts.

She will not leave the fairgrounds, she insists, unless George and Willie accompany her home.

But they are Shelton's children, he has the nerve to insist. They are his property. He even has documents, somewhere, paperwork proving that they have the same last name!

A scrum of Ringling executives arrives to try to shore up Shelton's claim, men in dark suits and fedoras—the people George and Willie call City Hall.

The police are on their way, too.

The Ringlings are powerful people, they remind the maid. They're multimillionaires who have the ear of presidents, their own railway lines, and mansions in several states.

Still, standing amid the sawdust in her dusty oxfords, Harriett refuses to budge.

In an act of extraordinary defiance, a stance that could have easily landed her in jail, she does not move when eight Roanoke police officers converge on the lingering, growing crowd, everybody eagerly listening and watching for her next move.

"They are my children!" she says.

And, pointing out the obvious: "Can't no white man birth two colored children."

So what happened?

According to newspaper accounts, Harriett tells the officers that years ago, she had contracted for George and Willie to travel with a carnival operator named Stokes, who was passing through the area. Conflicting news articles have her meeting the original carnival operators in Roanoke, Covington, and Clifton Forge. (One account even placed the transaction in an unnamed Tennessee city.)

But after a few months had passed, someone who she now believes is Shelton — *this man* — lured them away from Stokes, then refused, for thirteen years, to bring them back.

During their entire absence, George and Willie have told their mother, Shelton lied and told them she was dead.

Harriett had called on social service organizations to help her find them, she explains to police, and she'd been searching for them in crowds ever since. She even took out a notice in *Billboard*.

With nightfall approaching, the day's performances over, the candy butchers, troupers, and rousties begin folding up the show, preparing to depart for Lynchburg, the next stop.

But the drama is still unfolding. Shelton and the executives insist the Muse brothers join them as they prepare to take the gilly back to the train station.

Reluctantly, George and Willie say they'll get back on the train. "But only for a moment," the paper explains, awkwardly attempting to convey Harriett's dialect without directly attributing it:

"For anxious and beseeching words from the lips of their 'old mammy who yo all aint seen for all dese years' turned their thoughts.

"No, they would not go."

It wasn't a likely outcome, but by the end of the verbal tug-of-war, the police tell Shelton the Muses are free to leave with their mother if that is their wish. It was a shocking turn of fortune, given the widespread record of police abuse and unfair treatment of blacks by the courts in 1927. (That year, blacks were incarcerated at a rate three times higher than whites; by 2010, the rate differential had doubled. According to recent Bureau of Justice Statistics, one in three black men can expect to be incarcerated in their lifetime.)

But Harriett relayed her side of the story firmly and convincingly to police. "Off they went with their mother while beneath the big top disturbed showmen tore their hair and appealed to the law," a reporter recounts.

"The law was helpless. Eko and Iko are certainly privileged to go where they choose, the law averred." The brouhaha is presumably not big enough to draw Prosecutor Kent Spiller's attention, for at no point is he recorded as weighing in on the legal back-and-forth.

And so the Big One pulls away from Roanoke without its Martian ambassadors.

And so George and Willie, finally, are home.

Across town that night, George Davis prepares to lug out his monster camera. He imagines he just might nail the photograph of his career.

On Ten-and-a-Half Street, the Muse family reassembles, finally, in Harriett's humble abode. Word has spread throughout Jordan's Alley about her bold move, and the neighbors converge to greet the long-lost relatives—to see the showstopping spectacles for themselves.

The brothers oblige, pulling out their instruments and playing a few songs on the front porch.

"They had been gone since childhood," ninety-eight-year-old A. L. Holland recalled of the reunion. For years, he remembers, people talked about that magical, mysterious night. "It was like the prodigal sons coming home."

It's well past dark by the time the tired maid from Truevine rests her head for the night, with nary a rainbow in sight.

But Harriett pauses to thank God, finally, for delivering her sons from the storm.

The quarters are cramped in Jordan's Alley, the shotgun shacks crammed three and four to a lot—so close you can hear neighbors sneezing and shouting and doing all manner of Lord-knows-what. For the first time in recent memory, the brothers prepare to rest their heads not on a creaking train-car bed but on solid earth. The trains in the rail yard couple, and people couple, and soon the surprising cacophony of everyday life in Jordan's Alley gives way to the smell of something even more surprising—and delicious—coming from the oven. Ash cakes.

After all those years, they can't quite believe they're in a house with their dear mother, who after so many years is baking her humble bread.

10

Not One Single, Solitary, Red Penny

By the time Baby Dot's daddy came home from work that night, there were so many people crowding the Ten-and-a-Half Street porches and front yards that the very sight of it made Herbert Saunders's stomach sink. The neighbors were all out front, spilling onto the alleyway and dirt road.

There were strangers, too, a rare mix of black and white people who had converged from all quadrants of the city, drawn as if by some mystical, magnetic force.

So many people stood milling around the front of the clapboard shacks that Herbert's mind went to the worst-possible scenario: he thought Baby Dot had died.

But the beautiful two-week-old baby hadn't registered in visitors' minds. Martian brothers who'd become stars of the Ringling sideshow were now staying in this working-class enclave? For the next several days, everyone in town wanted a look.

They came by streetcar. They came by automobile and on foot.

Harriett's reunion with her sons had been "told of in the newspapers, others talking of it, all the while humming happy mammy songs," the *Roanoke Times* reported in its usual racist language. "And the chapter of difficulties was opened."

Twenty-four hours. That's how long it took before Cabell

thought to put out a tin cup for the "throng of curious" traipsing through the family's front yard. If all those white men had profited from exhibiting Willie and George, why shouldn't he?

By Sunday, the news was all over town. More than a hundred people had elbowed their way through the family's tiny house. The admission price was "a free will offering, tenderly taken at the door," a *Roanoke Times* reporter noted. "Eko and Iko sit with the two tin cups, grunting mystic words to the sweet accompaniment of falling dimes and quarters."

Candy Shelton found his way to Jordan's Alley, too. He offered Harriett Muse $100—a pretty pile of cash for the time, worth about $1,400 today—and the promise that he'd wire home $20 a month to her if she allowed her sons to return to the circus, which was due to perform in Richmond the next day. He pointed out the obvious—that the circus had more resources to keep the brothers fed, housed, and clothed than their parents could ever dream of having.

As the *Roanoke Times* described it, "To avoid any disturbance, detectives were called in to take a hand in the matter. The officers, however, could not settle the misunderstanding and departed."

The paper continued in its characteristic mocking tone: "Still the woman refuses. No doubt her resolve is strengthened by the sound of falling dimes."

The brothers would not return to Shelton and the circus, and despite "persistent efforts [that] failed to get them from the house, there was talk of resorting to legal channels for settlement of the affair, which causes the loss of two performers."

Harriett sent Shelton and his cronies away.

With Ringling now threatening to sue, Harriett would have to formulate a legal strategy of her own.

*   *   *

As the popularity of movies, radio, and professional baseball surged, the circus was now past its peak. There was increasing talk from some corners that the sideshow would soon be banished. "Nothing now makes anyone wonder or exhibit interest in freaks; the public is merely disgusted," the *Elmira (New York) Advertiser* claimed. The prediction was premature, though, as both the circus and its sideshow stepchild were still capturing the imaginations of rural and small-town Americans. In the 1920s, first-generation factory workers were seeking out paid leisure for the first time in their lives, and few thought to question the exploitation of people with disabilities.

In an era before Social Security disability or workers' compensation, most agreed with managers like Clyde Ingalls, who patted quarter-paying customers on the back as do-gooders for supporting people who might have otherwise had to rely on charity. What other jobs, they argued, could the limbless man or half-lady hold?

"Put yourself in the shoes of some of these poor folks back in time," Al Stencell told me. "Having some show guy come along and take two odd kids off your hands would seem like the right thing to do, for you and for them."

The circus's wave may have crested by the 1920s, but the brothers Ringling were still regarded as captains of industry, pointed out historian Greg Renoff, who has researched traveling amusements in the Jim Crow South. "The Ringlings had this aura of achievement and success; they were men of enterprise, on a par with the Carnegies. They employed thousands of people."

That a black domestic worker had challenged such a formidable white-owned company at the height of Jim Crow was exceptionally unusual. "Blacks could not count on law-enforcement support at the time," Renoff said. "The Klan was now a pseudo-respectable middle-class organization. Blacks couldn't testify in court in some cases.

"There was no reason for [Harriett] to think that anybody in a position of power was going to help her." The possibility of being lynched for confronting Ringling's lawyers and Roanoke's police probably crossed her mind, he said. (Of the 3,959 lynchings that took place in twelve southern states between 1877 and 1950, 83 of the victims were women.)

Why wasn't Harriett *arrested* inside the sideshow tent? Renoff recalled the bravery of the black women who challenged Jim Crow voting laws in North Carolina's small towns by storming their way into election offices in the 1920s, without being arrested or abused. The cult of motherhood in the South — where black maids helped raise most well-off whites — probably shielded Harriett Muse.

She hoped she'd be treated with deference because, back at home, the police chief probably had someone who looked just like Harriett washing his clothes and babysitting his kids.

She might not have held a lot of power, but what she did have she wielded as only a mother could.

Next came the battle with the bureaucrats. City officials turned up at Ten-and-a-Half Street to deliver the news that Harriett and Cabell had no right to convert their house into a theater without the proper permits. They stopped short of pressing charges but told them in no uncertain terms that George and Willie had to stop playing on the porch and drawing crowds.

"It all reverts to one simple question: Who will in the end collect the returns from the viewers of Eko and Iko — the mother or the showmen?" the *Roanoke Times* mused. The brothers had been "purchased" long ago by Barnum and Bailey showmen operating in California who had "keen business acumen," the paper explained, incorrectly citing the name of the circus and omitting the source of that information entirely. They'd been made to work without pay and without their mother's knowledge of their whereabouts — that much, it appeared, was fact.

The reporter fashioned a ballyhoo of his own as he described the scene on the Muse family's front lawn: "Right this way, ladies and gents, we have the original albinos! Seeing is believing. Step up and don't crowd the passageway. We know you want to see them but don't let's crowd!... They've appeared before the crowned heads of Irup, Europe, and Syrup. Ten cents, one dime, see the two albinos!"

Before the crowds quieted, before Harriett sent Candy Shelton packing, before the brothers had made up their minds about their own next steps, George Davis turned up with his gigantic camera.

Davis left no notes about his visit to the Muse family's abode, just a single photograph that went out over the wires, appearing in dozens of cities where Ringling had performed, from Troy, New York, to Pittsburgh to Winnipeg. Taken in the harsh late-afternoon sun, the portrait appears posed behind the house — away from the crowds.

The family stands in front of an unpainted outhouse, with a hole for a window, broken trim boards, and a pile of coal slag strewn on the ground.

The portrait suggests questions more than answers, heartbreak more than joy. Flanked by Harriett and Cabell, George and Willie stand on homemade rag rugs that look to have been hauled out for the occasion. While Harriett and Cabell stare directly into the camera, the brothers avert their eyes, squinting as if in pain and looking at the ground.

George slumps his shoulders forward, frowning. Usually the confident one, this time he looks grumpy, like a child placed in time-out — though it's possible the blazing sun is making him wince.

Maybe it has already dawned on George Muse what a fix the two of them are in: the life they've known for most of their time on earth has just left Roanoke for its next stop. Their stepdad is a brute who seems to have his own moneymaking schemes in mind.

Maybe someone else is standing off camera, coaching them to look miserable in the picture. A gloomy, hangdog expression would emphasize the mistreatment they've experienced at the hands of their circus captors. Maybe that someone else is an ambitious young lawyer hoping to shore up a lawsuit, down to the wrinkled handkerchief in George's hand.

Or maybe they truly are sad, relegated to living in a ramshackle and wholly unfamiliar new place, and a very cramped one at that. The house at 19 Ten-and-a-Half Street is a one-and-a-half-room affair measuring just 517 square feet. Counting a sister-in-law residing there (presumably because their youngest sibling, Harrison, is still away in prison) plus Cabell and Harriett, George and Willie are now living in less space than they had on the circus train.

T. Warren Messick was not surprised when Harriett Muse soon showed up at his downtown Roanoke law office. He'd read about the dustup in the papers. He was a young defense lawyer, just twenty-seven, but already he'd made a splash.

Members of the local bar association noted his ability to get charges dismissed or sentences lightened for defendants with little hope, particularly in the black community.

Squeak was his nickname. In the days before television, Roanokers used to leave their downtown offices to observe his oratorical courtroom antics. To confuse an eyewitness, Messick once had the identical twin brother of an accused client sit next to him at the defense table. He used him to underscore the fact that the witness could not positively pinpoint the accused — not when choosing between him and his twin, anyway.

Spectators were particularly enraptured by Messick's closing arguments, delivered in the lilting accent of a central Virginia gentleman — he'd grown up in Virginia's rolling Shenandoah Valley hills, the son of a farm manager — and punctuated by a rhythmic, repetitious flair. "Usually he would start his presentation with an appropriate story or joke that endeared him to his jury right away," recalled his son, T. Roger Messick, who declared his delivery "smooth as silk."

Messick was such a raconteur that he frequently moved *himself* to tears.

A military-school graduate, Messick spent his downtime grouse hunting in Montana or fishing at his riverside country home. He celebrated the end of every workday by drinking a Scotch at his desk, though not as many as the gossip-prone members of the local bar claimed, said his junior law partner, Harvey Lutins, whose nickname was Little Squeak.

While all the other lawyers in town showed up to court in austere black suits, Messick wore sport jackets. "He looked like he was going out for a party," recalled Lutins, at the time of our interview in his mideighties and still practicing law. (He died in late 2015 at the age of eighty-seven.) "Only Mr. Messick could do that and get away with it."

Later in his career, Messick and his second wife, Jean, lived above his law office, located in a sprawling Victorian home not far from downtown. The office was adorned with plush Oriental rugs, leather chairs, and game animals he'd hunted and had stuffed. He kept an African-American manservant named John on call, along with a live-in maid, Pearl. She regularly fetched drinks for Jean, who favored thick furs, diamonds, and toy-sized dogs. "It was really a circus over there," said Nancy Barbour, whose former husband, Stuart Barbour Jr., was another Messick protégé.

Messick's cases, his attire, his office — he kept it all teetering, barely, on the edge. His entire life was played as if it were all just one squeaker of a game, down to his final breath. (In 1962, Messick mistakenly thought he was dying of stomach cancer. To relieve himself and his family of the expected agony, he committed suicide by shooting himself in the stomach on the banks of the Roanoke River in front of Gray Rocks, his second home.)

Messick got so invested in his cases that he frequently let details he deemed unimportant slip. Lutins remembers showing up for work early in his career to find that the power to their offices had been turned off. His boss had forgotten to pay the bill.

Money didn't motivate him, Lutins said, adding that when Messick learned that one of his own partners had stolen the firm's funds, he testified at the trial — on the embezzler's behalf.

"Blacks thought Mr. Messick could do magic with the law, getting them off a charge or getting them less of a sentence, and sometimes he did," said Buster Carico, the longtime *Roanoke Times* reporter. He remembered a case in which an African-American man arrested for theft was convicted and sentenced to minor jail time. He'd been represented at trial by a court-appointed defense attorney.

"Next time I'm gonna steal enough to hire Lawyer Messick," the man said as he was led away to jail.

Messick adored his maid, Pearl. He trusted her so much that he tasked her with delivering the annual Christmas bonus — cash — to the underlings in his practice. "My wife and I were paupers in the early days, and every Christmas Eve, we'd wait for the knock, and say to each other, 'Is that Pearl at the door?'" recalled Lutins.

But Messick was more pragmatic than political when it came to race. "Mr. Messick was not a civil rights guy. He had no political party affiliation," Lutins said.

Once when examining a black witness on the stand in a rural Bedford County case, Lutins referred to her, politely, as Mrs. Smith. It was the late 1950s, and the judge was so incensed that he called a recess to excoriate Lutins and Messick, who was providing legal backup, as second chair, on the case.

"Mr. Messick, you did not tell your young associate how we examine colored people here in my court," the judge said firmly.

"You're right, Judge," Messick said, deferring to him. "Harvey, we don't call the witness *Mrs. Smith*. We call her *Mary*" — meaning, without deference and using only her first name.

The trial reconvened, and Lutins continued, this time peppering *Mary* with questions.

"That's the way it was, and nobody said nothing about it,"

Lutins said. "Colored folk were not entitled to the dignity. Women weren't permitted to sit on juries. It was a different world back then."

Warren Messick went along and got along. He would try just about anything to get his clients a break.

"He didn't mind the rough-and-tumble cases," Buster Carico said, citing the 1949 murder of a beautiful high school coed and class leader in a prominent Episcopalian church. Messick represented the defendant, an Eagle Scout and choirboy who admitted to police that he'd killed the girl. Pieces of his flesh were found under her fingernails, indicating a fierce struggle, and when he was arrested at school the next day, his face was marred by scratches. The case made national and international headlines, and it was featured in popular detective magazines of the day.

Not only did Messick keep his client out of the electric chair, the murderer would end up serving only a small portion of his ninety-nine-year sentence. During his closing remarks, Messick exhibited his usual flair. He pulled a metal case from the pocket of his sport coat, unfolding it to reveal photographs of his own teenaged children.

Addressing the jury, Messick turned up his upper-crust drawl.

"You are not trying a gang-stah," Messick said, arguing for leniency because the girl had, after all, not been raped. Because the choirboy had completed forty-eight merit badges, went to Sunday School faithfully, and taught swimming at the YMCA.

"You are not trying a mob-stah," he continued.

"You are trying a boy."

After a sixteen-year prison stint, the murderer started a new life in another state and went on to lead a remarkably unremarkable and upstanding life, with T. Warren Messick to thank for it all.

"I sued Ringling once," Messick mentioned to Little Squeak occasionally over the years, in typical understatement.

But Lutins did not recall Messick elaborating on the lawsuit he filed against the circus a few days after it left town in October 1927.

Lutins said he probably accepted the Muse case to build what was then a fledgling practice. "That case had 'sex appeal,' as he would describe it. He took it because he could get a lot of mileage out of it—you know, as long as they spell your name right. That's how you build a new practice: get the neighbors to know your name, and the newspapers to write it down."

Roanokers would soon know the name of T. Warren Messick.

Just three days after Harriett reclaimed her sons, he filed two pleadings for $50,000 each, against both Ringling and Candy Shelton, on behalf of George and Willie Muse.

The legal complaint was pure Messick: furious and fiery, as finely rendered as a Clyde Ingalls ballyhoo. In florid prose, he traced their kidnapping back to Robert Stokes, alleging they'd been lured away from their mother and displayed as freaks in a traveling sideshow "against their will for a period of time, the exact period your petitioner does not know." Though a *Roanoke Times* writer covering the reunion explained that Harriett had first "contracted to let her two tots go with a man by the name of Stokes" in 1914, it's unclear whether Harriett ever used the word *contract* or the name Stokes, and Messick certainly didn't mention her having a monetary agreement with Stokes in his legal brief, insisting only that the boys were "wrongfully taken...without the consent of their parents." (The reporter cited Roanoke police officers, not Harriett, as the source of his information.)

If she or someone else in the family did initially let them leave with a carnival operator, maybe Messick chose to omit that uncomfortable detail. It's also entirely plausible, given the media's treatment of African Americans, that the two written sources for Harriett's alleged culpability—the 1914 *Billboard* notice and the 1927 newspaper reunion stories—were one-sided affairs, entirely dictated by show managers and/or police.

Regardless, the brothers had indeed been wrongfully taken, if not initially by Stokes, then, a few months following their 1914 departure, certainly by Shelton.

The remainder of Messick's timeline has been backed up by numerous written accounts: sometime in 1922, Candy Shelton had sold their services to Ringling Combined Shows, whereupon the brothers were displayed "against their will" and turned into "slaves" for four and a half more years, Messick wrote.

The brothers could not read or write and had not gone to school. "They were carried to all parts of the United States" and made to "exhibit themselves against their will."

They would have "escaped from the said principal defendant, from its clutches, from the clutches of its agents, servants and employees," Messick wrote. "But at all times your petitioner and his brother were carefully guarded and as a further means to prevent their escape and in furtherance of the business of [Ringling], in order to enrich itself, [Ringling] has not paid them one single, solitary, red penny for their services...only board and very little clothing."

* * *

The Associated Press carried the lawsuit story, and so Messick's rhetoric was repeated — *not one single, solitary, red penny* — in dozens of cities and towns where the Ambassadors from Mars had played.

The *Danville (Virginia) Bee* headlined: LURED FROM HOME, KEPT IN SLAVERY.

The *Syracuse Journal:* MOTHER SUES CIRCUS TO GET BACK SONS.

In Harrisonburg, Virginia, where Messick's parents still lived, the *Daily News-Record* added more color to the report, calling the brothers "youngsters" and describing how they'd "longed for their mother and searched the crowds which viewed them daily for her familiar face," while she had enlisted the aid of humane societies and social agencies, to no avail: "They were tired of being considered wild men from the astral world, tired of shocking people by their queer forms and circus makeup, tired of the stares and the squeals of other children, tired of being exhibited without their consent and without the knowledge of their parents."

To the Big One, Messick's opening salvo was nothing more than a single bullet glancing off an elephant's hide. The next day, Ringling's own formidable lawyer fired back in the courts and in the press. The Muse "youngsters" were not at all tots, as Messick had led the public to believe, but "grown men of the age of 35 years." Rather than being stolen, John M. Kelley argued, they were "engaged by us through their manager exactly as we engage all our attractions."

The terms of the contract among Shelton, Ringling, and the Muses were not disclosed, nor could I find a copy of any

1920s-era contracts on file in the Circus World Museum archives or anywhere else, including in the Roanoke and Richmond courthouses. (As for the brothers' ages, they appear to have been closer to thirty in 1927, though no one, including their mother, could pinpoint with certainty when they were born. Official documents created for them later in life, such as draft registration and Social Security cards, say George was born in 1890 and Willie in 1893—their birth years seemed to gravitate further back in time the older they got.)

Bespectacled and with an ever-present cigar in his hand, Kelley was a Baraboo native who'd grown up with the Ringling brothers and represented them and the company from 1905 to 1937. Among his favorite stories was his response to a lawsuit sparked by a 1917 circus parade in Omaha. A runaway horse had destroyed property and injured several bystanders, resulting in a $25,000 claim. An especially damning eyewitness account from a socialite, the wife of an Omaha newspaper editor, had Kelley's case circling the drain. But Kelley had thrown the witness off-guard with a simple question—"How old are you, ma'am?"—that played on the socialite's vanity.

The woman responded exactly as Kelley had hoped.

She fidgeted, swayed, and "blushed in the throes of evident dread."

Kelley used her stammering to discount her entire testimony and won the case.

In the late 1910s and early '20s, Kelley had helped turn John Ringling into a tycoon. He had rushed to the scene of an Oklahoma oil strike, fortuitously located near one of John's newly acquired rail lines. Kelley quickly secured eight thousand acres of oil leases that would bring millions in profits and lead to the creation of Ringling, Oklahoma, a company town named for and laid out by John himself. Kelley had elevated the self-titled circus king to oil baron.

Though eventually their partnership soured, Kelley always exhibited a deep love for Ringling history, founding the Circus World Museum in 1959, long after he retired. He revered Baraboo, unlike John, who had looked down his nose at the hometown folk and called them Baraboobians.

Stepping into an intrafamily money squabble in the wake of Charles Ringling's death, in 1926, Kelley had accused the grand pooh-bah, John—then the remaining original partner and heir—of being lazy, distracted, and moneygrubbing. Six years later, he helped the remaining heirs incorporate the business and orchestrated a power shift from John to Samuel Gumpertz.

With offices in Chicago and, later, Manhattan, Kelley was no one to trifle with, and he was used to frying fish much larger than the ones Warren Messick caught along the river at Gray Rocks. He was a master at combing legal documents, down to the prenuptial agreements he'd insisted John nail down before his second marriage, after Mable died.

Still, Kelley prided himself on knowing the minutest goings-on of the Big One, including its sideshow contracts. A coworker recalled watching him unfold his long, gangly frame from his car, stomp into the circus office, and announce, "Boys, I have a great idea for next year. We will feature a sight denied past generations—a man...from the wilds of Borneo. Adam Forepaugh did it in 1864, and we will do it," too.

"The Ringlings paid their people ten percent less [than other circuses] because they had taken control of the market," said former Circus World Museum archivist Fred Dahlinger, who currently writes and does circus research for the Ringling Museum

of Art in Sarasota. Though Dahlinger knew nothing about the
1927 Muse case, he had strong doubts about the charges Messick
brought against Ringling and found it hard to believe that George
and Willie Muse had ever worked without pay.

"In terms of business practices, they were not fly-by-night;
they were very honorable," Dahlinger said of the company. "And
they would have known if they had talent that was not being
paid" or otherwise held in peonage by their manager, he
insisted. "They were rough people, but they did not welch on
financial obligations."

He did not at all buy the argument that Ringling might have
been just as culpable in exploiting the brothers' labor as Shelton, which is why Messick named them in the suit.

But Dahlinger was so insistent about the fairness of Ringling
business dealings that, since I was unable to find a contract
between the Muses and the circus *or* Shelton and the circus,
he suggested I look toward the contractual obligations written
for Clicko, the Wild Dancing Bushman, the Muse brothers'
sideshow coworker for many years. Franz Taibosh, who actually
did hail from South Africa, suffered at the hands of a brutal
early manager but was rescued by Ringling legal agent, or fixer,
Frank Cook, who found him near starvation and ill clothed in
an unheated Bridgeport, Connecticut, apartment. Taibosh had
been performing in the Barnum and Bailey sideshow, unpaid
and under the care of his harsh manager, Paddy Hepston. He
took his temper out on Taibosh in frequent alcoholic rages and
compensated him only in food, booze, and cigars.

Cook not only rescued Taibosh; he made him welcome to
such an extent that he lived with Cook's family, quite happily,
for the remainder of his career, as related in Neil Parsons's
2010 biography, *Clicko*. And not only that, he even adopted

Taibosh, "and by what political machinations I'll never know—since Taibosh could not read—got him made an American citizen," recalled circus heir Henry Ringling North, in a candid memoir.

Cook had wheel-greased Taibosh's emancipation, Parsons wrote, describing a relationship that was certainly parallel to dealings between the Muse brothers and Candy Shelton—but only to a point. Shelton did not have the clout of Cook, and therefore the brothers never enjoyed the "pet" status that Clicko had among many Ringling managers.

North fondly recalled playing with Taibosh as a kid: "He'd let me pull his kinky hair, which would stretch out a foot or more and, when I let go, snap back like a rubber band. He called my brother 'Johnny' and me 'Bonny' to save the bother of adding an entire new word to his limited vocabulary." When Taibosh learned of his impending American citizenship, he bounded up to young North and shouted, "Bonny, me American citizen now, no more nigger son of a bitch."

The Muses did not enjoy the insider status accorded Taibosh, who was treated like something between a fraternity brother and an eccentric, dementia-addled uncle. "Cook ensured Taibosh had all creature comforts, including those of the flesh; they partied and ate and drank" together, Parsons reported. "As Taibosh's manager, Cook dealt with all money matters. In essence the arrangement was that, in return for Taibosh's summer pay minus pocket money, Cook would provide Taibosh with a winter home." During the circus season, Taibosh slept in the same dormitory Pullman car as the other sideshow performers while Cook traveled separately, in a management car.

Not surprisingly, Parsons wrote, Taibosh's command of

English greatly improved after he became liberated from Hepston, and his lilting South African accent charmed the crowds in the sideshow and in the circus backyard. (His first language was Afrikaans, but Hepston had spent years hiding him away from potential paying audiences and instructing him to grunt and yell when onstage.)

Taibosh was not a fan of George and Willie Muse — "he was rather snooty about them," Parsons told me in an e-mail. But the brothers were well liked both in the press, which considered them good copy, and among the rousties, who recalled them pleasantly strumming guitars and "laughing and singing until the train started to roll" on humid summer nights.

As *The New Yorker* put it in the magazine's lawsuit coverage, the Muses were widely considered "good examples of contented freaks." They loved monkeys and kangaroos, the magazine reported. It also mentioned their appearance at the hairdressers' convention, where their dreadlocks were unveiled in a publicity stunt involving permanent waves. "If the waving machines on exhibition at the convention could wave Ecko's [*sic*] ropy locks, they could wave anything, even a telephone switchboard. But it never happened. The freak remained happily in a corner with a plate of ice cream."

Lawyer Kelley won the first volley in his battle against Messick, who could not squeak past the shortcut he'd taken in hastily writing his initial legal pleading. Like the press, Richmond judge Beverly T. Crump issued no comment at all about the brothers' claims of enslavement. But he agreed with Kelley that Messick had mistakenly labeled the circus a "corporation" when in fact no such entity existed. Despite becoming captains of industry, the Ringlings technically still operated the business as an informal family partnership, just as they had back in the old wagon days of Baraboo. (The circus incorporated several years later, in 1932. Its Baraboo winter quarters had moved to Bridgeport in 1919, and a decade later John Ringling bade the Baraboobians a final good-bye by shifting the operation closer to his mansion in Sarasota.)

There being no corporation to sue, Crump deemed the case quashed.

But Messick left the door open for another suit by persuading the judge to keep the matter under advisement while he took one more stab at it. Meanwhile, he angled quietly for a settlement, presenting it as a way to keep the kidnapping story out of the press and to preserve Ringling's "Sunday School" image.

Not that anyone in the press viewed the charges seriously. In fact, reporters took even greater liberties to embellish Clyde Ingalls's ballyhoo about the brothers by turning the brouhaha into yet another joke.

In Wisconsin, an editorial writer opined that sideshow customers, not the Muses, had suffered the most harm: it was a hard blow to patrons who had paid out their good coin to see authentic citizens from another planet. They felt they had been wickedly imposed on by those slick fellows of the circus.

In Norfolk, Virginia, an editorial writer reframed the story, comparing it to ghostwritten celebrity gossip: as long as the newspaper world can stomach this sort of faking in its own household without nausea, it is in no position to steam up over Ambassadors from Mars.

Nary a reporter wrote a word about how the Muses felt.

Meanwhile, a Kansas journalist reported—correctly—that life in Roanoke amid the drugstore crowds was not exactly brimming with excitement for the famous duo: now they sat around the fireside of the old home "shack" and seemed lonesome for the crowds who used to visit them each day.

In February 1928, Messick pulled out another squeaker—he got the Big One to settle with the Muses. Details of the settlement he brokered with Ringling were not reported in the media, though the Roanoke newspapers insisted it was "a highly satisfactory adjustment of their claim."

Evidence of the case no longer seems to exist in city or state holdings in Roanoke and Richmond beyond Messick's initial brief, Kelley's response, and myriad newspaper accounts. I have personally looked for them, hired a legal researcher to look for them, begged lawyer friends to cajole law librarians and clerks into looking *one more time* on my behalf, and combed accounts by sideshow historians, who have likewise come up dry.

"Efforts to bring an appropriate case against the circus were frustrated," the Canadian historian Jane Nicholas summed up, vaguely, in a 2014 article. She shared my exasperation about the difficulty of trying to envision lives that were seemingly well documented—only never from the subjects' point of view. "There are so many stories missing, especially of [sideshow performers who began as] child performers," she told me. "Young performers weren't seen as children, only as people who brought an economic benefit. They weren't hidden away from the public. They were *there* for the public. So even though the sideshow did provide them with work and a place to be, it was still exploitative."

Missing documents notwithstanding, Nicholas encouraged me to keep digging. If we only wrote the histories of the people who left detailed records, she said, "we would only get to know about the really privileged people. You have to piece together your evidence with empathy and conjecture," using the materials at hand.

At the stately Library of Virginia, where researchers are restricted to laptops and pencils for note taking and where I was asked to lock my belongings away (a routine part of theft prevention), a clerk who spoke in brief, hushed tones hauled out museum-quality storage boxes containing the court case on a large wheeled rack.

There wasn't much to see.

Folded into thirds and wrapped in neat bundles tied in orange lace bows, the trace legal leavings bore no hint of the reality of George and Willie Muse. The boxes contained fewer than ten pages, mostly just the original filing by Messick and Kelley's response.

Messick declined to disclose the amount Ringling ponied up as the brothers' unofficial back pay, nor did he offer his own lawyerly reflection. He hinted that a federal peonage suit might be in the works. We also know he gave a short press conference, with George and Willie on hand, "their long sheep-like hair waving like banners in the breezes that waft through the Federal Building. They talked, and not without a touch of longing, of the old trouping days," the *Roanoke Times* wrote. "The drab narrowness and cramped horizons of Ten-and-a-Half Street fail to touch the spark of their esthetic emotion as the Ringling ballyhoo of the big top once did."

Messick also implied that he and Kelley had come to a new agreement over the Muses' employment. He hinted that the brothers might be willing to return to the circus—but only if they were paid adequately and allowed to visit their family during breaks.

If their salaries were sent home, maybe their mother could get away from the neighborhood's noisy nip joints, its cinder-filled air, the screeching and clanking of all those rail-yard brakes. Maybe, instead of doing other people's laundry, she could just do her own, out of earshot from the loud racist parrots up the street.

Maybe she'd have a space for gardening, which she missed. Maybe she'd buy a respectable piece of property in Pinkard Court, the black suburban enclave on the outskirts of town.

Maybe, George and Willie hoped, Harriett would figure out a way to leave Cabell, who wanted, more than anything, not to buy his wife a home but to score the ultimate status symbol in 1928: a new car. Outside of the black doctors and lawyers in town, he'd be among the first African Americans in the city to own his own set of wheels.

Ringling dispatched Shelton back to Roanoke to further sweeten the deal: if George and Willie returned to the sideshow, he promised, the circus would find roustabout work for their younger brother Tom. He could tour the country now, too, helping erect the big top alongside scores of other, mostly black laborers. Shelton even hoped to land them all a wintertime gig in London with a British-owned circus called Bertram Mills. They could play before King George V!

The *Roanoke Times* pondered their predicament:

"The curtain of the drama has only commenced to rise" on the brothers' next act. "Eko and Iko sit snugly by a fat stove in their Ten-and-a-Half Street abode while the indulgent daddy supplies the fuel."

Given Cabell's behavior in the nip joints and at the back-alley craps matches, the family was surprised he hadn't already absconded with that chauffeur car he drove for work. And though they couldn't stand Candy Shelton, George and Willie had come to realize that the indulgent daddy was maybe even greedier.

That winter, the brothers found themselves engaged in much less glamorous work — playing music in the storefront window of a downtown Roanoke drugstore. Their frowns were even deeper set. A. L. Holland remembers watching them there when he was just ten years old. They were sitting on stools, playing a mandolin and guitar. They spoke very little but played beautifully, Holland said.

Before and after school, Holland worked as a blind man's assistant, leading him around town, helping him sell brooms for seventy-five cents apiece. "Every time he sold a broom, I got a nickel," Holland recalled.

"It had been a very happy time; everybody was glad to see the Muse brothers. The whole town was talking about it." But after a few weeks of it, "they looked real sad to me," he said. He had never before seen hair like theirs, and "as a kid, I was a little bit scared of them."

Holland was not the only one.

"We were afraid to get close to them," another Roanoke native told me in 2001. He recalled George and Willie standing inside the family's front door and waving shyly to passersby.

It was George and Willie's decision to heed Candy Shelton's plea and rejoin the circus in the spring of 1928, with Tom in tow, according to family members. They wanted to help support their mother, especially in light of the way Cabell was burning through the settlement money. They probably also missed the relative freedom of the circus backyard, a familiar place where a person happening upon them was not apt to walk the other way—or call the police about wild savages on the loose.

Maybe they believed their dark-skinned brother, with his normal vision and streetwise ways, could help them navigate a more independent life. Shelton would continue to manage their act, but they would not be so constantly under his thumb. Census records from 1930 show the three brothers living in the multiracial, immigrant-rich Hell's Kitchen section of Manhattan during the off-season, in an apartment building that also housed actors, theater ushers, and factory workers.

Were their fellow sideshow workers glad to see them back under the tent? Unclear. Did managers treat them better now? We'll never know.

Opening-day circus coverage in the *New York Times* noted only that George and Willie hadn't missed a beat during their Roanoke hiatus. The reporter only briefly noted the reunion drama and didn't even mention the lawsuit. In a Fellows-fed story subtitled EKO AND IKO ARE HAPPY, the brothers had been "found by their parents last Winter after they had been missing from home for some ten years," the paper explained.

The story was pure Fellows fodder, a page-three gimmick that mainly focused on Habu, the man with the iron tongue, who supposedly had just suffered two nervous breakdowns because he could not hoist an elephant, or even a baby zebra, with his tongue. He lifted items—a heavy-looking bucket, for instance—via a hook that was placed in his pierced tongue. ("This is actually a gaff," Al Stencell said of Habu's gimmicky hoax. "A U-shaped piece fits around the tongue" and is covered up with a cloth in front of the mouth while the hook is pretend-inserted.)

"Yah," the brothers were quoted as saying of Habu, as if in unison. "He's gloomy," they supposedly chorused.

Nothing was written about the conditions of their employment, past or present, by either the *Times* or the *New York Evening Post,* which noted only that the Muse "twins" had returned to Ringling "dressed to kill in their crimson flannel dress clothes."

A few years later, *The New Yorker* finally spelled their stage names correctly but cruelly recollected their 1928 return to the circus as being motivated by...food. "The fried chicken had soon given out at Roanoke. Their relatives and friends had at first looked on them as heroes and wonder men, but gradually came to regard them as flitter-witted gormandizers."

During Ringling's Madison Square Garden 1928 season opener, the brothers seemed captivated only by the menagerie, the *Post* reported: they watched the tigers pace, their heads turning "patiently, regularly, back and forth together as they leaned silently on the rail, as absorbed and fascinated as any bucolic from Jackson, Miss....[though] without a doubt they'd seen this phenomenon before."

During a June stop in Buffalo, the Muses were once again such a draw that six patrons came close to trampling over a reporter during their mad rush to get to the platform where they were playing. Annoyed, the reporter ended up with mud plastered across his trousers and shoes as he pondered how the crowd had come to be under the spell of the "bearded twins from someplace or other in the South Seas Islands."

In a pitch card taken around that time—a photo the size of a postcard that was sold as a souvenir in penny arcades, candy stores, and amusement parks—the brothers have graduated from Martian ambassadors to Eko and Iko, Sheep-Headed Cannibals from Ecuador.

George appears to be scouting out something in the distance—people to eat?—while Willie crouches on one knee, pointing stage right. They wear blousy shirts, comically over-sized vests, and pantaloons tucked into tights.

George has one hand on Willie's shoulder, and both sport long dreadlocks and beards. It was the height of the exhibition craze that sideshow managers tried to dignify with the euphonious word *Zulu*, a time when Clyde Ingalls not only featured Clicko *and* Eko and Iko, but had also begun to hire "foreign rarities scouts" to regularly recruit acts from genuinely far-off places like Burma and the Congo. During the time of Jim Crow restrictions, displaying such bloodthirsty warriors and Stone Age savages underscored the omnipresence of racial segregation. Besides, with circuses now struggling to compete with the marvels of radio and motion pictures, Ingalls hoped the imports would help him up his game.

As Ingalls told reporters, the Muse brothers "were taken from Ecuador to England when nine years of age by missionaries, and so have been brought up under English rules which forbid them eating each other—or the spectators!" But compared with the older pitch cards and circus publicity pictures, there's now a marked change in the expressions of George and Willie that belies the ballyhoo about their cannibalistic Zulu shtick.

"Black 'wildmen' were sometimes exhibited in cages as uncivilized brutes who subsisted on raw meat and bit the heads off chicken or snakes. But these two, in comparison, look like Boy Scouts," said Bernth Lindfors, the University of Texas scholar, of the photo.

Perhaps that's because George and Willie are now in on the joke. They're performers who are being paid—for a while, anyway.

"They may have been laughing at us, but backstage, we were laughing at *them* because they were paying to see us," Willie told his relatives.

Their younger brother Tom was not so enthralled. He had not grown up in the circus backyard, as the brothers had, and didn't understand the appeal. Besides, black rousties were paid two-thirds of what their lighter-skinned Euro-American immigrant coworkers earned, and unlike his brothers, they generally were segregated from whites in lodging and in the cookhouse.

They wielded giant sledgehammers in unison as the lot lice stood nearby, watching the feat of syncopation, a free show-before-the-show. It was grueling work, maybe even harder than the dawn-to-dusk sharecropping schedule of "can to can't." They were up early, up late, with long hours, and very little sleep.

Tom hated the work, but he did what he was told and dutifully sent most of his salary home to his mother. The brothers had seen enough of their stepfather's behavior to be wary of what would come of it, though.

And since their departure for the circus in the spring of 1928, things had only gotten worse.

Adultery's Siamese Twin

The money — first from the change cup on the porch, then from the Ringling settlement and the funds being sent home — changed everything at Ten-and-a-Half Street. The food went from pinto beans to steak. The nip-joint shot glasses turned into whiskey in a jar — bought by the case.

The black-owned *Baltimore Afro-American* painted the metamorphosis of Cabell Muse in a disapproving glare. The paper said he had long been "feared by men of lower strata," a well-known bully in the black community.

But now, emboldened by the sudden infusion of settlement cash, he was becoming even more "overbearing and brutish in his associations." He hogged the Muse brothers' back pay for himself, spending it on a brand-new car and other luxuries. Harriett's dream of buying property would have to wait.

For a young A. L. Holland, the behavior of Cabell Muse became a morality lesson that underscored his own father's sense of duty: instead of blowing money on a car, Gus Holland walked to his rail-yard job and squirreled away his earnings, giving him something that would buttress the family for generations rather than bleed it dry — home ownership.

The Hollands wasted little money buying food because they kept chickens in the backyard for eggs, and they canned vege-

tables they grew in the yard. Instead of buying coal to heat
their stoves, Gus Holland carted home leftover cross ties from
work, using the scrap wood for free fuel. The children, who
grew up chopping kindling for the stove every night before they
went to bed, would adopt a metaphor for their father's lessons:
"We made cotton, but we took that cotton and made silk."

Cabell was definitely the only blue-collar worker in town
with the fortune—and the audacity—to buy a car. To a person, blue-collar African Americans in Roanoke aspiring to join
the middle class in the late 1920s "walked to work. Didn't
nobody have a car," Holland recalled. "I mean, Dr. Pinkard and
Dr. Claytor and maybe the lawyer had a car."

Holland didn't recall what brand Cabell's car was (nor did
anyone in the family), just that "it was real nice." Buick models
introduced in 1928, at the peak of the stock market bubble,
ranged from $1,195 to $1,850, around the average American's
annual salary.

Back then, the speed limit outside city limits was forty-five
miles per hour. A trip from Roanoke to Charlottesville that
now takes two hours by way of the four-lane interstate then
took eleven. Roads were twisty and riddled with potholes. The
Roanoke Times was filled with morbid accounts of cars careen-
ing off mountainsides and ramming into each other. In one
instance, a Rocky Mount man was repairing a blown-out tire
on the roadside in the fall of 1927 when a speeding motorist
slammed into him, breaking most of his bones, then drove
away. The injured man died the next day.

Henry Ford's mass-production methods already had transformed the way Americans worked, played, and spent their
money. The car became *the* status symbol for aspirational
Americans. If you owned a car, it meant you had achieved the

"world's highest standard of living," according to a popular highway billboard featuring a smiling family of four taking a joy ride through the mountains.

For Cabell, the ride may have been joyful, but it was plagued with hairpin turns. Word was out all over Jordan's Alley: he had graduated from the women in the back rooms of the nip joints to something far more serious—another man's wife.

That man, Hope Wooden, worked for the Norfolk and Western Railway. He was fifty-eight years old and "comma, colored," in newspaper parlance. Holland could still visualize Wooden sweeping the stairs that led to the tracks of the downtown train station. Wooden had worked as a railroad mail carrier, porter, and janitor.

Word had reached Wooden that Cabell was flirting with his much younger wife, Edna. The Woodens had a teenaged son, Charley. And Cabell was known to stop by the Woodens' place before Charley got home from school or Hope from his train-station work. The neighbors all knew. It was impossible to miss, especially when the presence of Cabell's car announced it to everyone on the street. The car was not the accessory of choice for twenties-era adulterers—it was way too flashy—but Cabell was intoxicated by the power of that car.

Wooden made it clear to Cabell that he should stay away.

He threatened to kill him, the neighbors all said, if he didn't.

It was turning into another tumultuous year in Roanoke, with an average of one murder a month for nineteen months straight. A severe drought had everyone in the summer of 1928 on edge. The city council had adopted water restrictions, and gardens were drying up. Prosecutor Kent Spiller was still on a tear about his pet issues, liquor and gambling. His latest targets were cigar stores and confectioneries that sold bets on baseball games; he'd had twelve people arrested for such wagering on June 12.

No one in Roanoke or anywhere else in the nation paid much attention to the legal betting going on by the finance gangsters — soon to be called banksters — on Wall Street, where a record seven million shares of stock had just changed hands on a single day. Millions of Americans were about to lose their jobs; one in four were on the brink of losing their life savings. Those enjoying the excesses of the Roaring Twenties were about to find out that the stock market would not, in fact, rise indefinitely.

To facilitate his work, Spiller made great use of the federal "padlock law," which gave local police the authority to lock up any building being used for the sale of illegal liquor. But at 1:44 a.m. on June 13, bootleggers and liquor runners struck back. They went to the home of Samuel Atkins, the policeman known for being the most vigorous Prohibition enforcer in town. They snuck into the back alley behind his house, and they hit him where they knew it would hurt.

They firebombed his car.

The explosion shattered the windows of every house on the block.

A few weeks later, on a sweltering July day, Hope Wooden decided to surprise his wife by coming home for lunch. Finding not only nothing to eat but also no wife in sight, he went to see if Edna was at her mother's house, a few blocks away.

His lunch wasn't there either.

But Cabell Muse was.

He was upstairs, in bed, with Wooden's wife.

"Look, the man had been warned," Holland remembered. "A

man's wife was his beauty, and he took pride in taking care of his wife. Hope had warned him to stay away.

"But old Cabell didn't have the sense to do it."

Wooden made his presence known to Cabell, who was short but stocky with broad shoulders.

Cabell leapt from the bed swinging, and he charged at Wooden, hitting and kicking him, according to police accounts.

Shielding himself from Cabell's blows with one hand, Wooden used his other hand to draw a rusty pocketknife from his trousers, then wrangled the knife open with his teeth.

Wooden came back at Cabell—with the end of his rusty knife. He stabbed Cabell in the torso and the neck. He stabbed him in the back and legs.

Wooden stabbed him so many times that when police arrived no one could figure out how Cabell had managed to claw his way to the front yard, a line of blood trailing him down the stairs and through the back porch.

Cabell Muse's last act had been to crawl toward his only safe haven.

He collapsed in the front yard, a few feet from the car paid for by Willie and George. The brothers were far away, working a midseason show in Madison, Wisconsin, when Cabell drew his final breath.

His blood soaked into the parched grass, where it continued to draw spectators for several days.

Wooden did the only thing he knew to do: he went back to work at the train station, confessed to his superiors, and prepared for police to take him in.

At police headquarters, he admitted freely to committing the murder, leaning casually against the rail in the switchboard room.

When he noticed the antiquated knife in the hands of the desk sergeant, he even bragged to a reporter from the afternoon *World-News* that he'd used it to kill Cabell. The article was headlined FATHER OF EKO AND IKO, THE MARTIAN AMBASSADORS, KILLED.

The murder of Cabell Muse paled in comparison to other events making headlines in the southern black press in the late 1920s. (Outside Roanoke, the white press didn't mention it at all.) A record low of eleven lynchings had been reported across the South that year. The following year in St. Louis, five men had escaped slavery on a Mississippi plantation, one saying he'd been forced to work without pay since the age of nine. Another victim testified that plantation owners had "sold" his wife to another planter for $250. In 1926, the *New York World* published an exposé on southern slavery, reporting that a thousand prisoners had been sold into coal mines and forced-labor camps the previous year, generating the modern equivalent of $2.8 million for local officials and $6.6 million for the state government, according to Douglas Blackmon's Pulitzer Prize–winning book, *Slavery by Another Name: The Re-Enslavement of Black Americans from the Civil War to World War II*. Most of the inmates were impoverished sharecroppers, many of whom had been arrested for offenses as slight as trying to hop a train. They faced beatings with steel wire, hickory sticks, and shovels, and were locked up in what the *World* called "dog houses," rough-hewn boxes the size of coffins, for forty-eight hours at a stretch. The Alabama slave mines were finally closed in the summer of 1928, as Blackmon described it, with two columns of African-American men "blinking at the sudden brightness of the summer sun" and singing "Swing Low, Sweet Chariot" as they walked out of the mine shafts a final time.

On the same day a judge pronounced Wooden guilty of voluntary manslaughter, another black man was sentenced to three years in prison for a failed pickpocket theft at the Roanoke Fair. Just attempting to lift another's property, even "within a hair's breadth," constituted stealing, argued Prosecutor Spiller in his closing remarks.

The founder of Roanoke's Robert E. Lee branch of the KKK, Spiller was also the chief prosecutor against Wooden in the Cabell Muse murder case.

Spiller was proud of his tough-on-crime reputation. The same month Cabell was murdered, the press lauded him for asking police to call him "at any hour of the day or night when a slaying occurs within the city limits. It is [the prosecutors'] intention to be at the scene before the victim's body is removed, so that they may not be deprived of what may prove to be important evidence."

But with Cabell's death, justice had already been served, Spiller felt. He did not bother showing up to gather evidence, dispatching the coroner instead to Wooden's mother-in-law's lawn.

The coroner counted seven wounds in Cabell's back, three in his chest, and one each across his leg, head, and throat.

Wooden was sentenced to a single year in prison for the crime—one-third the time the clumsy pickpocket received.

When I first asked A. L. Holland about the crime, he was reluctant to weigh in—"It's nothing that's gonna make anybody feel real glamorous," he said.

And: "You didn't talk too much about old people's business back in the day; you kinda walked around it. But there was a big to-do about it when it happened." He remembered kids at school discussing it as well as customers on his broom-selling route.

When I mentioned that his cousin Nancy had told me about the murder—"You missed one, Scoop," she had teased me a few months earlier, pointing out that our newspaper research had failed to unearth that story—Holland finally opened up. Like so many other African-American men of that era, including George and Willie Muse, Holland thought Cabell got what he deserved. And Wooden, too, with his relatively light sentence.

Reginald Shareef, the social science professor and Muse family friend who has written about Roanoke's black community, explained the adultery-revenge mind-set, and the common stresses and indignities that fueled it. Black men working in a white Jim Crow world were under tremendous pressure everywhere they went—especially from white bosses and white policemen. That stress had driven Shareef's father, a railroad mail clerk, to become a functioning alcoholic, like his father before him, who preferred working the graveyard janitorial shift to avoid his supervisors entirely.

Shareef said he will never forget the horror of being suspended from school, only to learn that his principal was about to call *his father* out of work to fetch him instead of his mild-mannered mother, a librarian in an all-black elementary school.

As he waited for his father to make the short drive from the railway office building to the school, "I was like a condemned man." His father was now at risk of being belittled or disrespected by his white supervisor, who could have used the occasion to condescend to him about his parenting. His father was

very proud and very large—six feet four and 250 pounds—
and relatives feared that his suppressed anger would boil over
at the slightest provocation, Shareef said.

He remembers waiting for his father inside the double doors
of the school, "so when he grabs me and slams me up against
the car, only the kids on one side of the building will see me."

Many of the men in his childhood neighborhood were functioning alcoholics, which is why Shareef, who became a practicing Muslim at twenty-five, swore off intoxicants early in
adulthood.

Alcohol had been a constant source of stress between his
parents. He remembers his father calling him into the living
room one night.

"Reggie, your mother says I have an alcohol problem. Go
ahead and flip that switch and see if the lights come on."

Shareef dutifully flipped the switch.

Light dutifully bathed the room.

His father snapped: "I might drink, but I pay Appalachian
[Power Company] every month."

During forty-two years of working for the railroad, he took
only seventeen sick days.

"To survive, you see, you had to have these coping strategies,
and alcohol was the most popular one," Shareef recalled.

Even though it often led to bad choices and explosive out-
comes. Black laboring men were already so diminished in their
daily life that Shareef grew up believing "if you committed
adultery, you *would* be killed. I'd hear men say that at the barbershop on Henry Street," he said.

It was a pervasive part of the black-male psyche Shareef
absorbed growing up, he said, one that persisted for decades.

In the 1980s, his own barber (who also worked for the railroad) found his wife in bed with another man, and shot and killed them both.

In Shareef's world, black men were so routinely belittled, they believed that committing murder to avenge adultery was worth the risk of imprisonment—if it meant keeping their fragile dignity intact. The shame of everyone *knowing* another man had gotten away with sleeping with your wife outweighed the risk of going to jail for murdering the son of a bitch.

"That was the cultural environment I grew up in: adultery and murder were Siamese twins," Shareef said.

After a year in prison, Wooden returned to Roanoke and started his own shoe-shine business in the lobby of the train station, as if nothing had happened.

Even the Muse brothers shrugged. They were more concerned about their destitute widowed mother than the memory of her low-down cheating husband, who by now had frittered away all that money. The cash that was supposed to compensate them for all the years they'd been separated from their mother, lied to, and used. *Their* money.

George and Willie might have taken Cabell's last name. But they did not attend his burial.

Later, when the economy tanked and even jobs for washerwomen became scarce, the brothers recalled Cabell with even greater disdain.

"He just wasn't no good," Willie told his relatives.

After the murder, the family instructed the funeral home to send his body away, and it was buried immediately—in an unmarked grave tucked into the tobacco-rich foothills of Truevine.

*   *   *

As preparations began to put Cabell in the ground, the three Muse brothers prepared for the show in Madison. It's impossible to know whether they wanted to go home to comfort their mother and were denied the right. Judging from their later conversations about Cabell, family members doubt they would have wanted to pay him the respect.

"Remember, he was cheating on their mama, and then he was up in the bed with another man's wife after he'd been warned," Nancy says. "Plus, he'd spent all that money that wasn't for him.

"So that served him right."

A gravedigger in Truevine was hard at work, and the sideshow went on with the Martian ambassadors front and center.

It would be eight more years before the circus train rolled through the Blue Ridge Mountains and hoisted its tents in Roanoke again.

PART FOUR

12

Housekeeping!

She was "the World's Largest Ship." Weighing 56,551 tons and holding more than twenty-one hundred passengers, the RMS *Majestic* steamed across the Atlantic from England's Southampton to New York in five days, fourteen hours, and forty-five minutes. Run by the British shipping company White Star, the same group that operated the ill-fated *Titanic*, the *Majestic* displaced 64,000 tons of water. When she docked in New York, her stern projected into the Hudson River some forty-one feet past the pier.

With a swimming pool flanked by granite columns, she was so popular among elite passengers from the two countries she traveled between, including King George V and Queen Mary, that she was affectionately nicknamed the Magic Stick (a near-homophone of *majestic*) for the fortune she made her owners. The luxury liner's first-class section featured oak-paneled lounges with carved-wood ceilings and velvet draperies, and was peopled by such dignitaries as Wall Street bankers, Columbia University professors, and former president Wilson's assistant secretary of the treasury, Martin Vogel, who was on a mission in 1928 to bring back a prize-winning Airedale, which he planned to offer up to the White House as first dog.

The Muse brothers were not considered dignitaries when they crossed the Atlantic via the big ship in the middle of December 1928, but their accommodations nonetheless included dining rooms with linens and silverware, and cabins in which a steward could be summoned by a bell. They traveled third class, according to the manifest, which listed their occupations as showmen (George and Tom) and freak (Willie). The modest luxuries offered in steerage were designed to attract immigrants. Menu cards offered free postcards on the back so passengers could write to their relatives at home and talk them into traveling with White Star, too.

The ship made a big impression on the brothers, family members recall. Willie "told us as kids that he would have steak and caviar when they traveled," said the brothers' great-niece Louise Burrell. "He told us he was treated just exactly like he was white." When they reached London they stayed at the Strand Palace Hotel, where Willie would acquire the lifelong habit of announcing "Housekeeping!" in a joking, faux-British accent every time the doorbell rang.

According to Louise and Nancy, after the settlement, side-show managers began to treat the brothers better—to a point. "Once their mama located them, it was their choice to go back," Nancy said. A 1929 picture of the brothers underscores their newfound confidence. They're both wearing gold rings and impeccably shined shoes. Willie flashes a wry half-smile. He is no longer looking off gloomily or clenching his fists in every photograph, and his personality is beginning to emerge in the official record now.

Sideshow manager Clyde Ingalls had arranged everything for the transatlantic trip. He'd been taking his favorite performers to London in the off-season since 1921. They performed as part of the Bertram Mills Circus "Fun Fair" at Olympia, an exhibition hall in west London. The Fun Fair drew throngs of spectators during the Christmas season, including, frequently, members of the royal family, the lord mayor of London, and Winston Churchill.

Bertram Mills had cultivated a relationship with the royals by naming the earl of Lonsdale honorary president of his circus in 1922 and throwing lavish opening-day luncheons that attracted hundreds of baronets, knights, and bishops to the table. In 1926, learning that the prince of Wales (the future duke of Windsor) had quietly attended one of the performances, Mills had a private viewing box installed—to help shield the duke and Wallis Simpson, his lover and future wife, from the indignity of having to spectate among the masses.

Mills's show was the British equivalent of the Big One, though the British circus patron was beginning to grow offended by certain sideshow acts, even those affiliated with Ringling. Writing that same year, Kenneth Grahame, the British author best known for *The Wind in the Willows,* said the biggest change in show life in his generation was "the disappearance of freaks and monstrousities...a change entirely for good."

The *Times* of London offered a more nuanced view: "We are tired of gaping at those of our fellow creatures who occupy sideshows; we are anxious to understand them instead."

According to the historian Nadja Durbach, who has written about freak shows in Britain, the British were more sensitive to the treatment of people with disabilities than Americans in the wake of World War I, probably because far more veterans living in England suffered from war wounds and what would become known as post-traumatic stress disorder.

Exhibits popular before the Great War became "suddenly

distasteful," Durbach told me. "Some characters were able to survive it, but only because they inspired a kind of comic gentleness"—Clicko, for instance.

While Tod Browning's film *Freaks* caused an uproar in the United States in 1932—it was pulled from circulation after its New York run—British film censors banned it outright for thirty years. (The British found the showcasing of so-called pinheads the film's most disturbing aspect.)

With migration rules tightening throughout Europe, England's war-weary populace was bent on securing its borders and protecting its own workforce, so anti-immigration sentiments probably also contributed to British skepticism of Ingalls's sideshow imports, Durbach said.

In 1927, Mills's annual request to import Ingalls with his freaks hit a political snag: the Ministry of Labor denied the application, citing the 1920 Aliens Order. "We might be challenged for interfering with the legitimate activities of showmen; but it would be difficult for the Showmen's Guild or any other body to convince us that alien abnormalities are essential for their productions," one immigration official wrote. "They are curious, but not in my mind wholesome," he said of Ingalls's acts.

Mills was not shy about using his contacts and calling in favors, though. You could tell that from a behind-the-scenes letter he wrote to Sir William Haldane Porter, begging for the senior civil servant's personal intervention ("You were good enough to say on that occasion that at any time I was in difficulty about any aliens whom I wished to employ, I might see you on the subject"). Without the imported American freaks, Mills argued, his Fun Fair would be left to operate with "only about a half-dozen of them in this Country, the greater number always finding their way abroad, as they can earn so much more money in America and on the Continent than they could normally earn in England."

Mills drew on both humanitarian and labor arguments. Without employment, his British performers would have become a "serious handicap to their families," he wrote.

The next day, the committee reversed its decision. The Aliens Order would not be used to deny "exhibits who, though not to everybody's taste, are not indecent, repulsive or likely to bring in some disease with them," an officer ruled.

The ruling closed with the words "I think Bertram Mills must have his freaks."

But some of Ingalls's imports proved more popular than others, and between 1929 and 1935, the number of traveling fairground sideshows in Britain diminished from 298 to 43. "Nobody wanted to see those suffering from physical deformities which made them objects of pity," recalled Mills's son, Cyril, an MI5 agent who worked in the circus in his early years and wrote his father's 1967 biography. Mills once became so desperate for novelty acts and the publicity they generated that he offered £20,000 to anyone who could find the Loch Ness Monster for him to exhibit.

Back in 1921, Ingalls had been chosen for the Fun Fair because Mills was no dummy: nabbing Ingalls meant access to the popular giant Jack Earle and the little people who were his coworkers.

Mills was especially fond of a Fun Fair section he dubbed Tiny Town, and he spent a fortune on it, adorning it with miniature houses; miniature churches, hotels, and shops; tiny battery-driven motorcars; and even a diminutive pool hall.

Most important, hiring Ingalls to manage the Fun Fair initially meant scoring the biggest circus star on the planet—Ingalls's wife, Lillian Leitzel, even though early in their marriage it became clear the two were spiraling toward divorce.

During one heated argument, Leitzel had chopped off one of Ingalls's fingers—with a butcher knife.

By 1928, the couple had already been divorced four years, and Leitzel was remarried to Alfredo Codona, the trapeze artist. Still, Mills kept Ingalls on as his sideshow impresario.

The British didn't care much for bearded ladies or microcephalics, judging from a set of highlight reels from Mills's shows, and he encouraged Ingalls to bring along his best-looking acts—Jack Earle and the little people, especially the twenty-seven-inch-tall Lya Graf, a beautiful brunette and a Ringling favorite.

"Well, looky here," drawls the eight-foot-six-inch Earle in one of the films. He displays the diminutive Graf in his arms while several other Russian Lilliputians, as the producers call them, run circles between his legs.

"Where'd you come from, I wonder?" Earle says, grinning and blowing Graf a kiss.

And "Isn't she sweet?" he asks kindly, as the lot lice stare at them, mesmerized, from behind.

Ringling performers tended to scatter in the winter off-season, some to charity Masonic or Shrine circuses in the United States, others to Mills's show in London or to warmer climes, in Honolulu and Havana. With the exception of the 1924 trip to Hawaii and the winter 1928–29 journey to England, Shelton usually exhibited the Muse brothers in American carnivals and dime museums during the off-season. He hadn't accompanied the Muses to London.

Today it's unclear whether the brothers made that trip because they decided they needed to work more — so they could send money home to their newly widowed (and reimpoverished) mother — or whether Ingalls intervened and found them winter work before they had a chance to return to Roanoke at the end of the 1928 season.

"Once in a while somebody gets dissatisfied and quits to go into vaudeville or into a museum," Ingalls said a few years before the trip, explaining the constant challenges of staffing the sideshow. "It's part of my job to keep track of them while the show is in winter quarters. In the spring I have to round them up if any have dropped out; it's up to me to get busy and fill their places."

Ingalls's winter pilgrimages to London were his busman's holidays — but they were also a way for him to keep tabs on his best-earning acts.

Ingalls struck Mills's equestrian director, Frank Foster, as quintessentially American. He was loud — "a huge dominating man with a stentorian voice," Foster called him — and he was boastful.

As were his charges, according to Foster, who spent mornings hanging out with the Fun Fair freaks. "I have never met a freak who suffered from what is known as an inferiority complex," he wrote. "On the contrary, they had the highest opinion of themselves and were proud that they were not as other people.... Deformity gave them good jobs and saved them the anxiety and low standard of life which, to people of the class whence they derived, was the common lot."

Willie Muse may have developed his lifelong affinity for the London lifestyle — especially *housekeeping!* — but the city's residents did not return his warm feelings.

In a 1984 letter written to the University of Texas scholar Bernth Lindfors, Cyril Mills recalled of George and Willie's act that "the London public had no taste for that sort of thing." Mills's longtime ringmaster described the brothers as having "a peculiar sponge-like growth instead of hair, pink eyes, and a weird expression and mentality; they really *did* look like visitors from a strange planet."

The British found the Eko and Iko act "extremely distasteful," according to the letter. Mills equated them with Ingalls's Ubangi Duck-Billed Savages, the eight Congolese women who were an instant sensation in the Ringling sideshow in 1930 and '31. The Ringling press agent Roland Butler had come up with the word *Ubangi* after scouring a map and deeming it the most exotic-sounding locale, though the Ubangi district was far from their actual home.

The Ubangis' distinguishing feature was their lips, marks of beauty common among female tribe members. Wooden disks had been inserted into their lips in childhood, then gradually increased in diameter up to eight or ten inches, giving the lips a duckbill effect. Or so their manager spieled, saying that the lip-stretching practice initially developed as a way to make the women unattractive to kidnapping pirates and marauders. Over time, the elongated lips came to be considered beautiful, "and only the comeliest little girls were chosen for this adornment," Ringling's press agent Dexter Fellows recalled.

An anthropologist later traced the practice to a nuptial rite; it indicated that a girl was engaged to marry—until Ringling got hold of her, anyway.

The Ubangis had been discovered by the master freak hunter Samuel W. Gumpertz, a close friend of John Ringling's whose biggest coup had been the importation of 212 tribal headhunters from the Philippine Islands to his Dreamland amusement park in Coney Island, New York, another popular locale for sideshow performers in the off-season. Dubbed the freak czar, Gumpertz was a self-taught linguist who could bargain for acts in several languages and was particularly fluent in "a patois spoken in a section of the Pyrenees that had many midgets."

Circus agents had to pay bribes in Washington just to get the Ubangis, including their tribal chief and the chief's brother, past Ellis Island immigration authorities. The transition became awkward for everyone—including the stevedores working the docks—when the Ubangis disembarked and almost immediately...took off their tops.

Voilà! It was instant marketing: dockworkers quickly spread the word about Ringling's hottest new act.

Then the bill posters got busy putting up notices heralding the NEW TO CIVILIZATION attraction, FROM AFRICA'S DARKEST CONTINENT and WITH MOUTHS AND LIPS AS LARGE AS THOSE OF FULL GROWN CROCODILES. To highlight the range of acts, Ringling arranged for a photograph to be taken of two of the largest-lipped women seated between two beautifully adorned American dancing girls, clad in rhinestones and with picture-perfect smiles.

Attendance soared.

Sideshow managers pretended to be shocked every time the women took their tops off, knowing that sly male customers could now attend a peep show but tell their wives they were actually viewing an educational exhibit.

By 1930, their second season in America, the Ubangis had become terribly homesick, worried they would never see their children again. Two of the women attempted suicide together by throwing themselves in front of a car, which fortunately stopped before any damage was done.

Compared with George and Willie, whom longtime managers described as cheerful and compliant, the Ubangis were obstinate. They cried, complained, and cursed.

"Nothing that might be written about them could possibly be bad enough to describe them," Fred Bradna wrote. He was especially offended by their hygiene practices: they had cut four neat holes into a wooden train car—to use in place of a toilet—and hauled down blankets from the beds to sleep on the floor. During their stint with the Mills circus in London, the brother of one Ubangi had tried to wash his face in the toilet bowl.

Hotels refused to admit them, and the women were constantly feuding with their French manager, Eugene Bergonier. They had discovered that Bergonier was siphoning off most of their $1,500-a-week salary.

In response, the women crafted a miniature effigy of him, which they tortured continuously.

In response, Bergonier carried a revolver.

In response, the Ubangis announced a work stoppage, refusing to board the train from Chicago to Milwaukee unless Bergonier left the show.

Just as the show must go on, the train must pull out of the station on time. Every train, every station, every time. It was the American railroad, after all, that had driven the creation of standardized time in the United States in the 1880s—to prevent train wrecks. Back in Roanoke, railroad men synchronized their Hamilton pocket watches daily, and they manned the steam-powered factory whistle (nicknamed Old Gabriel), which blew to announce the beginning and end of work shifts, then and now. (Before, towns across the nation set their own times by observing the placement of the sun, so instead of Eastern Standard Time, there was Philadelphia Standard Time, for instance — until rail companies persuaded each region to abandon the chaos of local times.)

So the train schedule won out, as it was wont to do. And the circus train soon departed, leaving Bergonier to take another train, bound for Sarasota instead. Shortly after arriving in Florida, he was bitten by a tropical insect (though the medical examiner listed the cause of death as "septic pneumonia"). He died just as the circus was rolling into its Florida winter quarters.

When the Ubangis heard the news, they cheered, bragging that their hexes had caused his demise ("No die, we make 'em die"). The chief of the tribe demanded to see Bergonier's body at the funeral home, where he and four of the women spread powders and made gestures to repel his "evil spirit" before they approached the casket.

Then, according to Bradna, they stared at his remains with "a fierce hatred."

Setting profits aside, John Ringling finally agreed to let the Ubangis return to the Congo, at his expense, at the end of their second season. "At home...they bought a big ranch, stocked it with splendid cattle, and now live in high style among their grandchildren," Bradna wrote.

Of course a new, slightly more Westernized crop of Ubangis was imported the following year to take their place. They spoke not only their tribal language but also French, wore blue sweaters that they did not randomly take off, and generally mixed with their coworkers better than the first Ubangi crew.

Still, according to Mills, the British deemed both the Ubangis and the Muse brothers flops. "We made it clear that whereas a giant like Jake Earle would always be welcome, we did not want objects of pity of any kind," Cyril Mills recalled. "In my opinion, Eko and Iko were severely handicapped mentally, and if I am right it was stretching the law to the limits to exhibit them in public."

I flinched, again, when I read that portrayal. Having interviewed not just family members but also lawyers who deposed Willie Muse in later life, as well as caregivers who treated him, I'm convinced the brothers were not mentally incapacitated.

Uneducated, yes. Socially uncomfortable around white authority figures, yes.

As a young man in the late 1920s, A. L. Holland noticed they sometimes seemed to have trouble putting sentences together. But later in life and far away from the circus — settled snugly within the confines of their loved ones' homes — they conversed just fine.

I believe that Ingalls encouraged the Muse brothers to play dumb, just as P. T. Barnum and Zip's later manager, O. K. White, manipulated Zip. In an unpublished memoir on file at the Circus World Museum, a ballet dancer described Zip as just "a normal colored man" whose contract stipulated he remain silent onstage.

Tiny Kline wrote: "Should any folks have dropped into the side-show during the 'off' hours, between five and seven p.m., they would have found [Zip] down on his knees in the circle with the other men, before a blanket spread out on the ground, shooting 'crap,' and with typical Southern accent, repeating the magic words used in the game: *Come on, seven! 'leven! Baby needs new shoes!*"

Teasing out the Muse brothers' behind-the-scenes character is somewhat harder, not just because of the universally racist press accounts but also because few, if any, insiders bothered to record and report their point of view.

By the early 1930s, they were beginning to become slightly humanized by the media: two 1930 press accounts describe them being engaged in chess, but in a typically jokey tone. A *New York Post* article riffed for two long columns about what Eko and Iko thought of the fact that Herbert Hoover's widowed vice president, Charles Curtis, had his half sister living with him in Washington, serving as his hostess for social gatherings.

"Ambassador Eko reported that everywhere he is finding a growing interest in Mars and its exports, and a feeling of international amity," wrote the reporter. He then noted that Eko was from "Western Mars," whereas Iko hailed from the "rich tenderloin of East Mars." The premise of the article—the joke—was that the reporter interviewed them (or pretended to) as if they were indeed politicians representing the interplanetary state of Mars.

"What did get recorded is so one-sided and so full of holes," said Jane Nicholas, the historian. "You're like, I know there are *real people* in there somewhere and not just shells."

The sideshow might have given the Muses a place where they belonged, and they might indeed have been treated with more humanity than their family was in segregated Roanoke. But, without question, that place was also exploitative, Nicholas argued.

From London to Lansing, Michigan, George and Willie Muse were among the most widely celebrated people of their time, endlessly photographed and written about—yet never were they given a chance to tell their own story.

*   *   *

Accounts of managers who spoke of their midcareer period made the Muse brothers sound not like naïve Boy Scouts, as today's cultural anthropologists view them, but like wild savages who had to be looked after at all times. Sideshow bally Charlie Roark told Al Stencell he often had to escort the brothers from the sideshow tent to the cookhouse. He said they took turns announcing the various circus features they were passing along the way:

The menagerie tent was the monkey house.

The front end, where the bosses worked, was City Hall.

"I got the sense they needed supervision, from what Charlie said," Stencell recalled. "Every now and then, one would pick up a ladder [leading up to the sideshow platform], then run around swinging it in the air," as Roark remembered it. "People were ducking, and they'd be yelling out, 'Ham and bone! Ham and bone!' They'd have to run out and get Candy Shelton to come out and calm 'em down and put the ladder back up to the platform."

Whether they were wild savages or musical geniuses depended on who was telling the tale. Many of the show people were "racist Southern crackers. Not one of 'em was politically correct!" Stencell said.

The ham-and-bone bit? A good chance it was probably one more bit of theater trumped up by managers to entice another quarter from the rubes.

Whether the British liked them or not, the Muses were a mainstay for American circus-goers throughout the Depression. In fact, the brothers from Truevine would fare better—and longer— than many of their more respected (and better-paid) coworkers.

The kindly giant Jack Earle (real name Jacob Erlich) might have been ogled and admired by the royals, but he also suffered from disabling depression for much of his life, in addition to a pituitary fluke called acromegaly. Seven feet tall by the sixth grade, he was the target of schoolyard bullies and withdrew into himself, taking solace in books, painting, and sculpture. (His work, much of it circus-themed, has been the subject of museum shows. A bust he sculpted of Taibosh posing as Clicko and six paintings featured in a 1936 Fifth Avenue gallery show were found to be "promising," according to a critic quoted in the *New York Times*.)

On a mid-1910s childhood fishing trip to California designed by his parents to cheer him up, Earle had been "discovered" by silent-film scouts and ended up acting in forty-nine early movies — some with pioneering child star Baby Peggy. (They starred together in *Jack and the Beanstalk* and other films in which Earle typically played...the giant.) After a stunt accident temporarily blinded him, Earle was recuperating with his family in El Paso, Texas, when a group of friends took him to see the Big One as it passed through their hometown.

Clyde Ingalls spotted him on the midway. He could tell that Erlich was several inches taller than Ringling's longtime giant, Jim Tarver, according to Erlich's nephew. Andy Erlich is a psychologist who writes and gives motivational speeches about his uncle, whom he refers to by his nickname, Jake.

Ingalls offered him a job on the spot.

"But I don't want to be a freak," Jake told his father during a family meeting to discuss whether he would join the circus.

"And my grandfather told him, 'Being a freak is a state of mind,'" Erlich said.

"He couldn't make a living in El Paso; he didn't have a skill.

And everybody was worried if he stayed home he'd get depressed again," Erlich told me. So he went.

Ingalls outfitted Jake in outlandish clothes: red satin garments with gold buttons and epaulets, capped off by platform shoes that were twelve inches high. "I was so damn high in the air, I had to keep moving my toes to make sure it was really my feet down there," he once told an interviewer.

The locals peppered him with tedious clichés — "How is the weather up there?" — along with questions about his sex life and occasionally anti-Semitic remarks (Jake was the son of German-Jewish immigrants). He was so nervous during his first show that his knees were knocking — until a thin voice from below said to him, "Take it easy, Jake. And don't worry: there's more freaks out there in the crowd than there are up here."

It was the voice of Harry Doll (real name: Kurt Fritz Schneider), the dwarf who went on to be featured in *Freaks* and *The Wizard of Oz*, in which he played a member of the Lollipop Guild.

So began a long friendship between Jake and the Doll family and the other little people on the show. During one stop in Chattanooga, a patron tried to grab Harry as they walked along the midway, and Jake busted the man's jaw. "Ringling had to settle the guy's claims, and Jake never engaged in fisticuffs again," his nephew said.

For a long time, Andy Erlich felt conflicted about his uncle's story and didn't want to write about it. "I guess I felt his depression, and it kind of made me not want to go there. But when I looked at his art and his paintings and saw him expressing himself, I started to embrace it."

It reminded me of Nancy's response to our 2001 newspaper series. For the first time in her life, people came up to her—in her restaurant and when they bumped into her in stores. Rather than taunt her about George and Willie or make light of them, as happened often when she was younger, they congratulated her for preserving their legacy. A few even apologized for having complained about her intermittent restaurant hours—not understanding that when she'd been late opening the Goody Shop it was because she'd been home, tending Uncle Willie.

"Some of the things you're dealing with growing up, they just make you tougher. They make it so you learn to handle things," she said.

The often-brandished rock on the cash register; the prickly, defensive posture; her pride in her great-grandmother despite Harriett's possible role in George's and Willie's joining the circus—all of it was coming into focus now. I was also beginning to understand what Nancy meant when she told me, knowingly, at the start of my research for this book: "No matter what you find out...you have to remember: in the end, they came out on top."

Still, she remained defensive during our interactions. During a photo shoot I arranged for this book, a photographer friend casually asked if we could shoot her portrait at Uncle Willie's house, where she grew up and where she cared for him in retirement. She wheeled around and snapped at me, "Are you *senile* or something?" She'd said no to that request a few months earlier. Didn't I know better than to ask again?

When I complained that the brothers' interior existence was hard to report on, she told one of her younger relatives, "If she thinks it's hard for her to write this story, just think how hard it was for Uncle Willie and Uncle Georgie to live it! She better pick her ass up!"

But on the day of the photo shoot, on the way out of her house, Nancy also handed me an inspirational quote she'd saved from the newspaper. It was a line by Voltaire that resonated with the story of her uncles:

"To the living we owe respect, but to the dead we owe only the truth."

Unlike Nancy, Andy Erlich had not experienced any bullying related to his uncle. He knew nothing of the perils of growing up black in one of the most segregated cities in the South, or of the legacy of slavery and sharecropping on a gap-riddled family tree. Unlike Nancy, he can not only pinpoint the identity of all his great-grandparents; he can also place, with certainty, where they are buried.

While the Muse brothers' circus artifacts rest mainly in collectors' hands, the legacy of Jake could fill an Erlich family museum. Andy's father, Jake's brother, was extremely proud of the giant in the family, maintaining a trove of his artwork, press clippings, and a welter of books Jake himself had collected.

Andy's first memory was of being thrown into the air by his uncle and of his grandmother screaming, "Watch out, he's gonna hit his head on the ceiling!" Shortly before Jake died, in 1952, Andy's parents took him to see his uncle, who asked the boy to give him a kiss. "I can't reach you," Andy said.

Jake died at the age of forty-six, from complications related to acromegaly. He left behind his paintings and sculptures, a book of poetry, and a collection of souvenir rings that originally had sold for a quarter, inscribed with the words *Jack Earle, Circus Giant, Eight Foot Six.* The actress Diana Serra Cary—aka child star Baby Peggy—gave Andy hers as a gift.

During performances, Jake would take off one of his rings so that lecturer Charlie Roark could pass a fifty-cent piece through it—to demonstrate the massive size of his finger. "There is enough good metal in that ring that even the meanest junkman will get you a quarter for it," Roark would say, and the quarters clinked as sales added up. "Earle made a ton of money," Roark recalled. (And the lecturer, too, who typically pocketed 10 percent of souvenir sales.)

Tom Waits immortalized the winsome Texas giant in a song. At the suggestion of muralist Diego Rivera, a gallery in New York mounted a one-man show of his work. His nephew penned a book based on his life, closing it with what is perhaps the saddest sideshow ending of all: the fate of the German brunette Lya Graf.

"The World's Littlest Woman" was one of Jake's closest friends on the sideshow. Just as he'd done with Jake and Harry Doll, Ingalls often posed the two of them together for promotional photographs that exaggerated the difference in their size.

If you were charting Graf's height using Jake's body, the crown of her head would be even with his knees.

In 1933, a Ringling press agent—a Fellows minion and never one to miss a photo op—had the idea to boost circus attendance by staging a photograph: Graf would sit on the lap of Wall Street titan J. P. Morgan Jr.

The juxtaposition would be rich: Graf was adorable. Morgan was a bankster.

It turned into a twofer promotion: The photo would also make Morgan appear grandfatherly, the company bankers hoped, more "of the people"—despite his $2.5 million yacht, *Corsair*, and his four homes, not counting the Scottish estate he rented annually so he could shoot grouse with King George VI.

In 1933, snagged in the crosshairs of congressional hearings about the 1929 stock market crash, the world's most powerful banker was being hammered in the press about income taxes. He stood accused of selling stocks at below-market prices to favored, politically connected clients.

In the middle of the monthlong hearings, Senator Carter Glass casually told reporters that the proceedings needed only pink lemonade and peanuts to turn them into a three-ring circus. That was all the juice Fellows and the Ringling publicity machine required to turn the spectacle into one of the country's first media circuses. (Glass is the same Lynchburg senator who had shouted out "Discrimination! Why, that is *exactly* what we propose" during debate about the 1902 Virginia Constitution.)

Morgan had always been private and press-shy, but now, even he admitted, he needed a media boost.

He smiled stiffly as handlers placed a beaming Graf onto his lap. She wore a blue satin dress, a red straw hat, and Mary Jane pumps, her ankles daintily crossed.

The twofer backfired. Published worldwide, the photo went on to become an emblem of Wall Street's fallen state.

But Graf was more than a circus joke, more than a footnote to the stodgy Wall Street titan. Like Jake, she was sensitive, and she grew weary of being ridiculed about the famous picture. She found off-color jokes about her relationship with Morgan unbearable, she told Jake and other sideshow friends.

To escape the media's glare, she quit the sideshow in 1935 and retreated to her native Germany, where she'd been born Lia Schwarz.

By the late 1930s, Jake was working as a sales rep for Roma Wine. The shtick: here was the largest man hawking product for the largest wine company. It was so good you would have thought Dexter Fellows had personally dreamed it up.

The Muse brothers were still traveling the country, still reliant on the imperfect legal system that was supposed to govern their settlement agreement — and protect them from the whims of Candy Shelton, the former captor who was still managing them. And their money.

But they were faring a lot better than their brother Tom, who'd quit the circus after two years and returned to Roanoke. In December 1930, he was arrested for felony assault after shooting "Johnny Clark, colored," in the stomach, as the newspaper put it, and was sentenced to three years in prison.

"He was a rough man, very rowdy," said Mary Davis, whose aunt was married to him, briefly, in the 1920s.

Lya Graf's life after the circus had a much sadder ending. The Nazis rounded her up in 1941 and arrested her. They eventually sent her to Auschwitz, where she died in the gas chambers. She was twenty-eight years old.

Deemed "useless" by the Nazis, she had been triply cursed: half Jewish, physically different, and forever connected to a despised American capitalist — who lived to the ripe old age of seventy-five.

13

Practically Imbeciles

Harriett wasn't sure what to do. It was 1936, and the Great Depression had only just begun to plateau, with nearly ten million Americans still out of work. Jobs were still almost impossible to find, and drought was gripping the Southeast again. In her native Franklin County, money was so scarce that a farmer's choices were to make whiskey, steal, or starve. Many made whiskey, judging from the ongoing conspiracy case that had swept up fifty-five of the county's moonshiners and haulers, plus dozens of sheriff's deputies, Prohibition agents, and even the commonwealth's attorney—who were all thought to be on the take.

Though Prohibition ended in 1933, the multi-tentacled case extended back to 1928 and drew national attention. Between 1930 and 1935, local still operators and their business partners had sold a volume of whiskey that would have generated $5.5 million in excise taxes. Juries were tampered with, bribes offered, and a deputy who happened to be a key government witness was gunned down in his car on a country road, along with a prisoner he was carting to jail on unrelated business— all to keep the deputy from testifying.

President Franklin D. Roosevelt had pushed to end Prohibition for good. It hadn't kept people from drinking anyway, judging from all the swinging nip joints in Jordan's Alley alone. But money trumped morals when politicians finally conceded that the new liquor taxes were helping fund federal jobs projects. (One such program, the Federal Writers' Project, employed writers to collect oral histories from across the country—including, for instance, some stories of the Franklin County ex-slaves drawn on earlier in this book.)

Roosevelt himself came to the Roanoke Valley, visiting nearby Salem to dedicate a huge new Veterans Administration hospital complex in 1935. But Harriett Muse, now in her early sixties, had no way of getting to a VA cleaning job even if she'd been lucky enough to land one.

She missed the country. She missed her sons.

And she was dead broke, now dependent on her daughter and son-in-law—who had mouths of their own to feed.

The checks sent home by Ringling Brothers had stopped coming in the early 1930s, according to court records. Though Ringling did swing through Roanoke in the fall of 1935—the local newspaper described it as a "clean show"—there was no mention of Eko and Iko, which we now know was because they were no longer part of the lineup.

Harriett had no idea where or how Willie and George were, and no real way of finding out. In a repeat of what happened to them in their early careers, Candy Shelton had switched the brothers to another show, abruptly cutting off their paychecks—and all contact with their mother.

Having abandoned the contract Warren Messick had negotiated as part of the 1928 settlement package, he was also avoiding the ire of Ringling's lawyers by finding them all a new employer who played looser with contractual details than Ringling did.

In circus lingo, he had blown the show.

But Shelton had forgotten what a worthy adversary Harriett Muse was. Even her descendants had no idea how consistently fierce she'd had to be, the stories of her heroic actions in 1927 eclipsing any reports of her subsequent battles.

Though the voluminous documents don't relay her precise motivations, they do reveal that every time the money stopped coming home, Harriett took forceful legal action. While we'll never know where Willie and George preferred to be as they aged, or how much oversight they had over their earnings — including their mother's cut — it's clear from the records that their family connection remained strong.

She had risked her life in 1927, standing up for her sons against lawyers, circus showmen, and the police. That was all true. But her bravery then was simply a prelude to what she would spend the remainder of her life doing: holding the showmen legally accountable. The next case became so convoluted and so protracted that it would persist longer, even, than the moonshine-conspiracy trial.

Harriett hadn't seen George and Willie for "three to five years," according to court documents filed in the fall of 1936. The brothers were performing in a carnival called Beckmann and Gerety Shows now, working for a sideshow operated by the Greek-born Canadian Pete Kortes, whose name was pronounced, maybe ironically, "courts."

If Shelton had dominated the first half of the Muse brothers' careers, Kortes would dominate the last. And so would the courts.

About a third the size of Ringling, the B&G carnival still was not a small operation. Described as a "Stupendous Spectacle of Inconceivable Magnificence," promising "Fun and

Thrills for the Entire Family," the traveling show had enough performers, rides, and animals to fill thirty train cars. Major acts included the Singers Midget Band, John Ruhl's Flea Circus, and Marjorie Kemp, a curvaceous brunette daredevil who rode the pitched walls of the motordrome in a tiny race car—with a lion seated next to her.

Run by Fred Beckmann, a longtime showman with deep jowls, the show was visited by twenty-five million people annually. It traversed eighteen thousand miles a year, mostly in the midwestern, central, and southwestern states, where its stops lasted five or six days. Among the larger traveling carnivals, B&G was sizable enough that it issued its own "brass," or scrip—tokens performers used as part of their pay to buy food and other items on the show lot.

Kortes ran the sideshow, paying rent to Beckmann for his exhibit space, which he grandly titled the Kortes World's Fair Museum. Along with myriad showmen of that era, Kortes routinely ripped off the World's Fair moniker, hoping to profit from the association with wildly popular and much grander events and harking back, most notably, to the 1893 Chicago World's Fair, a six-month exposition that drew twenty-seven million visitors and heralded America's emerging prowess in science, technology, and anthropology.

But whereas the nineteenth-century presentation of exhibits was rooted in the flawed, xenophobic science popular at the time—people actually believed Zip might have been a member of a brand-new species combining elements of human and ape—Americans were increasingly familiar with medicine and more knowledgeable about people living on the other side of the world. Accordingly, the sideshow began to reflect a more comic, almost tongue-in-cheek view of human differentness.

Kortes's 1935 version of a world's fair featured Barney Nelson, the Colored Armless Wonder and the Most Amazing Man You Ever Saw, and the sixty-pound Shadow Harrow, the Thinnest Man in the World, placed alongside Tiny, the World's Largest Girl. It was fronted by Miss Gibbons, whose back featured a giant tattoo of *The Last Supper*.

The once-heralded space travelers were absent, though, having been replaced by Eko and Iko, the Sheep-Headed Men from Ecuador. Why, for ten years, bragged a newspaper in Rockford, Illinois, they had even been "one of the ace attractions" of Ringling!

Working alongside his brother, George Kourtis (who refused to Americanize his surname), Pete Kortes had started out in the business as a fire-eater during World War I. George had been the manager for Schlitzie, the microcephalic performer (or pinhead, in offensive showman parlance) featured in the film *Freaks,* and he later managed Athelia, another microcephalic, believed to be Schlitzie's sibling. Unlike Harry Lewiston, who admitted to binding the limbs of two microcephalics — so they couldn't masturbate — George treated them relatively well, providing a nurse to supervise them and manage their hygiene. They were incontinent, which is why microcephalic males were typically presented as females. When they wore dresses, it was easier to change their diapers.

For a time, Pete Kortes also managed Schlitzie. "But he didn't need both of them, and as he became older, Schlitzie was a little rangy and hard to get along with," said Ward Hall, who eventually bought Kortes's show.

While the Muse brothers abhorred Shelton, Nancy Saunders recalled, they were quite fond of Kortes and his wife, Marie, who cooked meals and planned off-hour outings for the per-formers. Kortes was a fun-loving, friendly sort, Willie told her, a heavy drinker but not abusive when drunk. His trips were more relaxed, and it was he who would make possible one of their favorite experiences: swimming with dolphins.

In a picture of the Kortes gang taken in Honolulu, the Muses pose happily for a group sideshow portrait, the clenched fists and nervous glances of their earlier photos long gone. George has his arm draped over Athelia's shoulder. The group is at a restaurant, with Pete at the head of the table, wearing thick black-framed glasses and holding a cigarette. He's seated next to the "fat man" Jack Connor, who required the extra space at the table's edge. As the Muses entered middle age, their hair-lines seem to retreat in direct proportion to their expanding waistlines.

As one writer of that era described them: "Their hobby is music, and they play it on their platform, softly practicing on saxophone and guitar, hour after hour, when not called upon by the inside talker to stand up and be seen."

It was the life they were used to.

But the happy-go-lucky sheen of the photographs and news clippings belies the seamier side of the business arrangement with Shelton and, likable or not, with Pete and Marie Kortes.

According to dozens of court documents filed on the Muse family's behalf in the mid- to late 1930s, Shelton was back to his old tricks and had been for several years: he was stealing the brothers' pay again and keeping them as far away from Roa-noke as possible.

Harriett had no idea where they were. Again. But period documents show they were all over the place with Kortes, after Shelton joined forces with the sideshow carnival showman in

1931. Two years later, Shelton switched back to Ringling, and it was business as usual with the Big One again, though he and the Muses still traveled annually with Kortes in the off-season: with the tacit approval of both Ringling and Kortes, Shelton continued stealing their earnings. No money was sent home, nor was any news about the brothers, including their whereabouts.

Harriett would strike back legally in 1936. But by that time, Ringling wasn't as invested as it had been in 1927 in holding on to its sideshow stars. The Big One was preoccupied with turbulence of a much bigger sort throughout the 1930s, extending from its biggest big-top performers to the men putting up the tents.

The opening salvo hit in March 1931, when Leitzel, the most beloved circus performer of all time, fell to her death in Copenhagen. The brass swivel on her performing rope had snapped, and she shot from her trapeze, landing on a floor protected only by a thin rubber mat. Just moments before, a crowd of hundreds had been applauding so wildly for her that the crystals on the performance hall chandelier shook.

The news devastated the circus community, especially John Ringling, who considered Leitzel and her husband, Alfredo Codona, dear friends. He used to chew his cigar to bits during their most dangerous routines.

A few years later, Codona was still mourning Leitzel and in the midst of the breakup of his second marriage, to Vera Bruce, a circus bareback rider who'd frowned on the shrine he maintained to Leitzel—in their bedroom. "I am going back to Leitzel, the only woman who ever loved me," he wrote in a suicide note. Then he shot and killed Bruce before turning the gun on himself.

Leitzel and Codona had been the glimmering showstoppers adorning the cake, but the foundational layers, too, were beginning to cave. A power grab orchestrated by lawyer John Kelley against John Ringling had wrested the circus out of the potentate's hands, crippling his finances, which in turn — aided by decades of late-night meals and myriad poor lifestyle choices — crippled his health.

The takeover was payback for a poor business decision Ringling had made in 1929, when he took out a $1.7 million loan to buy the Peru, Indiana–based American Circus Corporation. Ringling purchased the company purely out of spite after Madison Square Garden changed the terms of his opening-day contract, eliminating Friday shows for the circus, which the Garden now wanted to devote to the more lucrative spectacle of prizefighting.

According to his nephew Henry Ringling North, John Ringling initially responded by telling "them with anatomical exactitude precisely where they could put their contract, and announced that the circus would open at the 22nd Regiment Armory."

When the Garden promptly contracted with Ringling's only serious rival, ACC, "John Ringling was thunderstruck," his nephew recalled. Some form of the family circus had been opening at Madison Square Garden for more than fifty years. "His rage consumed him. And destroyed his business judgment."

Ringling tried to trump the deal the only way he knew how. He *bought* the American Circus Corporation for $2 million.

But putting his circus into so much debt proved to be unduly risky in 1929.

With only a little cash down, he'd taken out the note for $1.7

million from the Prudence Bond and Mortgage Company, which financed the deal. His plan was to incorporate a new company and sell its shares to the stock-frenzied public, thus paying off the note, according to his nephew.

But before he could sell an issue of circus stock, the market crashed.

The ACC purchase had been childish, and it was, ultimately, Ringling's undoing. By 1936, his competitors had filed an antitrust lawsuit, and his real estate holdings were so entangled that almost every lawyer in Sarasota was engaged in a suit either for or against him. (There were at least one hundred lawsuits pending against him.)

After his own family members and many longtime associates—including lawyer Kelley—had taken control back to save the debt-plagued circus, John Ringling was now simply a figurehead, forbidden from making any commitments in the name of the circus. His personal life was equally fraught. After his beloved wife, Mable, died in 1929, Ringling had married a sophisticated (and very spoiled) socialite. So tone-deaf was Emily Ringling to the needs of Depression-starved folks that she went to a Sarasota country-club party themed "How to Have Fun Though Broke" costumed as she imagined the poor might dress—wearing a native Cuban outfit with a string of new potatoes around her neck.

In the months leading up to his death, in 1936, Ringling wasn't even allowed to mingle with the crew at the circus. Employees were forbidden to speak to him, and he was mostly alone in his rapidly deteriorating Florida mansion with only his private nurse, who stayed on to work for him—though she hadn't been paid since 1933—and his yacht captain from happier days, who now "did his best to keep the grounds and gardens from going back to the jungle," according to Henry North. North (whom Ringling dubbed Buddy) also filled in gratis as his uncle's business agent, chauffeur, handyman, cook, and butler. To keep Ringling's art collection from deteriorating in the sea-damp climate, he borrowed library books and Harvard University technical papers and gave himself a DIY course in art restoration.

In 1938, Henry and his brother, John Ringling North, took over management of the Big One, determined to restore its reputation as the greatest show on earth. But labor disputes were raging across the country, and that June, in one twenty-four-hour period in Erie, Pennsylvania, sixty-seven crewmen walked off the job. John Ringling North had announced that everyone, executives included, would be taking a 25 percent pay cut. Aggrieved employees responded by sabotaging the brakes on twelve train cars. Delayed train departures created delayed performances, in turn creating mayhem under the tents. Pinkerton detectives were called in to guard the trains.

A falling tent pole shattered a spectator's shoulder. Then the North brothers' latest menagerie star, a gorilla named Gargantua they'd bought from an eccentric woman in Brooklyn (and managed to get featured on the cover of *Life* magazine), turned on his keeper, attacking him in front of the crowd.

Circus managers, who had historically responded to roustabout wage demands by simply replacing the men, could no longer ignore workers' pleas. The rousties had recently organized for the first time ever as an affiliate of the American Federation of Labor, so when John Ringling North decided to cut wages, a full-on strike was called.

The show went on. In Janesville, Wisconsin, managers broke picket lines with elephants. In New York City, John Ringling North himself helped clowns and midgets hoist ropes and rig performers' nets. At another stop, the cage serving as the panther's arena was moved and reassembled by Clyde Ingalls and Jack Earle while Harry Doll assisted by securing the trapdoor ropes—and the audience assumed it was all just part of the show.

During a late June stop in Scranton, Pennsylvania, the Norths could no longer finagle a work-around. As Henry North described it, "We were in considerable danger" from labor activists, some of whom were pelting performers with rocks. "For five days we were besieged in the Casey Hotel, with the circus stalled on the lot. We could not move it out, and the left-wing mayor of Scranton was disinclined to help us or offer protection."

This time the North brothers couldn't round up enough strikebreakers to move the circus out, not even with the elephants on standby. At the end of the standoff, Henry paid $12,000 in "strike costs" to the union before taking the circus back to winter quarters midseason.

To save the show, John Ringling North, thirty-four at the time, had the moxie to talk the best performers into moving west and switching to the Ringling subsidiary, Al G. Barnes-Sells Floto Combined Shows, whose employees were not unionized. Its workers had already agreed to accept the 25 percent pay cut.

Even Gargantua the Great, the World's Most Terrifying Living Creature, joined the twenty-one railcars leaving Sarasota for South Dakota. Adding the Ringling performers doubled the size of the Barnes-Sells Floto show, which pushed the media superlatives into overdrive as the circus publicity machine tried to overshadow news mentions of labor struggles. The gorilla performed alongside Mabel Stark, the World's Only Lion and Tiger Trainer, and along with aerialist Janet May, who could pull off one-arm flips from her rope but "lacked the polish of the celebrated artist" she was trying to evoke—Leitzel. Or maybe it was still too soon after Leitzel's death for critics to fully embrace May's efforts.

The gorilla's backstory grew more elaborate as the train made its usual fall journey south: captured at the age of two, traded by a sea captain, five feet six and "growing more evil tempered" by the moment—with a daily diet that included sixteen bananas, twelve oranges, three milk shakes, and a half-pound of calf liver brought to a boil.

"We yielded, but we made the most of it," North wrote. The brothers called in press photographers to record John Ringling North handing over a wad of cash to union leader Ralph Whitehead, under the caption "Whitehead Getting His Pound of Flesh." Republicans blamed the closure on the New Deal, with one congressman declaring, "Not even this great circus can compete with the circus the New Deal is giving us."

With movies and radio threatening to eclipse the circus in cash-strapped Americans' eyes, the big top struggled to maintain a luster of novelty. As one longtime showman described it: "The kids of today ain't so wide-eyed and amazed at what they see at a circus as they was a quarter of a century ago. So many marvelous things goes on all the time in this day and age that kids probably expect more from a circus now than it's humanly possible to give."

Maybe the Muse brothers' next act would add some drama, if not in front of the stage, then certainly behind the scenes.

*　　*　　*

Attorney Warren Messick had not been available for Harriett's hire this time around. Wrapped up in the multifaceted moonshine-conspiracy trial, he was representing two West Virginia moonshiners in an ancillary case connected to the Franklin County trial: the men were accused of murdering a sheriff's deputy as payback for his role in the death of their brother in a whiskey-running car chase. Messick, ultimately, lost the murder trial, though his defendants' sentences were considered light.

It isn't clear how Harriett found her way instead to the downtown law offices of Roanoke lawyer Wilbur Austin. But she did, sometime in the early fall of 1936, around the time her sons were being photographed outside a sideshow tent in Lincoln, Nebraska. In a backyard candid shot—"caught by the cameraman here sunning themselves," as the local newspaper put it—George and Willie sit next to a tent with Athelia perched on their laps, her long dress draped over their knees. The splendor of their pre-Depression tuxedos has been replaced by simpler white blouses and loose, looping ascots.

Austin's personality mirrored the economic mood, too. He was not nearly as flashy as Messick. "Compared to Squeak, Mr. Austin was deadly dull," according to Harvey Lutins, Messick's longtime coworker and protégé. Lutins strenuously and repeatedly tried to steer me to write more about Messick, who still fascinated him fifty years after Messick's death.

Unlike the disheveled Messick, the buttoned-up Austin had no oratorical flair for fallback. He had to pay attention to every detail. And he did.

Descended from a prominent family in nearby Botetourt County, Austin was politically connected in the state capitol of

Richmond — his sister was married to the man who advised several Virginia governors of that era. His father-in-law's family included a governor and several influential Virginia lawmakers.

Austin may have been dull, but he was also the perfect person to come up with a permanent, court-approved solution for getting Candy Shelton out of the Muse brothers' lives. The fix would take care of Harriett Muse — and her sons — and reward Austin, too.

In an extended guardianship case called *Harriett Muse v. George and Willie Muse,* Harriett petitioned a Roanoke court to have her sons declared "practically imbeciles," though the ploy was likely Austin's idea, according to scholars and lawyers who analyzed the legal records at my request. The "boys," as the petition called them (though they were now in their forties), "are not mentally capable of entering into a contract or attending to business for themselves," the petition stated.

It was a cruel-sounding but pragmatic legal maneuver that guaranteed every paycheck would henceforth be monitored by a court and divvied up accordingly. At Austin's request, the Roanoke judge and future Virginia governor Lindsay Almond appointed Austin to be the committee (pronounced "com-a-TEE"), in charge of their financial affairs. (The term today would be "conservator" or "guardian.")

The judge then ordered Austin to negotiate with Ringling lawyers, winning the brothers a three-year contract that began in November 1936. As far as the money was concerned, Shelton was bypassed entirely now.

The circus would pay the Muses $115 a month, including during the off-season. Harriett would get $60 of their monthly salary, set aside "for her care and maintenance," and Austin $15 for his monthly legal fee.

The rest, or about a third, would go into a savings account established for the brothers, reserved as a kind of retirement fund—a novel idea, considering that Social Security payments for retired Americans were still four years away.

The case would spawn ongoing filings for more than three decades. Financial records, called settlement accounts, would be filed regularly with the courts, documenting every dollar earned and every dollar spent on the brothers' behalf, from groceries to expenses for trips home to visit family to property, including, even, their grave sites.

Austin was also court-ordered to track down, if he could, the back pay owed by Kortes during the Beckmann and Gerety stint. And if Shelton tried to insert himself into the pay process—they had reason to believe he would—judicial repercussions would be triggered. Austin would eventually talk the judge into decreeing that George and Willie "could not be taken from the jurisdiction of this Court by J. H. Shelton or anyone else" without Almond's permission. All future showmen seeking to employ the brothers had to be approved, in person, by the court.

It was an astonishingly twisted legal end run, unusual if not singular among sideshow performers of the time. "The judge did it because I'm sure it was the only way to get justice for them," said Richmond lawyer Tom Word, who writes about Virginia legal history. He doubted the court even had a doctor present to weigh in on George's and Willie's alleged imbecility.

Indeed, the files contain no medical evaluation from a doctor or any professional testimony about the brothers' mental status. Their illiteracy, combined with their near-blindness and dancing eyes, was probably convincing enough. They were likely led into the courtroom by relatives, judging from another photo from this period that shows them being flanked by circus minders outside a tent: George and Willie are squinting in the late-day sun with two men and a woman clutching their arms, presumably so they won't stumble or trip over the nearby tent ropes.

The agreement was probably a backroom deal between Austin and the judge. "It allows the person to have control of them physically but, more importantly, to collect the money on their behalf," said Paul Lombardo, a Georgia State University law professor and bioethics expert who reviewed the filings. "It's about creating a conduit for the money because the guardian has a motive for collecting: he gets paid, and the mom gets paid.

"It's weird... but what else did she have the power to do?"

It was also illegal, by today's standards, from the rubber-stamping of the brothers' mental status to the payments to Harriett Muse, whom Austin described in a subsequent legal filing as "a very good old colored woman."

In a 1938 letter, Austin called Harriett "penniless and absolutely dependent on the stipulation allowed by the Court each month." Unemployment was back on the rise, after slight declines in 1936 and 1937. And though members of the Roanoke Country Club were delighted to learn that a swimming pool would soon be constructed for their recreation, people in Jordan's Alley were none so fortunate.

Those who couldn't pay their rent were beholden to white landlords who refused to fix broken fixtures or repair structural flaws and sent their collectors out to terrorize renters in arrears — some of whom were forced to pay in sexual favors, recalled multiple elderly residents who grew up in Roanoke's West End in the 1930s and '40s.

There were no real protections in place for low-income renters. It would be five more decades before Roanoke hired adequate rental-property inspectors, and only in the wake of an elderly resident freezing to death just a few yards from Harriett's house, on Ten-and-a-Half Street. "I can remember as a kid, riding on that old narrow Tenth Street trestle bridge," said Dan Webb, the city's current code-compliance coordinator. "You'd look over to the side and see those shotgun shanties with no paint and no front yard, all crammed together."

The rail-yard bridge that Harriett's grandchildren had to cross, along with Sweet Sue and Mother Ingram, to get to the all-black Harrison School? Webb described it as wooden planks topped by asphalt. He remembered hearing the *ka-clunk, ka-clunk* of the boards when his father's car crossed the bridge. "You smelled the creosote, and, as a kid, to me, that was the smell of poverty."

V. Anne Edenfield, a Roanoke lawyer who handles guardianship cases, also reviewed Austin's filings at my request. "It's a huge breach of fiduciary duty to use a ward's money to pay a family member," absent court approval, she said. "You could not get away with that now." The guardianship would also be legally impossible to obtain without proof of incapacity presented to the court, she added.

Considering that getting the circus to pay up regularly had already proven impossible, though, the ploy was "not so horrible," Edenfield conceded. She thought that paternalism, more than greed or self-interest, motivated Austin to keep the case going. "My hunch is that Austin was probably a decent guy trying to do good for his client."

Besides, as she pointed out, the likelihood of an illiterate George and Willie Muse demanding their own pay, given their lack of social capital in the circus hierarchy, was minimal.

From his office in Roanoke, Austin not only managed the paperwork; he also won the court's authority to seek legal restitution the minute the checks failed to appear—or to clear the bank. Most years, Austin seemed to earn every penny of his monthly fifteen bucks. Adjusted for inflation, in today's money, his salary from the case typically amounted to about $2,000 annually.

Frugal his entire life, Austin never learned to drive. He raised his family in the side wing of a sweeping Roanoke mansion owned and occupied by his in-laws. In 1925, his father-in-law, Samuel Harris Hoge, had lost the governor's race to Harry Byrd of the Byrd Machine, which dominated Virginia politics for much of the twentieth century. It was Byrd and his minions who would go on to godfather Virginia's "massive resistance" scheme to protest the Supreme Court's 1954 *Brown v. Board of Education* decision. They forged new state laws and policies in defiance of the decision, and many Virginia schools were closed in an attempt to block desegregation.

Austin was no champion of civil rights, according to his grandson, Robert M. Brown, a lawyer in Newport News, Virginia, who writes crime fiction on the side. Brown preferred his great-grandfather Hoge to his grandfather Austin, who seemed to live under the elder man's shadow.

Wilbur Austin "lived rent-free, no utilities or anything, in this giant house owned by his father-in-law," Brown said, along with other members of the extended family. "I can remember they had a black maid, Bessie, a large lady, and she would ring the dinner bell, and everybody would come down from their rooms in coats and ties, and they'd all eat together at this massive dining room table."

Hoge, Austin's father-in-law and law partner, was a friendlier and more socially savvy man. When his clients couldn't pay during the Depression, he accepted homegrown tomatoes as compensation. "It got to the point where he had to ask [his] children to help pay for their own food," Brown recalled.

But Austin refused to contribute. "So here's this lawyer, and his law partner is his father-in-law, and my grandfather started 'taking his meals out,' if you can believe that," Brown said.

It was cheaper, Austin believed, to forgo the family meals and eat in diners.

According to his family, Austin was an odd man with no sense of humor. He was super-meticulous with his clients' money — and quite stingy with his own. After his death, in 1972, the family learned he'd hoarded away money in accounts strategically placed with several different banks.

A Civil War buff with a Mathew Brady photograph collection, Austin was more comfortable among his legal books than with members of his own family, relatives said. He was not warm toward Brown's mother, Austin's only child, to the point that Brown's father later had him banned from their home.

"But as standoffish as he was with his family, he took his profession very seriously," Brown said. "I can see how he would have done everything within his power to help his client." Especially a very good old colored woman.

Though he was never revered by his family, on the red-dirt streets of Jordan's Alley, Wilbur Austin was something of a miracle worker.

*   *   *

It was not so difficult to have people declared mentally incapacitated in the 1930s, a period when Virginia had one of the nation's most active eugenics programs. Between 1924 and 1979, the state forcibly sterilized more than eight thousand Virginians on the alleged grounds of mental illness, physical deformity, "feeble-mindedness," or even just homelessness—to keep them from procreating and to protect the "purity of the American race."

Virginia was in the vanguard of a national movement promoting the so-called science of racial superiority and inferiority. With broad support from the federal government, prominent jurists, research scientists, and the Carnegie Institution, the Eugenics Record Office was initially formed in 1910.

For four decades, the office was the nerve center of a nationwide campaign to promote sterilization for ostensibly inferior genetic stock and strict laws against racial intermarriage, and to quell the immigration of Jews and others from Southern and Eastern Europe, all deemed racially inferior to their whiter-skinned Northern European counterparts.

Such sentiment explains the 1939 appearance of George and Willie's photo—courtesy of Ringling, of course—in the textbook *You and Heredity*. As the author notes, clinically, in his caption, "They have white skins (note their throats), pale blue eyes and flaxen hair (the odd effect produced by combing out the woolly strands and letting them grow for exhibition purposes). They also have nystagmus (oscillating eyeballs) and teeth defects, characteristic of many Albinos."

The author writes, "By sterilization and birth control we might reduce somewhat the proportion of the 'unfit,' and by stimulating births in other quarters we might increase somewhat the proportion of the 'fit.'"

But how to measure who is "fit"? Some eugenics victims were criminals, and some were mentally incapacitated.

Many were just poor.

Nazi war-crimes defendants, on trial in Nuremberg after World War II, claimed that Virginia's eugenics law had been the model for a German program that sterilized thousands. The practice is sometimes said to have declined in the wake of Nazi revelations, but Lombardo says that in fact Virginia sterilized more people in 1949, '50, and '51 than it had in the mid-'30s. "There were lots of reasons for that, but the most important point is that people in Virginia may have been shocked by the Holocaust, but not necessarily by German sterilizations," he added.

In 2015, finally, the Virginia General Assembly voted to compensate victims who had been involuntarily sterilized at six institutions in the state with payments of $25,000 each. Only eleven were still alive.

Such was the legal backdrop for having two illiterate circus freaks declared "practically imbeciles" in 1936 at the request of their destitute mother and her nervous but well-connected lawyer. The State of Virginia's definition of an adult imbecile was a person "with the mentality of a normal child six or seven years old; can do little house errands such as washing dishes and dusting."

The statute does not mention the ability to play music on multiple instruments fabulously well while pretending to be cannibals from Ecuador or ambassadors from Mars.

"In those days it was pretty easy to get this done," said Lombardo, who wrote the definitive book about Virginia's role in the eugenics movement, centering on the landmark Supreme Court case *Buck v. Bell* (1927).

During the off-season, the Muse brothers often played in dime museums, at Coney Island and also at the Dreamland Circus Side Show, shown here in the early 1930s, as a headliner act. *(Courtesy of Bob Blackmar)*

Candy Shelton promised the Muse brothers the chance to sail to England to play before the queen, alongside two of the most famous Ringling Brothers & Barnum-Bailey Circus performers ever, aerialist Lillian Leitzel (right) and her husband, Alfredo Codona, shown here in a candid circus backyard photo. *(Courtesy of the Milner Library Special Collections, Illinois State University)*

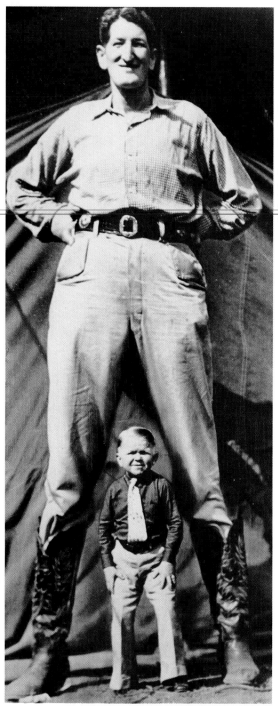

Circus publicity photographs often juxtaposed sideshow performers, such as in this 1920s-era photo of Harry Doll standing in between the legs of his friend the Texas giant Jack Earle. *(Courtesy of Dr. Andy Erlich)*

Manager Candy Shelton, shown here working as a sideshow talker for Ringling Brothers & Barnum-Bailey Circus in 1938, skimmed the Muse brothers' wages whenever he could, forcing Harriett Muse and her lawyers into a protracted legal battle. (*Courtesy of Al Stencell*)

A rare photograph of George and Willie together on the bally platform, during the tumultuous 1938 season on a late-season stop in Green Bay, Wisconsin, for the Ringling-owned Al G. Barnes Circus. It was one of their last performances under the management of Candy Shelton. (*Courtesy of the John and Mable Ringling Museum of Art, Tibbals Collection*)

Wilbur Austin Jr. (standing on right) was frugal, detail-oriented, and eccentric. His young family, shown here on the porch of his father-in-law's grand Roanoke, Virginia, house, in the 1930s, boarded with his in-laws (seated) for free until the Depression hit and a conflict arose over meal payments. (*Courtesy of Robert Brown Jr.*)

Wilbur Austin Jr. was the attorney who most influenced the Muse family's lives, fashioning a legal scheme that was very unusual but court-approved and court-ordered—and thus ensured that the brothers' employers finally paid them their wages. (*Courtesy of Robert Brown Jr.*)

Fred Beckmann was one of the co-owners of Beckmann & Gerety Shows, one of the many carnivals the Muse brothers performed with in the 1930s and 1940s under the sideshow management of Pete and Marie Kortes. *(Courtesy of Circus World Museum)*

The Muse brothers seemed to have more agency during the last half of their careers, performing across North America with the Pete Kortes sideshow for much of the 1940s and 1950s—although Austin periodically had to take Kortes to court, too, when his checks failed to clear. *(Courtesy of Bob Blackmar)*

George Muse was frequently spotlighted on the bally toward the end of their careers, shown here with an unknown lecturer or talker, with the Clyde Beatty Russell Brothers Circus, in the mid-1940s. (*Courtesy of Bob Blackmar*)

George (left) and Willie Muse worked as "The Sheep-Headed Men" during the latter portion of their careers, the splendor of their pre-Depression tuxedos now replaced by simpler white blouses and loose, looping ascots. The reduction in their finery seemed to mirror the decline of the circus and of the sideshow itself. (*Courtesy of Bernth Lindfors*)

Willie and George Muse (third and fourth from left, upper row) learned to play xylophones in the late 1940s, and were so popular in Texas and Mexico that radio stations in Juárez invited them to perform on air as "The Sheep-Headed Cannibals." Al Tomaini is on the far right, upper row, while his wife, Jeanie, is fourth from left, bottom row. In retirement, the Tomainis ran the Giant's Camp in Gibsonton, Florida, turning it into a mecca for sideshow performers and managers, including Candy Shelton. *(The North American Carnival Museum & Archives)*

Roanoke judge J. Lindsay Almond presided paternalistically over the Muse brothers' case in the late 1930s and 1940s at the urging of their mother's attorney, Wilbur Austin Jr. Later, as governor of Virginia from 1958 to 1962, he was the chief defender of *massive resistance,* the state's official refusal to desegregate schools in the wake of the U.S. Supreme Court's *Brown v. Board of Education. (Courtesy of The Library of Virginia)*

Jordan's Alley natives Madaline Daniels and Sarah Woods Showalter (right) recalled the neighborhood slumlords who bullied tenants. Showalter's adopted father, John Houp, was a store owner, bail bondsman, and assistant to Roanoke lawyer Wilbur Austin Jr., and he helped Austin manage the Muses' extended legal case. "The houses were ramshackle and facing all kindsa different ways," Showalter said of Ten-and-a-Half Street, where the Muse family lived. "It was the ghetto." (*Photograph by Beth Macy*)

Roanoke civic leader A. L. Holland, who died in late 2015, had a front-row seat to the Muse brothers' story, witnessing their reunion with their family and its circuitous aftermath—and life in general for African Americans during segregation. He's photographed here in front of a boarded-up storefront in Gainsboro, once a thriving African-American business-and-entertainment district in Roanoke. (*Photograph by Kyle Green, courtesy of the* Roanoke Times)

The author with court researcher, map collector, and title examiner Betsy Biesenbach (left), who figured out where Harriett Muse purchased her first piece of property in 1939, in the southeast Roanoke County settlement of Ballyhack—with this view—thanks to the money her sons were sending home. She bought a 16.8-acre mini-farm in a black enclave, a place with a view so vast and so spectacular that, decades later, developers eyeing it for the first time would one day dream of building vineyards and exclusive golf resorts. (*Photograph by Jerry Trammell*)

This photograph, titled *A Dentist Visits Ballyhack*, was a choreographed picture taken by an unknown photographer, near the turn of the twentieth century. It spotlights the scenic, quiet setting that must have attracted Harriett Muse to buy property in the rural, predominantly black community. (*Courtesy of Frank Ewald, originally from the Collection of George Davis*)

Annie Belle Saunders was the younger sister of George and Willie Muse. She and her husband, Walter, along with their daughter, Dorothy "Dot" Brown, and, later, Dot's daughter, Nancy Saunders, helped look after the brothers in their retirement. As a child, when her great-uncles were home on vacation, Nancy once exclaimed, "Grandma, your brothers need a haircut!" (*Courtesy of Nancy Saunders*)

Dorothy "Dot" Brown was the niece who helped care for George and Willie Muse in their retirement. She raised her daughter, Nancy, in the northwest Roanoke home her uncles paid cash for with the savings accrued—painstakingly, and with not a little bit of legal action—from their circus earnings. (*Courtesy of Nancy Saunders*)

Throughout most of the 1940s, the Muse brothers performed for the Pete Kortes Sideshow, which traveled with various circuses, including the Clyde Beatty Russell Brothers Circus. (*Courtesy of Bob Blackmar*)

During the last half of their careers, the Muse brothers frequently traveled to Hawaii, Venezuela, and Mexico in the off-season, performing with the Pete Kortes Sideshow. Whenever Kortes's checks failed to clear, lawyer Austin would have to go find them—and make the circus pay what it owed them. Pete Kortes is fourth from left, upper row, shown next to his brother, who has his arm around Athelia. (*Courtesy of Bob Blackmar*)

The brothers were often photographed wearing Hawaiian shirts during late-career tours with the Pete Kortes Sideshow and fondly remembered learning to swim with the dolphins in Hawaii. As one elderly black Roanoker recalled, "They were the first black folks I ever knew to ride a plane!" *(Courtesy of Bob Blackmar)*

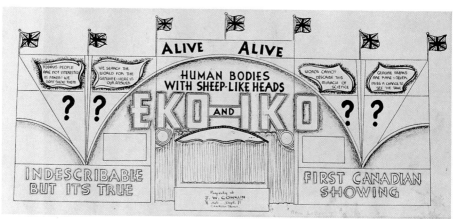

This is a sketch of a proposed banner line for Eko and Iko, advertising their "first Canadian showing" with the Conklin carnival, sometime in the 1950s. *(Courtesy of the North American Carnival Museum & Archives)*

This is the block of Jordan's Alley where the seventy-six-year-old domestic worker Madeline Tate froze to death on Tenth Street in 1985; the houses were shotgun shacks and very similar in appearance to the Muses' home at 19 Ten-and-a-Half Street, just around the corner. All have since been demolished, most of them replaced by a Habitat for Humanity development. (*Photograph by Wayne Deel; copyright* Roanoke Times, *reprinted by permission.*)

Even though he was blind in late life, Willie Muse always kept this framed photo of his mother, Harriett Muse, next to his bed. (*Courtesy of Nancy Saunders*)

Willie Muse played his guitar so often in retirement that he wore down its frets with his finger pads. (*Photograph by Josh Meltzer; copyright* Roanoke Times, *reprinted by permission.*)

Nancy Saunders sits on the bed of her recently departed great-uncle Willie Muse, whom she cared for over a period of decades. "It still smells like him in here," she said, shortly after his 2001 death, referring to the lingering smell of the baby lotion and baby powder that she and other caregivers applied to his fragile skin. (*Photograph by Josh Meltzer; copyright* Roanoke Times, *reprinted by permission.*)

Nancy Saunders was her great-uncle Willie Muse's staunchest caregiver, advocate, and supporter. She is seen here holding a family snapshot of her centenarian Uncle Willie. *(Courtesy of Nancy Saunders)*

Reggie Shareef, now a social science professor, grew up in segregated Roanoke near the Muse family. He remembers thinking it was bunk when his mother said to him, "Be careful, or someone will snatch you up" like Eko and Iko—until he learned the story was true. "That is one exceptionally guarded family," he said. *(Courtesy of Dr. Reginald Shareef)*

Nancy Saunders, photographed in 2015, said she does not "and will not believe that Harriett let her children go off with no circus. As a mother, that's all she had to cling to—her children and her Christ." (Photograph by Josh Meltzer)

In a segregated cemetery in Roanoke, Virginia, Nancy Saunders walks near the newly discovered unmarked grave of her great-grandmother, Harriett Muse, whom she considers a hero. "I lost track of how many times she had to take those circus men to court," she said. (Photograph by Beth Macy)

"I'm sure it was all the lawyer's idea." Given the money being set aside for the Muse brothers' retirement, Lombardo said, "the support for the mom and the fee for the lawyer do not seem excessive. Fifteen a month would have been generous, but not unconscionable, for the lawyer."

Everything went according to Austin's plan for getting Ringling Brothers to pay up per the new contract signed in 1936. The checks arrived monthly, with Harriett and Austin getting their allotments and the rest piling up in savings accounts for Willie and George. Then in the fall of 1938, Shelton took full advantage of the tumultuous, strike-filled Ringling season by blowing the show, again, without a word to Harriett or Austin.

It took months for me to suss out Austin's response to that move. First I had to locate all the court files, two of which had been misfiled in an off-site storage facility, far from the Roanoke courthouse. But when the first of the missing documents was finally unearthed, the whole of Candy Shelton's quarter-century of mistreatment came into focus. So did the enormity of Austin's influence—and the astonishing persistence of Harriett Muse.

For the remainder of the brothers' careers, chauffeurs were hired to accompany the nondriving Austin to various locales to bring them home. New contracts had to be renegotiated when the checks coming in from Kortes bounced.

More than once, Austin hired Pinkerton detectives to track the missing brothers down.

More than once, he coached Harriett and her Roanoke relatives to call him if Shelton showed up during their visits home, trying to whisk the brothers away. He ordered them to "refuse to let [Shelton] in the house." In November 1938, at Austin's request, Judge Almond even issued a temporary restraining order against Shelton.

"My grandfather did that?" Brown said, astonished and, seemingly for the first time in his life, impressed by Wilbur Austin.

When the last missing court file from 1938 still hadn't turned up after multiple searches by myself and a hired researcher, I asked the clerk of the Roanoke City Circuit Court to intervene. Brenda Hamilton accompanied me on a walk down the paneled, third-floor corridor that borders the courtrooms. Along the walls hang large oil paintings of Roanoke judges dating back to 1880s-era Roanoke.

I was also hunting for a portrait of the man behind that file, Wilbur Austin, who, following his work with the Muses, had become a traffic-court judge and, later, a juvenile and domestic-relations judge.

It was beginning to dawn on me that stalking the Big One was probably the most exciting work of Austin's life.

I described the case to Brenda as we walked. When she reminded me she'd been the first African American ever elected to the Roanoke position of clerk of courts, I pointed out that we were standing directly in front of Judge Lindsay Almond's portrait. As Virginia governor in the late 1950s, a Byrd ally, and a chief defender of massive resistance, Almond was the judge who handled the Muse brothers' case.

Brenda was all too familiar with Almond's defiance of the U.S. Supreme Court orders, his insistence on closing, rather than integrating, many Virginia schools. In 1959, she was seven years old and living in the Prince Edward County seat of Farmville, where the school board had closed the county schools for five long years. Wealthy whites in the region built private, whites-only academies.

As Almond put it in a 1959 radio address, his baritone drawl reverberating:

> To those who [support] the livid stench of sadism, sex, immorality, and juvenile pregnancy infesting the mixed schools of the District of Columbia and elsewhere... Let me make it abundantly clear for the record: As governor of this state, I will not yield to that which I know shall be wrong and will destroy every rational semblance of public education for thousands of the children of Virginia. Be not dismayed by recent judicial deliverances.

Brenda missed the entire first grade.

During what should have been her second year of schooling, her parents arranged to drop her off at a family friend's home in the next county, where she was then put on a bus headed to a one-room school. It was a shack with a tar-paper roof that leaked when it rained and had no space for quiet learning. There was only one teacher to accommodate scores of black students ranging from grades one through twelve.

"I used to cry every day," she said.

When her father died the following year, the family moved to Roanoke. As massive resistance began to collapse, Brenda was one of a handful of blacks in a newly integrated Roanoke County school, where attendance was now booming due to white flight.

I told her what Almond and Austin had done for the Muses. That their legal maneuver had ultimately helped the Muse family but that the ploy was also racist, patronizing, and illegal. It was one more of the thousands of stories, told and untold, that illuminated the brutal legacy of 250 years of slavery and a half-century of Jim Crow.

Having located no pictures of the mousy and bespectacled Wilbur Austin that day in the Roanoke courthouse, I was still eager to find that missing file, hoping it contained more clues about the case.

"I'll call you tomorrow," Brenda said. "I *will* find that file."

In her forty-two years of working for the city, Brenda had often walked past the portrait of the man responsible for her patchwork education. When I offered her my copy of a book on massive resistance in Prince Edward County, by journalist Kristen Green, she was eager to read it.

The following week, she e-mailed to say she'd already had to walk away from the book, twice.

"It's like pouring gas in an open wound," she wrote.

It was the spring of 2015, the sesquicentennial of the end of the Civil War. And yet racial wounds seemed to be growing deeper by the day: police shootings of unarmed black men occurred in so many cities, it was hard to feel one had been mourned before another happened.

A crazed gunman hoping to incite a race war killed nine worshippers inside a historic Charleston, South Carolina, church.

Then outside the statehouse in Columbia, South Carolina, the Confederate flag would lower for the last time. Closer to home, Virginia governor Terry McAuliffe ordered the flag's removal from a specialty state license plate.

And Brenda was still contending with the regal portrait of the man who'd stained her childhood — not twenty paces from her door. Outside her office window in downtown Roanoke, a pickup with giant white poles erected on the rear corners of its truck bed sported twin flags, the Rebel Stars and Bars snapping in the summer breeze.

Brenda called the day after our courthouse stroll with information that not only filled gaps in the Muse timeline but also must have sparked interest under the sideshow tent in the late fall of 1938. She had found the missing case file. Signed by Lindsay Almond himself, a petition inside it described a courtroom gathering on November 2. The Muse brothers and their mother were there with Wilbur Austin.

And so was a very unhappy Candy Shelton.

As Austin argued in his petition to the court, Shelton "has been availing himself of the services of the wards of this court without making just compensation to this Committee, and without any express or implied authority from this Committee, by reason of which he is indebted to this Committee for the services of said wards."

The court records don't say where exactly Shelton had taken the brothers after Ringling ended its season following the Scranton standoff in June. But judging from his 1938 employment card and other circus records, Shelton had been among the scores of Ringling staffers who switched midseason to the Ringling-owned Al G. Barnes affiliate, and he took the Muse brothers with him. (I also found a bally photograph of Willie on guitar and George on the ukulele during a 1938 Barnes stop in Green Bay, Wisconsin.)

The checks from Ringling abruptly had stopped going to Roanoke, again.

In a September 1938 letter, Ringling auditor J. F. Wadsworth indicated that the Muse "twins," as he called them, were working with the Barnes circus in Texas. Austin was stirring up trouble, Wadsworth explained to the Barnes circus assistant treasurer: "From the letter of Austin, you will notice that he expects us to continue the payment of their wages each month and that he suggests it is up to us to get them back on the job."

Wadsworth conceded that it was the company's responsibility to return them to Austin after the contract expired. "At any rate, this should be taken up with Mr. [John Ringling] North and whatever action, if any, is necessary to protect us should be taken at once." The contract for the "imbeciles" and "rope-haired wonders," as Wadsworth called them, was once again in flux.

Wadsworth looped in Ringling's legal adjuster, John Reddy, and made a point of telling the treasurer that he should return the "file of legal papers connected with this case" to Ringling offices, pronto.

I found no such file attached to the Ringling papers archives on file at Circus World—only a brief exchange between Austin and Wadsworth—but Brenda's court records were now reassembled and could tell their story.

If the kids of the time expected more from a circus than it was humanly possible to give, how convenient that the Ecuadorian cannibals were ready to morph back into their Ambassadors from Mars attire.

Just three days before Austin's November 2 petition to the Roanoke court, Orson Welles had terrified the country with his radio drama, *War of the Worlds,* a simulated newscast that suggested an alien invasion from Mars was in progress—landing in New York and New Jersey.

RADIO LISTENERS IN PANIC, TAKING WAR DRAMA AS FACT blared an above-the-fold headline on the front page of the *New*

York Times, which described household disruptions, interrupted religious services, and communication-systems logjams. This scene unfolded in a single block of Newark:

> More than twenty families rushed out of their houses with wet handkerchiefs and towels over their faces to flee from what they believed was to be a gas raid. Some began moving household furniture.... Thousands of persons called the police, newspapers and radio stations here and in other cities of the United States and Canada seeking advice on protective measures against the raids.

A Syracuse reporter who happened to have the radio beat bundled his family into the car and headed north for Watertown, New York, "about the time the Martians were wading the Hudson and starting upstate," *Variety* magazine reported. He'd stopped en route to rescue his mother-in-law when he learned that it was not a real attack.

Calls from more than 350 readers flooded the switchboards of the *Roanoke Times:* "So frantic were some of the callers that the entire matter soon ceased to be funny, even for the newsmen, who were kept busy, jumping from one telephone to another, and back again."

Austin was no Messick, but he was savvy enough to make extraterrestrial hay out of the biggest entertainment snafu in radio history. I can just envision him in the courtroom: a champion fidget, running his hands through his hair, nervously adjusting his necktie, removing his Coke-bottle glasses in the middle of an argument only to put them back on again a few seconds later.

I can see Shelton there, dressed in his bally best, his mangled hand tucked into the pocket of his suit pants.

Austin pointed out that Shelton hadn't paid the brothers in more than two months, the last time wiring the $115 payment via Western Union. He pleaded to the judge:

> Your Committee would further show that George Muse and Willie Muse are known to the public of North America and the Continent of Europe as "Eko and Iko, the gentlemen from Mars," and are Albinos of such similar appearance, and such freakish nature as to make them particularly desirable for public exhibition at this time, due in part to a widespread public interest in all Martian affairs, a hoax concerning the Planet Mars having recently been perpetrated upon the American public.

Orson Welles could not have had better timing.

The following week, Almond ruled that no one—including Shelton—would be permitted to remove Willie and George from the jurisdiction of his court until a proper contract had been written, signed, and approved.

Six weeks later, Pete Kortes sent his company treasurer—his wife, Marie—from their home in California to Roanoke to offer Austin a deal. The Kortes show would match the Ringling salary, and to prove they operated in good faith, they proposed something unheard of in the circus world of the 1930s: they would pay six weeks in advance. The Korteses would also cover all food, clothing, and travel expenses for the brothers.

More meaningfully to Harriett Muse, from now on she would know where her sons were performing.

Marie promised to mail regular letters to Austin, who would read them to Harriett when she came to the office to retrieve her monthly checks.

After more than two decades of being in the dark, Harriett would now receive monthly updates advising her "where George & Willie Muse are, and how they are."

Shelton would never come in contact with them again.

The gentlemen from Mars were now under the "exclusive custody and control" of Pete and Marie Kortes.

Marie signed for her husband in his absence. Below her loopy cursive, Wilbur J. Austin Jr. signed the contract for Willie and George, who were present but could not write their names.

On February 20, 1939, the contract was initialed by Lindsay Almond Jr., then stamped with his official seal. And so was finalized the ruling of the racist, benevolent judge.

PART FIVE

14

Very Good Old Colored Woman

This time Harriett had a better plan for the money being sent home for her benefit. On a balmy late-winter day in 2015, I set out to explore exactly what she bought with the remittances from her sons, seventy-six years after the fact, and to track the rippling impact of first-time property ownership on a woman whose parents and children had been themselves considered property. My guide was Betsy Biesenbach, a Roanoke court researcher, title examiner, and map collector.

We drove southeast from Roanoke toward an unpopulated knoll near the Blue Ridge Parkway to find Harriett Muse's first and only piece of land. Cars cruising the parkway hummed in the distance. A warm breeze skirted thickets of denuded trees. Wrinkled horse-nettle fruit clustered in tiny orange bunches, and dried milkweed pods spiked from fields of overgrown, butter-colored grass.

Even though our chances of discovering Harriett's motivations were slim, here Betsy and I were, standing outside my car, each of us pivoting in a circle, as if on cue. Bookended by Fort Lewis Mountain to the west and Peaks of Otter to the east, the panorama demands that kind of attention.

It's as if God reached his hand down four hundred million

years ago and crimped a hundred miles of piecrust into sedimentary rock.

The only evidence of human habitation here, on what was once Harriett's 16.8 acres, was the occasional pocket of daffodils marking long-gone property lines and a few stretches of rusted wire-mesh fencing. And lots of trash, in the form of more recently discarded tires, a toilet, and bottles of Yoohoo and Mad Dog 20/20.

People once lived here, first the Sioux and Powhatan and Iroquois, then the English and their African slaves, and the German and Scots-Irish settlers after them. In the late 1930s, whites owned most of the land, but several black subsistence farmers lived amid them, too, descendants of the slaves, most of them in an enclave called Ballyhack.

From 1939 to 1942, they were Harriett Muse's neighbors.

For the first time in her life, the widowed maid owned something of her own—with a view so vast and so spectacular that, decades later, developers eyeing it for the first time would dream of one day building vineyards and exclusive golf resorts.

We were there to explore Ballyhack, a community that took its name from a bloody election-day brouhaha in the mid-1800s between rival political factions. If oral history is true, the fight took place at a voting precinct, where brawlers struck one another with boots, clubs, and knives (hence Bally*hack*).

A milder-sounding name was later suggested, which is why most people now refer to the area as Mount Pleasant, for the views and high-elevation breezes. The black history of Ballyhack seems to have evaporated among all but the very old and the George Davis archives: his photograph *The Dentist Visits Ballyhack* features the outdoor pulling of a tooth by a neighborhood healer, with the entire family looking on, and its details offer a stop-time moment of rural daily living, from pigs at the feeding trough, to a collapsed porch roof cobbled from sticks, to bedsheets hanging from tree-limb fence rails.

The Ballyhack name did recently reenter the local lexicon, though, attached to an ultra-exclusive golf club a few miles down the road. Virginia Tech football icon Frank Beamer and NFL great Archie Manning are members, and many in the club travel to the region by private jet and chauffeur.

There were neither golfers nor brawlers in sight the day Betsy and I set out to locate the plot of land Wilbur Austin bought in George's and Willie's names for $790 in early 1939. He paid $400 cash down, accrued from the money he'd been setting aside for the brothers' savings and retirement, followed by $10 monthly payments by Harriett. The house on the plot had been built sometime around 1905, Betsy surmised from the deeds, by a farmer named General Grant Maxey. It was a bit unusual, having the same name as the Union commander General Ulysses Grant in the midst of Rebel territory. But Maxey was born in 1862 in nearby Bedford County, and though he had many black families as neighbors, he was actually white, census records show.

Technically, we were trespassing as we walked atop the knoll where Harriett's house had been located, long before her plot was sold and resold. We were trespassing on what had become, long after Harriett's tenure there, the final resting spot for more than two million tons of the region's garbage between 1977 and 1994. Two years later, Roanoke Regional Landfill officials had it capped off and covered with dirt and grass, moving operations to a newer and more environmentally sound facility elsewhere in the county.

On auspicious days, it's possible to stand at a nearby parkway overlook and catch sight of a bald eagle or a red-tailed hawk swooping in and out of the undulating blue haze.

Within fifteen minutes of our arrival on this day, a worker monitoring leachate seepage spotted us walking on the old landfill and told us to move along, and we did.

In 1939, Harriett Muse was one of fifty-six black homesteaders living in Roanoke County. Her dwelling was a five-room frame house, including a ceiling, as the real estate assessor noted. She also owned a barn built of oak with a roof that badly needed repair. Among the amenities of Ballyhack—a smattering of black homes spread out along a single meandering road, not unlike the tiny crossroads of Truevine—were a segregated "colored school," two black churches, a black cemetery, and a black-owned store. As the crow flies, Ballyhack was just four miles southeast of the Roanoke city line, but the road there from Roanoke was winding and ill maintained, making the journey rugged and long.

Ballyhack was a tight-knit community, recalled ninety-three-year-old Veron Holland, who grew up spending weekends at her grandparents' farm next door to Harriett's. Veron pulled weeds in the garden, helped care for the chickens and cows, and went to church at the Ballyhack African Methodist Episcopal church. When she was lucky she got to shop in a little store run by Ardelia Jones, "a very, very pretty woman who would sell us a penny's worth of candy," the retired teacher told me.

Veron described the forty homes clustered around Ballyhack as "shanty and shackly," small country houses built of wood-frame construction, some of them lopsided, but for the stick-straight house built by hand by her grandfather Jordan Holland, the son of former slaves.

"I tell you the truth, black folks had a hard time trying to live back then. Money was a very scarce thing," Veron said. Her father, Garrett Holland, worked as a Norfolk and Western railroad laborer, the family grew its own food, and her parents squirreled away money to send Veron and her sister by train to Bluefield State, in West Virginia. "Hollins College was right here in Roanoke County, but blacks couldn't go," she said. (Another retired black educator told me the same story, remembering that students had to sit in the back of the train car until the moment it crossed the state line into West Virginia, at which point they all rose and moved forward.)

The name Harriett Muse did not ring a bell with Holland. But as a longtime elementary schoolteacher at Roanoke's segregated Harrison School, she recalled hearing her students whisper, gossip, and giggle about Harriett's sons. "Oh, Eko and Iko, Lord yes, I knew about them," she said. "Everybody would get out and try to get a peep at 'em when they came to town. They were famous boys, but it was sad, too. They had a hard time."

She remembered the time someone spotted them walking through Washington Park, up the street from her school, and called police to report that two wild men were on the loose.

Back then, forty-five tons of trash got deposited every day right next to that park—in the heart of Roanoke's black community. The city's landfill was also within smelling range of three black schools and the black hospital.

In the 1960s, when black Roanokers protested the fact that their children had to walk past the steaming, reeking, and rat-infested dump to get to school, the black PTA president A.

Byron Smith appealed to the white city council's own sense of safety. He reasoned: the black maids hired to cook and care for the councilmen's kids might infect them with sickness picked up from the Washington Park landfill. (For decades after, the newspaper ran an angry-looking picture of Smith from that meeting with every story that quoted him. "Mr. Smith, you aren't as ugly as the paper's making you look," a woman from across town told him years later, astonished. "You're nice-looking.")

But only the threat of a mass protest spurred the council to move. No matter how much agency the black community began to have in its affairs, it could not overcome the mind-set of most white decision makers that their children and their homes should be far from view. On the eve of a sit-in organized by Smith, officials finally announced they would close the dump and move it way out to southeastern Roanoke County—to the one black neighborhood in that part of the countryside.

To Ballyhack.

But capped landfills and venture-capitalist golfers were still decades away in 1939. Back then, Ballyhack was the kind of remote piece of heaven that Harriett's young grandchildren loathed, relatives recalled. It was a half-hour drive from the city on winding bumpy roads, and there was no electricity. The roads were so bad that, a year earlier, the "Parent-Teacher Association of the Ballyhack school (colored) appeared before the Roanoke County School Board...to request adequate roads over which the school's pupils can travel to and from school," the *Roanoke Times* reported.

"Mama never did like to go out there," Nancy recalled of her mother, Dot, who preferred the Henry Street nightlife in the city. (Dot was *gorgeous,* one Jordan's Alley native said, recalling a teenager who wore beautiful clothes, stylish haircuts, and bright-red lipstick—very much against the wishes of her ultra-religious Pentecostal mother, whose salt-and-pepper hair was "so long she could sit on it.")

Dot "didn't like that it was so dark in the country, not like in the city with all the lights," Nancy said. "She never wanted to spend the night out there."

Nancy had never been there herself and had no idea where Harriett had lived beyond "somewhere in Ballyhack." But Betsy had spent three hours piecing together exactly where her long-gone property lines were by comparing and superimposing old maps and surveys, and tracking down titles to adjoining properties.

A visitor making the trek from Jordan's Alley would have arrived on Harriett's property only to realize that the journey to her actual home was far from over. To get to her house on the hill (at an elevation of eleven hundred feet), you had to traverse a long and rutted dirt lane. After a hard rain it was impassable. The soil was too rocky to be of adequate fertility. It was typical, Betsy said, "of the kind of property white landowners would sell to blacks."

But Harriett loved her hilltop house, especially the view. She kept her own chickens and pigs, and neighbors sold her butter-milk and meats. A church friend from the city brought her other groceries, and Annie Belle and Herbert looked after her, too.

She was never alone. In 1940, her son Tom, divorced now and working in a coal yard (probably for his brother-in-law), lived with her, as did a nephew and niece from West Virginia, who rented rooms from her and worked nearby as a miner and a maid.

On breezy summer nights, Harriett liked to sit on her front stoop and sing her favorite gospel tune, "Hallelujah, It's Already Done":

Faith is the substance
Of things hoped for
The evidence of things I've seen
So even before you get it
Go praise God for it
Tell the world it's already done....

She could not have imagined owning such land during all those years she'd spent picking worms off tobacco plants and washing other people's clothes.

She was sixty-six years old and, for the first time in her life, at peace.

I imagine her sitting on the stoop, clasping the letters Marie Kortes wrote to her, maybe asking her niece or nephew to reread them to her at night, though no one in the family today remembers ever seeing the letters. She now knew where George and Willie were and where they were heading—in a typical month, from Denver to San Antonio to New Orleans.

During the regular season, the show traveled across America and Canada attached to larger affairs, usually the Clyde Beatty Circus but sometimes Beckmann and Gerety or the Conklin Shows. During the off-season, Kortes rented storefronts for his sideshow, erecting a kind of small indoor circus.

No longer traveling by rail during World War II, Beatty's circus moved in forty-two trucks and vehicles, working around gasoline and tire rationing as well as worker shortages prompted by the war. Candy butchers had to put up the menagerie tent in 1944, and clowns had to build their own dressing facilities, which made them so mad they went on strike, or tried to— until the boss "gave us a hard look and said it didn't make any difference whether we were on the show or not," Beatty clown Walt Matthie recalled. "So we went back to hauling the trunks and putting up the tent and tearing it down."

George and Willie helped with grunt work, too, according to relatives' accounts. But they often did more than their share, and not necessarily of their own will, according to a letter written in the summer of 1946 by a Walnut Grove, Illinois, grocer to the Chicago division of the FBI. Harry E. Friend said he traveled with the show for several summers and believed the Muse brothers were seriously mistreated.

"For giving this information it would cost me my life if it were known," the letter began.

Friend wrote to complain about the "almost impossible conditions" that George and Willie were forced to live under in 1946: "There [*sic*] sleeping quarters while on location is or was a lousy show wagon, thousands of bed bugs in their beds possibly body lice, to have money they were forced to carry water and do other show peoples [*sic*] flunky work, including doing showmens' washing."

Unless there is a trust fund being set aside for them, Friend wrote—which there was, unbeknownst to him—"it seems to me there [*sic*] present owner is as guilty of kidnapping as the criminal ones that kidnapped these 2 colored Boys" years ago.

Circus collectors I interviewed roundly dismissed the letter after it entered online circulation a few years back thanks to a peonage researcher who found it in Department of Justice records on file at the National Archives. They believe Friend had an ax to grind with Clyde Beatty. Sideshow historian Bob Blackmar even suggested that Kortes and Beatty must have fled the Walnut Grove region without settling their grocery bill—not so uncommon among show people operating with slim profits and sometimes in the red—and Friend was seeking payback.

Scanning personnel lists in Beatty's souvenir programs, I found no mention of Harry Friend working for Clyde Beatty, which made me wonder if the letter was written by a person using a *Friend*-ly alias.

The letter was forwarded to FBI assistant attorney general Theron L. Caudle in August 1946. Thirteen days later, Caudle sent a memo to Director J. Edgar Hoover, advising him that "from the information presently available it appears that the institution of criminal proceedings is not warranted. No further investigation is warranted."

As Douglas Blackmon recounted in *Slavery by Another Name,* peonage cases were not a priority of the FBI's in the 1930s or '40s. Only the most egregious cases were investigated, and punishment was rare for those convicted. A man who pleaded guilty in federal court in Mobile, Alabama, for holding a black man named Martin Thompson against his will received a $100 fine and six months of probation. "The futility of combating [peonage] was clear," Blackmon wrote.

It wasn't until 1951, following the return of black and white World War II soldiers who'd witnessed the violent horrors of the Nazis' racial ideology, that Congress passed explicit statutes deeming any form of slavery indisputably a crime. Then, three years later, came *Brown v. Board of Education.*

"It was a strange irony that after seventy-four years of hollow emancipation, the final delivery of African Americans from overt slavery and from the quiet complicity of the federal government in their servitude was precipitated only in response to the horrors perpetrated by an enemy country against its own despised minorities," Blackmon wrote.

Mississippi-based Antoinette Harrell, who first published Friend's letter online and in her book about peonage, doubts that Friend's complaint was investigated at all. An activist and author, she's researched and lectured about scores of peonage claims, past and present, in six southern states, including in twenty-seven Mississippi counties. In secluded parts of rural Mississippi, there are some families, entrapped for generations and predating emancipation, who still farm in exchange for the privilege of living in a shanty on someone else's land, she said.

Harrell doesn't doubt that Harriett Muse loved her sons, but she doesn't believe George and Willie were able to give informed consent when they decided to rejoin the circus in 1928 and continue performing. "If you had spent twenty years, and this was the way you supported yourself, and this is all that you know, then you may not be able to make a wise decision for yourself, especially if you've been brainwashed to believe that no one would hire you because you're a misfit."

Without proper training and education, victims of involuntary servitude generally gravitate back to what they know, she said.

Harrell's insistence that George and Willie weren't capable of deciding to rejoin the circus represents another parting of the story streams: it seemed there would always be people suggesting that the brothers weren't mentally capable, just as there would always be a family and supporters who vehemently believe they were.

Jordan's Alley native Myrtle Phanelson, ninety-seven, recalls them visiting Roanoke in the 1940s. "They'd visit their mama out in Ballyhack, and they'd bring 'em to church down here at Mount Sinai," the Pentecostal Holiness church where Annie Belle sometimes preached. Myrtle's mother-in-law, Esther, was the minister of the tiny white church with wooden pews, where Wednesday-night services sometimes went till 1:00 in the morning. (At Mount Sinai, they banged tambourines to floor-stomping hymns, and "they felt like you wasn't saved unless you spoke in tongues.")

"I knew Iko and Eko, yes," Myrtle said. "One did all the talking, and the other one would just sit and listen. The one who talked [George], he seemed very smart, he really did. They'd been gone a long time with the circus, but, finally, they'd gotten 'em back," she said.

As with the other African Americans I interviewed in Roanoke, it didn't occur to Myrtle to think that George and Willie were victims of a family that stood to benefit from their work. While Harriett was literally living off their salaries during the last years of her life, she was also enforcing their work contracts and building a substantial retirement nest egg for them—something Harrell and Friend knew nothing about.

Within ten years, their savings had accrued to $10,635—worth about $106,000 in today's money—and the Ballyhack property was fully paid off and accounted for, and in George's and Willie's names. At a time when black families struggled to get low-interest mortgages, when the Federal Housing Authority guaranteed very few loans in low-income and minority neighborhoods, Harriett was now a rarity. She was among just 20 percent of black Americans who owned their own homes.

*   *   *

Friend's concern for the brothers did seem sincere (if poorly worded and spelled). His account of their musicianship and faith rang especially true, according to people I interviewed: "Even though they were not gave any schooling, they are good Christians and are able to play almost any musical instrument yet never had a lesson, and were you to ask how they account for this, their answer would be it was a gift from God, and truly it must have been. Now they can neither read nor write yet I think they are good enough to be in Vaudeville."

Indeed, judging from photographs of that time, George in particular seems to enjoy a higher status among his peers. He has a ladies'-man reputation, relatives and circus chroniclers say. And he's regularly highlighted on the bally for solo performances while the lecturer teases the crowd, trying to turn the tip. In one mid-1940s photograph, George peeks out from under a sheet, and it's unclear whether he and the lecturer are working the crowd, or if George is just trying to prevent a sunburn.

The Mars madness having run its course, the banner that year bills the brothers as the Sheep-Headed Men from Ecuador. They've taken up the xylophone too, now, and their playing is so popular along the Texas-Mexico border that radio stations in Juárez invite them to perform on air. By 1948, they are Eko and Iko, the Sheep-Headed Cannibals. (Kortes was a champ at name switching, aiming to give returning prospective audiences at least the promise of seeing something new.)

Former circus-bill poster Dave Price remembers meeting the brothers as a boy at the Tennessee State Fair during that time. He walked up to the platform inside the tent and watched them play a spirited, flawless version of "The Stars and Stripes Forever," with Willie on guitar and George on mandolin.

Price, a certified member of the lot lice, introduced himself to George and Willie. They politely and easily conversed with him and others in the crowd. Price asked them about a family friend and sideshow artist whose trick was stuffing his mouth with dozens of golf balls. The brothers fondly remembered working with Paul McWilliams, the Big-Mouthed Man, on Ringling in 1937, they said.

Press accounts from the 1940s do not describe them peering endlessly at the menagerie or grabbing fried chicken by the fistful. Since Kortes was a much smaller affair than Ringling, they are rarely mentioned at all, in fact, except in puff pieces Kortes himself provided to *Billboard*.

Indeed, though they are still referred to as "boys," at least one author looking back on that time bestowed George and Willie, finally, with manly attributes and appetites. "The boys had saved up enough money for either a woman or a new suit of clothes and couldn't decide which they wanted more," one wrote of the Muses' time with Kortes. "They debated this important issue for three days."

They were already almost totally blind by late middle age, recalled another writer, Albert Tucker, a carnival cook during that period. It was hard for them to recognize objects or people unless they were brought within a few inches of their faces.

As workers waited for the train to pull out for the next stop, show people would lounge around the backyard, listening to the Muses playing and singing, some of them joining in. "Everyone on the circus loved them and would gather around, laughing and singing until the train started to roll, and then what a scramble to get aboard," Tucker wrote.

For the first time in their careers, the Muse brothers were being treated with a modicum of respect. By the late 1940s and '50s, their costumes shifted to floral Hawaiian shirts, as Kortes began producing winter shows around the Pacific, rotating acts in and out of various island resorts by boat and plane. "They were the first black folks I ever knew to ride a plane!" several elderly black Roanokers said, proudly.

Though Willie never got used to riding in a car—especially on four-lane highways—he loved flying during the early days of commercial aviation, when an airplane trip was usually reserved for the upper-middle and upper classes. People dressed up, and in-flight service was elegant, often including champagne. "When I was on that airplane, God never did let that plane crash," he told his relatives, marveling.

Most of their coworkers were more collegial, more inclusive, than in decades past, when George and Willie are usually described as being off to themselves, with only the menagerie—and each other—for companionship. Kortes was never a household name like Ringling, but his operation was every bit as colorful, maybe even more so, with a legacy that spanned fifty years and several countries. Among the Muses' longest-running coworkers were the Kortes fixtures who were pitched as the World's Strangest Married Couple: the sideshow giant Al Tomaini and his "half-lady" acrobat wife, Jeanie, a pretty brunette born without legs or lower torso. In publicity pictures, eight-foot-tall Al holds the thirty-inch Jeanie on his lap. In some photos, she poses on the ground next to him, the crown of her head reaching just above the top of his cowboy boots (size 22).

"My mother said the Muse brothers could play instruments very well, but they were kind of shy," recalled the Tomainis' adopted daughter, Judy Rock. "During the Depression when most people weren't working, the sideshow people were still working, and it was decent money, especially for blacks. They got to travel the world. They got to meet people they'd never have otherwise met," she enthused.

Born in 1916 and originally exhibited by her mother, who died when she was thirteen, Jeanie had come under the abusive care of an adoptive mother who locked her up between performances. When she met Al Tomaini at a Cleveland fair in 1936, he vowed to protect her, and they became part of each other's acts, marrying the following year.

By the time the Tomainis retired, in 1949, they had built a combination trailer park, motel, restaurant, and bait shop in Gibsonton, Florida, about twelve miles southeast of Tampa, called the Giant's Camp. It helped launch "Gibtown" and surrounding communities as a retirement mecca of sorts for all kinds of sideshow managers and performers, including Percilla Bejano, the Monkey Girl, and her husband, Emmett, the Alligator-Skinned Boy—who were also billed as the World's Strangest Married Couple. (Percilla spent her retirement puttering in the garden outside her bungalow—at the end of a dead-end street in nearby Lutz, fenced in to keep curiosity seekers out and her menagerie of cats, dogs, and goats in, Al Stencell recalled.)

But when strangers dropped in to the Giant's Camp for a free freak show, Al Tomaini welcomed them. "I don't mind," he said, especially if they stayed to fish or buy lunch. "I'm peek-proof."

Al was revered in Gibtown, where he served as the World's Tallest Fire Chief and the president of the local chamber of commerce. (He once gave every stick of furniture in his home to a family that had lost theirs in a fire he'd been called to fight.) After his death, in 1962, widowed Jeanie remained in Gibtown, getting around the trailer park on an electric tricycle, until her death, in 1999.

Robert Bogdan, the sociologist, likened the Kortes gang's career path to one that many workers face in their careers: as they grew older, "their value as exhibits declined," he said. The shift mirrored both the downward pattern of sideshows generally and the upward pattern of technologically enhanced entertainment.

The Muses were among the last of their kind, not unlike the production guys who set hot type at my first newspaper job — the backshop, we called them — the luckiest of them old enough to retire just as the first digital equipment was coming through the doors.

When I interviewed Judy Rock in 2001, she was still running the Giant's Camp, where diner regulars included Petie the Midget Terhune, who ate fire, handled snakes, and juggled; Melvin Burkhart, the Human Blockhead, another longtime Kortes performer, who hammered metal spikes into his nasal passage; and Bruce Snowdon, aka Falstaff the Fatman. They had all worked for the longtime sideshow operator Ward Hall, who bought the Pete Kortes Sideshow in 1973, a year before Kortes's death.

Some of them had direct knowledge — or at least opinions — about George and Willie Muse.

Terhune, who died at age eighty-two in 2012, worked for Hall as a performer and rode shotgun to keep the manager from falling asleep at the wheel of his truck. Burkhart and Snowdon have also since died — Burkhart at ninety-four in

2001, and Snowdon at sixty-four in 2009. ("He literally ate himself to death," Hall said of Snowdon.) Even the Giant's Camp, sold to a local phosphate company after the last of the Tomaini family left town, closed in 2006.

Hall had seen the Muse brothers perform several times in the 1950s. He noted that Willie had lost so much hair toward the end of his career that Kortes commissioned a dreadlocked wig for him to wear during shows. In a backstage photo of the brothers from that time, they sport flowery Hawaiian shirts, and George has his arm around Willie's shoulder. Willie is bearded but bald while George has a short blond Afro and beard.

It still pains Hall that he threw Willie's old wig away after buying Kortes's show and finding it inside an old storage crate.

"It'd be worth a lot of money today!" he said.

Not everyone cared so much about the Muse brothers' legacy. Burkhart, also known as the Anatomical Wonder, was living in a Gibtown trailer with his wife and daughter when we met in 2001. He demonstrated his act with gusto. At age ninety-four, he was still happy to pound a spike up his nose for anyone who asked. (A source who introduced us did suggest we take him and his wife out to lunch for the interview; "they're on a fixed income," he said.)

When Burkhart was a teen, his nose had been squashed in the boxing ring and twenty-two bone fragments removed, creating a cavity behind one nostril that was just big enough for a thick nail. He could also make the two sides of his face do different things—grimace and laugh—at the same time.

His memories of the Muse brothers underscored the caste system George and Willie operated under for so many decades. Burkhart had worked alongside them, both with Ringling in the 1930s and, later, with Pete Kortes. People didn't come to see reality, he told me. "They came to be entertained." Customers liked the spontaneity, never knowing what was going to happen onstage. Burkhart rolled his eyes, recalling the questions the public threw at them, especially regarding their sex lives. "The half-lady used to say she'd stand onstage and marvel at the freaks in the audience," he said.

He remembered George and Willie introducing themselves: "We're Eko and Iko, and we come from Mars." They were "backwards," Burkhart said.

Asked if black performers were generally looked down on, he said, "Nobody wanted to lose a good black act, so if you started picking on them, you'd hear about it."

But he never bothered getting to know them, he conceded, and wasn't surprised by stories of exploitative managers. "Some of the bosses were good, and some weren't."

He'd heard something about a kidnapping and, later, after their mother found them, that they still sometimes went unpaid.

"But I also heard they were from Mars," he quipped.

Then he laughed dismissively and changed the subject.

For the life of him, he couldn't figure out why anyone would want to write about George and Willie Muse.

The brothers came home every year or two. They usually stayed with their mother in Ballyhack or with their sister, Annie Belle, in Jordan's Alley, where family friends and relatives treated them like celebrities, according to eighty-eight-year-old Madaline Daniels, who was born in the shotgun house across from Jerusalem Baptist Church and remembers the homecomings.

An occasional lay preacher, Annie Belle tried to isolate her family from others in the neighborhood, maintaining a pious-ness that came across as snobbery to some. "The Pentecostals looked down on the rest of us," Madaline and another neighbor told me. They wore tightly buttoned long dresses and eschewed makeup, and they spoke in tongues on a mourning bench posi-tioned near the front of their church, for penitent sinners seek-ing salvation.

"Don't be unevenly yoked," they preached, which meant: stay away from the Baptists and other ne'er-do-wells, or their sin-ning might rub off on you.

Occasionally during visits home, George and Willie traveled with Harriett back to Truevine, where nonagenarian Mozell Witcher recalls them playing guitar and banjo at house parties in the countryside, held to celebrate the pulling of the season's last tobacco-bud leaves. It was the early 1940s, and Mozell remem-bered being fascinated, and slightly scared, by the novel sight of dreadlocks. (Another elderly resident recalled George telling one of the children at the party, "Come sit on my big fat knee.")

"People said they'd been stolen off the street," Witcher told me.

That wasn't a provable truth.

Some evidence suggests that Harriett had temporarily let them go, presumably for pay, and *then* they'd been stolen and she'd had to fight to get them back.

But Harriett did not correct the stories as they arose, nor did the brothers. "When I saw 'em, their mother was right proud of all they'd accomplished and all the places they'd been," Witcher said.

Harriett was especially proud of their musical talent, remem-bered Truevine native J. Harry Woody, ninety-four, who also recalled their attendance at house parties.

"They played guitar and they played banjo, and it wasn't like the music you hear today. This was *real country* blues, and they could make those instruments talk to you like a man talks."

The parties were such spirited affairs that hosts often added extra nails and other reinforcements to the floorboards to keep the structures from sinking under the weight of the merriment.

In his ongoing role as sideshow coordinator and subcontractor, Kortes coordinated as many as six wintertime sideshows for a Hawaiian-based carnival owner named E. K. Fernandez, known as the Barnum of the Pacific Rim. The Muses flew to Cuba, Puerto Rico, the Dominican Republic, Guatemala, across the Hawaiian Islands, and into Venezuela, where the Kortes group also worked for carnivals operated by Charlie Cox, according to photographs and *Billboard* notices. Other show owners had tried, and failed, to make money operating in the Caribbean, and "some... lost all their equipment, even their elephants!" marveled Bob Blackmar. But Cox must have had "some kind of in with the Cuban government," he said, because he handled the immigration transitions with ease.

In a typical year, the performers' route ranged from San Juan, Puerto Rico, to Maui to Mexico City to Montreal, then down through the southern United States, into Nashville and New Orleans. They played indoors and outdoors, and Kortes's assistants often gave one-off lectures to local Kiwanis or chamber of commerce groups titled "The Home Life of Freaks."

"Sympathy is wasted on human oddities," said a Kortes lecturer at a Cleveland stop. "Besides, I'll bet they make more money than you do."

But whether the checks arrived on time — and didn't bounce when Harriett tried to cash them — was another issue entirely.

15

Wilbur and John

Though Pete Kortes followed the employment contract with more integrity than Candy Shelton ever had, Harriett's move to draw Wilbur Austin into the process proved prescient and astute.

Especially when the checks home from Kortes began to bounce, as happened on September 9, 1943.

And again in 1952.

And again in 1954, when Austin had to commission the Missing Persons Bureau to locate the brothers first in Vancouver and later in Montreal.

Every time the checks bounced, Austin had to figure out where they were, then travel there to personally collect the back pay Kortes owed, sometimes as much as $1,500.

How did he manage it? How did he track Kortes down across several states and into Canada? Those questions nagged at me, given what I'd heard about his mousy demeanor from relatives and fellow bar members.

Then I met Sarah Woods Showalter, who grew up in Jordan's Alley with a front-row seat to the backroom dealings of Wilbur Austin Jr.

Austin's secret weapon was John Houp. I'd seen Houp's name in court documents and Muse financial accountings. He was the man—and the muscle—who accompanied Austin on his money-shaking journeys. I imagine he was also the man who'd told Shelton, in no uncertain terms, what might happen to him if he showed up in *his neighborhood* again.

Houp, a black bail bondsman and well-known store owner throughout Roanoke's West End, and his polio-stricken wife, Miss Irene, unofficially adopted three-year-old Sarah after her mother abandoned her. An unwed pregnant teenager, Sarah's mother had walked and hitchhiked the fifty miles north from Martinsville to Roanoke in 1936 after her father kicked her out. Four years later, little Sarah wandered into Miss Irene's store—a block away from the home of Annie Belle Muse Saunders.

"I went to stay one night, and I stayed till I got grown and left for college," recalled Showalter, who, at seventy-nine, still works part-time as a nurse in a drug-rehab facility. "Miss Irene instilled in me that you can do anything you want to do."

Young Sarah became Miss Irene's legs, fetching items from shelves for customers and taking the money to her in the back room of the store, where they lived. Irene would count out the customers' change, then Sarah delivered it to them at the checkout counter.

Miss Irene became Sarah's savior and personal hero, and Houp spoiled her with all the RC Colas her heart desired. One year, her biological grandparents in Henry County, near Martinsville, insisted she spend the summer on their farm. She was made to work from dawn to dusk, "can see to can't see." Her grandfather was employed by Bassett Furniture Company, where for many decades blacks earned much less than whites. To make ends meet, the family raised chickens and pigs and grew their own vegetables. Her cousins terrified her by throwing dead snakes in her path. If she shrieked, they teased her for being a city slicker.

Houp visited her every Sunday. She would cry, then he would cry. "He wanted me to come back," but her grandparents were enjoying the extra labor and insisted she stay.

Finally, Miss Irene paid a visit and demanded, "Give her back now, or I'm not going to ever let her come back." The ploy worked, but not exactly because of family sentiment, as there was no way the family could afford another mouth to feed during the winter.

"Lawyer Austin," as Sarah called him, was in and out of the Houps' store and home constantly; she described him with equal parts respect and bemusement. He was disheveled, with wrinkled suits and poorly cinched neckties—which he fiddled with constantly. In terms of confidence, Houp had him beat by a mile.

The two men called each other by first names, which was highly unusual between the races in the 1940s. In his brand-new gray Packard, Houp drove Austin to appointments, but he was definitely more colleague than chauffeur. (Besides, Houp owned the car.)

"They were like brothers, Wilbur and John; they were crazy about each other," Sarah recalled.

As store owners and extenders of credit, the Houps occupied a place of prestige in the Jordan's Alley pecking order, on a par with the minister of Jerusalem Baptist Church. White insurance men and postmen working in the neighborhood also stopped by regularly and ate the lunches Miss Irene cooked from her wheelchair.

Sarah remembers delivering groceries by foot across the community, especially to Jordan's Alley, which old-timers still refer to as Jerden's Alley. She walked the red-dirt roadway next to Harriett's old house, the one on Ten-and-a-Half Street, and around the corner to Annie Belle and Herbert Saunders's house, on Jackson Avenue, which had a backyard that abutted the noisy rail yard.

"It looked like West Virginia back then," she recalled, pointing out where the Muse rental homes once stood. "The houses were ramshackle and facing all kindsa different ways. It was the ghetto."

When we drove around Jordan's Alley together looking at it, I asked her to elaborate on what she meant by *ghetto,* and she said: "Ghetto is…you know, the kind of poverty that doesn't ever quit."

The next day, she phoned me back; the word *ghetto* had been niggling at her. She wanted me to know about a now-defunct company, Boswell Realty, which owned the slummiest homes in Jordan's Alley for many decades. The company had hundreds of units, in fact, in the wider West End and other low-income neighborhoods. Boswell hired imposing rent collectors who often cruised the neighborhood proudly in their long black Buicks. A few manipulated and sometimes forced teenaged girls in the neighborhood to have sex with them. "You know, give them a dollar or two," longtime resident Madaline Daniels said.

If Jordan's Alley was the most impoverished section of town, the people living in Boswell housing were a micro-community representing the poorest of the poor. According to old city maps, Boswell crammed two to four dwellings on a single lot. Mention that company to anyone who grew up there during that time, and they all flinch, remembering the rent collectors in their Buicks and those Boswell Realty signs.

"We had a Boswell house where the toilet was on the alley," recalled Lawrence Mitchell, a retired city landscaper in his mid-seventies. "We had sewage but not water to it. So you had to take a bucket of water and pour it in there to get it to flush. The city eventually made my mother put the toilet on the back porch."

Mitchell said they referred to the ramshackle Boswell dwellings as a "half-a-house." Until the late 1950s, he remembered, most people in Jordan's Alley shared backyard water spigots with their neighbors.

J. W. Boswell had been an early Roanoke rental-property magnate, with strong ties to bank boards, city officials, and tax assessors. One of his earliest tenants recalled him collecting rent on horseback and, later, in a Reo automobile with a crank on the side. His son, John Boswell Jr., inherited the company and was a city councilman in the 1960s, when two of Roanoke's black neighborhoods, Old Northeast and Gainsboro, were torn down. It was part of the nation's postwar "urban renewal" efforts to clear out the so-called slums, often by the power of eminent domain.

It was happening in cities across the country. In New York, urban renewal director Robert Moses oversaw the evictions of a half-million residents, most of them poor and black, to make way for expressways, luxury apartments, parks, cultural centers, and the United Nations, among other developments. Moses's FDR Drive shares some traits with a four-lane expressway that would cut through Roanoke; for the purpose of clearing land for such amenities as the Roanoke Civic Center, a postal headquarters, and a sprawling white-owned Ford dealership, the city used federal dollars to demolish (and burn; it was faster) some sixteen hundred black homes, two hundred businesses, and twenty-four churches. "People look at urban renewal, but it was Negro removal. That's all it was," a black civic leader remembered.

Officials forced the migration of thousands into the brand-new housing projects they were building on the outskirts of the old neighborhoods, as well as to the edge of Jordan's Alley in Southwest, where they were aptly named Hurt Park. Other, smaller portions of Southwest were demolished — including Annie Belle's church — so the city could erect a four-lane bridge across the railroad, replacing the two-lane trestle bridge that smelled of creosote.

But most of the Boswell properties survived urban renewal, as did many of the original shotgun homes in Jordan's Alley. A few of them — including Madaline Daniels's century-old house, weathered and worn but with huge boxwoods that border her cozy, glassed-in front porch — are still intact, still bearing witness the way old places do.

Boswell didn't own the Muses' old shack at 19 Ten-and-a-Half Street, but most of the surrounding lots had Boswell's company as a landlord for many decades. Which was just one reason Harriett wanted so badly to buy the Ballyhack property. It was only a half hour away but, mentally and culturally, it was another world. And that world inspired her to make sure George and Willie would have a home waiting for them when they retired, too — far from Jordan's Alley.

Boswell did own the house across the alleyway on Tenth Street. In 1985, both shacks were still standing, barely, when a seventy-six-year-old domestic worker named Madeline Tate froze to death inside a one-story duplex at 21 Tenth Street during minus-11-degree weather.

Police found her body lying next to her woodstove, the only source of heat in a house that rented for $50 a month.

She'd bundled herself up in a dress, two blouses, a sweater, a bathrobe, and a pair of boots. Her arms were folded casually, as if she'd planned to get up soon and put more wood on the fire.

"We're very sorry it happened," Boswell's daughter told a reporter. But the company was not responsible, she said, referring to the clause in the contract requiring renters to provide their own heat.

In the wake of Tate's death, the city increased the number of inspectors from two part-timers to thirteen full-time positions. Boswell's daughter, who had inherited the company, sold it to a real estate consortium, and Tate's house was demolished soon after.

In 1989, the city paid a demolition contractor $1,000 to tear down the Muse shack, a sum that was greater than its assessed worth.

Tate's house and several others surrounding it—including the Muses' old shack—had been condemned as unfit for habitation shortly after her death, and the city said it might have been able to save her if someone had complained earlier about the bad conditions.

But neighborhood activist Florine Redick told a *Roanoke Times* reporter she had complained, only to be dismissed by city officials, who said that none of the houses were bad enough. "Anybody with eyes can see there's something very wrong," she said.

A newspaper photograph of Tate's house showed a weather-worn shack with a slanted porch, rickety wooden steps, badly broken latticework fronting the house beneath the porch, and very little paint but for peeling white flecks. On a similarly slummy house next door was the sign FOR RENT. BOSWELL REALTY COMPANY.

"If people complained and housing inspectors came by, the slumlords would boot the tenants, then rent the dump out again to someone who would not complain, for a time at least," remembered former *Roanoke Times* reporter Doug Pardue, who investigated Tate's death and helped keep the story on the front page for weeks.

More than a decade later, a cluster of Easter egg–colored Habitat for Humanity homes was built to replace the Muse and Tate shacks, and several nearby properties. The development was named for a retired railroad executive and a General Electric engineer, both of whom had been active Habitat volunteers. One had traveled south to spend a week in Pikeville, Kentucky, repairing homes for low-income people.

At the homes' dedication, no one spoke of the old front-porch concerts put on by Martian ambassadors, or even of the little girl who'd been born just around the corner, though an astute reader of best-selling nonfiction might recognize her name. Loretta Pleasant, born a half-block from Jordan's Alley in 1920, would grow up to become the unknowing donor of cells that contributed to groundbreaking medical research, as chronicled in Rebecca Skloot's *The Immortal Life of Henrietta Lacks*.

Like Madeline Tate, Henrietta Lacks (as she later became known) died penniless. Whereas Lacks was buried without a marker in a private family cemetery in rural Virginia, only a number — 978 — marked Madeline Tate's grave in a pauper's cemetery in the countryside of another county. At Tate's graveside service, a chaplain read aloud: "It's better to rely in the Lord than put any trust in flesh."

A few months later, seven people gathered at her grave in a springtime ceremony, after which the *Roanoke Times* described Tate as now being "more privileged than her neighbors—something she probably never dreamed of during her life." Tate's number had been replaced by a proper tombstone: MADELINE ADAMS TATE, 76 YEARS OLD, JAN. 20, 1985, FROZE TO DEATH.

A vigorous opponent of providing public housing to African Americans back in the 1960s, city councilman John Boswell Jr. had driven the bumpy red-dirt alleyways in his cushy Buick, bullying tenants who were late paying, and refusing to insulate or make repairs in the worst properties. "You didn't want to rent from Boswell, but you had to because he was the cheapest," said JoAnne Poindexter, the *Roanoke Times'* first black reporter. She grew up attending Jerusalem Baptist and, now sixty-five and retired, still does.

Some of her friends and relatives were among the five thousand or more people displaced by urban renewal in Roanoke. Between 1951 and 1955, JoAnne's family lived in a new housing project called Lincoln Terrace. When school integration triggered white migration to the Roanoke County suburbs, her father bought a house in a nearby neighborhood called Rugby. Just a few years before white flight hit, all Rugby homes had been deemed salable only to whites.

Boswell had been the lone dissenting voice against the construction of federally subsidized housing, trying to protect his own bottom line. If his Jordan's Alley renters could find better, cleaner, and cheaper housing in the projects, he knew he would lose tenants. "Unmitigated socialism," Boswell harrumphed when the 105-unit Hurt Park housing project complex opened in 1965. "In my opinion, three persons in Roanoke who have been pushed around too much are the real estate owner, the taxpayer, and the man who is trying to operate a business."

That same week, Johnny Cash performed at the Roanoke Fairgrounds, where the Muse brothers had once played. His hit that year was, fittingly, a train song—"Orange Blossom Special."

And the U.S. Office of Education told the Roanoke school superintendent that his plan to desegregate the city's schools— eleven years after the *Brown v. Board of Education* decision— had finally been approved.

If Boswell had been the neighborhood heavy, then Wilbur Austin was his antidote, especially once he'd joined forces with Houp in the late 1930s. "Lawyer Austin was very well known among blacks," Sarah said. "You know how you always have one lawyer who's pretty cheap? That was him."

Once Austin latched on to Houp, he had an entrée into the entire African-American community. That's likely how Harriett Muse came to hire him, how the unlikely duo came to travel the continent seeking justice for her sons. "They were always planning and anticipating what would happen when they were going places," Sarah said.

Houp and Austin were a formidable one-two punch when it came to collecting on Kortes's bounced checks.

Especially Houp. While Austin was paunchy and fidgety, Houp was trim, confident, imposing; a dark and handsome ladies' man with a broad nose and shoulders. He wore suits with bright white shirts and impeccably shined shoes.

Sarah doesn't recall meeting Harriett Muse, but she remembers George and Willie visiting the store several times during their trips home. Their family had a credit account with Miss Irene, and the brothers, wanting to avoid the stares of people in the neighborhood, usually waited in the car while their relatives shopped.

Harriett was heading to Roanoke to grocery shop, in fact, on a sweltering day in July 1942. She was riding the winding road from Ballyhack, on her way to collect her wartime sugar rations. A baker extraordinaire, she had moved beyond ash cakes as her budget allowed and was now known for her yeast rolls and cakes—though she still made ash cakes, on request, every time George and Willie came home, served with apple butter she'd canned herself.

It was two in the afternoon. The heat was getting to her, she told the friend who was driving the car, and just as he pulled off the road to check on her, Harriett slumped over.

"Mother Muse," her friend cried out. But her death was instant. She was sixty-eight years old.

It fell to Houp to handle the arrangements, and to collect the brothers from Kortes, this time so they could pay their respects to the woman who had done so much for them, and whose actions had both complicated and simplified their lives.

Willie was especially distraught. "He always had that attachment to his mama," Nancy said.

After Harriett's death, her funeral expenses and outstanding debts were logged by Austin and approved by the court, like everything else. She owed one neighbor $13.41 for butter and milk, and another $2.05 for meat. Austin directed another $9.52 to pay off the credit account she'd kept back in Jordan's Alley—at Miss Irene's store.

*   *   *

At the funeral, congregants sang Harriett's favorite hymn:

> *One more thing here*
> *Don't wait till the early dawn*
> *Shall now it should be done*
> *Speak things with a loudness as though they were*
> *And know the Bible has already won*
> *Go on and shout, it's already done.*

After the service, the brothers sat with the rest of their family on their sister's front porch in Jordan's Alley, a place they would soon leave behind, thanks to Harriett, Austin, and Houp.

They were a block away from Miss Irene's store, close enough to the rail yard to feel the falling cinders. Neighbor kids gathered, trying to get a peep at their peculiar hair, their milky skin, their fluttering blue eyes.

"Mama's gone," George said, shaking his head.

"Mama's gone," Willie repeated, shaking his head.

16

God Is Good to Me

The house on Mercer Avenue is a two-story American Foursquare. It's made of wood-frame construction and painted white, with four bedrooms upstairs. The year is 1961. And as with all houses in the Rugby section of Roanoke, the deed stipulation on the home has just shifted from whites-only to come-one-come-all. *Good-bye, white people.*

Compared with Harriett's house in Ballyhack, the Mercer home is a major improvement, with indoor plumbing and electricity, with water that doesn't have to be fetched from the well. The porch is not rickety, its latticework fully intact.

Compared with the shacks in Jordan's Alley, it's draft-free and downright palatial. There's no gaping hole in the wall, no woodstove to feed.

Chances are slim that an elderly woman might freeze to death here in her bathrobe, blouses, and boots.

White flight has descended on Rugby, which is fine with Annie Belle Saunders; her daughter, Dot; and Dot's only child, eleven-year-old Nancy.

Dot and Nancy are the latest recipients of the largesse of Uncle Georgie and Uncle Willie, as they call their soon-to-retire uncles and great-uncles.

The women in the family have just purchased the house on Mercer, in their uncles' names. The sale has been court-approved, for a lump sum of $8,000, the paperwork all taken care of by the knee-jiggling, hair-kneading Wilbur Austin.

There's just one caveat:

Annie Belle, Dot, and Nancy may live in the Mercer home indefinitely, as long as they agree to take care of George and Willie for the "rest of their natural lives."

The money has come from the nest egg Austin has been channeling their wages into since 1938. The fund has now grown to $23,000, a small fortune for a working-class family (the equivalent of around $183,000 today). The family has pulled off a feat in minority home ownership; the brothers are now among the 38.1 percent of home-owning black households in the nation, compared with 64.3 percent among whites.

The savings have accrued from Austin's myriad trips to track the Muse brothers down when the circus checks bounced, from the threats and muscle employed by John Houp to force the skinflint showmen, finally, to honor their word.

Mostly, it comes from George's and Willie's fifty years of sideshow work. It's hard to say how big that nest egg would be had the brothers been getting paid all along.

Willie is almost totally blind. Georgie's heart is weak.

They don't mind if a family friend or a Rugby neighbor asks them to play a few bars from a song. But they don't like it when strangers bang on the door at two or three in the morning, demanding to see them, demanding to see the wild savages who eat raw meat.

The family hires a barber who makes house calls to cut their hair—so they can avoid the stares. At the segregated elementary school Nancy attends, kids tease her. They want to know: Which one is Eko and which is Iko?

"Neither," she tells them, clutching her fists, so ready for a fight.

"Their names are *Mister* George and *Mister* Willie Muse."

They share a bedroom at the top of the stairs, across the hall from Nancy's room. Years from now, long after they're gone, friends looking back will pause to remark on the color of that room.

They are always so certain of the shade.

"When you walked into the bedroom, everything was white," recalls the doctor who made house calls regularly to treat Willie Muse. "The ceiling, the walls, the curtains, the beds, and even Willie. He was also basically white."

The first time the doctor sees Willie in the room, he is singing along with the radio. In the doctor's memory, the bedroom is so blanketed in white that he finds himself thinking: *I've just walked into a Stephen King novel.*

But everyone's memory of that bedroom is skewed, wrapped in a dreamy, protective web. Having visited the room myself—the one time Nancy let me inside the Mercer house, in 2001—I, too, could have sworn the walls were painted white.

But Nancy says no. And later, looking at photographs, I see that she's right. The walls are the hue of ferns unfurling, of Easter-basket grass, of springtime in Virginia.

It must have been something about Willie that projected an air of calm, white, and stillness, long after he departed this world. I can't think of anything else.

*   *   *

More than anyone, it is Nancy who makes good on the Mercer Avenue promise. She and her mother, Dot, take care of Georgie until his death of heart failure, in 1972.

They fret watching Willie grieve for his lifelong protector and best friend; they worry that he'll soon die, too. He has never been without his brother. "Georgie was almost more like a father to him," Nancy says, though they were only three years apart.

But God is good to Willie Muse.

He tells that to everyone he meets, as if by greeting.

He says it as he prays before every meal, before every snack.

He says it when Nancy brings the balloons and gifts that will mark the birthday his family celebrates as his eightieth, then ninetieth, and all the holidays in between.

"He talks to God the way he would talk to you and me," one of his at-home nurses remembers, still referring to him in the present tense.

He outlives everyone he has crossed paths with in the circus — the showmen who exploited him, his colleagues in the sideshow, the lawyers who opposed and defended him.

When he's ninety-nine, doctors install a pacemaker with a battery designed to last seven years.

"God is good to me," he says, again, when the battery keeps ticking beyond seven years, then eight.

And so does Willie Muse.

If the circus was his first real home, the property on Mercer is his first real house. At birthdays and Christmas, he wants it stocked with stuffed animals, music boxes, and snow globes — his novelties, he calls them, in circus parlance popular fifty years earlier. "She's touching my novelties," he tattles on his great-niece Louise when she borrows a favorite stuffed alligator from his bed.

While George embraced playing with children in the family—*Come sit on my big fat knee*—Willie kept them at a distance. If they tried to roughhouse with him, he complained, "You're messing up my clothes."

He's living the childhood he never had. He gives Nancy the motherhood she never had, too.

He shakes his snow globes. Though he can't see the flakes floating inside, they transport Willie to Truevine. He thinks of the pale-white snow cream his mother once made from vanilla, sugar, eggs, and new-fallen snow—a poor man's ice cream.

Before suffering a stroke in 1990, Willie plays his Marquis guitar every day. After the stroke, his left arm is compromised, but he gets the guitar out anyway just to hold it in his lap. The neck looks like dominoes, the fretboard finish worn down in rows of ovals by his finger pads. He runs his hands along the frets, not so long removed from the clatter of train cars and cookhouses.

He asks Nancy to buy him a harmonica. Then he asks her to send it back for another, "one with more sharps."

He plays "Tipperary" first, then "The Stars and Stripes Forever," which they used to play before, during, and after the world wars: *Hurrah for the flag of the free...*

There's the tune he sings in memory of a lover from a town he no longer recalls: *Put your arms around me, honey / Squeeze me tight / Pull up and cuddle up / With all your might.*

There's the song he sings every day to Nancy: *You are my sunshine, my only sunshine / You make me happy when skies are gray...*

When she's had a bad day, he counsels her, "When you walk

around angry, Nancy, you lose a lot of blessings the Lord has in store for you."

Willie craves the French fries she makes for him—extra long so he can pick them up easily. When Nancy's on vacation or out of town, Willie cons Louise into making him cheeseburgers, a meal that taskmaster Nancy (the Warden, they call her) forbids. Cheeseburgers are too rich, she says, too hard for someone his age to digest.

Louise and Nancy have placed old telephone cords at hip height around the room, to help Willie feel his way when he walks. Nancy's husband, Ike, has placed the bed diagonally into the corner, so when Willie stands he can hold the rail Ike has affixed to the wall.

Willie is proud of his age, calling it a blessing from the Lord. He explains to all who visit that God has *entrusted* him to live as long as he has.

But he has a sense of humor about it, too. When visitors ask for the secret to his longevity, he deadpans, "Because I never got married."

Every morning the Warden counts out the numbers as she lifts and rotates his arms and legs, five times each, to keep him limber. When he hears Louise enter the room, he says loud enough for her to hear, "You missed a number, Nancy."

When a new nurse arrives to care for him, she tends to speak too loudly at first.

"I *hear* ya," Willie says. "I'm blind, you know. I'm not deaf."

His ear is as sharp as his other faculties. When he hears a nurse coming up the stairs, he calls out, "Who is it?"

"The nurse" comes her reply.

"Does the nurse have a name?" Willie wants to know.

* * *

The centenarian Willie Muse is another person entirely from the timid, fist-clenched younger Willie Muse. He's gone from cautionary tale to wise elder. The photo-card caricature has a personality now, and that personality is finally being recorded in a voice all its own, in the memories of all who hear it and live to tell. It has advice to give, lessons to impart.

Brutally honest, Willie tells his great-great-nephew Jason, who grows up in the Mercer house, that he needs to practice his tuba more if he expects to progress in the high school band.

He hates the thumping of rap, which he calls "that mess." Willie prefers listening to the blues, bluegrass, country music, and spirituals. His favorites are Louis Armstrong, Minnie Pearl, Mahalia Jackson, and the Reverend Billy Graham. He loves whistling along with the theme song to *The Andy Griffith Show*. ("Good Lord, could that man whistle!" recalls his nurse Diane Rhodes.)

He's lived through nineteen presidents, two world wars, and the advent not just of Hollywood and television but also of microwaves ("That's an oven?"), CD players ("Amazing!"), and commercial airplanes, which he still prefers to riding in cars.

He asks Nancy to record him singing his favorite songs on a cassette so he can play them back to himself at night. He reminds her often that he was a better musician than George.

Me and my lady lover, walkin' down the street...

Beginning on his 103rd birthday, Baskin-Robbins gives him a free ice cream birthday cake, with a rainbow painted in icing — to remind him of his mother. A home-health nurse comes to the party and brings along several visitors. Her brother plays the banjo, a niece the violin, her husband the autoharp.

"Get my recorder," Willie says to Nancy, so he can enjoy

hearing it again later. He especially loves the niece's violin rendition of "Ashokan Farewell," the lonesome fiddle waltz and theme of Ken Burns's miniseries *The Civil War.*

Every night before bed, Willie stops to straighten his mother's picture, displayed in a pretty silver frame on the wall near the foot of his bed. He thinks about a black maid standing up to all those policemen ("'leven of 'em!"), the circus bigwigs in their fedoras and suits ("City Hall!"). Never in his life will he forget the moment Georgie spotted her, then elbowed him in the ribs, both of their lives upended once more ("'There's our dear old mother!' he said to me").

In his mind, Willie sees her the way she appears in the picture: her face long-suffering and serene, wearing her homemade dress and black felt hat. There's a vague pile of work she's tending on her lap—a sewing project, maybe, or some laundry, perhaps.

It's hard to tell whether she's squinting defensively or cracking a half-smile.

Like her great-granddaughter Nancy, Harriett keeps her stories quiet. She holds her cards close.

Uncle Willie has outlived his mother, his siblings, and every one of the showmen who exploited him—including the only one he ever hated. "Scum of the earth," he still calls Candy Shelton. When he's feeling feisty, he'll add his favorite curse—"Cocksucker!"—a sly grin turning up the right corner of his mouth.

While Willie lives to be a centenarian, adored by everyone he meets, Shelton spends his waning days in a sheet-metal trailer at the Giant's Camp in Gibtown.

A writer exploring the state of Florida for a book-length travelogue stumbles upon him there, living alongside other retired sideshow workers. The year is 1973.

In nearby Sarasota, the last two remaining members of the Doll family won't let the man inside their door, telling him they are finished with the press, period. "We quit the gaggle," one of the sisters says, politely. "We done that all our lives."

And indeed, they had. I picture Grace Doll next to Clyde Ingalls on the bally, as in that early silent film, nervously tugging her sundress and answering all questions that are thrown her way.

Shelton, though, clad in trousers and an undershirt, seems lonely and invites the writer in.

After failing to regain control of the Muse brothers, Shelton had spent his final days in the circus as a Ringling ticket seller and lecturer — a bally boy. He had once been an insider, chummy with management and performers alike. Now he'd come full circle. At a Halloween party for the cast and crew in 1946, he prepared an old-fashioned chicken dinner for the entire bunch.

Soon after, he retired and returned to his farming roots, this time in rural Virginia, just south of Richmond. He ran a poultry shop and chicken farm, doing the same kind of rote chore that had gotten his fingers lopped off as a young teen.

"Cocksucker!" I imagine Willie Muse saying, had he ever known.

"Serves the cocksucker right!"

Shelton is nostalgic for the sideshow. A vagabond most of his life, he's now a widower with no children. His only relatives are two nephews he no longer keeps in touch with. "I don't remember a lot of laughter or joking," says one of the nephews, who lived with him briefly as a teen.

After his stint running the Virginia poultry farm, "we lost touch with him," another nephew says.

With the smell of simmering lima beans wafting through the trailer, the writer helps Shelton haul a trunk out of his closet. It's stuffed with yellowed clippings, circus route books, and pictures. Together they peruse the 1937 Ringling route book. It contains a schedule of the last full season Shelton managed George and Willie Muse.

That year he had pitched the brothers as Eko and Iko, Ministers from Dahomey, after the long-gone West African kingdom. That year they and 1,606 other circus workers traveled more than fifteen thousand miles and gave 404 performances.

"You people your age never seen a real circus," Shelton tells the writer. "It was a wonderful institution."

By the 1970s, the sideshow has mostly come and gone, caught in the crosshairs of changing sensibilities and disability rights. The freak show is not only offensive, now reserved mainly for "circus buffs and a few nonconformists in the humanities," as the sociologist Robert Bogdan writes, it's now long in the tooth, and so is Shelton.

It's to disabled people what the striptease is to women, what stereotypically offensive shows like *Amos 'n' Andy* are to blacks.

"It's a darn shame they don't exist anymore," Candy Shelton says in what was probably the last interview he gave before his death, in 1974, at age seventy-six.

She makes bread and she has guts, just like her great-grandmother.

Nancy is the new Harriett, the tough matriarch of her tight-knit clan. At the Goody Shop, she bakes yeast rolls by the hundreds while Dot makes the cookies and pies. Customers flock there every early November to get in their holiday orders.

And just like Harriett, Nancy is not one to be pushed around. There is a gooey center at the heart of her, but it can take a long time—twenty-five *years,* in my case—to discover it.

Growing up, Nancy didn't want people to ask about her famous uncles, so she erected a wall of toughness that projected as aloof, her classmates recall. "The family didn't talk about Eko and Iko because it reflected the powerlessness of black people at the time; that somebody could come along and take your children, and you had no power over it," recalls Reginald Shareef, the social science prof and family friend who frequented the Goody Shop. (His mother, Maxine "Mac" Thomas, was the revered librarian at the elementary school Nancy attended.)

Nancy graduated in 1967 from Lucy Addison High School, which was named for the Reconstruction-era teacher who rose from slave to champion of black education in Roanoke. She went to work at Singer Furniture Company, a Roanoke factory, where she began dating a coworker named Howard (nickname: Ike), a quiet sort who by chance had the same last name. They married, and the city of Roanoke eventually hired Ike Saunders to maintain its traffic lights. It was Ike's salary that financed the purchase of the Goody Shop, whereupon Nancy promptly hired her mother, aunt Martha, and cousin Louise.

"I could write a case study for the *Harvard Business Review* on small entrepreneurship, and the family then might really understand what they accomplished in successfully launching and operating the Goody Shop," Shareef says. "But in many ways, it's like that book Ralph Ellison wrote in the fifties about the invisible man." With little recognition from the broader community, blacks who succeed without moving out of their neighborhoods too often remain invisible to the white community, while the minority criminals and misfits among them get most of the ink.

Nancy may have seemed unmoved by my 1993 feature on the Goody Shop—"It brought out a bunch of crazy white people, that's all!"—but I later learn that one of those crazy white people is a prominent banker named John Clarke. Known far and wide as Big John, Clarke used to phone me with juicy story tips, which he uttered in a booming Virginia drawl. When I needed his help researching a story, he used to say, "Let me go dip my toes in the creek and get back to you on that," and he would.

He and Nancy get along so well that they tell people they are first cousins. For Christmas one year, he buys her a beautiful silk scarf. "When you ran that article about me, Big John showed up the first day, and from that day till the day he died, he was my customer," Nancy tells me in 2015. "They always came for the Thanksgiving and Christmas rolls, him and his cronies. They'd stop on their way home from the country club, and they'd be about half-tipped."

He was one of a very select group of customers who could request "an extra kick of brandy" with his sweet potato pie order and, astonishingly, the Warden would comply.

Nancy leaves the restaurant "three, four, sometimes five times a day to check on Uncle Willie," recalls Elaine Stovall, a retired schoolteacher and Mercer Avenue neighbor. "You just can't imagine how good she was to him."

She does everything she can think of to restore the family time he lost as a child. So he no longer has to sign with an X,

she teaches him to print his name, which he does proudly—
even though he can't see his work.

At Christmas, she puts a live Norfolk pine in his bedroom so
he can inhale the scent.

It's just before Christmas 1995 when Uncle Willie begins complaining of severe stomach pain. Fearing a bowel obstruction,
the doctor admits him to the hospital.

Nancy leaves Roanoke Memorial Hospital after she gets him
settled in. Soon after, a nurse applies a piping-hot electric heat-
ing pad to his stomach. A shift change occurs, and no one stops
by to check on him or the device.

By the morning, Willie has huge, blistering third-degree
burns. He's in so much pain, he can't speak. He's 102.

When Nancy arrives the next morning and sees him writh-
ing, "she really [lets] them have it," says Jason, her nephew.
(He's responsible for the Warden nickname.)

But she doesn't blow her top, not yet. The one thing the Warden has taught her nephew: you never let someone see that
they made you upset.

"She took that anger, and she took her time, and then she
took them to task. I would not have wanted to be them, not at
all," Jason says, shaking his head.

The presence of the railroad has diminished significantly since
the sharecroppers from Truevine migrated to booming Roanoke. *When you marry, marry a railroad man / Every Sunday,
dollar in your hand.*

In 1982, Norfolk and Western merges with the Southern
Railway and switches names to Norfolk Southern, then shifts

its headquarters to Norfolk. Roanoke's corporate Big Daddy ups and leaves, just like that, sparking anxiety and hand-wringing among laid-off employees and economic developers alike. (Roanokers have to chuckle, though, when the marquee for new corporate offices in Norfolk is unveiled to contain a stunner of a spelling error: NORFORK SOUTHERN RAILWAY.)

After a few years, a nonprofit hospital corporation with an invented, focus-grouped name comes barreling along in the railroad's wake, and by 1995 Carilion is well on its way to becoming the largest employer in Roanoke, with plans of launching a medical school with nearby Virginia Tech and satellite hospitals across the western half of the state.

It would be an intimidating move for anyone to sue Carilion, let alone a black woman operating a tiny soul-food restaurant out of a strip mall in one of the poorest sections of town.

But the Warden is not intimidated. She's about to give the biggest game in town a dose of sit-down-and-shut-up.

Nancy summons her ancestors. She is Harriett under the sideshow tent. She is Dot Brown threatening her groping employer with a knife.

She is Mabel Pullen back in Truevine, now taking the lunch that has just been tossed out the window at her and throwing it in the landlord's face.

She's the pretty girl in Jordan's Alley, telling the rent collector "No you don't."

She gets behind the wheel of her Honda Civic hatchback, bought new in 1990 as a point of pride, and drives herself to the law firm of Richard Lawrence, one of the scrappiest and most formidable lawyers in town. (She still drives that car, by the way, also as a point of pride. When she can no longer take care of herself, she says, she plans to drive it to a nursing-home parking lot, beep the horn, and say, "Come and get me!")

By the time she and Mr. Lawrence are done with them, the corporate suits will pay for what the inattentive nurses have done to Willie Muse, to the tune of a settlement worth $250,000, which Nancy, acting as his legal guardian, administers. To stretch the money as far as possible, Big John Clarke offers her free banking and investment advice.

And not only that, Carilion nurses who specialize in burns will personally come to the house on Mercer, to clean the wound and change the bandages. Twice a day, for going on two years.

Early on in the process, hospital staffers had offered to train Nancy to tend the burn instead, but she declined. "I'm not the one that caused it," she tells them.

And: "If I had caused it, I would probably be in jail."

They are not there to calm Willie in the middle of the night, when the nightmares arrive, no matter how much he has prayed for them to go away.

"I'm hot. Help me. It's burning," Willie calls from his room.

It's his relatives, not the nurses, who jostle him awake and chase the night terrors away.

By his 106th birthday, Willie's smooth Harry Belafonte voice has turned raspy. He can no longer walk, not even with the aid of the telephone cord. He spends most of the day in his room seated in his favorite chair, a La-Z-Boy recliner, looking forward to visits from Nancy and his nurses.

"This man, even though he was blind, he just *knew* things," nurse Diane Rhodes recalls. "He could tell in your voice after one sentence how you were feeling that day. He'd say, 'So you've had a rough day at work today, Diane?'"

If Diane has been impatient with a meddling coworker, Willie senses it. He counsels her not to speak her mind "until you've figured out the right way of saying it."

If she's snapped back at a scolding colleague with a harsh tone, Willie knows. He tells her, "Feed 'em honey instead of vinegar. It's good to keep the peace."

He has reason to be bitter, Diane knows from the stories he sometimes tells. During the earliest days of commercial aviation, people stared at him and Georgie on the airplanes. "Like we're some kinda monsters."

He chooses not to dwell on past slights, even though his memory has recorded them all. But, like the songs on his cassette player, he can play back the lessons from them anytime he wants.

"Feed 'em honey, Diane," he tells her.

"Be better than the person who is mistreating you."

In March 2001, a month before his 108th birthday, Willie Muse wants to know, "Nancy, how old am I?"

"A hundred and seven," she tells him.

"That's old," he says.

They chuckle.

His life has overlapped three centuries, from Grover Cleveland to George W. Bush. He was born the same year two musical sisters composed the most popular song in the world, "Happy Birthday to You."

"After my birthday I'm going to go live with God and with Georgie," he tells his great-niece.

The hospital settlement has allowed Nancy the cushion, with Big John's advice, to hire near-constant caregivers.

"My mother came for me and Georgie when we were young," Willie tells a nurse named Margaret.

"Did you ever marry, Willie?" she wants to know.

"No, but I had a girlfriend."

"I bet you were cute."

"Yeah, I was a right handsome man."

Margaret, June, Marsha, and Diane—Willie has fed them all, his nurses, with honey. And they are his loudest cheerleaders now.

"I don't know how to explain it," Margaret says. "It was just never monotonous with Willie. You looked forward to seeing him. Every day."

A month later, on April 5, the 108th birthday arrives. Nancy has gotten the rainbow-decorated cake, this time with a pot-of-gold flourish.

The nightmares have faded. Willie's sleep is deeper. He slumbers most of the time.

When he wakes, he asks Nancy if she can see Georgie in the room.

"No, Uncle Willie. I can't see Uncle Georgie in the room."

"Well, he's here," Willie tells her, then drifts back to sleep.

A week later, daffodils give way to tulips. Ferns shoot up and unfurl from the ground.

Just before midnight, Willie's labored breathing turns into intermittent gasps.

Birthday balloons still hover above his four-poster bed. The snow globes are next to the stuffed animals, the picture of Harriett on the wall. Nancy punches the button on his cassette player, and out comes the voice of Andy Griffith singing "Just As I Am."

A hospice worker urges her to give her uncle permission to leave. Tell him it's OK to go.

Shortly after midnight Nancy crawls into bed beside him, curls up by his side.

"God has left you here on earth for a hundred and eight years," she whispers. "So I know y'all must have a special connection.

"Uncle Willie, will you please tell God, 'We're still struggling.'"

At 1:40 in the morning, eight days after his 108th birthday, Willie Muse dies exactly the way he wants to.

It's Good Friday, 2001. *God is good to me.*

The Monday after Easter is bright but blustery. At the funeral home, a family friend sings:

He knows what's best for me
Although my weary eyes, they can't see.
So I'll just say thank you, Lord.
I won't complain.

Mourners process to the segregated cemetery, and clouds descend as they enter the gate. The morning had been bright, the temperature in the mid-40s, but suddenly a wind gusts in and the mercury abruptly drops.

As a line of cars wends its way into C. C. Williams Memorial Park, snow flurries begin to descend. It's so confusing at first that people mistake the flakes for blossoms blowing off the spring trees.

The preacher reads as the casket is lowered, and all heads are bowed.

When the last *amen* is uttered, the wind dies down and, abruptly, so does the snow, the flakes melting at everyone's feet. The sun comes out again, bright.

More than a decade later, mourners are still talking about the burial of Willie Muse, and not just because of the wind or the snow but mainly because of what happened next.

"It had been so warm that morning and then so cold," says Diane Rhodes, the nurse.

"And then, just like that, a rainbow appeared, and everyone just stood there stunned. And we were all of one accord:

"Heaven was opening the gates. To welcome Uncle Willie home."

But Nancy hasn't spotted the rainbow, not yet. She's busy pulling out large bags from the back of a cousin's van. Then she's untying the bags.

Then one hundred and eight balloons float into the air, and all eyes are on them, squinting.

It's an Uncle Willie trifecta, a performance spectacle featuring his three favorite things: balloons, snow, and a rainbow— *God's promise after the storm.*

As the balloons ascend, they split into two distinct clusters. The groupings seem to hover for a moment, as if taking one last look. Then they rise higher and smaller and, finally, drift out of sight.

Half the balloons are white, for purity. And half are blue, for the color of his eyes.

Epilogue

Markers

The trains still pass by Jordan's Alley, their cars still brimming with coal, though the fuel in many of them is now destined for markets overseas.

The ones that head south roll past the site of the old fairgrounds, the spot where an illiterate washerwoman, the daughter of slaves, managed to find and claim her long-gone sons, even though she was the wrong color, in the wrong neighborhood, on the wrong side of the law.

Harriett Muse's bravery remains unmarked in Jordan's Alley, and it goes unrecognized here, just south of downtown, where the trains now parallel a thirteen-mile greenway path meant to connect the various Roanoke Valley communities, provide outdoor recreation, and, in so doing, attract new industry to the region to replace the waning influence of the railroad and of coal.

Riding my bike on the Roanoke River Greenway path, I parallel the passing trains, too. I pass dog walkers and runners, young and old, black and white. It's one of the rare places in Roanoke where the racial makeup actually reflects the diversity of the city's census count, down to the immigrant soccer league playing Sunday mornings across the street.

My friend Zeor, a refugee from Liberia, comes to watch her

sons play on those fields. "We were never called 'black people' before — until we moved here," she tells me, tapping into Americans' innate and unconscious belief in the reality of race as unequivocal divider. Our history of categorizing human beings as immutably black or white before we even know their names.

It's one year after Ferguson, fifty years after the Watts riots, 150 years since the end of the Civil War. In the past year, thirty-two states have enforced new voter identification requirements that disproportionately disenfranchise poor and minority voters, and twenty-six unarmed black men have been fatally shot by police across the United States of America. Even Atticus Finch, it turns out, wasn't the progressive lawyer we thought he was.

On the greenway, near the old fairgrounds and the new medical school, I ride over a freshly scrawled graffiti bomb on the asphalt. SLAVERY IS OVER! someone has spray-painted.

I think of Nancy's young cousin, the auburn-blond Erika Turner, when I see it. She has cried, imagining the travails of her great-great-great-uncle Willie and his brother George. When she cries, Erika tells me, her hazel eyes turn green. A rising senior at a Roanoke County high school, she's one of a handful of African Americans, occasionally the only one, in her advanced classes. When riots broke out in Baltimore her junior year, her classmates criticized the protesters and looters, asking, "What's the sense in them burning businesses? What does that prove?"

The course was psychology, and Erika, one of three blacks in that class, pointed out that the riots were not happening in a vacuum. They were precipitated not only by police killings, but also by a government-sanctioned history of violence, discrimination, and injustice as old as the country itself.

But this is a conversation that most white people, if suburban classrooms and greenway graffiti are to be believed, do not wish to have. More than half of white Americans think the country spends too much time talking about race, while just 18 percent of black Americans do.

In July 2015, I'm driving Nancy to the cemetery where Willie Muse is buried. She tells me she's inspired by my account of her great-grandmother's efforts to make the circus pay for her sons' work. "I lost track of how many times she had to take those circus men to court. And if she was like that back then with no education, just think what she might be like today. She was . . . *bad*."

There's just one real problem with the facts as I've assembled them, she says, and it's big:

"I do not and I will not believe that Harriett let her children go off with no circus," she says. "As a mother, that was all she had to cling to—her children and her Christ."

I remind her about the *Billboard* notice Harriett took out with the help of Anna Clark. I remind her of the initial 1927 newspaper coverage of the case, in which Harriett was said to have "contracted" to let her sons leave with the mysterious Mr. Stokes.

She reminds me of the institutional racism exhibited by countless publications during the Jim Crow era; of the *Roanoke Times'* mocking attempt to capture the family's voice—"for anxious and beseeching words from the lips of their 'old mammy who yo all aint seen for all dese years'"—without ever actually quoting anyone named Muse.

She reminds me of the story that Willie himself told—about a man luring him and his brother into the back of his wagon with a piece of candy. I asked if Willie had used the word *kidnapped*. "No," she snaps. "His word was *stolen*."

"I'm not questioning what you found," Nancy says. "I'm telling you how I feel about it, based on the love and connection that Uncle Willie had with his mama."

What exactly transpired between Harriett Muse and an itinerant showman in the summer of 1914 will probably never be known. After drilling down more rabbit holes than I can count, I've had to settle for an imperfect and incomplete story line, uncertain but for its ripple-free reflections on memory, power, and race.

It's late afternoon and 90 degrees, the sky so cerulean the Blue Ridge Mountains are visible for miles in every direction. We enter the gates of the cemetery, which holds more than twenty thousand graves—many of them Roanoke's earliest black rail workers and domestics, still housed in unofficial segregation, like most of the people in the surrounding neighborhood.

In one of the cemetery's oldest sections, the physician I. D. Burrell—the man who died on the train to Washington after Roanoke's white hospitals refused to admit him in 1914—is buried beneath a tall granite obelisk. Three of the city's five Tuskegee Airmen are buried nearby with dignified headstones, including a pair of brothers who joined the elite group of African-American military pilots. (One died in a 1943 training exercise, and the other, who signed up to complete his brother's mission, died in a 1949 crash during the Berlin Airlift.)

We pass the cinderblock cemetery office, and near a cluster

of stately hickory trees, Nancy points to the section with Willie's grave. She comes here several times a year — before Christmas, on his birthday, and on Mother's Day, when she also visits the graves of her mother, Dot, who died in 2004, and her grandmother Annie Belle, who died in 1983.

Crabgrass creeps over the right side of the granite marker, which is flush with the ground, and dried grass clippings lie heaped on one side.

WILLIE MUSE, the bronze marker says in raised capital letters, and beneath an outline of praying hands, it reads GOD IS GOOD TO ME.

A week later we return, this time during office hours. We need help paying our respects to the unmarked graves created before the family could afford memorial niceties: George's in 1972, and Harriett's in 1942. Cemetery employees only know exactly where George is buried, since records before 1952 were not retained when the cemetery changed hands decades ago. (Nancy didn't realize Harriett was buried here, too, until I found her death certificate earlier in the summer.)

Groundskeeper Brian Nichols takes us to the far edge of an area referred to as the space graves, the humble unnamed section behind the office where people were buried in order as their bodies arrived, one next to the other, in largely unmarked graves and typically nowhere near their relatives. We walk out to the section he figures was dug in July 1942, when Harriett died.

If you look closely down the row, he shows us, you can make out the indentations where the ground is sunken in just so, the outline of the graves as straight and rectangular as a set of xylophone keys.

"Is it true he used to play tunes on a plastic string guitar, and you could tell what songs he was playing?" the groundskeeper asks Nancy. Yes, and Willie could also play songs using a range of notes he created solely by snapping his fingers.

In the car we put in Willie's homemade recording, now converted from cassette to CD. And, like an aural apparition, there he is, his a cappella baritone steady and clear.

I replay the CD after I drop Nancy off. As I cross the Tenth Street bridge over the railroad tracks, I make my way back to Jordan's Alley—that name only rarely crossing the lips of the area's oldest residents. The new Habitat houses here are vinyl-sided and modest; a few have posted NO TRESPASSING signs.

Their backyards are so deep they've erased all traces of the red-clay road that once passed for Ten-and-a-Half Street. Lodged between two backyard chain-link fences is the only visible remnant of No. 19—a scrubby, half-dead mulberry tree, a tangle of ivy and periwinkle rooted at its base. I snap a few pictures, pick up a single lichen-covered mulberry twig, and return to my car.

The rail yard still clatters in the distance. But it's barely audible over the music of Willie Muse: *It's a long way to Tipperary / It's a loo-ong way to go.*

It's the Irish war ballad, of all things, that sticks with him the longest—a song with the power to summon, with pride and astonishment, the memory of his "dear old mother" under a sideshow tent.

Acknowledgments

This book began with a picture of George and Willie Muse posted about two years ago on Facebook, of all things. I was midway through a shared bottle of wine on a Friday night when I spotted a familiar, circa-1927 picture shared by my inimitable friend Mim Young, a lifelong circus aficionada. The enthusiastic response to Mim's post gave me my first, albeit flushed, idea that just maybe I could resurrect the *Roanoke Times* newspaper series I'd cowritten in 2001 and, if enough new material could be gathered, turn it into a book. It helped immeasurably that my former newspaper cowriter, Jen McCaffery, had carted her sixteen-pound box of Muse files around with her through several moves to multiple cities, always hoping in the back of her mind that one of us would write that book. Jen, I will forever owe you for sending that box to me, plus postage!

My agent, Peter McGuigan, was his usual cheerful, opinionated, and bulldogging self throughout the arc of this project. A hearty thanks to Peter and the entire team at Foundry Literary + Media, especially Bret Witter, Kirsten Neuhaus, Jessica Regel, Richie Kern, and Matt Wise; and to Caspian Dennis at Abner Stein in London.

I remain so lucky to get to work with editor John Parsley, who has now shepherded two of my books into print — and made them smoother, more nuanced, and ultimately more honest. Thanks also to my Macmillan editor, Georgina Morley, and to all my stalwart champions at Little, Brown and Company, including Malin von Euler-Hogan, Miriam Parker, Sabrina Callahan, Alyssa Persons, Sarah Haugen, Fiona Brown, Reagan Arthur, Craig Young, and Karen Torres. Copyeditor Deborah P. Jacobs and production editor Pamela Marshall were eagle-eyed and diligent, and I'm so grateful this book was in their care.

There's no chapter in this book that doesn't owe some fact-finding debt to my estimable cadre of librarians, researchers, historians, and court-records sleuths. Librarians are so much cleverer, cooler, and cheerfully subversive than they get credit for, and they are my favorite tribe, especially razor-sharp Piper Cumbo at Roanoke College and the amazingly resourceful staffs of the Virginia Room at the Roanoke City Library, and of that system's very special Gainsboro branch. Special thanks for the research assistance of Pat Ross of the Bassett Historical Center; Diane Adkins of the Pittsylvania County Public Library; Franklin County genealogist Beverly Merritt; Linda Stanley at the Franklin County Historical Society; retired journalist and all-around historical stickler George Kegley; Harrison Museum of African American Culture director Charles Price; Aiesha (the intern!) Krause-Lee at the College of William and Mary; and historian John Kern.

Title examiner and court-records researcher Betsy Biesenbach dedicated herself to this project as if it were her own, as did Belinda Harris, who spent many weekends combing through newspaper archives. Others who helped me navigate tricky subjects included Evalyn Chapman, Mark and Elizabeth Jamison, Greg Renoff, Andy Erlich, Gladys Hairston, Jane Nicholas, Bev Fitzpatrick, Randy Abbott, Virgil Goode, the late

Harvey Lutins, and Roddy Moore and Vaughan Webb of the Blue Ridge Institute and Museum at Ferrum College. Editor/historian Rand Dotson's amazing *Roanoke, Virginia, 1882–1912: Magic City of the New South* guided much of my Jim Crow–era research. Sarah Baumgardner cheerfully plunged into dusty map archives at the Western Virginia Water Authority, as did Dan Webb at the City of Roanoke. Kate and Kamran Khalilian made their home my Richmond bureau, and Kate scoured archives at the Library of Virginia when I couldn't make the trek.

Mary Bishop's coverage of black Roanoke history for the *Roanoke Times* schooled me countless times, and the impact of her almost three decades of journalistic counsel is palpable an every page of this book.

Dr. Reginald Shareef coached me and shared important insights about growing up in segregated Roanoke, as did Sarah Showalter, Willie Mae Ingram, ace journalist JoAnne Poindexter, Lawrence Mitchell, and the late A. L. Holland. Thanks to Regina "Sweet Sue" Peeks, I will never drive past a vacant urban lot again without imagining the racist parrots she recalled — a reminder that archives and documents only carry you so far: nothing beats strangers sharing their memories and desires. Nothing. To Janet Johnson, Mabel Pullen, Johnny Angell, J. Harry Woody, and A. J. Reeves in Truevine: God bless *you* a double portion.

Leading my own version of a circus backyard was the endlessly fascinating Al Stencell, whose love of sideshow history is as unparalleled as his colorful stories. I'm equally grateful to circus historians Dick Flint, Warren Raymond, Bob Blackmar, Bob Bogdan, Bernth Lindfors, Fred Pfening III, LaVahn Hoh, Glenn Charron, and Fred Dahlinger, and to historical costume expert Joshua Bond. Pete Shrake at the Circus World Museum, in Baraboo, was especially helpful, as were Maureen Brunsdale and Mark Schmitt at the Milner Library's Circus and Allied Arts collection at Illinois State University; and Kelly Zacovic, Heidi Taylor, and Howard Tibbals of the John and Mable Ringling Museum of Art, in Sarasota. My research into British sideshows was greatly aided by Clare Moore and her research at the Stoole-Tott collection of the University of California–Santa Barbara library; Matthew Neill at the National Fairground Archive, University of Sheffield, England; and John Woolf.

Lawyers who helped search for case files and/or protected me from misinterpreting them included Paul Lombardo, V. Anne Edenfield, Lori Lord, Nick Leitch, and retired circuit court judges Cliff Weckstein and Diane Strickland.

The month I spent at the MacDowell Colony was crucial to the completion of this book, especially the early feedback from other fellows. Support from the Virginia Foundation for the Humanities boosted my ability to delve into archives near and far; I'm especially grateful to David Bearinger, Jeanne Siler, Jane Kulow, Rob Vaughn, Tucker Lemon, and Margot Lee Shetterly.

For traversing journalism challenges, I'm obliged to my all-star advisory team of Carole Tarrant, Martha Bebinger, Doug Pardue, Annie Jacobsen, Roland Lazenby, Lisa Mullins, Rob Freis, Sue Lindsey, Frosty Landon, Gary Knight, Rob Lunsford, Josh Meltzer, Stephanie Klein-Davis, Ralph Berrier Jr., Dr. Frank Ochberg, Andrea Pitzer, Anna Quindlen, Mary Bishop, Mike Hudson, Laurie Hoffman, Joana Gorjao Henriques, Bill Steiden, Rich and Margaret Martin, and Bob and Nancy Giles.

On the home front, I'd like to thank Will Landon (and apologize for my inability to write with his near-constant whistling), Max Landon, Chloe Landon, Barbara Landon, and Chris Landon; my mom, Sarah Macy Slack, for teaching me to love books; my sister, Terry Vigus, for her dedication to Mom; tireless support from Jean and Scott Whitaker, Lee and Nancy Coleman, Angela Charlton, Sharon Rapoport, Dina and Reggie Bennett, Cheri Storms and Joe Loughmiller, Chris and Connie Henson, Bonny Branch, Frances and Lee West, Libba Wolfe, Dotsy Clifton, Emily and Elizabeth Perkins, and Lezlie and Keno Snyder at Parkway Brewing; and Tom Landon, who steers everything through, steadily, from the idea's first flush to the final word.

And for never failing to remind me that I didn't want to be "just another white person stirring up shit," my deepest regards go to Nancy Saunders. While you didn't exactly invite me into Dot's kitchen, you also never *quite* kicked me out. For that and for your vast mother wisdom about so many things, I will always be in your debt.

Notes

Prologue. I Am the True Vine

Interviews: Diane Hayes, A. J. Reeves, Nancy Saunders, Dot Brown, Rand Dotson

Tobacco growing in Virginia's piedmont in nineteenth century: Outlined in Samuel C. Shelton's "The Culture and Management of Tobacco," *Southern Planter* (April 1861): 209–218.

Sharecropping life: Gleaned from Tom Landenburg's "The African-American as Sharecropper," http://www.digitalhistory.uh.edu/teachers/lesson_plans/pdfs/unit6_7.pdf, and in Marshall Wingfield's *Franklin County: A History* (Berryville, VA: Chesapeake Book Co., 1964).

"whole race trying to go to school": Booker T. Washington's *Up from Slavery* (New York: Doubleday, Page, 1907), http://docsouth.unc.edu/fpn/washington/washing.html.

Early Lucy Addison history: From an undated history of African-American schools in Roanoke, on file at the Harrison Museum of African American Culture, museum annex. The report also describes a two-room building, "the earliest colored school," called Old Lick School, a log structure opened in 1872.

Lucy Addison's teaching Oliver Hill: Beth Macy, "She Touched on Us to Eternity," *Roanoke Times*, Feb. 5, 2006.

Delayed literacy among black sharecroppers: From 1870 Franklin County census figures culled in Audrey Dudley and Diane Hayes, eds., *Oh, Master* (six-volume set of local African-American history), self-published in 2002, held at Franklin County Historical Society: four of thirty-three blacks with the surname Muse could read and write; three of twenty resident blacks with the surname Dickenson/Dickerson (Harriett's maiden name) could read and write.

Harriett Muse's protective nature: Author interviews, Nancy Saunders, June 2, 2014, and Nancy Saunders and Dot Brown, April 2001.

First school in Truevine: Author interview, A. J. Reeves, Sept. 15, 2014.

Freak hunting, as exemplified by a typical ad from *Billboard*: "WANTED—Freaks, Curiosities for Pit Show...fat man, lady midget, glass blower, magician, anything suitable for high-class Pit Show," Sept. 13, 1919.

Freak-hunting ad: *Billboard*, April 25, 1914.

Scant evidence to prove lynch-mob victims guilty of 1890 Rocky Mount arson: The black-owned *Richmond Planet* opined that the case "tells in no uncertain tones the prejudiced conditions existing in that community, and makes one wish in vain for the resurrection of those human beings hanged for a crime which possibly they never committed," Dec. 20, 1890.

Bird Woods's last words: *Daily Virginian*, Aug. 23, 1890.

Thomas Smith's lynching in 1893: Details from Rand Dotson's "Race and Violence in Urbanizing Appalachia: The Roanoke Riot of 1893," and Bruce Stewart's *Blood in the Hills* (Lexington: University Press of Kentucky, 2012). Also recounted in Suzanne Lebsock's *A Murder in Virginia: Southern Justice on Trial* (New York: W. W. Norton, 2003).

eighth known lynching in southwest Virginia that year: Dwayne Yancey, "'And the Harvest of Blood Commenced,'" *Roanoke Times*, Sept. 20, 1993.

Chapter One. Sit Down and Shut Up

Interviews: Richard L. Chubb, Reginald Shareef, Nancy Saunders, Dot Brown, Louise Burrell, Brian Sieveking, Frank Ewald, Frosty Landon

Black mothers in Roanoke wouldn't let children pick up odd jobs at the circus: Author interview, Richard L. Chubb, Oct. 16, 2014.

Photography book with brothers' picture: Reginald Shareef's *The Roanoke Valley's African American Heritage: A Pictorial History* (Virginia Beach, VA: Donning, 1996), 185.

"Your uncles eat raw meat!": Author interview, Nancy Saunders and Dot Brown, April 2001.

double curse of differentness: Author interview, Louise Burrell, talking about her albino mother, Sept. 22, 2014.

Nancy Saunders's request to remove picture of brothers from photo exhibit: Author interview, Frank Ewald, Sept. 18, 2014.

Young Roanoker's fascination with brothers: Author interview, Brian Sieveking, Sept. 2, 2014.

Brothers featured in genetics book: Amram Scheinfeld, *You and Heredity* (New York: Frederick A. Stokes, 1939), 147.

Author's initial article on Nancy Saunders and her restaurant: Beth Macy, "Made with Love for Twelve Years Now, Customers Have Been Coming Back for the Goody Shop's Southern Cooking," *Roanoke Times,* Jan. 9, 1991.

"one exceptionally guarded family": Author interview, Reginald Shareef, Sept. 7, 2014.

***Roanoke Times*' refusal to print wedding announcements for black brides:** Author interview, Frosty Landon, former editorial-page editor, Oct. 13, 2014.

"Nobody can write about Freaks": Leslie Fiedler, *Freaks: Myths and Images of the Secret Self* (New York: Anchor, 1978), 171.

Chapter Two. White Peoples Is Hateful

Interviews: Johnny Angell, Diane Hayes, Janet Johnson, A. J. Reeves, Andrew Baskin, Thelma Muse Lee

Life of twentieth-century sharecropper: Author interview, Johnny Angell, Franklin County tobacco farmer, Oct. 14, 2014.

Connection between slavery and lingering black poverty and family structure: "It is true that many slaves were involved in social units that looked like nuclear families, but these were largely reproductive associations based on fragile male-female relationships," Patterson told journalist Craig Lambert in "The Caribbean Zola," *Harvard Magazine* (November–December 2014). "Parents had no custodial claims on their children, who at any time could be sold away from them. To call these units 'families,' as revisionist historians have done, is a historical and sociological travesty."

Blacks' reluctance to discuss slavery: Author interview, Diane Hayes, Oct. 22, 2014. Hayes and Audrey Dudley spent years compiling records on African Americans in Franklin County for a six-volume set they self-published called *Oh, Master*—named not for the slave owners but as a tribute to God. "They shouldn't have taught those black people to pray because praying's what got them out of slavery," Dudley told Hayes as they were working on the series.

Sabotage of recording about slavery at Colonial Williamsburg: Michael S. Durham, "The Word Is Slaves: A Trip into Black History," *American Heritage Journal* (April 1992).

"about the same as getting into paradise": Booker T. Washington, *Up from Slavery* (New York: Doubleday, Page, 1907), 7, *http://docsouth .unc.edu/fpn/washington/washing.html.*

Slave narrative of Armistead Reeves: Recounted by Janet Johnson to author, Nov. 11, 2013, and again by his grandson A. J. Reeves, Sept. 15, 2014.

How sharecroppers were often cheated out of pay: Jay R. Mandle, *The Roots of Black Poverty: The Southern Plantation Economy After the Civil War* (Durham, NC: Duke University Press, 1978), 25.

Dishonesty of farmers on "settling-day": Among the complaints logged in *Records of the Bureau of Refugees, Freedmen, and Abandoned Lands: Virginia, Rocky Mount, Letters Sent, 1866–1868,* pp. 45–48, compiled by U.S. National Archives and Record Service [n.d.]: A former slave was starving with her three children and deemed she was "better off before freedom"; a former slave trader told blacks in the region not to vote, then whites tried to incite blacks to hang him (they would have been blamed for the riots); and several complaints from sharecroppers who didn't get paid at all, 182.

no choice but to return: Ibid., 48. In some cases, interest rates were as high as 200 percent, according to Richard Wormser, *The Rise and Fall of Jim Crow* (New York: St. Martin's, 2003), 36.

only a fool would question the landlord's math: Andrew Baskin, author interview, Oct. 28, 2014. Baskin also coauthored *Studies in the Local History of Slavery: Essays Prepared for the Booker T. Washington National Monument* (Ferrum, VA: Ferrum College, 1978).

Violence against sharecroppers questioning landlord's accounting: Theodore Rosengarten's *All God's Dangers: The Life of Nate Shaw* (Chicago: University of Chicago Press, 1974).

"I find an inclination": Freedmen's Bureau Records, p. 200, as noted on the copy held at Franklin County Library, Rocky Mount, VA.

"It was the onliest way we had to make money": Author interview, Thelma Muse Lee, Sept. 15, 2014.

Muse and Dickerson descendants in Franklin County: Elizabeth Muse and Martha Dickerson/Dickinson/Dickenson (spellings varied) were prominent slave owners in the region. Harriett Dickerson Muse may have been born on Dickerson land. (Her parents were Edmund and Martha Dickerson, according to her Franklin County marriage license.) Ex-slaves by the last names Muse, Finney, and Pullen purchased farm-working equipment from Martha Dickerson in 1867, according to a slave inventory abstract compiled for Audrey Dudley and Diane Hayes, eds., *Oh, Master* (self-published, 2002), suggesting that they lived near one another.

Remarkable story of former slave Samuel Walker: Bill Archer, "Samuel Walker: Slave, Freedman, and Pensioner, 1842–1933," *Virginia Cavalcade* (Winter 2001).

Railroad presence in West Virginia coalfields: Ronald Lewis, "From Peasant to Proletarian: The Migration of Southern Blacks to the Central Appalachian Coalfields," *Journal of Southern History* 55, no. 1 (1989): 77–102.

Black men's eagerness to join cash economy: Wormser, *Rise and Fall of Jim Crow,* 58.

Documentation of Cabell Muse's first paid work alongside other Truevine natives: 1900 U.S. Census figures: Cabell/Calvin Muse (first-name spelling varied; he was sometimes even listed as Calbert) "works on track" in Rock, WV, and shared a household with Franklin County–born blacks, including N. H. Pullen (Charles Pullen's grandfather), William Belcher, and Patrick Payne. A. J. Reeves's father, Robert Reeves, was living with William Muse and Jack Hopkins in the same locality and working as a blacksmith.

The hard labor of building railroad track: Sheree Scarborough, *African American Railroad Workers of Roanoke: Oral Histories of the Norfolk and Western* (Charleston, SC: History Press, 2014), 11.

Railroad-camp violence: "Murdered by Tramps: Special Policeman and Telegraph Operator Shot in N. & W. Yards," *Washington Post,* July 27, 1904.

Masterless men: Wormser, *Rise and Fall of Jim Crow,* 54.

Du Bois's description of "race feud": W. E. B. Du Bois, *The Souls of Black Folk* (New York: Dover, 1994), 23, 65.

black people lacked the necessary intelligence: Baskin, *Studies in the Local History of Slavery,* 94.

Treatment of blacks as subhuman: Douglas A. Blackmon, *Slavery by Another Name: The Re-Enslavement of Black Americans from the Civil War to World War II* (New York: Doubleday, 2008), 235.

Sad parallel story of Ota Benga: Pamela Newkirk, *Spectacle: The Astonishing Life of Ota Benga* (New York: Amistad, 2015). The story is also told by Phillips Verner Bradford and Harvey Blume in *Ota Benga: The Pygmy in the Zoo* (New York: St. Martin's, 1992).

National media's racist coverage of Ota Benga: Mitch Keller, "The Scandal at the Zoo," *New York Times,* Aug. 6, 2006.

Ota Benga's suicide: Mike Hudson, "The Man They Put in the Zoo," *Roanoke Times,* Feb. 7, 1993.

"about as near to nowhere": Booker T. Washington, *An Autobiography by Booker T. Washington: The Story of My Life and Work* (Atlanta: J. L. Nichols, 1901), 15.

Chapter Three. And Still the Cry Against Us Continues

Interviews: Rand Dotson, A. L. Holland, Bev Fitzpatrick, Oliver Hill, Willie Mae Ingram, Regina "Sweet Sue" Holmes Peeks

The inception of Roanoke: Roanoke's growth was fastest between 1880 and 1890, according to Rand Dotson, *Roanoke, Virginia, 1882–1912: Magic City of the New South* (Knoxville: University of Tennessee Press, 2007), 105.

How Norfolk and Western Railway ended up in Roanoke: Ibid., 15.

Origin of city's name: The name Roanoke comes from the American Indian word *rawrenoc,* meaning "shell money," from Beth Macy, "What's in a Name?," *Roanoke Times,* Feb. 21, 2002.

How Roanoke businesses exploited state's coal deposits: *New York Times,* Aug. 27, 1883.

Growing pains in Roanoke: Clare White, *Roanoke: 1740–1982* (Roanoke, VA: Roanoke Valley Historical Society, 1982), 87.

Early Roanoke drinking culture: Dotson, *Roanoke, Virginia,* 21.

"Big Lick to Bigger Lick": Ibid., 232.

Ridiculing of country people in Roanoke's early days: Ibid., 115.

Racism in early Roanoke: Ibid., 23.

"Roanoke was incredibly hostile to African Americans": Author interview, Rand Dotson, Oct. 2, 2014.

Cabell Muse's first job in Roanoke: Water job listed on Cabell (spelled Cabble) Muse's World War I draft registration card; labor details confirmed by contemporary George Davis photos of the Roanoke Water Company, now part of the Western Virginia Water Authority.

Early 1900s restriction of black voting: Ben Beagle, "The 1902 Constitution: A Bleak Era for Blacks," *Roanoke Times,* special series reprint on race, "Black Virginia: Progress, Poverty & Paradox," 1984. The number of African Americans qualified to vote dropped from 147,000 to 21,000 immediately.

The Reverend R. R. Jones's escape from Roanoke and reaction in black press: *Richmond Planet,* as quoted in *Roanoke Times,* April 6, 1904.

Racist sentiments in wake of Shields case: Between 1880 and 1930, twenty-four blacks were lynched in southwest Virginia alone, according to a chart compiled by historian John Kern, Kern Collection, Virginia Room, Roanoke City Library.

Roanoke ordinance codifies housing segregation: Naomi A. Mattos, "Segregation by Custom Versus Segregation by Law, 1910–1917, City of Roanoke," written for Roanoke Regional Preservation Office, 2005; on file with Kern Collection.

Summary of Jim Crow laws and their impact from *Richmond Planet* editor: Ann Field Alexander, *Race Man: The Rise and Fall of the "Fighting Editor" John Mitchell Jr.* (Charlottesville: University of Virginia Press, 2002), 173.

National resurgence of Ku Klux Klan: Benjamin Quarles, *The Negro in the Making of America* (New York: Macmillan, 1964), 192.

Blues song about marrying a railroad man: "Berta, Berta," quoted in August Wilson, *The Piano Lesson* (New York: Penguin, 1990), 40.

Memory of early black migration pattern to Roanoke: Author interview, A. L. Holland, Nov. 11, 2014, and cited in Sheree Scarborough's *African American Railroad Workers of Roanoke: Oral Histories of the Norfolk and Western* (Charleston, SC: History Press, 2014).

Jim Crow humiliations for black workers in railroad work camps: Mason Scott, worker, interview by historian Michael A. Cooke, March 16, 1991, in Cooke, "Race Relations in Montgomery County, Virginia, 1870–1990," *Journals of the Appalachian Studies Association* (March 1992).

How Jordan's Alley got its name: In 1882 a man named John N. Jordan bought a rooming house owned by the son of early Roanoke developer Ferdinand Rorer. It had a bar that made the adjoining narrow alleyway a popular .thoroughfare and earned the nickname Jordan's Alley. Raymond Barnes, *A History of the City of Roanoke* (Radford, VA: Commonwealth Press, 1968), 97.

Description of rail yard's impact on Jordan's Alley: Author interview, Bev Fitzpatrick, Virginia Museum of Transportation executive director, on 1920s-era roundhouse conditions, Aug. 11, 2015. The roundhouse was later moved westward to Shaffer's Crossing.

Description of Muses' block in Jordan's Alley: Drawn from a 1929 Appraisal Map, Office of City Engineer, Sheet No. 111, on file at Roanoke City Hall.

Dr. I. D. Burrell's death: Mary Bishop, "A History of Strength," *Roanoke Times*, April 25, 1993.

Oliver Hill's description of segregated black school conditions: Beth Macy, "She Touched on Us to Eternity," *Roanoke Times*, Feb. 5, 2006.

Hill's description of threatened racial violence: Jonathan K. Stubbs, ed., *The Big Bang: Brown v. Board of Education and Beyond: The Autobiography of Oliver W. Hill, Sr.* (Winter Park, FL: Four-G, 2000), 34.

Du Bois's "Talented Tenth": Du Bois believed a black man had a one-in-ten chance of becoming a leader but needed classical education to reach full potential, in contrast to the industrial education and trades proposed by Booker T. Washington. "The Negro race, like all races, is going to be saved by its exceptional men," he wrote in "The Talented Tenth," September 1903: http://teachingamericanhistory.org/library/document/the-talented-tenth/.

Living conditions in Jordan's Alley: Author interview, Willie Mae Ingram, Nov. 11, 2014.

Family life in Jordan's Alley: Author interview, Regina "Sweet Sue" Holmes Peeks, Nov. 11, 2014.

Poverty in Roanoke's West End today: Hurt Park Elementary statistics at Virginia Department of Education, Office of School Nutrition Programs, as of October 2014: http://www.pen.k12.va.us/support/nutrition/statistics/free_reduced_eligibility/2014-2015/schools/frpe_sch_report_sy2014-15.pdf.

Chapter Four. *Your Momma Is Dead*

Interviews: Warren Raymond, Howard Tibbals, Richard Dillard, Joshua Bond, Bonnie LeRoy, Robert Bogdan, Al Stencell, Fred Dahlinger

Freaks as "aristocrats": Patricia Bosworth's *Diane Arbus: A Biography* (New York: W. W. Norton, 2006), 177.

Description of sideshow exhibits: Richard W. Flint, "Promoting Peerless Prodigies 'To the Curious,'" in Kristin L. Spangenberg and Deborah W. Walk, eds., *The Amazing American Circus Poster: The Strobridge Lithographing Company* (Cincinnati: Cincinnati Art Museum, 2011), 48–54.

Lew Graham's definition of a good freak act: Fred Bradna, *The Big Top: My Forty Years with the Greatest Show on Earth* (New York: Simon and Schuster, 1952), 236.

Sideshow pecking order: Author interview, Warren Raymond, Feb. 26, 2015.

a hyperbolic spiel: A pitchman, also known as a talker but never a barker, would deliver the pitch, according to a pamphlet written by retired showman Joe McKennon, *Circus Lingo* (Sarasota, FL: Carnival Publishers of Sarasota, 1980), my go-to source for circus slang throughout this book.

"The brothers were descended from monkeys": As recounted in Bradna, *Big Top,* 237.

"Two Ecuador white savages": How Lee Graham first spun the Muse brothers' act, "Lew Graham Made One of Finds of His Career," *Billboard,* July 27, 1922.

"All for the insignificant sum": Felix Isman, *Weber and Fields: Their Tribulations, Triumphs and Their Associates* (New York: Boni and Liveright, 1924).

Diane Arbus's portrayal of sideshow subjects: Arbus's photograph of Jack Dracula was not printed in the magazine, but the final image, selected as AR00570, is in the holdings of the Tate and National Galleries of Scotland, "Jack Dracula, the Marked Man, N.Y.C.," available at http://www.tate.org.uk/art/artworks/arbus-jack-dracula-in-a-bar-nyc-al00191/text-summary.

Howard Tibbals's circus collection: Billy Cox, "Howard Tibbals and the Huge Miniature Circus," *Sarasota (FL) Herald Tribune,* Jan. 19, 2012.

"I hate sideshows": Author interview, Howard Tibbals, Dec. 3, 2014.

James Baldwin on freaks: "Freaks and the American Ideal of Manhood," in Toni Morrison, ed., *James Baldwin: Collected Essays* (New York: Library of America, 1998). Also published in *James Baldwin: The Price of the Ticket: Collected Essays, 1948–1985* (New York: St. Martin's, 1985).

"the freaks are the good people!": Author interview, Richard Dillard, Nov. 24, 2014.

Freak pride "in being a burden to nobody": A. W. Stencell, *Seeing Is Believing: America's Sideshows* (Toronto: ECW Press, 2002).

Zip's supposed last words: Leslie Fiedler, *Freaks: Myths and Images of the Secret Self* (New York: Anchor, 1978).

Press agents' influence on circus coverage: "I am a creature born of the minds of newspapermen, a genie of journalistic paste jars, a fantastic flower nurtured in a pot of printer's ink, a product of the freedom of the press," longtime Ringling press agent Dexter Fellows writes in his autobiography, Fellows and Andrew A. Freeman, *This Way to the Big Show: The Life of Dexter Fellows* (New York: Viking, 1936), prologue.

Barnum's controlling of Zip: Robert Bogdan, *Freak Show: Presenting Human Oddities for Amusement and Profit* (Chicago: University of Chicago Press, 1988), 136.

Zip paid not to talk: Ibid., 135.

Popularity of sideshow portraits during Victorian era: Ibid., 12.

Analysis of clothing in photo of Muse brothers: Author interview, Joshua Bond, Nov. 18, 2014.

Incidence of albinism: Armand Marie Leroi, *Mutants: On Genetic Variety and the Human Body* (New York: Viking, 2003), 254.

Poor eyesight among albinos: Author interview, Bonnie LeRoy, June 4, 2015.

Negative views of albinos: Maryrose Cuskelly, *Original Skin: Exploring the Marvels of the Human Hide* (Berkeley, CA: Counterpoint, 2011).

Possibility of Noah's being an albino: Damon Rose, "The People Who Think Noah Had Albinism," BBC News, April 3, 2014.

"start seeing beauty in difference": Rick Guidotti, "From Stigma to Supermodel," TED Talk, https://www.ted.com/talks/rick_guidotti_from_stigma_to_supermodel.

Background on history of science, albinism, and early entertainment-venue draws: Taken primarily from Bogdan, *Freak Show,* and author interview, Bogdan, Sept. 2, 2014, and from Charles D. Martin, *The White African American Body: A Cultural and Literary Exploration* (New Brunswick, NJ: Rutgers University Press, 2002), from which the story of Jefferson's fascination with albinism is also summarized.

Jefferson's fascination with albinos: The first *Notes on the State of Virginia* was compiled in 1781, then updated in 1782 and 1783. Topics covered ranged from natural resources, religion, and economy to Jefferson's belief that blacks and whites could not live together in a free society; later printed in Julian P. Boyd, ed., *The Papers of Thomas Jefferson,* vol. 6, May 1781–March 1784 (Princeton, NJ: Princeton University Press, 1950), 423.

Jefferson's suggestion that Africans had sex with apes: Joe Feagin, sociologist and race scholar, interviewed by George Yancy, "American Racism in the 'White Frame,'" *New York Times,* July 27, 2015.

Charles Willson Peale's museum: Bogdan, *Freak Show,* 29.

Argument for vitiligo as cure for blackness: Dr. Benjamin Rush put forward his theory in a 1796 letter to Thomas Jefferson, according to John Wood Sweet, *Bodies Politic: Negotiating Race in the American North, 1730–1830* (Philadelphia: University of Pennsylvania Press, 2006).

Barnum adding the bling: Bogdan, *Freak Show,* 32.

Freak hunting described: Freddie Darius Benham, "The Side Show Manager," *Circus Scrap Book* 1, no. 4 (October 1929): 27–30.

Account of Unzie: As written in Frederick Drimmer's *Very Special People: The Struggles, Loves, and Triumphs of Human Oddities* (New York: Amjon, 1973), 31.

Premature sideshow obituary: "Tragic Retreat of Human Freaks Before Picture Shows," *Washington Post,* Feb. 26, 1911.

Freak-wanted ads: *Billboard,* March 13, 1915, and Sept. 13, 1919.

First description of brothers' first carnival: J. A. Forbes, "Great American Shows," *Billboard,* Feb. 7, 1914.

Background on Miller's carnival: Ibid.

lot lice: Gene Plowden, *Circus Press Agent: The Life and Times of Roland Butler* (Caldwell, ID: Caxton, 1984).

Importance of lot lice: Author interview, Al Stencell, March 1, 2015.

Miller's carnival acts described: *Billboard,* Aug. 1, 1914.

First description of brothers as "monkey-face men": *Fort Wayne (IN) Journal-Gazette,* Sept. 4, 1914.

Typical ballyhoo for albino acts: As described in Harry Lewiston's *Freak Show Man: The Autobiography of Harry Lewiston as Told to Jerry Holtman* (Los Angeles: Holloway House, 1968).

"Sunday boil-up": Bogdan, *Freak Show,* 75.

Description of various carnival acts: "Great American Shows Will Be One of the Big Features on the Fair Grounds Next Week," *Fort Wayne (IN) Daily News,* Sept. 10, 1914.

Cyclist drafted into German army: *Billboard,* Oct. 24, 1914.

Carnival murder: "Snake Charmer Involved in Tragedy," *Billboard,* Oct. 24, 1914.

"The Southern darky is in clover this fall": "Shows Cleaning Up," *Billboard,* Nov. 11, 1916, p. 64.

Complicated lives of sideshow acts and managers: Author interview, Stencell, Nov. 14, 2014.

"A question that needs to be answered": Author interviews (via e-mail), Fred Dahlinger, November and December 2014.

"How are the wonders 'Eko' and 'Iko' doing?": Notice posted by C. E. Williams, *New York Clipper,* Oct. 3, 1914, p. 12.

Notice possibly dictated by Harriett Muse/Hattie Cooke, saying she wants her sons back: Readers' Column, *Billboard,* Dec. 26, 1914.

Lack of diversity in New Castle: 2010 census figures put the percentage of African Americans in Craig County at 0.2.

Chapter Five. *Some Serious Secrets*

Interviews: Jane Johnston, Lori LeMay, Jerry Jones, Don Charlton, Bernth Lindfors, Jane Nicholas, Nancy Saunders, Bonnie LeRoy, Al Stencell, J. Harry Woody.

Social history of Fenwick Mines: From "Geologic Wonders of the George Washington and Jefferson National Forests," Pamphlet No. 3 in a series, U.S. Department of Agriculture, Forest Service, Southern Region, 2001.

Diversity among Fenwick workers: Ibid. and author interview, Jane Johnston, Craig County Historical Society, Nov. 24, 2014.

Italians' goal to earn enough money to return home: Lori Barfield, "Fenwick Mine Complex," for U.S. Department of Agriculture, Forest Service, Southern Region, June 5, 1990. The quote comes from an interview with Craig County native "Boots" Hutchinson, who attended school in Fenwick. (Researcher's name is now Lori LeMay.) Author interview, Lori LeMay, May 26, 2015.

Preponderance of minority labor in mining camps: Michael B. Barber et al., "Industry as Rural Landscape: The Fenwick Iron Mining Complex, Craig County, Virginia," for Jefferson National Forest, April 1995.

Recollection of brothers in New Castle as children: Author interview, Jerry Jones, Nov. 25, 2014.

Recollection of life in New Castle: Author interview, Don Charlton, Nov. 24, 2014.

Family name misrecorded as Mules instead of Muse: In the 1920 census, a ninety-three-year-old grandmother named America Cook lives with Harriett and Cabell Muse, along with their three youngest children, all of whom are wrongly filed under the Mules surname.

America Cook's probable whereabouts in 1870: Found in the 1870 census living in the Maggoddee Creek section of Franklin County, Virginia; the name "America" was likely mistyped as "Avram."

"My great-grandfather was a white man": Author interview, J. Harry Woody, April 1, 2016.

Race relations in New Castle region: A trusted former colleague who is now retired, JoAnne Poindexter is a lifelong member of Jerusalem Baptist Church and was the same source who helped in Chapter Three by introducing me to Regina "Sweet Sue" Holmes Peeks and Willie Mae (Mother) Ingram and, later, Sarah Showalter.

Italians had the most dangerous mining jobs: Barber et al., "Industry as Rural Landscape."

Child workers at Fenwick: Author interview, Lori LeMay, May 26, 2015.

Public records for Cookes/Muses, including marriage certificate: Moses and Hattie Cooke lived in the Big Lick magisterial district of Roanoke County in 1900, sans children. But I could find no accounting of Moses Cooke after that in city directories or public records, including marriage records, criminal complaints, and death records. When Harriett married Cabell Muse in 1917 in Franklin County, she used her maiden name, Harriett Dickerson.

Erratic documentation of Muse children using Cook/Cooke family name: 1930 U.S. Census documents a Virginia-born Thomas

Cook living with George and Willie Muse in Manhattan, along with three other nonrelatives; the brothers were all listed as circus employees. (By 1940, Thomas told census takers his name was Thomas Muse; he was living in Roanoke County's Ballyhack with his mother, listed as Harriett Muse.)

End of Fenwick Mines: Emmette Milton Sr., "Rise and Fall of Prosperity in Craig County," *New Castle (VA) Record*, Aug. 22, 1974.

Craig County crime that captured public's attention: Harvey D. Looney broke out of Craig County Jail on April 24, 1914, according to *New Castle (VA) Record.*

"the last trace of him being a set of bloody footprints": Escapee Harvey Looney returned to New Castle a few years later—incognito, dressed as a woman—in order to attend his mother's funeral. Burks Mountain was later renamed Nutter Mountain. Author interview, Don Charlton, April 22, 2016.

Remnants of Fenwick: Barfield, "Fenwick Mine Complex," 20.

KKK picnic: Laura Fasbach, "Out-of-State KKK Group to Meet Today," *Roanoke Times,* July 11, 1998.

family's long-accepted timeline: According to the 1910 census, George and Willie were born in 1899 and 1901, respectively. All other official records, including death certificates and employment records, line up with the family's account that they were born in 1890 and 1893.

Nancy's reaction to Hattie Cooke revelation: Author interview, Nancy Saunders, Dec. 5, 2014.

Black American sideshow acts pretending to be from Africa: Author interview, Bernth Lindfors, Oct. 13, 2014.

Barnum's claim of discovering Zip: Bernth Lindfors, *Early African Entertainments Abroad: From the Hottentot Venus to Africa's First Olympians* (Madison: University of Wisconsin Press, 2014).

Zip's being initially coerced to perform: James W. Cook Jr., "Of Men, Missing Links, and Nondescripts: The Strange Career of P. T. Barnum's 'What Is It?' Exhibition," in Rosemarie Garland Thomson, ed., *Freakery: Cultural Spectacles of the Extraordinary Body* (New York: New York University Press, 1996).

More varying accounts of Zip's early career: When the novelist Charles Dickens asked, "What is it?" P. T. Barnum allegedly replied, "That's what it is, a What Is It," as recounted in Fred Bradna, *The Big*

Top: My Forty Years with the Greatest Show on Earth (New York: Simon and Schuster, 1952).

Klein's description of carnival's acts, travels, and reception: Ben H. Klein, "Carnival News: Great American Shows," *Billboard,* Sept. 5, 1914.

"strange creatures": "Completing Arrangements," *Fort Wayne (IN) Daily News,* Sept. 10, 1914.

Description of Austin and Stone's: The main attractions were plays, operas, and traveling Broadway shows (hired at cut rates for the off-season); the sideshows were supplemental attractions typically housed on the second or third floor, according to author interview, Al Stencell, March 1, 2015.

"Marvelous, marvelous!": Fred Allen, *Much Ado About Me* (Boston: Little, Brown, 1956).

large blocks of ice: David Kruh, *Always Something Doing: Boston's Infamous Scollay Square* (Boston: Northeastern University Press, 1989).

Milton Berle's early career: Ibid., 30.

Background on Albert R. Bawden: "1925 Officers for Local Pin League Elected," *Davenport (IA) Democrat and Leader,* May 1, 1925.

Eli Bowen's desire to return to sideshows in old age: "Legless Eli Bowen Dies in Dreamland," *Brooklyn Daily Eagle,* May 5, 1924.

Ads documenting range and popularity of sideshow acts: Classified ads, *Billboard,* Jan. 22, 1916.

Nascent child labor laws in Roanoke: Raymond Barnes, *A History of the City of Roanoke* (Radford, VA: Commonwealth Press, 1968), 515.

Lewis Hine's photographs documenting child labor in Roanoke: Taken when he was working for the National Child Labor Committee between 1908 and 1924, now held by Library of Congress, Washington, DC.

"These people are going to stare at me anyway": Author interview, Jane Nicholas, Feb. 26, 2015.

How Eli Bowen became a sideshow performer: Robert Bogdan, *Freak Show: Presenting Human Oddities for Amusement and Profit* (Chicago: University of Chicago Press, 1988), 213, and Susan Burch, ed., *Encyclopedia of American Disability History* (New York: Facts on File, 2009).

adults could legally and literally mail children: May Pierstroff, a child of five, was mailed between two Idaho towns in 1914, according to Nancy A. Pope, "100 Years of Parcels, Packages, and Packets," Feb. 19, 2013, on file at Smithsonian Institution, National Postal Museum, http://postalmuseumblog.si.edu/2013/02/.

Minik's railing against American Museum of Natural History: Michael T. Kaufman, "A Museum's Eskimo Skeletons and Its Own," About New York, *New York Times*, Aug. 21, 1993.

Repatriation of Minik's father's remains: Kenn Harper, *Give Me My Father's Body: The Life of Minik, the New York Eskimo* (Frobisher Bay, NU: Blacklead, 1986), 227–229.

Minik's description of loneliness: Ibid., 34.

Minik's fear of being returned to museum: Ibid., 44.

Zip's career around 1914: "Old Favorites in the Circus Ring," *New York Times*, April 5, 1914.

How Hiram and Barney Davis became sideshow acts: Bogdan, *Freak Show*, 122.

"they were not freaks": Ibid., 126.

Popularity of "A Long Way to Tipperary": "Christmas 1914: The Day Even WWI Showed Humanity," Associated Press, Dec. 20, 2014.

Chapter Six. A Paying Proposition

Interviews: Fred Pfening III, Don Nicely, Rand Dotson, Al Stencell, Nancy Saunders, Kinney Rorrer

throwing his hat into the ring: Fred Bradna, *The Big Top: My Forty Years with the Greatest Show on Earth* (New York: Simon and Schuster, 1952), 118.

Size of traveling circuses in early 1900s: Janet M. Davis, *The Circus Age: Culture and Society Under the American Big Top* (Chapel Hill: University of North Carolina Press, 2002), 5–9.

Timing and plotting of circus routes: Dexter Fellows and Andrew A. Freeman, *This Way to the Big Show: The Life of Dexter Fellows* (New York: Viking, 1936), 220–221.

"a nonintellectual activity": Author interview, Fred Pfening III, Nov. 10, 2014.

Ringlings recruit drummers: Fellows and Freeman, *This Way to the Big Show*, 180–182.

"Quite often the carnivals would change their name": Author interview, Warren Raymond, Feb. 26, 2015.

"nature's greatest mistakes": "Big Street Fair This Week," *White-wright (TX) Sun*, Aug. 10, 1917.

Shelton's rise in carnival hierarchy: The first press mentions of Shelton were "Deep Water Jubilee" notice, *New York Clipper*, May 23, 1914 (Shelton is listed as a candy butcher), and "Carnival Rosters," *Billboard*, March 18, 1916 (Shelton was listed as an announcer for Paul's United Shows).

Description of Shelton's hand deformity: Author interview, Don Nicely, Feb. 26, 2015.

Biographical details for Shelton: Billboard directories have him first listed in 1916 as an "announcer." He was born on April 6, 1897, in Grainger County, Tennessee, according to census records.

Origin of "candy butcher": Joe McKennon, *Circus Lingo* (Sarasota, FL: Carnival Publishers of Sarasota, 1980), 23.

Pinkard's developing black subdivision: Reginald Shareef, *The Roanoke Valley's African American Heritage: A Pictorial History* (Virginia Beach, VA: Donning, 1996), 39–40, and Kevin Kittredge, "Recalling the 'Yarb Doctor,'" *Roanoke Times*, July 19, 2006.

Pinkard's fashion flair: When Pinkard's Court was razed in 1998 to make room for a Lowe's and a Walmart, one former resident lamented, "They should have left that arch"; Christina Nuckols, "The Life and Times of Pinkard Court," *Roanoke Times*, Nov. 9, 1997.

shortly after marrying Cabell Muse, in 1917: Harriett's 1917 marriage certificate is on file at the Franklin County courthouse. For it, Harriett gives her maiden name as Dickerson. No mention was ever made of her marriage to Moses Cook, and no courthouse marriage records for Moses Cook and Harriett Dickerson could be found.

the right to live without fear of being lynched: Author interview, Rand Dotson, Jan. 12, 2015, and Isabel Wilkerson, "When Will the North Face Its Racism?," *New York Times*, Jan. 10, 2015.

Examples of Jim Crow restriction: Benjamin Quarles, *The Negro in the Making of America* (New York: Macmillan, 1964), 129–130.

Virginia poll taxes: "Virginia Constitutional Convention (1901–1902)," *Encyclopedia of Virginia*, Virginia Foundation for the Humanities, http://www.encyclopediavirginia.org/Constitutional_Convention _Virginia_1901-1902.

Brothers as "big money getters": "Metropolitan and Loos Shows Open 1917 Season," *Billboard*, March 3, 1917, p. 34.

Booger Red's Congress of Rough Riders: "Big Crowd at Carnival," *Corsicana (TX) Daily Sun*, Oct. 3, 1916. Ad copy from *Billboard*, Jan. 31, 1920.

"the shows are all clean and meritorious": "Big Grist of Indictments," *Corsicana (TX) Daily Sun*, Oct. 28, 1919.

they oddly shared a left-hand deformity: "Second and third fingers of left hand grown together," according to John George Loos's World War I draft registration card.

Freak- and talker-seeking ad for J. George Loos Shows: *Billboard*, June 10, 1916.

Comparison of Muses' and other performers' contracts: Copies of contracts for Zip, George Bell, and James G. Tarver (the white giant) were provided by collector and sideshow researcher Fred Pfening III.

"I am sure Bell was of at least average intelligence": Author interview, Pfening.

George Bell, "the colored giant" and minstrel: Bell died in 1919 at sixty-five, after being shot by a fellow circus worker, Maceo Ealy, according to "Negro Giant Dead," *Evening Telegraph (IL)*, March 25, 1919.

plant shows: Author interview, Al Stencell, March 18, 2015.

Shelton exaggerates his position: "Circus Men Are Hetterich's Guests," *Journal News (OH)*, May 1, 1923.

shortchanger's code of honor: Harry Lewiston, *Freak Show Man: The Autobiography of Harry Lewiston as Told to Jerry Holtman* (Los Angeles: Holloway House, 1968), 89.

Shortchanging was frequent: Author interviews, Al Stencell (via phone and e-mail), December 2014–January 2015.

Wives were "time-wasters": Henry Ringling North and Alden Hatch, *The Circus Kings: Our Ringling Family Story* (Garden City, NY: Doubleday, 1960), 102.

Preponderance of gay men in circus: Author interviews, Stencell, and Fellows and Freeman, *This Way to the Big Show*, 183.

Stockholm syndrome: "When someone holds you totally powerless, totally isolated and has complete power of life and death over you, and then he lets you live, you think, 'He could have killed me but he didn't,'" the psychiatrist Martin Symonds told reporter Erik Eckholm, "Out of Captivity; Hostage Bond of Captors Is Common," *New York Times*, July 1, 1985.

Shelton's reputation: Multiple ads the summer of 1920, including on p. 93 of *Billboard,* July 31, 1920.

Barnes's dog-and-pony show: Dave Robeson, *Al G. Barnes, Master Showman* (Caldwell, ID: Caxton, 1936), 30.

Showmen's cashing in on America's fascination with the exotic: To hone his tribal knowledge for the spieling of Wu Foo, supposedly a Ghanian tribal chief but actually a black native New Yorker, Harry Lewiston bought books on Africa and memorized country names, according to Lewiston, *Freak Show Man,* 187–189.

Barnes "quickly realized [the Muses'] possibilities": Robeson, *Al G. Barnes, Master Showman,* 276–277.

the Muse brothers morphed: Various ads from the Barnes sideshow of that era also cast them as Ecuadorian Twins and/or Ecuadorian Cannibals.

Mabel Stark's prowess: Miss Cellania, "Mabel Stark: The Lady with the Tigers," Feb. 7, 2013, http://mentalfloss.com/article/48808/mabel-stark-lady-tigers.

fireworks would emanate from her head: Robeson, *Al G. Barnes,* text and photographs, and "Barnes' Circus Scores a Hit in Cincinnati," *Billboard,* Sept. 20, 1919.

Barnes dedicates lion: *Billboard,* May 10, 1919, p. 84.

Tusko's death at forty-two: "Death Takes Tusko, Big Elephant That Lived Stormy Life," *Chicago Tribune,* June 11, 1933.

"Displays of sex, horror, and strangeness": A. W. Stencell, *Seeing Is Believing: America's Sideshows* (Toronto: ECW Press, 2002), 4.

Barnes show described as "all beauty and muscle": *Billboard,* Sept. 20, 1919, pp. 48, 68.

"too much for one pair of eyes to see": "Deming Was Out En Masse to See the Big Circus," *Deming (NM) Highlight,* Nov. 9, 1923.

"Bodies of Zanzibar Youths": *Scranton (PA) Republican,* June 23, 1923.

Coverage, with brothers' picture, in Scranton: "Barnes Big Circus Will Be in This City Today," *Scranton (PA) Republican,* June 26, 1923.

Shelton may have been co-managing the Muses earlier: There are brief descriptions of Barnum's Monkey Men being managed by "Messrs. Shelton and Stone," *Billboard,* March 3, 1917, p. 34, and *New York Clipper,* March 14, 1917. The "Shelton" is presumably Candy Shelton. Judging by 1918 *Billboard* ads, Shelton is their sole manager.

Barnes's stormy marriage record: "Al G. Barnes Dies," *Around the White Tops* (Circus Fans of America publication), September 1931; on file at Circus World Museum, Baraboo, WI.

"his zest for life": "Al G. Barnes Dies; Noted Circus Man," *New York Times,* July 25, 1931.

George and Willie feigned servitude: Stanley Elkins's views were influential during the development of affirmative-action programs designed to counteract the lingering effects of slavery on black culture; Quarles, *Negro in the Making of America,* 74–75, and Elkins, *Slavery: A Problem in American Institutional and Intellectual Life* (Chicago: University of Chicago Press, 1959).

frustration behind a façade of happiness: Paul Laurence Dunbar, "We Wear the Mask," *Lyrics of Lowly Life* (New York: Dodd, Mead, 1896). Dunbar's poem inspired Maya Angelou's "The Mask."

"It's still not uncommon for people to misdiagnose albinism": Author interview, Bonnie LeRoy, June 4, 2015.

"rigid caste system of the circus": Lewiston, *Freak Show Man,* 213–214.

Freaks said to be moody and illiterate: Bradna, *Big Top,* 236.

Novelty was always the goal: "Curiosities as Drawing Cards," *Billboard,* May 24, 1901.

But as Willie himself told the story: Author interview, Nancy Saunders, Nov. 5, 2015.

"Eko and Iko could play anything": Author interviews, Al Stencell (via phone and e-mail), December 2014–January 2015, with primary source Charlie Roark, as noted in Stencell, *Circus and Carnival Ballyhoo: Sideshow Freaks, Jabbers and Blade Box Queens* (Toronto: ECW Press, 2010).

Background on minstrelsy: Jan Harold Brunvand, ed., *American Folklore: An Encyclopedia* (New York: Routledge, 1998), 122.

Barnum's jig-dancing contests: Stencell, *Seeing Is Believing,* 174. In his memoir, *The Life of P. T. Barnum* (Buffalo, NY: Courier, 1888), Barnum himself described John Diamond as a "Negro break-down dancer" and said Diamond occasionally swindled him.

The term "Jim Crow": One African-American's perspective on Jim Crow is the Reverend Walter H. Brooks's poem "The 'Jim Crow' Car," published in the black-owned *Richmond Planet,* Sept. 15, 1900: *"This too is done to crush me, / But naught can keep us back; / 'My place,' forsooth, a* *section / 'Twixt' smoker, front and back, / While others ride in coaches / Full large and filled with light,/ And this our Southern Christians / Insist is just and right."*

Clawhammer-style banjo playing and analysis of second known Muse brothers photo: Author interview, Kinney Rorrer, Sept. 26, 2014.

"a sense of freedom and spontaneity": John Kenrick, *Al Jolson: A Biography*, 2003 (Musicals101.com).

Bert Williams, one of the highest-paid black entertainers: Kevin Young, "Wearing the Mask," *New York Times,* Nov. 16, 2012.

"the funniest man I ever saw": Cary D. Wintz and Paul Finkelman, eds., *Encyclopedia of the Harlem Renaissance* (New York: Routledge, 2004), 1210.

Rabbit Muse's attempt to leave home and join a traveling show: Ralph Berrier Jr., "Remembering Rabbit," *Roanoke Times,* Feb. 27, 2007.

Rabbit Muse's family band: "Darkness on the Delta," from *Blues* (1976), recorded in Franklin County, VA, https://www.youtube.com/watch?v=x8caDIplsAg.

Background on Rabbit Muse and blues of Virginia's western Piedmont: Liner notes, "Virginia Traditions: Western Piedmont Blues," produced by Blue Ridge Institute of Ferrum College, available for download here: http://www.folkways.si.edu/virginia-traditions-western-piedmont-blues/african-american-folk/music/album/smithsonian.

"a better offer from another circus": Robeson, 277.

a dozen large railroad shows competed: Stencell, *Seeing Is Believing,* 58.

Ringling Brothers played to as many as two and a half million people: Dean Jensen, *Queen of the Air: A True Story of Love and Tragedy at the Circus* (New York: Crown, 2013).

Chapter Seven. He Who Hustleth While He Waiteth

Interviews: Rob Houston, Nancy Saunders, Louise Burrell, Robert Bogdan, Al Stencell

Silent film of circus: Film archives are searchable online at the Circus World Museum website at http://www.cwmdigitacollections

.com/cwm-fm-326.html. The brothers are featured twice in Part One, at 1:04 and again at 1:59.

Black performers portrayed as white in banners: Author interview, Rob Houston, Jan. 14, 2015.

"dunk the nigger": Grace Elizabeth Hale, *Making Whiteness: The Culture of Segregation in the South, 1890–1940* (New York: Random House, 1998), 205.

Anderson sisters optimized the exposure of their spots: Edward J. Kelty, *Congress of Freaks with Ringling Brothers and Barnum & Bailey Combined Circus,* 1926 promotional shot, on file at Circus World Museum, Baraboo, WI.

Kelty's drinking: Described by his son, Ed Kelty Jr., in Ellen Warren, "The History of E. J. Kelty," *Chicago Tribune,* Feb. 7, 2003.

Kelty pawned his negatives: Miles Barth, "Edward J. Kelty and Century Flashlight Photographers," in Kelty et al., *Step Right This Way: The Photographs of Edward J. Kelty* (New York: Barnes and Noble, 2002).

Soaring KKK membership: C. Vann Woodward, *The Strange Career of Jim Crow* (New York: Oxford University Press, 1955), 115.

"considered white when they traveled": Author interview, Nancy Saunders and Louise Burrell, Sept. 14, 2014.

As whites: George and Willie were also listed as "white" on their World War II draft registration cards.

managers plied Clicko with beer: Robert Bogdan, *Freak Show: Presenting Human Oddities for Amusement and Profit* (Chicago: University of Chicago Press, 1988), 192, and A. W. Stencell, *Circus and Carnival Ballyhoo: Sideshow Freaks, Jabbers and Blade Box Queens* (Toronto: ECW Press, 2010).

Cook bailed him out of trouble: After Clicko had been arrested for drunken and disorderly conduct, Cook gave the jailers a big book of circus tickets and left with Clicko, according to Albert Tucker, "The Strangest People on Earth," *Sarasota (FL) Sentinel,* July 7, 1973.

Doll family's tiny furniture and Jack Earle's extra-long bed: Dexter Fellows and Andrew A. Freeman, *This Way to the Big Show: The Life of Dexter Fellows* (New York: Viking, 1936), 225.

Ingalls kept 10 percent of the door: Ibid., 224.

Lewiston's errors: A. W. Stencell, *Seeing Is Believing: America's Sideshows* (Toronto: ECW Press, 2002), 6.

Ingalls's verbal flair: Harry Lewiston, *Freak Show Man: The Autobiography of Harry Lewiston as Told to Jerry Holtman* (Los Angeles: Holloway House, 1968), 201–203. Ingalls ballyhoo as quoted in Dean Jensen, *Queen of the Air: A True Story of Love and Tragedy at the Circus* (New York: Crown, 2013), 145.

Lowery's personal mantra: Clifford Edward Watkins, *Showman: The Life and Music of Perry George Lowery* (Jackson: University Press of Mississippi, 2003).

Sideshow band timing and setup: Ibid.

Sideshow revenues as estimated by Ingalls: "Circus Side Show Brought Up to Date," *New Bedford (MA) Sunday Standard,* July 2, 1916.

"No secret can survive long": Dean Jensen, *Queen of the Air: A True Story of Love and Tragedy at the Circus* (New York: Crown, 2013), 146–147.

Alfredo Codona: John Ringling signed the Flying Codonas to be the headliners for RB&BB in 1927, according to Jensen, *Queen of the Air,* 171.

James Bailey's humble beginnings: "A Caesar Among Showmen," *New York Times,* April 19, 1891.

German military studies Bailey's methods: Ibid. Bailey's wizardry in logistics is also described in Fred Bradna, *The Big Top: My Forty Years with the Greatest Show on Earth* (New York: Simon and Schuster, 1952), Chapter 3.

The Bailey vs. Barnum battle over Columbia: Fellows's account (Fellows and Freeman, *This Way to the Big Show*) says Barnum offered Bailey $10,000 for the elephant, the first born in captivity, while Bradna's (Bradna, *Big Top*) says he offered him $50,000.

Bailey as silent but canny partner for Barnum: Bradna, *Big Top,* 33.

"an awful exhibition of faltering nerve": Henry Ringling North and Alden Hatch, *The Circus Kings: Our Ringling Family Story* (Garden City, NY: Doubleday, 1960), 65.

The Ringling Brothers' initial circus jobs: Fellows and Freeman, *This Way to the Big Show,* 175–176.

Lou Ringling's double duty: Charles Philip Fox, *A Ticket to the Circus: A Pictorial History of the Incredible Ringlings* (New York: Bramhall House, 1958).

Al Ringling's exaggeration of circus size: David C. Weeks, *Ringling: The Florida Years, 1911–1936* (Gainesville: University Press of Florida, 1993), 9.

Al Ringling's plow balancing: "Wisconsin Museum Dedicated to the Big Top," *New York Times,* Aug. 2, 1959.

"almost impregnable": North and Hatch, 116–117, 123–125.

Ringlings' purchase of Barnum and Bailey: Fellows and Freeman, *This Way to the Big Show,* 184. Other accounts of the sales price differ, including that in John and Alice Durant, *Pictorial History of the American Circus* (New York: A. S. Barnes, 1957), which put the sale at $410,000 (186).

John Ringling's appetite: Taylor Gordon, *Born to Be* (Seattle: University of Washington Press, 1975), 113.

John Ringling's looks and voice: Weeks, *Ringling,* 1.

Ringlings' quest to absorb their competitors: Bradna, *Big Top,* 71–73.

"Kill Diamond in some humane way": Durant, *Pictorial History of the American Circus,* 206–207.

Media's love of and reliance on Fellows: "Dexter Fellows, Press Agent, Dies," *New York Times,* Nov. 27, 1937.

"He could improvise the type": Ibid.

"pride of calling": Fellows and Freeman, *This Way to the Big Show,* 292–293.

"built-in incentive to keep the sideshow exhibits happy": Author interview, Robert Bogdan, Sept. 2, 2014.

RB&BB's announcement about Eko and Iko: "Lew Graham Made One of Finds of His Career," *Billboard,* Aug. 5, 1922.

fifty-eight-pound Human Skeleton: Robinson was married to Baby Bunny Smith, the 467-pound fat lady; Robinson was best known for his role in the horror film *Freaks* (1932), according to http://www.imdb.com/name/nm0732977/bio?ref_=nm_ov_bio_sm.

A paper in Syracuse: "Bodies Covered With Wool," *Syracuse (NY) Journal,* July 16, 1923.

one of the few photos I found of Shelton from that era: From Stencell, *Circus and Carnival Ballyhoo.*

Possibly hyped-up claim about sideshow workers' pay: "Circus Freaks Are Well Paid," *Sun (NY),* April 1, 1924. The article described Lionel as being the highest-paid freak on the Ringling sideshow at the time, at $250 a week, with Clio the snake charmer being the lowest-paid, at $75 a week. George and Willie, it said, "are drawing $400 a week between them." The story noted that pitch cards typically brought in an additional $50 to $100 a week. Bradna wrote: "An outstanding freak is worth from $200 to $2,500 a week. Others with specialties that are easily duplicated are content with $42.50," *Big Top,* 236.

Shelton's friendships and associations: Noted from *Billboard* mentions on Nov. 9, 1922; Dec. 22, 1923; Jan. 19, 1924; and Oct. 17, 1925.

Christmas poem: Barry Gray, "A Side-Show Review," *Billboard,* Dec. 25, 1926.

The Ringling brass hadn't bothered: "I don't know which is Eko and which is Iko," wrote Ringling manager I. W. Robertson in an internal memo, Feb. 25, 1937, on file at Circus World Museum.

Description of 1924 backstage Halloween party: "R-B Halloween Party," *Billboard,* Nov. 25, 1924.

they reprinted his every word: Scott M. Cutlip, *Public Relations History: From the 17th to the 20th Century: The Antecedents* (New York: Routledge, 1995), 178.

Chapter Eight. *Comma, Colored*

Interviews: Rand Dotson, Melville "Buster" Carico, Nancy Saunders, Dot Brown

Fellows mislabels Muse brothers' home state: Dexter Fellows and Andrew A. Freeman, *This Way to the Big Show: The Life of Dexter Fellows* (New York: Viking, 1936), 309.

the lamentations of a poem: From Paul Laurence Dunbar's "The Haunted Oak," as recounted in ibid., 62. Written in 1900, Dunbar's anti-lynching poem could have been based on one of 105 lynchings that occurred that year. Scholar Edward F. Arnold has theorized that Dunbar wrote it after hearing the story from an old ex-slave who lived near the grounds of Howard University.

Smith's lynching was the city's last: Author interview, Rand Dotson, Jan. 12, 2015.

one-twelfth of what it was planning: Beth Macy, "Community by the Book," *Roanoke Times,* March 12, 2006.

"a little prayer that God": Ibid.

the most prolific filmmaker of the silent period: Gerald R. Butters Jr., "From Homestead to Lynch Mob: Portrayals of Black Masculinity in Oscar Micheaux's *Within Our Gates," Journal for MultiMedia History* 3 (2000). Micheaux's Roanoke office operated from 1922 to 1925, according to the documentary *The Czar of Black Hollywood,* Block Starz TV, 2014. He also had offices in Chicago and Harlem.

Roanoke Times' response to The Birth of a Nation: Raymond Barnes, *A History of the City of Roanoke* (Radford, VA: Commonwealth Press, 1968), 527.

Lynchings of World War I veterans: Butters, "From Homestead to Lynch Mob," part 2.

Lynching as spectator sport: Ibid., 207.

Micheaux explored the negative traits: Ibid., part 1.

"Oscar was just light-years ahead of his time": Public lecture by Bayer Mack on *The Czar of Black Hollywood,* which he wrote and directed, Grandin Theatre Film Festival, Roanoke, May 3, 2015.

Blacks now owned $53 million in property: "Negroes in Virginia Owners of Property Valued at $53,516,174," *Roanoke Times,* July 20, 1924.

three-quarters of African Americans living in the South were still working as day laborers or sharecroppers: Jill Quadagno, "Unfinished Democracy," in Louis Kushnick and James Jennings, eds., *A New Introduction to Poverty: The Role of Race, Power, and Politics* (New York: New York University Press, 1999), 77–78.

stringent Jim Crow laws: In 1902, Virginia adopted a new state constitution that was never put to the voters for ratification; it had provisions for a poll tax and a literacy test for voting, according to C. Vann Woodward, *The Strange Career of Jim Crow* (New York: Oxford University Press, 1955), and Geoff Seamans, "A Quarter Century of Racial Change," *Roanoke Times and World-News,* May 13, 1979.

Visiting Swedish writer's take on segregation: Woodward, *Strange Career of Jim Crow,* 117–118.

Black-white interactions could now be as bizarrely intimate: Naomi A. Mattos, "Segregation by Custom Versus Segregation by Law, 1910–1917, City of Roanoke," written for Roanoke Regional Preservation Office, 2005; on file with Kern Collection, Virginia Room, Roanoke City Library.

more than seventy African Americans had been lynched: Woodward, *Strange Career of Jim Crow,* 115.

Spiller, who would go on to serve as the city's commonwealth attorney: Barnes, *History of the City of Roanoke,* 509, 649, 652.

Roanoke Klan parade and rally: "Klansmen Stage Big Celebration," *Roanoke Times,* Oct. 17, 1925; also recounted by Mike Hudson, "Visible Empire," *Roanoke Times,* Dec. 2, 2001.

Spiller and company declared: Barnes, *History of the City of Roanoke,* as initially reported in *Roanoke Times.*

law-and-order defender of racial integrity: Spiller biography from Philip Alexander Bruce et al., *History of Virginia,* vol. 4 (Chicago: American Historical Society, 1924), 312–313.

At ninety-eight years old, retired but still a legend: Author interview, Melville "Buster" Carico, Jan. 20, 2015.

During Prohibition: Prohibition took effect in Virginia in 1916 and was legalized federally in 1920 via the Eighteenth Amendment.

illegal '20s drinking: Clare White, *Roanoke: 1740–1982* (Roanoke, VA: Roanoke Valley Historical Society, 1982), 98–99.

"permissive law-breaking": Ibid., 98.

Spiller's campaign against gambling: Barnes, *History of the City of Roanoke,* 665.

Black-crime coverage: "Police Court Notes," *Roanoke Times,* Feb. 27, 1923.

"Fifty and thirty": "Police Court Notes," *Roanoke Times,* Feb. 28, 1923.

Arrest of Harrison Muse for assault: Case No. 3761 in Corporation Court for City of Roanoke, filed March 1923.

Cabell Muse as Oscar Micheaux–type character: Ralph D. Matthews, "Tragedy in Wake of Circus Freaks," *Baltimore Afro-American,* June 1, 1929.

Chapter Nine. The Prodigal Sons

Interviews: Frank Ewald, Rand Dotson, Nancy Saunders, Dot Brown, Melville "Buster" Carico, Jerry Jones, A. L. Holland, John Molumphy

officials had gone to the trouble: In 1914, the State of Louisiana mandated that all circus and tent exhibitions provide two separate entrances and exits, separate ticket offices, and at least two ticket takers to divide black and white patrons, requiring that they be at least twenty-five feet apart: http://chnm.gmu.edu/acpstah/unitdocs/unit5/lesson5/jimcrowimages.pdf.

back-end blues: A. W. Stencell, *Seeing Is Believing: America's Sideshows* (Toronto: ECW Press, 2002), 178.

"Mr. Ringling's niggah": Taylor Gordon, *Born to Be* (Seattle: University of Washington Press, 1975), 105. "Niggah didn't mean anything, but to be a rich man's niggah—that established the amount of liberty the individual niggah was to have," Gordon wrote.

Dot Brown's recollection of Harriett's dream: Author interview, Dot Brown, March 2001, with *Roanoke Times* cowriter Jen McCaffery.

Prohibition violence in Roanoke: "Liquor Blamed for Five Deaths: Four Officers Have Lost Lives," *Roanoke Times,* Oct. 9, 1927.

George Davis's camera and borrowed car: Author interview, Frank Ewald, Sept. 18, 2014.

Lynching picture from Davis's collection: Says author/historian Rand Dotson, who has written several articles about Virginia lynchings, "That image is very likely from a lynching of four black miners in Clifton Forge in 1891. It could also be from a lynching of four black men in Richlands, Virginia, in 1893. Both of these events were covered (i.e., celebrated) in the *Roanoke Times*. Indeed, some of the rope used in the Richlands murder was presented to a reporter in Roanoke." E-mail to author, Oct. 2, 2014.

"all strange oddities": *Roanoke Times,* Oct. 14, 1927.

Ringling's route in 1927: "Ringling Bros and Barnum and Bailey Combined Shows Official Route," Season 1927, on file at Circus World Museum, Baraboo, WI.

they were found floating off Madagascar: Fred Bradna, *The Big Top: My Forty Years with the Greatest Show on Earth* (New York: Simon and Schuster, 1952), 237, and "They Got Permanent One Back at Home in Madagascar," *Sun (NY),* March 31, 1925.

Treatment of Clicko's hair: Neil Parsons, *Clicko: The Wild Dancing Bushman* (Chicago: University of Chicago Press, 2010), 98.

Patrons could have their picture made with the brothers: "Soar on Clouds of Circus Canvas," *Plain Dealer (OH),* June 4, 1928, and "A Camel Has Zero on Eko and Iko," *Fairfield (IA) Weekly Ledger,* Aug. 10, 1922.

"as a chicken moults": "Strange People," Talk of the Town," *The New Yorker,* Nov. 5, 1927. The writer misspelled Eko's moniker as Eeko.

hampered in terms of sentence construction: Author interview, A. L. Holland, Oct. 27, 2014.

Willie Muse's intelligence: Author interview, John Molumphy, Aug. 4, 2015; mental competency seconded by lawyer Nick Leitch, who also deposed Willie Muse in 1996.

"Mr. Fellows's stories are taken for granted": Guy Fawkes, "The Wayward Press: Spring Fret," *The New Yorker*, May 10, 1930.

Eko and Iko were often among the top tier of sideshow headline grabbers: One such headline was MEN FROM MARS SNUB OTHER FREAKS, *New York Evening Post*, April 23, 1927. The bogus story that ran beneath it claimed, "Iko and Eko do not fraternize with the other 'strange people.' For that matter they don't talk to any great amount with each other. By the hour they stand before the monkey cage, wrinkling up their foreheads and shaking their shaggy heads."

Muses and others reportedly mourn Zip's impending death: "Fellow Freaks Sad as Zip Nears Death," *New York Evening Post*, April 9, 1926.

Brothers' names chosen for side of gilly: "Reo Speed Wagon in New Role," pictured in April 17, 1921, *Fort Worth (TX) Star-Telegram*; purpose of vehicle explained in "Reo Holds Freak Job," *Oregonian*, Jan. 8, 1928.

Gertrude Stein review mentioning Eko and Iko: John Chamberlain, "Books of the Times," *New York Times*, Nov. 7, 1934.

Photo from Christmas 1926: According to handwritten notes on the back of the picture, the snapshot originated with Langley Charlan, who in 1940 was renting out a room in his Miami house to Candy's ex-wife, Cora "Frankie" Shelton, then a fifty-six-year-old restaurant waitress, according to U.S. Census documents.

"home planet was in the ascendancy": "Bearded Lady Pays Debt to Lady Luck," *New York Times*, April 21, 1927.

Krao Farini's funeral wishes: "Shy Bearded Lady of Circus Orders Hairy Body Cremated," Associated Press, April 17, 1926.

civic leaders had fretted that Roanoke: "Circus Pleases Huge Audience," *Roanoke Times*, Oct. 15, 1927.

Reunion of "Miss Leslie" with brothers at fairgrounds: Author interview, Jerry Jones, Leslie Crawford's nephew, Nov. 25, 2014.

Segregation often broke down inside sideshow tent: Author interview (via e-mail), Rand Dotson, Feb. 9, 2015, citing Gregory J. Renoff, *The Big Tent: The Traveling Circus in Georgia, 1820–1930* (Athens: University of Georgia Press, 2008).

Description of tug-of-war over brothers: "Circus United a Negro Family," *Roanoke Times*, Oct. 15, 1927.

Black and white incarceration rates: "Ratio of proportion admitted to prison to share of population, by race, 1926–1993," Figure H, and other analyses, Robynn J. A. Cox, "Where Do We Go from Here? Mass Incarceration and the Struggle for Civil Rights," *Economic Policy Institute,* Jan. 16, 2015: http://www.epi.org/publication/where-do-we-go-from -here-mass-incarceration-and-the-struggle-for-civil-rights/.

"disturbed showmen tore their hair": Scott Hart, "Vexing Problem Develops over Two Circus Albinos," *Roanoke Times,* Oct. 17, 1927.

Chapter Ten. Not One Single, Solitary, Red Penny

Interviews: Nancy Saunders, Al Stencell, Greg Renoff, Harvey Lutins, Nancy Barbour, Melville "Buster" Carico, T. Roger Messick, Fred Dahlinger, Neil Parsons, Jane Nicholas, Ralph Reddick, A. L. Holland, Bernth Lindfors

he thought Baby Dot had died: Author interview, Nancy Saunders, Feb. 11, 2015.

***Roanoke Times* reported in its usual racist language:** Scott Hart, "Vexing Problem Develops over Two Circus Albinos," *Roanoke Times,* Oct. 17, 1927.

Reunion account mocked by reporter: Ibid.

Decline of sideshow: A prediction for sideshow banishment was made by the president of the American Association of Fairs and Expositions in 1921, according to A. W. Stencell, *Circus and Carnival Ballyhoo: Sideshow Freaks, Jabbers and Blade Box Queens* (Toronto: ECW Press, 2010), 199.

"Nothing now makes anyone wonder or exhibit interest": Quoted in ibid., 199.

Sideshow customers as do-gooders: Rachel Adams, *Sideshow U.S.A.: Freaks and the American Cultural Imagination* (Chicago: University of Chicago Press, 2001), 14.

Sideshow was "right thing to do": Author interview, Al Stencell, March 1, 2015.

Ringlings as captains of industry: Author interview, Greg Renoff, Feb. 17, 2015.

Female lynching victims: "The Anti-Lynching Crusaders: The Lynching of Women," NAACP Papers, 1922, http://womhist .alexanderstreet.com/lynch/doc7.htm; overall lynching numbers, "Lynching in America: Confronting the Legacy of Racial Terror," compiled by the Equal Justice Initiative, 2015, http://www.eji.org/files/ EJI%20Lynching%20in%20America%20SUMMARY.pdf.

"It all reverts to one simple question": Hart, "Vexing Problem Develops over Two Circus Albinos," *Roanoke Times*, Oct. 17, 1927.

Square footage and description of Muse property: Recorded on a building appraisal permit, on file at Roanoke City Hall. The property was worth $395 in 1970. The lot registered 26 by 52 feet, according to an engineering survey and map recorded in 1943. Harriett's sister-in-law's residence there is documented in the 1927 city directory.

Messick's oratorical flair: Author interview and follow-up letter, T. Roger Messick, Nov. 3, 2014.

Messick's work habits: Author interview, Harvey Lutins, Feb. 5, 2015.

Messick's home and office life: Author interview, Nancy Barbour, Nov. 12, 2015.

Messick's suicide: Cause of death was "gunshot wound of abdomen," according to his February 1962 death certificate. The wound was self-inflicted, according to his obituary.

"Next time I'm gonna steal enough": Author interview, Melville "Buster" Carico, Jan. 20, 2015.

Messick represented the defendant: "Why Did Lee Scott Kill Dana Weaver?," *True Detective*, October 1949.

Messick's closing arguments on behalf of Lee Scott: Clarence Whittaker, "Lee Scott Convicted of First Degree Murder, Given 99-Year Sentence," *Roanoke Times*, July 3, 1949.

remarkably unremarkable and upstanding life: In 2002, I spent several weeks researching the murder of Dana Marie Weaver for a history article in the *Roanoke Times* but ultimately did not publish it, at the request of the murderer's widow, who said it would devastate her, and her children, who knew nothing of their father's criminal past.

The reporter cited Roanoke police officers, not Harriett: "Circus United a Negro Family," *Roanoke Times*, Oct. 15, 1927, front page.

"not paid them one single, solitary, red penny": Filed in Law and Equity Court of City of Richmond, VA: *Georgie Muse v. Ringling Brothers and Barnum and Bailey Combined Shows, Incorporated, and Herman Shelton*; on file at Library of Virginia. Willie's lawsuit is similarly named, only it's filed on behalf of "Willie Muse, an infant under the age of twenty-one years who sues by Cabell Muse, his next friend," Oct. 17, 1927.

"They were tired of being considered wild men": "Mother of Freaks Sues Big Circus," *Daily News-Record (VA)*, Oct. 19, 1927.

no one could pinpoint with certainty their dates of birth: "Their Mother does not know the day they were born, and as far as I know, they were born in a County that does not have a record of their births," wrote their attorney, Wilbur Austin, in a 1937 letter to Ringling pertaining to their lack of Social Security numbers. Indeed, neither Franklin nor nearby Pittsylvania County birth records have the brothers' birth records under the Cook or Muse surname. Most family records, including obituaries and death certificates, list Willie's birth year as 1893 and George's as 1890, although George's death certificate says he was born Dec. 24, 1901. Various ship and plane manifests list their birth years as between 1893 and 1902.

Kelley's legal strategies: Joe Botsford, "Legal Eagle of Circus Spins Yarn," *Milwaukee Sentinel*, May 30, 1963.

John Ringling's forays into real estate, railways, and oil: David C. Weeks, *Ringling: The Florida Years, 1911–1936* (Gainesville: University Press of Florida, 1993), 62.

Ringling's snobbishness: Henry Ringling North and Alden Hatch, *The Circus Kings: Our Ringling Family Story* (Garden City, NY: Doubleday, 1960), 62.

Kelley's power grab against Ringling: Ibid., 226–228.

Kelley's insistence on prenuptial agreements: Weeks, *Ringling*, 227–229.

Kelley's attention to detail: Letter of tribute written by Circus World Museum Director Chappie Fox, on Kelley's death, on file in Circus World Museum, Baraboo, WI, November 1963.

"The Ringlings paid their people ten percent less": Author interview, Fred Dahlinger, Jan. 29, 2015.

Abuse of Clicko by Paddy Hepston: Neil Parsons, *Clicko: The Wild Dancing Bushman* (Chicago: University of Chicago Press, 2010).

Clicko was embraced by Frank Cook and family: Ibid., 96.

Cook adopts Clicko: North and Hatch, *Circus Kings*, 18.

Clicko's hair and limited vocabulary: Ibid.

"Cook ensured Taibosh had all creature comforts": Parsons, *Clicko*, 129–132.

Brothers performing for colleagues in circus backyard: *Billboard*, Easter 1922.

"good examples of contented freaks": "Strange People," Talk of the Town, *The New Yorker,* Nov. 5, 1927.

Incorporation papers for RB&BB Circus: On file at Circus World Museum, filed by John M. Kelley, July 1932.

Lawsuit suspended for a time: "Move to Quash Circus Cases," Associated Press, Oct. 27, 1927.

it was a hard blow to patrons: "The Way of the Circus," *Manitowoc (WI) Herald-Tribune,* Nov. 10, 1927.

an editorial writer reframed the story: "Circus and Other Ethics," *Norfolk Virginian-Pilot,* Nov. 6, 1927.

seemed lonesome for the crowds: "Ambassadors From Mars, Stolen Twins, Return Home to Their Ma After 12 Years," *Belleville (KS) Telescope,* Nov. 17, 1927.

Roanoke papers' response to settlement: "Eko and Iko, Ambassadors, Have Received Financial Settlement," *Roanoke Times,* Feb. 20, 1928.

"There are so many stories missing": Jane Nicholas, "A Debt to the Dead? Ethics, Photography, History, and the Study of Freakery," *Social History/Histoire Sociale* 47, no. 93 (May 2014): 139–155.

"piece together your evidence with empathy and conjecture": Author interview, Jane Nicholas, Feb. 26, 2015.

"Eko and Iko sit snugly": "Eko and Iko, Ambassadors, Have Received Financial Settlement," *Roanoke Times,* Feb. 20, 1928.

That winter, the brothers found themselves engaged: Author interview, A. L. Holland, Oct. 16, 2014.

Neighbors afraid to get too close: Author interview, Ralph Reddick, May 2001.

Brief *New York Times* mention of reunion: "Habu Still Scowls Even on the Radio," *New York Times,* April 8, 1928.

***The New Yorker* credits brothers' return to circus to gluttony:** Alva Johnston, "Sideshow People—III," *The New Yorker,* April 28, 1934.

the brothers seemed captivated only by the menagerie: "The Phillies Might Watch Those Circus Midgets Sock," *New York Evening Post,* May 1, 1928.

"bearded twins from someplace or other": Clement V. Curry, "Circus Antics Renews Youth with Thrills," *Buffalo (NY) Courier Journal,* June 7, 1928.

"foreign rarities scouts" and "savage" displays meant to reinforce racial inferiority: Janet M. Davis, *The Circus Age: Culture & Society Under the American Big Top* (Chapel Hill: University of North Carolina Press, 2002), 223, and Bernth Lindfors, *Early African Entertainments Abroad: From the Hottentot Venus to Africa's First Olympians* (Madison: University of Wisconsin Press, 2014), 158–175.

Brothers "look like Boy Scouts" in comparison: Author interview, Bernth Lindfors, March 30, 2015.

Black rousties earned less than whites: Davis, *Circus Age,* 70–71.

Chapter Eleven. Adultery's Siamese Twin

Interviews: A. L. Holland, Reginald Shareef, Nancy Saunders

Cabell "overbearing and brutish": Ralph D. Matthews, "Tragedy in Wake of Circus Freaks," *Baltimore Afro-American,* June 1, 1929.

"We made cotton": Author interviews, A. L. Holland, Oct. 27, 2014, and May 2001; Sheree Scarborough, *African American Railroad Workers of Roanoke: Oral Histories of the Norfolk and Western* (Charleston, SC: History Press, 2014), 29–37.

The injured man died: "Injuries Fatal to Roanoke Man," *Roanoke Times,* Oct. 4, 1927.

Importance and status of car in America: David E. Kyvig, *Daily Life in the United States, 1920–1940: How Americans Lived Through the "Roaring Twenties" and the Great Depression* (Chicago: Ivan R. Dee, 2002), 27–52.

Billboard promoting cars: Ibid., 47.

Drought conditions in 1928: Raymond Barnes, *A History of the City of Roanoke* (Radford, VA: Commonwealth Press, 1968), 686.

Economic conditions in 1928: "Banksters" was a term that came out of the Senate hearings to regulate the American banking system: Gilbert King, "The Man Who Busted the 'Banksters,'" *Smithsonian,* Nov. 29, 2011.

Prohibition-era car bombing: Barnes, *History of the City of Roanoke,* 686–688.

Account of Hope Wooden's murder of Cabell Muse: *Roanoke World-News,* July 24, 1928. (The newspaper incorrectly reported his name as Calvin Muse.)

Peonage accounts from elsewhere in the South: "Five Peons Escape," *Baltimore Afro-American*, June 1, 1929.

Alabama slave mines: Douglas A. Blackmon, *Slavery by Another Name: The Re-Enslavement of Black Americans from the Civil War to World War II* (New York: Anchor, 2008), 369.

Spiller liked to be called to crime scenes: "19 Convicted on Murder Charge: Average Is One a Month," *Roanoke Times*, Oct. 5, 1928.

Stab wounds causing Cabell's death: Ibid. and "Father of Circus Freaks Is Killed," *Roanoke Times*, July 25, 1928.

"adultery and murder were Siamese twins": Author interview, Reginald Shareef, Sept. 10, 2014.

Willie thought Cabell "wasn't no good": Author interview, Nancy Saunders, Sept. 14, 2014.

Cabell's burial: Certificate of Death, State Board of Health, filed July 25, 1928. Muse was buried in Pin Hook (most likely a misspelling of Penhook, just up the road from Truevine) on July 25, 1928. Directories for Truevine Baptist Church Cemetery and Muse Cemetery show a total of six unmarked graves, and Cabell Muse is likely buried in one of those; cemetery maps and inventories courtesy of Virgil Goode.

"So that served him right": Author interview, Saunders, Aug. 6, 2015.

It would be eight more years: According to Ringling route books on file at Circus World Museum, Baraboo, WI, the circus next returned to Virginia in 1933, when it performed at stops in Norfolk, Newport News, and Richmond. It didn't play again in Roanoke until 1935.

Chapter Twelve. Housekeeping!

Interviews: Louise Burrell, Nancy Saunders, Nadja Durbach, Jane Nicholas, Al Stencell, Andy Erlich, Erika Turner, Ward Hall, Mary "Sug" Davis

Size and history of ship: The *Majestic*, built before World War I, was passed into the possession of England and then the United States, respectively, as part of the German indemnities: "Belfast Will Build World's Biggest Ship," *New York Times*, Feb. 12, 1926, and whitestarhistory.com.

Accommodations aboard ship: "2,593 on *Majestic*, a Record Since War," *New York Times*, Sept. 12, 1928, and "Vintage brochure — S. S. Majestic": second-class accommodations boasted a "light and airy" dining room and bunk-style beds with double sinks, third-class description not included, http://www.gjenvick.com/HistoricalBrochures/WhiteStarLine/RMS-Majestic/1922/StateroomsAndSuites.html#axzz3iW2E3fXJ.

"Housekeeping!": Author interview, Louise Burrell, Sept. 14, 2014.

Bertram Mills had cultivated a relationship: "The Renovator of the British Circus," http://www.circopedia.org/Bertram_Mills.

"the disappearance of freaks": Kenneth Grahame, *Fun o' the Fair* (London: J. M. Dent and Sons, 1929), 27.

"we are anxious to understand them": "With Bertram Mills," *Times (London)*, Jan. 21, 1938.

The British were more sensitive: Author interview, Nadja Durbach, March 16, 2015. Britain had been in the war five years as opposed to America's one (1917–1918); it also had eight times as many soldiers return from the war wounded; and the British military counted 107,000 civilian deaths and 1.01 million total deaths versus 117,465 American military-only deaths. The British population experienced more than double the percentage of per capita deaths than the United States did in World War I. Vera Brittain's *Testament of Youth* (London: Macmillan, 1933) offers a sobering personal account of World War I losses in Britain, particularly among middle-class military and civilian families.

British response to *Freaks*: David J. Skal and Elias Savada, *Dark Carnival: The Secret World of Tod Browning* (New York: Anchor, 1995), 181.

Ministry of Labor denied the application: "Aliens Branch File," document no. 574881, with minutes of meetings gathered at British National Archives, box marked "Misc. 5189," letter dated Sept. 11, 1927.

Mills appeals ruling: Ibid., from a letter by Bertram Mills to Sir W. Haldane Porter, Home Office, Ministry of Labor, Queen Anne's Chambers, London, Nov. 22, 1927.

Mills drew on both humanitarian and labor arguments: Nadja Durbach, *Spectacle of Deformity: Freak Show and Modern British Culture* (Berkeley: University of California Press, 2010), 177.

Sideshow performers granted entry: Approval letter, as noted in minutes, collected in "Aliens Branch File," British National Archives, Nov. 23, 1927.

traveling fairground sideshows in Britain diminish: "Travelling Showmen and Taxation," *Times (London)*, Jan. 16, 1935.

Cyril Bertram Mills: Author of his father's biography, *Bertram Mills Circus: Its Story* (London: Hutchinson of London, 1967), 27. Mills was the case officer who for a time controlled the double British-German agent Joan Pujol Garcia—whom he code-named Garbo, for Greta Garbo—during World War II.

Mills offers £20,000: Circus performance notes, *Times (London)*, June 29, 1934.

Mills's fondness for Tiny Town: Frank Foster, *Pink Coat, Spangles and Sawdust: Reminiscences of Circus Life with Sanger's Bertram Mills and Other Circuses* (London: Stanley Paul, 1948), 109.

Leitzel chopping Ingalls's finger: Henry Ringling North and Alden Hatch, *The Circus Kings: Our Ringling Family Story* (Garden City, NY: Doubleday, 1960), 187.

Jack Earle's British foray: Author interview, Andrew Erlich, nephew of Jack Earle, who said Earle was particularly close to Graf and the Doll family.

Film clip of Earle and Lya Graf: *Queer and Quaint,* 1931, filmed at Olympia London and archived by British Pathé, http://www.britishpathe.com.

"It's part of my job": *Circus Scrap Book* no. 10 (April 1931).

keep tabs on his best-earning acts: "Hartman's Broadcast," *Billboard,* Jan. 27, 1934.

"Deformity gave them good jobs": Foster, *Pink Coat,* 111–113.

"really [did] look like visitors from a strange planet": Letter from Cyril B. Mills to Bernth Lindfors, Aug. 1, 1984, shared with the author from Lindfors's collection.

Ubangi Duck-Billed Savages' backstory: Janet M. Davis, *The Circus Age: Culture & Society Under the American Big Top* (Chapel Hill: University of North Carolina Press, 2002), 135.

Scouring maps for exotic names: Dexter Fellows and Andrew A. Freeman, *This Way to the Big Show: The Life of Dexter Fellows* (New York: Viking, 1936), 295–296, and "African 'Beauties' Here to Join Circus," *New York Times,* April 1, 1930.

Beauty marks of Ubangis: Lindfors, *Early African Entertainments Abroad: From the Hottentot Venus to Africa's First Olympians* (Madison: University of Wisconsin Press, 2014), 159–160.

Dubbed the freak czar: "Samuel Gumpertz, Showman, 84, Dies," *New York Times,* June 23, 1952.

Cook's skillful dealings with immigration authorities: Fred Bradna, *The Big Top: My Forty Years with the Greatest Show on Earth* (New York: Simon and Schuster, 1952), 244.

Ubangis' homesickness: Fellows and Freeman, *This Way to the Big Show,* 295.

Ubangis' hygiene: Bradna, *Big Top,* 243–247.

tried to wash his face in the toilet bowl: Foster, *Pink Coat,* 109.

Feud with French manager: Bergonier stole their salary, allowing them to keep only the proceeds from their postcard sales: Davis, *Circus Age,* 135.

Railroad's influence on standardization of time: "In the days before battery-powered watches and telephones, Old Gabriel was Roanoke's Big Ben. A reminder of the stability—and authority—of the railroad, it gave order to a town known for its whorehouses, saloons, and the pigs rooting in its streets," from Beth Macy, "The Blast of the Past," *Roanoke Times,* Feb. 25, 1996.

the chaos of local times: "On Time," National Museum of American History, http://americanhistory.si.edu/ontime/synchronizing/zones.html.

Ubangis celebrate Bergonier's death: "Famed French Explorer Dies Here," *Sarasota (FL) Herald,* Oct. 13, 1930.

Second round of Ubangis fit in better than first: Neil Parsons, *Clicko: The Wild Dancing Bushman* (Chicago: University of Chicago Press, 2010), 148.

Allegation that Muse brothers were "severely handicapped mentally": Letter from Mills to Lindfors, Aug. 1, 1984.

Backstage behavior of Zip: Davis, *Circus Age,* 182–183, citing Tiny Kline, "Showground-Bound," unpublished memoir, on file at Circus World Museum, Baraboo, WI.

***New York Post* joke interview:** "Ambassadors From Mars Give Mr. Gann a Status," *New York Evening Post,* April 13, 1929.

"they needed supervision": Author interview, Al Stencell, Nov. 14, 2014.

Review of Jack Earle's artwork: "Talented Giant," *New York Times,* May 10, 1936.

Andy Erlich felt conflicted about his uncle's story: Author interview, Andrew Erlich, March 14, 2015.

"She better pick her ass up!": Author interview, Erika Turner, May 17, 2015.

Earle's giant ring: A. W. Stencell, *Circus and Carnival Ballyhoo: Sideshow Freaks, Jabbers and Blade Box Queens* (Toronto: ECW Press, 2010), 151.

Earle as successful businessman: Author interview, Ward Hall, Sept. 5, 2014.

Earle-inspired Tom Waits song, "Get Behind the Mule": Some of the lyrics: *"Big Jack Earle was eight foot one / And he stood in the road and he cried / He couldn't make her love him, couldn't make her stay / But tell the good Lord that he tried."*

New York gallery showing of Earle's work: Andrew Erlich, *The Long Shadows: The Story of Jake Erlich* (Scottsdale, AZ: Multicultural Publications, 2012).

Morgan's hunting habits and friendships with royalty: "J. P. Morgan Dies, Victim of Stroke at Florida Resort," United Press International, March 13, 1943.

one of the country's first media circuses: Michael Corkery, "A Midget, Banker Hearings and Populism Circa 1933," *Wall Street Journal,* Jan. 12, 2010.

Media stunt with Graf and Morgan: Morgan appeared before the Senate Subcommittee on Banking and Currency hearings, formed to inform "constructive legislation" that might get America's economy back on its feet. The investigation led to a major overhaul of the financial regulatory system, which brought about the Glass-Steagall Act and the creation of the Securities and Exchange Commission. "The Man Who Will Question Morgan," *New York Times,* May 21, 1933.

Graf retreated to Germany: Sherwin D. Smith, "A Midget Sat on J. P. Morgan's Lap and Showed the Great Banker Was Only Human," Thirty Years Ago, *New York Times,* May 26, 1963.

Tom Muse's legal troubles: *Commonwealth of Virginia v. Thomas Muse,* indictment for malicious assault with intent to maim, disfigure, disable, and kill, filed Dec. 1, 1930, Hustings Court, City of Roanoke, VA, and "Bryan Gets Life in Penitentiary," *Roanoke Times,* Dec. 11, 1930.

"a rough man, very rowdy": Author interview, Mary "Sug" Davis, Nov. 11, 2014.

Graf's death: John Brooks, *Once in Golconda: A True Drama of Wall Street 1920–1938* (New York: John Wiley and Sons, 1999).

triply cursed: Clark Hoyt, "Consistent, Sensitive and Weird," *New York Times,* April 18, 2009.

Chapter Thirteen. Practically Imbeciles

Interviews: Warren Raymond, Bob Blackmar, Ward Hall, Tom Word, Paul Lombardo, Robert M. Brown, Dan Webb, Sarah Showalter

make whiskey, steal, or starve: Thomas S. Word Jr., "The Whiskey Business (A Book Review)," *Virginia Bar Association News Journal,* Summer 2009.

Illegal whiskey sold in Roanoke region: Raymond Barnes, *A History of the City of Roanoke* (Radford, VA: Commonwealth Press, 1968), 753, and "The History and Culture of Untaxed Liquor in the Mountains of Virginia," Blue Ridge Institute, http://www.blueridgeinstitute.org/moonshine/the_franklin_county_conspiracy.html.

Ringling's 1935 return to Roanoke: Barnes, *History of the City of Roanoke,* 760.

Contract details for brothers' work with Pete Kortes: Hustings Court, Chancery Order Books No. 28–31, orders delivered by Judge J. Lindsay Almond from the period 1936 to 1939.

Description of Beckmann and Gerety Shows: Details from letter from Fred Beckmann to a potential client in Rockford, IL, June 23, 1932, on file at Circus World Museum, Baraboo, WI.

Scrip issued by Beckmann and Gerety: Author interview, Warren Raymond, Feb. 26, 2015.

Kortes's version of World's Fair: "Carnival Will Open Six-Day Stand Monday," *Register Republic (Rockford, IL),* July 7, 1934.

Microcephalics dressed as women: Harry Lewiston, *Freak Show Man: The Autobiography of Harry Lewiston as Told to Jerry Holtman* (Los Angeles: Holloway House, 1968), 1–15, and author interview, Bob Blackmar, Feb. 16, 2015.

Schlitzie's "rangy" behavior: Author interview, Ward Hall, Sept. 5, 2014.

Honolulu stint: Photograph from collection of Bob Blackmar, noted as "Pete Kortes' Circus Sideshow — Honolulu T.H. 1950."

Daily-living details with Kortes show: William Lindsey Gresham, *Monster Midway: An Uninhibited Look at the Glittering World of the Carny* (New York: Rinehart, 1948), 101.

Brothers' movement back to Ringling via Shelton, without pay: "Willie and George Muse have been in the possession of the Beckman & Gerety Shows and Pete Kortez [sic] for from three to five years; and the said parties have paid practically nothing for the services of Willie and George Muse," Hustings Court, Chancery Order Book No. 29, Jan. 29, 1937.

Leitzel's death: Dean Jensen, *Queen of the Air: A True Story of Love and Tragedy at the Circus* (New York: Crown, 2013), 244–248.

Leitzel's closeness to John Ringling: Fred Bradna, *The Big Top: My Forty Years with the Greatest Show on Earth* (New York: Simon and Schuster, 1952), 194.

Codona and murder-suicide: Jensen, *Queen of the Air,* 285.

John Ringling's purchase of ACC: The ACC was composed of five smaller circuses: Sells-Floto, Hagenbeck-Wallace, Al G. Barnes, Sparks, and John Robinson.

John Ringling's rage: Henry Ringling North and Alden Hatch, *The Circus Kings: Our Ringling Family Story* (Garden City, NY: Doubleday, 1960), 219.

Lawsuits against John Ringling: David C. Weeks, *Ringling: The Florida Years, 1911–1936* (Gainesville: University Press of Florida, 1993), 224.

at least one hundred lawsuits: North and Hatch, *Circus Kings,* 249.

Depression-era party behavior among Sarasota's rich: Weeks, *Ringling,* 229.

North fills in as uncle's handyman: Ibid., 250, and North and Hatch, *Circus Kings,* 230.

Henry and John Ringling North's takeover: North and Hatch, *Circus Kings,* 257–259.

Gargantua's backstory: "67 Baggage Stock Men Walk Out After Supt. Asks to Be Paid Off," *Billboard,* June 25, 1938.

broke picket lines with elephants: "Circus Men Strike, But Show Goes On," *New York Times,* April 13, 1938.

Clyde Ingalls and Jack Earle pitch in as rousties: Bradna, *Big Top,* 143–144.

Brouhaha in Scranton: North and Hatch, *Circus Kings,* 283.

Movement to Barnes-Sells Floto Combined Shows: Ibid., 283–285.

Aerialist not as polished as Leitzel: Account from *Independent (MT),* July 2, 1938.

Gorilla's backstory exaggerated: "Enlarged Circus Brings Gargantua," *Kerrville (TX) Daily Times,* Oct. 6, 1938.

North nephews pay off union leader: Ibid.

Circus closure blamed on New Deal: Boyd Sinclair, "The Theater-Goer," *Daily Texan,* Oct. 2, 1938.

"The kids of today": Janet M. Davis, *The Circus Age: Culture and Society Under the American Big Top* (Chapel Hill: University of North Carolina Press, 2002), 229, quoting nonagenarian circus trouper W. E. "Doc" Van Alstine from 1938.

Messick not available for Harriett's hire: Author interview, Tom Word, April 1, 2015, and T. Keister Greer, *The Great Moonshine Conspiracy Trial of 1935* (Lawrenceville, VA: Brunswick, 2002). Greer's book was also a primary source for the 2012 movie *Lawless.*

Depression-era costumes: "State Fair Freaks and Frolics," *Lincoln (NE) Evening Journal,* Sept. 11, 1936.

"Compared to Squeak, Mr. Austin was deadly dull": Author interview, Harvey Lutins, Aug. 14, 2014.

Austin's lineage: Documented in S. E. Grose, *Botetourt County, Virginia, Heritage Book 1770–2000* (Summersville, WV: Walsworth, 2000), p. 74; Carter O. Lowance was the brother-in-law, as outlined in Harry Hone, *Community Leaders of Virginia 1976–1977* (Williamsburg, VA: American Biographical Center, 1977); author interviews with family members.

"practically imbeciles": The legal terms used today would be "person with intellectual disabilities" or "person with special needs."

Brothers' alleged mental disabilities: Petition for guardianship: *Harriett Muse v. George and Willie Muse,* filed Oct. 26, 1936, Hustings Court.

Social Security payments: The Social Security Act was signed by President Franklin D. Roosevelt in 1935. Taxes began being collected for it in 1937, and regular ongoing benefits began in January 1940, according to the official Social Security website, http://www.ssa.gov/history/hfaq.html.

Future managers had to be court-approved: Hustings Court, Chancery Order Book No. 30, p. 339. Ordered by Judge J. Lindsay Almond, Nov. 10, 1938.

"It allows the person to have control of them physically": Author interview, Paul Lombardo, Aug. 17, 2015.

Harriett "penniless": Letter from Wilbur Austin Jr. to John Ringling North, Nov. 22, 1938, Circus World Museum.

Rich in Roanoke doing OK during Depression: Barnes, *History of the City of Roanoke,* 773.

"You smelled the creosote": Author interview, Dan Webb, Aug. 13, 2015.

Austin seemed to earn every penny: He earned more for the occasional filings and errands he made on the brother's behalf. Looking over the settlement of accounts filed with the court, attorney Edenfield commented on a 1954 two-day trip to locate the brothers, for which he charged $250. "It looks like small potatoes now, but actually for the time, it was a lot of money," worth $2,171 today.

Family's negative views of Austin: Author interview, Robert M. Brown, April 8, 2015.

Virginia in vanguard of eugenics movement: Douglas A. Blackmon, *Slavery by Another Name: The Re-Enslavement of Black Americans from the Civil War to World War II* (New York: Anchor, 2008), 240.

Eugenics research: Though the Eugenics Record Office was closed in 1939, today the Cold Spring Harbor Laboratory maintains full historical records and artifacts for historical, teaching, and research purposes: http://archives.cshl.edu/R/GDJ9IJNMX99HH5I8ITX3KQV HIHLLCPCKBS3XB5999YJM8UHHL8-00603?&pds_handle =GUEST.

Albinism as genetic flaw: Amram Scheinfeld, *You and Heredity* (New York: Frederick A. Stokes, 1939), 147.

"By sterilization and birth control": Ibid., 404.

Virginia sterilized more people: Author interview, Paul Lombardo, Aug. 17, 2015.

Survivors' payouts: Gary Robertson, "Virginia Lawmakers OK Payout to Forced Sterilization Survivors," Reuters, Feb. 26, 2015.

State definition of imbecility: "Mental Defectives in Virginia: A Special Report of the State Board of Charities and Corrections to the General Assembly of 1916, on Weak Mindedness in the State of Virginia," 1915, http://readingroom.law.gsu.edu/buckvbell/2.

Temporary restraining order against Shelton: Letter from Austin to North, Nov. 22, 1938.

Almond's defense of "massive resistance": Though the state ended massive resistance under Almond's governorship, his initial response to the Supreme Court's ruling of massive resistance as unconstitutional was sheer defiance. The speech in its entirety was recorded by WRVA Radio, Jan. 20, 1959, and digitized by Library of Virginia: http://www.lva.virginia.gov/exhibits/brown/resistance.htm.

"It's like pouring gas in an open wound": Author interview and follow-up e-mail with Brenda Hamilton, April 13–14, 2015. The book I gave her was an advance copy of Kristen Green, *Something Must Be Done About Prince Edward County: A Family, a Virginia Town, a Civil Rights Battle* (New York: Harper, 2015).

In a September 1938 letter: Letter from J. F. Wadsworth, Ringling auditor, to Mr. F. C. De Wolfe, assistant treasurer of the Al G. Barnes Circus: Sept. 30, 1938, on file with "RBBB Papers," Box 36, Circus World Museum.

Orson Welles's broadcast: "Radio Listeners in Panic, Taking War Drama as Fact," *New York Times*, Oct. 31, 1938.

A Syracuse reporter: "Radio Editor Duped," *Variety*, Nov. 9, 1938.

Calls from more than 350 readers: "Roanokers Become Alarmed Over Radio Dramatization," *Roanoke Times*, Oct. 31, 1938.

Austin's nervous tics: Author interview, Sarah Showalter, April 29, 2015.

Almond's order that all brothers' movements must be court-sanctioned: Hustings Court, Chancery Order Book, p. 330, issued Nov. 10, 1938.

Harriett would now receive monthly updates: Contract with Pete and Marie Kortes, filed Feb. 20, 1939, in Hustings Court, found in misfiled file in records annex by clerk Brenda Hamilton.

"exclusive custody and control": Hustings Court, Chancery Order Book No. 30, p. 482.

Chapter Fourteen. Very Good Old Colored Woman

Interviews: Betsy Biesenbach, Veron Holland, Richard L. Chubb, Antoinette Harrell, Dave Price, Myrtle Phanelson, Judy Rock Tomaini, Ward Hall, Melvin Burkhart, Sarah Showalter, Cutie Muse, Bruce Snowdon, Mozell Witcher, Bob Blackmar, J. Harry Woody

Ballyhack's name: Deedie Dent Kagey, *When Past Is Prologue: A History of Roanoke County* (Roanoke, VA: Roanoke County Sesquicentennial Committee, 1988), 317–318. The name is supposedly a perversion of "Battly-whack" or "Battle-hack."

Exclusive golf course: *Golf* magazine ranked Ballyhack number three on its 2009 list of new private courses. The club facility, which measures 11,400 square feet, is an ultra-private facility that will accommodate "only 60 local and 240 national members" and require membership deposits from $40,000 to $130,000, "depending on a member's location and status," according to Randy King, "Finishing Touch," *Roanoke Times,* July 8, 2011.

General Grant Maxey's property: 1880 census records. In contrast to Grant Maxey's unusual name, the Muse name was already common in Ballyhack. In 1860, a white settler named Thomas R. Muse owned ten slaves in Ballyhack, and his descendants inherited land just across the Roanoke River from Harriett's — "probably not a coincidence," Betsy said, especially given the land's relative proximity to Franklin County, where Muse is a common name.

Percentage of black homesteaders in Roanoke County: Workers of the Writers' Program of the Work Projects Administration in the State of Virginia, *Roanoke: Story of County and City* (Roanoke, VA: Federal Works Agency, 1942), 164. There were 1,531 farms in Roanoke County in 1939; average size was 62.6 acres.

Ardelia Jones, Ballyhack storekeeper: Author interview, Veron Holland, April 23, 2015.

Blacks attending college out of state during Jim Crow: Author interview, Richard L. Chubb, Oct. 16, 2014.

A. Byron Smith: Mary C. Bishop, "He Has Overcome," *Roanoke Times,* May 6, 2001: A man wrote to the newspaper saying Smith was too strident for Roanoke and ought to leave. A black City Hall janitor reluctantly quit buying from Smith's oil business because his white supervisor told him that Smith had a "big mouth." The janitor feared he would lose his job if he didn't.

"request adequate roads": Belinda Harris, Looking Back column (1937), reprinted Oct. 8, 2012, *Roanoke Times.*

"Mama never did like to go out there": Author interview, Nancy Saunders, June 2, 2014.

Dot's teenaged beauty: Author interview, Sarah Showalter, April 28, 2015.

Details of Harriett's daily life: Culled from bills noted in "Second Settlement of Accounts," April 1938 to December 1949, Hustings Court, City of Roanoke, VA, Chancery Order Book No. 49, pp. 4–8.

Harriett's household: 1940 U.S. Census, Big Lick Township, Roanoke County. Richard Muse, eighteen, is also listed as a son of Harriett's living in the home (but he was actually a grandson).

Circus adjustments during World War II: Chang Reynolds, "Clyde Beatty in Person: Season of 1944," *Bandwagon* (May/June 1969), 10–19.

Complaint mailed to FBI on brothers' behalf: Letter from Harry E. Friend of Friend's Grocery, Walnut Grove, IL, to FBI Chicago office, July 25, 1946.

thanks to a peonage researcher who found the letter: Antoinette Harrell self-published *Department of Justice: Slavery, Involuntary Servitude and Peonage* in 2014.

FBI rules it will not investigate Friend's letter: Letter from Caudle to Hoover is dated August 28, 1946, on file at National Archives; letter scans courtesy of Antoinette Harrell, Peonage Research.

only the most egregious peonage cases were investigated: Douglas A. Blackmon, *Slavery by Another Name: The Re-Enslavement of Black Americans from the Civil War to World War II* (New York: Doubleday, 2008), 376–377.

"quiet complicity of the federal government in their servitude": Ibid., 382.

Doubts that brothers could give informed consent: Author interview, Antoinette Harrell, May 7, 2015.

Brothers' visits home to Ballyhack and Jordan's Alley: Author interview, Myrtle Phanelson, Aug. 5, 2015.

Ballyhack deed paid off: "Second Settlement of Accounts," April 1938 to December 1949, Hustings Court, City of Roanoke, VA, Chancery Order Book No. 49, p. 9.

FHA guaranteed few loans to blacks: Trevor M. Kollmann and Price V. Fishback, "The New Deal, Race, and Home Ownership in the 1920s and 1930s," Department of Economics, University of Arizona, 2010.

Harriett rarity in home ownership: William J. Collins and Robert A. Morgo, "Race and Home Ownership: 1900 to 1990," National Bureau of Economic Research, Cambridge, MA, 1999. Among white Americans in 1940 figures, 43 percent owned their own homes. The white-black home ownership gap was at its highest in 1960.

Sheep-Headed Men: *Clyde Beatty Russell Brothers* photograph from circus photo collection no. 18, Circus World Museum, Baraboo, WI, 1944.

Brothers popular along Texas-Mexico border: "Kortes El Paso Biz Holding Up," *Billboard*, Jan. 1, 1944.

Brothers conversed easily with Price: Author interview, Dave Price, Jan. 26, 2015.

fondly remembered fellow performer: Paul McWilliams worked 185 days in 1937 and earned $1,266.17—about double Willie's pay at the time, according to Ringling pay-scale sheets on file at Circus World Museum. (Willie earned $1,007.25 in 1937 for 347 days worked.)

Debated whether to spend money on clothes or woman: Daniel Mannix, *Freaks: We Who Are Not As Others* (Brooklyn, NY: power-House Books, 1976), 89.

"Everyone on the circus loved them": Albert Tucker, "The Strangest People on Earth," *Sarasota (FL) Sentinel*, July 7, 1973.

Ship and airline manifests from 1940s and '50s: George and Willie list Kortes's address in Pasadena, CA, as their home base, ancestry.com. They also list him as their primary contact on the World War II draft registration cards.

Brothers recalled as shy: Author interview, Judy Rock Tomaini, April 25, 2001.

Al Tomaini "peek-proof": "Life Visits Carnival Town," *Life*, June 1983.

Al Tomaini's generosity: Judy Rock Tomaini, interview by Kim Wilmath, *Tampa Bay (FL) Times*, Sept. 2, 2010.

Jeanie Tomaini's tricycle: "Life Visits Carnival Town," *Life*, June 1983.

"their value as exhibits declined": Author interview, Robert Bogdan, via e-mail, Aug. 10, 2015.

Life on Ward Hall show: Author interview, Bruce Snowdon, May 5, 2001: "You get asked the same question over and over; just a total lack of imagination. Sometimes I address the whole group: 'Just listen carefully—I weigh 712 pounds,'" from Jen McCaffery and Beth Macy, "Where Did All the Freaks Go?," *Roanoke Times*, July 13, 2001.

Hall recalls final acts: Author interview, Ward Hall, Sept. 5, 2014, and "Melvin the Human Blockhead Dies," National Public Radio, Nov. 13, 2001.

Closing of Giant's Camp: Kim Wilmath, "Big Boot to Return to Former Gibsonton Giant's Camp," *Tampa Bay (FL) Times*, Sept. 9, 2010.

Willie's old wig: Author interview, Ward Hall.

Melvin Burkhart's start on sideshow: "Life Visits Carnival Town," *Life*, June 1983.

Burkhart's memories of brothers: Author interview, Melvin Burkhart, April 26, 2001.

"Don't be unevenly yoked": Author interview, Sarah Showalter, April 29, 2015.

"Come sit on my big fat knee": Cutie Muse, interview by Jen McCaffery, *Roanoke Times* series, Spring 2001.

Harriett "right proud": Author interview, Mozell Witcher, Nov. 8, 2013.

The brothers' musical prowess: Author interview, J. Harry Woody, April 1, 2016.

Shady Caribbean dealings: Author interview, Bob Blackmar, Feb. 16, 2015.

Typical show route with Kortes: "Heavy Traveling Kortes Attraction Plays San Juan," *Billboard,* Nov. 24, 1951.

Chapter Fifteen. Wilbur and John

Interviews: Sarah Showalter, Dan Webb, Madaline Daniels, Douglas Pardue, JoAnne Poindexter, Mary "Sug" Davis, Willie Mae Ingram, Lawrence Mitchell

Checks from Kortes bounced: "Second Settlement of Accounts," April 1938 to December 1949, Hustings Court, City of Roanoke, VA, Book No. 49, pp. 4–8. The bad check was written for $113.85, and Austin's committee had to pay almost $5 in bad-check charges.

Austin's travels to collect back pay: Hustings Court, Chancery Order Book No. 43, p. 313, July 2, 1954.

Miss Irene and John Houp as community leaders and store owners: Author interviews, Sarah Showalter, April 28 and 29, 2015.

Boswell as slumlord: Author interview, Dan Webb, Roanoke City housing inspector, Aug. 13, 2015.

Rent collectors forcing sex on young women who couldn't pay: Author interview, Madaline Daniels, Aug. 5, 2015.

Running water availability in Jordan's Alley: Author interview, Lawrence Mitchell, April 1, 2016.

J. W. Boswell, realty-company founder: Raymond Barnes, *A History of the City of Roanoke* (Radford, VA: Commonwealth Press, 1968), 283, 309, 403, 419, 540.

Collecting rent on horseback: "An elderly woman on Gregory Avenue N.E. told me before World War II that she remembered my father coming on horseback to collect rent," John Boswell Jr. said of his father. "Later he drove a Reo automobile that cranked on the side. Our oldest rental account dates from August 1893," from M. Carl Andrews, "Early Realtor Came with Rails," *Roanoke World-News,* March 9, 1976.

Urban renewal as "Negro removal": Mary C. Bishop, "How Urban Renewal Uprooted Black Roanoke," *Roanoke Times,* Jan. 29, 1995.

Madeline Tate's death: Douglas Pardue, "Madeline Adams Tate: Now She Is a Number," *Roanoke Times,* Jan. 26, 1985.

Demolition of Tate's house: Author interview, Webb.

Conditions of Tate's house: Douglas Pardue, "Death Leads City to Act Against Poor Housing," *Roanoke Times,* Feb. 2, 1985.

How slumlords dealt with tenant complaints: Author interview (via e-mail), Douglas Pardue, July 28, 2015.

Henrietta Lacks born half-block from Jordan's Alley: Loretta Pleasant was born at 28 12th St. S.W. "A midwife named Fannie delivered her into a small shack on a dead-end road overlooking the train depot, where hundreds of freight cars came and went each day," according to Rebecca Skloot, *The Immortal Life of Henrietta Lacks* (Crown, 2010).

Lacks's memorial: A marker for Lacks was eventually erected in 2010, paid for by a scientific researcher working at the Morehouse School of Medicine, according to Denise M. Watson, "After Sixty Years of Anonymity, Henrietta Lacks Has a Headstone," *Virginian-Pilot,* May 30, 2010.

Tate's tombstone: Belinda Harris, 1985 Looking Back column, reprinted May 24, 2010, *Roanoke Times.*

Boswell was the cheapest: Author interview, JoAnne Poindexter, May 2, 2015.

Housing codes in Rugby: Harris, 1965 Looking Back column, reprinted Aug. 17, 2015, *Roanoke Times.*

"Unmitigated socialism": "John Boswell, Ex-Councilman, Dies at 67," *Roanoke Times and World-News,* Feb. 28, 1979. The quote was recycled in his obituary, like an epitaph.

Harriett's outstanding debts at time of death: "Second Settlement of Accounts," Hustings Court, Chancery Order Book No. 49, pp. 4–8.

"Mama's gone" repeated: Author interviews, Mary "Sug" Davis and Willie Mae Ingram, Nov. 11, 2014.

Chapter Sixteen. *God Is Good to Me*

Interviews: Dr. Craig Mitchell, Margaret Ursprung, Diane Rhodes, Jason Banks, June Lowe, Nancy Saunders, Louise Burrell, George Nicely, Bob Shelton, Reginald Shareef, Teresia McNabb, David Lawrence

feat in minority home ownership: 1960 U.S. Census figures and "African Americans and Home Ownership: Separate and Unequal, 1940 to 2006," Joint Center for Political and Economic Studies, Brief no. 1, November 2007.

House calls to Willie: Author interview, Dr. W. Craig Mitchell, April 27, 2001.

"He talks to God the way he would talk to you and me": Margaret Ursprung, interview by Jen McCaffery, *Roanoke Times*, April 2001.

Willie's fond recollections of snow cream: Author interview, Diane Rhodes, April 29, 2001.

He plays "Tipperary" first: Willie Muse's singing recorded by Nancy and Howard Saunders, 1998–2001.

Willie's advice to Jason: Author interview, Jason Banks, April 25, 2015.

Willie's visits with nurses and children: Author interview, June Lowe, May 11, 2015 .

Candy Shelton's later life: Alex Shoumatoff, *Florida Ramble* (New York: Harper and Row, 1974), 46–47.

Shelton's last circus gig: "Dressing Room Gossip," *Billboard*, Nov. 16, 1946.

Shelton's life after circus: Author interviews, George Nicely and Bob Shelton, and city directories for Petersburg, VA, 1952 and 1955; Candy and Lillian Shelton lived in Centralia, VA, in the early to mid-1950s.

Shelton lost touch with extended family: Author interviews, Don Nicely and Bob Shelton, May 10, 2015.

Ministers from Dahomey: A major center in the Atlantic slave trade, Dahomey was taken over by the French in 1894 and, after independence, was renamed Benin.

the sideshow has mostly come and gone: Robert Bogdan, *Freak Show: Presenting Human Oddities for Amusement and Profit* (Chicago: University of Chicago Press, 1988), 2, 280.

Shelton's death: Florida Death Index, 1877–1998, ancestry.com. He was buried next to his wife, Lillian, in Oak Ridge Cemetery, in Inverness, FL.

Largely unnoticed success of Goody Shop: Author interview, Reginald Shareef, Sept. 10, 2014.

Big John Clarke as regular customer and friend: Author interview, Nancy Saunders, Feb. 11, 2015.

stunner of a spelling error: "Norfolk Southern Building Has Engraving Error," *Richmond (VA) Times–Dispatch,* July 12, 1982.

Nancy's lawsuit against Carilion on Willie's behalf: Teresia McNabb, interview by Jen McCaffery, *Roanoke Times;* author interview, David Lawrence, May 12, 2015.

a settlement worth $250,000: Sandra Brown Kelly, "104-Year-Old Wins $250,000 Settlement; Man Suffered Burn at Carilion Hospital," *Roanoke Times,* Sept. 9, 1997. According to documents on file at the courthouse, the settlement covered the duration of Willie's home-health care. At the time of his death, he had cash assets of $7,004, $4,000 of which was divided equally among his four nieces, and the rest went to Nancy. Also listed among his belongings were his hospital gown, some clothing, and his guitar.

"Happy Birthday to You": Originally written as "Good Morning to All" was written by sisters Patty and Mildred Hill in 1893, and the "Happy Birthday" change was copyrighted by their publisher in 1935, according to Paul Collins, "You Say It's Your Birthday," *Slate,* July 21, 2011.

Funeral hymn: Ronald Lanier sang the hymn "I Won't Complain."

Epilogue. Markers

Interviews: Erika Turner, Nancy Saunders

Recent voter-restriction efforts: "Voter ID in the States," ballotpedia.org; see also Jim Rutenberg, "A Dream Undone," *New York Times Magazine,* Aug. 2, 2015.

Increase in police brutality against unarmed black people: "The Counted: People Killed by Police in the U.S.," as of August 2015, *Guardian,* http://www.theguardian.com/us-news/ng-interactive/2015/jun/01/the-counted-police-killings-us-database.

Racial divide over discussions of race: 2015 YouGov survey: https://today.yougov.com/news/2015/03/18/whites-blacks-divided-whether-we-talk/.

Tuskegee Airmen buried in cemetery: LeRoi S. Williams, a second lieutenant in the 332 Fighter Group, was killed in a midair collision over Selfridge, Michigan, at the age of twenty-four. His younger brother, Eugene W. Williams, also a second lieutenant, died during the

Berlin Airlift, also at age twenty-four. Roanoke's Ralph V. Claytor, also a second lieutenant during World War II, died in 1993. All were alumni of Lucy Addison High School. From Tuskegee Airmen roster, obituaries, and Matt Chittum, "The Tuskegee Airmen," *Roanoke Times*, Feb. 19, 2012.

Index

House Behind the Cedars
(film), 162
Hutchings, William S., 101–2

Ingalls, Clyde: as bally master,
144–48, 187, 188, 203, 211,
218, 328; and Jack Earle,
247–48; and hairdresser for
George and Willie Muse, 180;
roustie work of, 264; as
sideshow manager, 155, 195,
234–35, 236, 237–40,
244, 251
Ingram, Willie Mae, 51, 53–54,
79, 270, 363n

Jefferson, Thomas, 73–74, 94,
361n
Jews, 166, 253, 273, 274
J. George Loos Shows carnival,
118–20, 124, 125, 135
Jim Crow laws: entrenchment of,
164; and Great Migration, 117,
144; injustices of, 50, 98;
legacy of, 277–78; origin of
term, 137; and race relations,
8, 23, 45, 49, 133, 143–44,
158, 163–64, 218; in Virginia,
45, 117–18; and voting
restrictions, 196. *See also*
segregation
John Robinson Circus, 65, 174
Johnson, Janet Pullen, 27–31, 32,
33, 92
Johnson, William Henry "Zip":
Phineas Taylor Barnum's
display of, 75–76, 99–100, 107,
114, 140, 244; contract of, 244,
368n; costume of, 75–76, 123,
257; death of, 185; George and
Willie Muse compared to, 101,

114, 244; George and Willie
Muse working with, 156;
illness of, 183; on lifestyle of
freaks, 67–68; O. K. White as
manager of, 119, 133
Jones, Jerry, 87–88
Jones, R. R., 45–46

Kelley, John M., 205–7, 210,
212–13, 261, 262
Kelty, Edward J., 142–43
Klein, Ben H., 79–80, 100–101
Kortes, Marie, 258–59,
282–83, 294
Kortes, Pete: and Wilbur Austin,
282–83, 308; back pay for
George and Willie Muse owed
by, 268, 275, 308, 317; death
of, 303; as manager of George
and Willie Muse, 283, 294,
296, 299, 300–301, 304, 308,
318, 397n; and James Herman
Shelton, 157, 259–60; as
sideshow manager, 256,
257–59, 296, 301, 303–5, 307,
390–91n
Ku Klux Klan: chapters of, 85,
94, 164–65, 166, 174, 226;
conventions of, 177–78;
influence of, 196; membership
of, 47–48, 94, 144, 162, 165,
166–67; parades of, 165, 166,
177; rallies of, 173

Lacks, Henrietta, 315, 399n
Lawrence, Richard, 333–34
Lee, Robert E., 34, 47, 164–65
Lee, Thelma Muse, 32–33
Lee, Virginia Y., 161–62
Leitzel, Lillian, 140, 147–48, 157,
158, 178, 238, 260–61, 265

About the Author

BETH MACY writes about outsiders and underdogs, and she is the author of the *New York Times* bestseller *Factory Man*. Her work has appeared in national magazines and newspapers and the *Roanoke Times*. Her reporting has won more than a dozen national awards, including a Nieman Fellowship for Journalism at Harvard and a Lukas Prize.

Reading Group Guide

TRUEVINE

by

Beth Macy

A conversation with
Beth Macy

What prompted you to write this book?

I was a young newspaper feature writer when I first landed in Roanoke, Virginia, in 1989. A white photographer had told me the bones of the story while we were driving around one day, saying, "It's the best story in town, but no one's been able to get it." One of the brothers, Willie Muse, was still alive, and the lore about him had a Boo Radley ring to it. I'd never heard anything quite like it in my life: two albino brothers kidnapped by a circus? A mother who risks her life to get justice for them? The story's gatekeeper, Nancy Saunders, who was Willie's great-niece and caregiver, was a story herself. But she wanted nothing to do with me, initially.

I eventually saw a great parallel between Nancy and her great-grandmother. So you have these two remarkable African-American women overcoming so many odds, against a historical backdrop of the circus and Jim Crow—segregation laws. It represented a big opportunity for me, a chance to bring a largely erased history to life, tell a fascinating story, and try to better understand why racism remains America's deepest stain.

Truevine covers over a century of family, industry, and regional history, and you yourself spent twenty-five years trying to get to the bottom of this story. How did you do your research and reporting?

I combed the written records, including doing a deep dive into the dozens of photographs I found of the brothers. There were two court cases to examine, the second one spanning decades. There were also hundreds of media accounts of the Muse brothers' act in the circus. But the entirety of the written record was recorded in dismissive, racist tones that never once gave the brothers or their family a voice. To view the documents in context, I called experts in race, eugenics, entertainment history, even photography and historic costuming.

But the best anecdotes in the book were stories I heard from ordinary people who lived in Truevine and Roanoke and had a connection to the family. I have always known that documents and records can only take you so far; that there's no substitute for talking to people on the ground. You can read endless accounts of sharecropping, but when you're sitting next to a kerosene heater in the kitchen of someone who sharecropped for sixty years, learning about how "they would feed you outdoors," and you weren't allowed to go to school when the crop came in, and many seasons you went unpaid—that brings the story viscerally alive.

Despite the international success of the Muse brothers, many people were not aware of them before Truevine.

Can you tell us a bit about their lives during the peak of their "fame," so to speak?

The Muse brothers performed with the Ringling Brothers and Barnum & Bailey sideshow throughout most of the 1920s and 1930s, traveling on trains and putting on hundreds of shows in a single year across America, and internationally, too. They said of their audiences, "They were laughing at us, but we were laughing at them, too, because they were paying to see us." Once they knew their mother was alive and they could return home in the off-season to see her—and once they were regularly being paid for their work—they liked being in the circus and even had a pride of calling about it. They were heralded far and wide for their musicianship, and you can tell especially in the older photographs that they had friends in the circus and were comfortable. In one photo from the 1940s, George has his hand casually draped on a white woman's bare shoulder—a rarity for a black man and a white woman during that period, but they are clearly at ease in the picture. In the earlier pictures and accounts from the 1910s and 1920s, the brothers seem uncomfortable and scared, surely the result of being exploited and ripped from their family, perhaps with some attendant Stockholm syndrome. They got to see the world and experience things most black people didn't, but at great personal and family expense.

Can you tell us more about the Muse brothers' mother, and the difficulty she faced while trying to get her sons back?

In 1927, the year Harriett Muse got her sons back, she was an illiterate black maid toiling in Roanoke, a city that was home to the largest KKK population in the state. From all accounts, she was entirely alone when she made her presence known under the sideshow tent and was forced into a tug-of-war with their manager, eight police officers, and several Ringling lawyers. Her bravery was something Willie Muse marveled at for the rest of his life — she could have been arrested, beaten, or killed. And yet she persisted in the face of those possibilities, and ultimately she prevailed. It's an astonishing story of guts, family, and faith. As Nancy put it: "She was *bad*." In the most awesome way.

While *Truevine* has a focused narrative about the exploitation of these brothers, it is really a larger story about love and determination. Do you find this emblematic of the era?

I do. There are countless stories of African Americans enduring against so many odds, but many accounts have been lost to history because of illiteracy and lack of educational opportunities, or because the white press deemed such stories unworthy of recording. I feel very lucky that I was able to piece together most of what happened to George and Willie while there were still people alive who had crossed paths with them. Some of the people I interviewed, sadly, passed away before the book came out. But there are others who are still going strong. A. J. Reeves is 102!

You've spent most of your career in Virginia and live quite close to the original crossroads of Truevine. Do you think your relationship with the area was an asset

in your reporting? How did it shape your perspective and understanding?

I couldn't have written either of my books without the insights and contacts that come from living in and writing about one place for thirty years. A. L. Holland, for instance, was ten years old the day Harriett Muse risked her life to bring George and Willie home; he had firsthand accounts about many developments in the story. A well-known Roanoke civil rights leader, Holland was in his eighties when I first interviewed him for my newspaper, for a story about a young college-bound woman from the projects who had just gotten a full ride to Harvard. By the time I came back to talk to him fifteen years later for this book, he knew and trusted me. The same was true with Nancy Saunders, whom I'd first profiled for my newspaper in 1991, for a feature about her soul-food restaurant. As for the Truevine tobacco farmer I interviewed: I'd met Johnny Angell in 2005 when I followed his guest workers back to their village in western Mexico for a newspaper series on immigration. I'm not some big-city reporter helicoptering in for a big scoop; these people know how I operate. I'm transparent with my story subjects; they know I'm attempting to tell the truth, fairly, even the dark parts.

Early in my career, I used to think you had to live in a big city to do big journalism. But there's power in delving deeply, over the course of many years, into a single community, no matter the size. I'm drawn most to unlikely heroes, people who have been marginalized and underestimated and, by some force of will or talent, end up upending society's expectations.

What surprised you most during the course of writing this book? What do you think was most surprising for your readers?

Most of us know about separate schools and separate drinking fountains, about Malcolm X and Martin Luther King Jr. What surprised me most were the daily indignities of the Jim Crow era, the quotidian realities as relayed by people in their eighties and nineties remembering what it was like to be taunted by parrots trained to squawk racial epithets at them as they walked to school, or the memory of slumlord rent collectors who took sex as partial payment. The quaking of a ninety-four-year-old's voice as he described his grandfather knowing he'd been conceived in violence—a white landowner raping his maid, then refusing to claim his child—and beseeching me to believe the horror he described because, as he put it, "ain't nobody making any of it up."

What's your relationship like with the relatives of the Muse brothers, particularly Nancy Saunders, and what did they think of the book?

Nancy has never told me she likes the book, but she's shown me that she does. When I asked if she would will me the homemade sign from her Goody Shop wall—the one that said, SIT DOWN AND SHUT UP—she deadpanned that I could have it..."after you deliver my eulogy." That was pretty nice! Also, for the first time in our twenty-seven-year history, she made me her homemade yeast rolls for Christmas. Mmmmmmm. (She reminded me that she inherited both her bread-making skills and her guts from Harriett Muse.)

How does the Jim Crow South era that you've written about in this book compare to what's going on today with race relations in this country?

The brothers' great-great-great-niece, Erika Turner, has this 2015 anecdote near the end of the book. She's in a high school psychology class just following the riots in Baltimore over police treatment of Freddie Gray. Her predominantly white, suburban classmates are criticizing the looting as she tries to point out that these events weren't happening in a vacuum; they were precipitated by centuries of systematic exploitation and bias, conscious and unconscious. So many white people don't want to talk about race. It's uncomfortable. Slavery happened more than a century ago, and people alive today had nothing to do with it, many reason. But the particulars of these stories, from slavery to segregation to civil rights and mass incarceration—they are at the marrow of life in America today. The racist parrots. The sharecropper who was forced to eat outside in bad weather because the rule was, "No [n-words] in the house." Racism was so much more insidious and ingrained than separate water fountains. And even though I've spent three decades writing largely about marginalized people, the Jim Crow Virginia I came to know in this book was much harsher than I had understood.

Blacks were considered subhuman beings by most whites, including most of our own white ancestors, many of whom benefitted from the systematic exploitation of a black underclass. (Turns out I'm not the only one in my neighborhood with an old toilet and sink in the basement that had once been installed for the help; friend after friend described something similar, and none of us understood the origins.)

I think we all need to own a little raw piece of this history.

And to own it, we need to understand it and acknowledge it. As Julius Lester has said, "History is not just facts and events. History is also a pain in the heart, and we repeat history until we are able to make another's pain in the heart our own."

What's your next book about?

My next book is about the heroin and opioid epidemic, a crisis unfolding in all corners of America. I'm going deeply local with families from three Virginia communities, tracing how the epidemic transpired from painkiller pills to heroin, from the rural hinterlands to the cities, suburbs, and towns. Unlikely heroes range from a country doctor to an octogenarian nun to a host of ordinary moms trying their damnedest, against so many odds, to save lives.

Questions and topics for discussion

1. Why do you think the story of George and Willie Muse varies so much, depending on who is telling it?

2. Do you think the Muse brothers were kidnapped, sold, or forsaken to the circus? Why?

3. What surprised you most about the trajectory of the Muse brothers' careers as performers?

4. How did racial stereotypes of the time play into the stage names George and Willie were given?

5. How did Harriett Muse fight to win back her sons?

6. Now that you've read *Truevine*, how do you think the history of a region affects the contemporary lives of its citizens? Do you believe it is important that people study the history of their own hometowns?

7. What role did Jim Crow laws play in the continued separation of the Muse brothers from their mother?

8. How does the treatment of the Muse brothers and their peers highlight exploitative practices within the circus? How did this extend beyond members of the sideshows?

9. How did George and Willie's financial status change during their lives? What impact did it have on them and on their family?

10. What parallels does Beth Macy draw between the lives of African Americans in Jordan's Alley and those in Roanoke, Virginia, today?